Textbook of Pharmaceutical Inorganic Chemistry
Theory and Practical

Textbook of Pharmaceutical Inorganic Chemistry
Theory and Practical

Prof VN Rajasekaran

Formerly
Joint Director of Medical Education (Pharmacy)
Tamil Nadu
Professor of Pharmaceutical Chemistry
Madras Medical College, Chennai
Madurai Medica College, Madurai

CBSPD

CBS Publishers & Distributors Pvt Ltd

New Delhi • Bengaluru • Chennai • Kochi • Kolkata • Lucknow • Mumbai
Hyderabad • Jharkhand • Nagpur • Patna • Pune • Uttarakhand

Textbook of
Pharmaceutical
Inorganic Chemistry
Theory and Practical

ISBN-13: 978-81-239-2943-9
ISBN-10: 81-239-2943-9

First edition 1997
Second Edition 2005

Reprint: 1999, 2001, 2003, 2004, 2007, 2008, 2009, 2010, 2011,
2012, 2013, 2014, 2015, 2018, 2019, 2020, 2022, 2023, **2024**

Published by **Satish Kumar Jain** and produced by **Varun Jain** for

CBS Publishers & Distributors Pvt Ltd
4819/XI Prahlad Street, 24 Ansari Road, Daryaganj, New Delhi 110 002, India.
Ph: 011-23289259, 23266861   Website: www.cbspd.com
                                    e-mail: delhi@cbspd.com

Corporate Office: 204 FIE, Industrial Area, Patparganj, Delhi 110 092
Ph: 011-4934 4934   Fax: 011-4934 4935
                           e-mail: publishing@cbspd.com; publicity@cbspd.com

Branches

- **Bengaluru:** Seema House 2975, 17th Cross, KR Road, Banasankari 2nd Stage, Bengaluru 560 070, Karnataka, India
  Ph: +91-80-26771678/79   Fax: +91-80-26771680   e-mail: bangalore@cbspd.com
- **Chennai:** 7, Subbaraya Street, Shenoy Nagar, Chennai 600 030, Tamil Nadu, India
  Ph: +91-44-26680620, 26681266   Fax: +91-44-42032115   e-mail: chennai@cbspd.com
- **Kochi:** 42/1325, 1326, Power House Road, Opp KSEB, Power House, Ernakulum Kochi 682 018, Kerala, India
  Ph: +91-484-4059061-65,67   Fax: +91-484-4059065   e-mail: kochi@cbspd.com
- **Kolkata:** 147, Hind Ceramics Compound, 1st Floor, Nilgunj Road, Belghoria, Kolkata-700056, West Bengal, India
  Ph: +033-25633055, 033-25633056   e-mail: kolkata@cbspd.com
- **Lucknow:** Basement, Khushnuma Complex, 7 Meerabai Marg (Behind Jawahar Bhawan), Lucknow-226001, UP, India
  Ph: +0522-4000032   e-mail: tiwari.lucknow@cbspd.com
- **Mumbai:** PWD Shed, Gala no 25/26, Ramchandra Bhatt Marg, Next to JJ Hospital Gate no. 2, Opp. Union Bank of India, Noorbaug, Mumbai-400009, Maharashtra, India
  Ph: 022-66661880/89   e-mail: mumbai@cbspd.com

Representatives

• Hyderabad	0-9885175004	• Jharkhand	0-9811541605	• Nagpur	0-8692091830
• Patna	0-9334159340	• Pune	0-9664372571	• Uttarakhand	0-9716462459

Printed at SRK Graphics, Delhi (India)

PREFACE

It is no secret that there is no proper text book available in India catering to the needs of the pharmacy students at the undergraduate level for any subject. Mostly the students have to fend for themselves sourcing their requirements here and there. This applies with great force especially to the subject of "Pharmaceutical Inorganic Chemistry". The only British text book does not cater to the requirements of B. Pharm students in India and it is also woefully outdated.

After the publication of an inorganic chemistry text book for Diploma in Pharmacy which has been very popular for about 13 years now, pressure has been brought on me by many of my students, colleagues and other teachers to write a text book with a professional approach on "Pharmaceutical Inorganic Chemistry" meeting the needs of the degree students.

So this is a humble effort on my part and a labour of love to fill the void and give a comprehensive, lucid, informative and useful textbook to the students. I hope I have succeeded in my effort and I leave it to the better judgement of the users of the book to pronounce the verdict

This book has been written covering mainly the syllabus of the Tamil Nadu Dr. M.G.R. Medical University and it is hoped that it will meet the requirements of the course in other Southern Universities also. The book contains two sections, Theory and Practical. In Theory all the inorganic drugs official in I.P. '96 are exhaustively dealt with and the I.P. standards, tests for identity, tests for purity, storage conditions, assay etc., are fully covered. Where some of the drugs do not have monographs in I.P. '96, the standards in B.P. '93 or I.P. '66 have been adopted if they have monographs in any one of them. However even inorganic substances which are not official in any of the above pharmacopoeias like nitrogen are also dealt with if their importance in pharmacy practice warrants it. Wherever it is simply mentioned as I.P., it refers to I.P. '96 only. Similarly simple mention of B.P. indicates B.P. '93.

In addition to the official drugs and formulations, other topics such as atomic structure, electronic theory of valency, periodic table, coordination compounds, quantitative analysis of inorganic compounds, etc. have been extensively and exhaustively dealt with incorporating the latest concepts to give indepth knowledge for the study of the chemistry and official requirements and standards of the inorganic drugs. A chapter on "Radioactivity and Radioisotopes" has also been included since many radioisotopes are being increasingly used in medicine and surgery.

The Practical section has chapters on limit tests, systematic qualitative analysis of inorganic salts and assays. The material in this section has been so designed as to enable the students to get a clear understanding of the nuances and intricacies of both qualitative and quantitative analyses.

I will be highly pleased if this book proves to be of good service to the B.Pharm students.

V.N. RAJASEKARAN

PREFACE TO SECOND EDITION

It is observed that almost all the universities in India have discarded the system of study of inorganic drugs based on chemical classification and switched over to pharmacological classification.. Hence this book has been redesigned and revamped completely on the basis of pharnacological classification to meet the newly arising needs of the students. Even though this lays more stress on the pharmacology than on the chemistry of drugs, the treatment of the subject is such that good emphasis is laid on the chemistry also to the extent necessary since almost all the drugs are chemicals only. A good knowledge of their chemical properties will help to understand the rationale behind the tests for identity and also the storage conditions prescribed.

New chapters dealing with "Essential and Trace Ions", "Consumer Dental Products", "Medical Gases"," Major Intra and Extracellular Electrolytes", "Inorganic Pharmaceutical Aids", and "Inorganic Reagents in Organic Synthesis" in tune with the changed syllabus have been introduced, while the chapters dealing with "Quantitative Analysis of Inorganic Compounds" and "Commonly Used Reagents" in theory and the chapter on "The Practical Aspects of the Quantitative Analysis of Inorganic Compounds" have been omitted as they now come under the purview of another subject in B.Pharm

I have again tried to present a comprehensive, lucid, informative and instructive text book with a professional approach. I again hope that I have succeeded in my efforts and leave it to the better judgement of the users of the book to pronounce the verdict. Suggestions for the improvement of the book are welcome.

V.N.RAJASEKARAN

CONTENTS

SECTION B - PRACTICAL

SOLUBILITY DESCRIPTIONS

The solubility descriptions in this book denote the following ranges:

Description	Approximate quantities of solvent by volume required to dissolve 1 part of solute by weight.
Very soluble	Less than 1 part
Freely soluble	From 1 to 10 parts
Soluble	From 10 to 30 parts
Sparingly soluble	From 30 to 100 parts
Slightly soluble	From 100 to 1,000 parts
Very slightly soluble	From 1,000 to 10,000 parts
Practically insoluble	More than 10,000 parts

VAPOUR PRESSURES OF HYDRATES
AND THEIR EFFECTS

The water present in crystalline solids as water of crystallization exerts a vapour pressure. The amount of this vapour pressure is a measure of the tendency of the solid to lose or gain water to or from the atmosphere. In other words if the vapour pressure of the water in the hydrate differs from the vapour pressure of the water in the atmosphere, the hydrate will tend to gain or lose water until an equilibrium is established with the water in the atmosphere.

Efflorescence: The loss of water of crystallization or hydration by a crystalline solid or hydrate to the atmosphere to form an anhydrous salt or a hydrate containing lesser number of water molecules is known as efflorescence. Example is sodium sulphate, $Na_2SO_4.10H_2O$. It has a vapour pressure of 16.3 mm at 20°C. When the aqueous vapour pressure of the atmosphere is below this value, the hydrate effloresces or loses water to the atmosphere to give an anhydrous substance. Borax, $Na_2B_4O_7.10H_2O$ and sodium phosphate, $Na_2HPO_4.12H_2O$ are other examples.

Deliquescence: When the aqueous vapour pressure of a saturated solution of a solid is lesser than the aqueous vapour pressure in the atmosphere, it tends to absorb water from the atmosphere till an equilibrium is established. In this process, the solid continues to absorb moisture from the atmosphere, forms a hydrate first and then a solution as it dissolves in the water absorbed. Hydrated calcium chloride has a very much lower vapour pressure than the aqueous vapour pressure in the atmosphere. So it continues to absorb water from the atmosphere till it forms a solution. All *deliquescent* substances are very soluble in water. Other examples of deliquescent substances are zinc chloride, potassium carbonate, potassium hydroxide and sodium lactate.

Hygroscopicity: However many substances absorb water but do not dissolve in the water absorbed forming a solution. They are said to be *hygroscopic.* In these cases it is possible that water is attracted to these solids by forces of adsorption. The most unique feature here is that water is absorbed but the solid remains the same without changing form. The classic example here is silica gel which is usually found in bottles containing capsules. It absorbs moisture from the atmosphere thus protecting the capsules. Other examples are sulphuric acid and glycerin.

Section A
THEORY

CHAPTER 1
INTRODUCTION

I. SYMBOLS OF ELEMENTS

Elements enter into many types of reactions and form large numbers of compounds. During some of these reactions many radicals are also formed. To follow these reactions chemical equations must be written. One such chemical equation is the formation of water by the combination of hydrogen and oxygen which can be written as below :-

Hydrogen + Oxygen = Water

Apart from the fact that writing the equation like this denoting the elements and compounds involved in the reaction is cumbersome, it does not convey any other information other than that of hydrogen and oxygen combining to form water. So symbols have been coined for denoting the elements in the shortest possible way.

A symbol is a concise representation of an element. Elements have been given symbols in three different ways :-

1. *Elements represented by a single letter:-*
   Examples : Carbon - C, Hydrogen - H, .Boron - B, Sulphur - S, Oxygen - O, Iodine - I, Fluorine - F, Nitrogen - N, Phosphorus - P. Vanadium - V, Uranium - U.

2. *Elements represented by two letters :-*
   (The first letter is given in capital and the second in small)
   Chlorine - Cl, Bromine - Br, Calcium - Ca, Barium - Ba, Zinc - Zn, Silicon - Si, Cobalt - Co, Magnesium - Mg, Aluminium - Al, Helium - He.

3. *Elements which derive their symbols from their Latin names:-*
   Mercury   - Hg (from Hydrargyrum)
   Sodium   - Na (from Natrium)
   Copper   - Cu (from Cuprum)
   Iron   - Fe (from Ferrum)

1

Tin	-	Sn	(from Stannium)
Lead	-	Pb	(from Plumbum)
Antimony	-	Sb	(from Stibium)
Potassium	-	K	(from Kalium)
Silver	-	Ag	(from Argentum)
Gold	-	Au	(from Aurum)

II. VALENCIES OF ELEMENTS

Valency can be simply described as the combining capacity of elements. It is defined as the number of hydrogen atoms or twice the number of oxygen atoms with which one atom of an element may combine.

Thus to form hydrogen chloride (HCl) one atom of chlorine is combining with one atom of hydrogen. So the valency of chlorine is 1. Similary one atom of nitrogen is combining with three atoms of hydrogen to form ammonia (NH_3). So the valency of nitrogen is 3.

In the case of magnesium oxide (MgO), one atom of magnesium combines with one atom of oxygen. So the valency of magnesium is 2. However same elements have variable valencies which means they have different valencies in different compounds. So the above concept is no longer tenable and valency is now better described as *the number of bonds formed by an atom of an element to form one molecule of a compound*. Examples are carbon, nitrogen, iron and phosphorus. For more and fuller information on this, please refer to the chapter on "Electronic Theory of Valency" in this book.

A *radical* consists of a group of atoms formed during the course of a reaction without free existence. It behaves as if it is a single atom and is soon converted into a compound. For example sulphate (SO_4^{2-}) is a radical. It does not exist in the free state but is combined with various elements forming compounds like sodium sulphate (Na_2SO_4), potassium sulphate (K_2SO_4) etc. Radicals may be monovalent, divalent or trivalent as in the case of elements. The radical ammonium is monovalent and sulphate is divalent, whereas phosphate is trivalent.

2

Examples of Monovalent Radicals

Chloride	-	Cl^-
Bromide	-	Br^-
Iodide	-	I^-
Ammonium	-	NH_4^+
Bicarbonate	-	HCO_4^-
Nitrate	-	NO_3^-
Hydroxyl	-	OH^-
Nitrite	-	NO_2^-
Chlorate	-	ClO_3^-
Perchlorate	-	ClO_4^-
Permanganate	-	MnO_4^-

Examples of Divalent Radicals

Sulphate	-	SO_4^{2-}
Carbonate	-	CO_3^{2-}
Chromate	-	CrO_4^{2-}
Dichromate	-	$Cr_2O_7^{2-}$
Oxide	-	O^{2-}
Sulphide	-	S^{2-}
Sulphite	-	SO_3^{2-}
Thiosulphate	-	$S_2O_3^{2-}$

Examples of Trivalent Radicals

Arsenite	-	AsO_3^{3-}
Phosphate	-	PO_4^{3-}

III. WRITING EMPIRICAL AND MOLECULAR FORMULAE

We know that the formula for hydrochloric acid or hydrogen chloride is HCl. The formula for magnesium oxide is MgO. What are the different types of chemical formulae and how are they derived ? The first type is the *empirical formula* which gives the *relative* number of different atoms present in a compound. The second type is the

.*nolecular formula* which gives the *correct or exact* numbers of the various atoms present in a compound. For example CH is the empirical formula of benzene. Its molecular formula is C_6H_6. From the empirical formula, we understand that in benzene, the two elements carbon and hydrogen present are in equal proportion. But the molecular formula gives the exact numbers of the atoms of carbon and hydrogen present actually in benzene.

To find out the empirical formula, the compound is subjected to chemical analysis and the percentage composition of the elements is determined. Usually the percentage of oxygen is not found out. It is obtained by subtracting the total of the percentages of all other elements from 100. The next step is to convert the percentage composition to mole composition. The mole composition is obtained by dividing the weight of each element by its atomic weight. Then we can obtain the mole ratio of the different elements in the compound. Any fraction of the mole ratio can be eliminated by dividing or multiplying by a suitable number.

Example

8 grams of copper chloride on being subjected to chemical analysis are found to contain 3.780 g of copper (Cu) and 4.220 g of chlorine (Cl). What is the empirical formula of copper chloride?

% of copper in copper chloride $= \dfrac{3.780}{8} \times 100 = 47.3\%$

% of chlorine in copper chloride $= \dfrac{4.220}{8} \times 100 = 52.7\%$

Mole ratio of Copper $= \dfrac{47.3}{63.55} = 0.743$

Mole ratio of Chlorine $= \dfrac{52.7}{35.45} = 1.487$

Dividing by 0.743, we obtain
    1 Cu : 1.999 Cl
 = 1 Cu : 2 Cl

So the empirical formula of copper chloride is $CuCl_2$.

4

The molecular formula of the above compound can be found out by using the empirical formula and the molecular weight of the compound.

Let us say that the molecular formula is $(CuCl_2)_n$. The mass of the compound as per empirical formula is the sum of the atomic weights of the elements in the compound. That is one atom of copper = 63.55 (atomic weight of copper). One atom of chlorine = 35.45 (atomic weight of chlorine). Actually as per empirical formula there are two chlorine atoms present. So the atomic mass of chlorine is 70.90 (ie. 35.45 × 2). For copper chloride($CuCl_2$), the empirical molecular mass is 134.45 (ie. 63.55 + 70.90). The actual molecular weight (amu) (as determined by experiment) is 134.45 only. So by dividing the actual molecular weight by empirical molecular mass, we get a value of 1 for n. So in this case, the empirical formula of $CuCl_2$ is also the molecular formula.

In another example the empirical formula mass of CH (for benzene) is 13.018 amu. (12.01 for carbon + 1.008 for hydrogen). But the actual molecular weight is found to be 78. So by dividing 78 by 13.018, we get 5.99 = 6. Therefore the molecular formula of benzene is C_6H_6.

IV. MOLECULAR AND IONIC EQUATIONS

Consider the reaction between sodium chloride and silver nitrate,both in aqueous solution. The products are a white precipitate of silver chloride and sodium nitrate.

The reaction can be written as below :-

$$NaCl + AgNO_3 = AgCl\downarrow + NaNO_3$$

This is a *molecular reaction*. However since the reactants are completely *ionized* in solution, the reaction actually takes place between the ions of the reactants as given below :-

$$NaCl + AgNO_3 \longrightarrow AgCl\downarrow + NaNO_3 \text{ (molecular)}$$

$$Na^+ + Cl^- + Ag^+ + NO_3^- \longrightarrow AgCl\downarrow + Na^+ + NO_3^- \text{ (Ionic)}$$

Since Na^+ and NO_3^- ions are present equally on both sides of the equation, these may be cancelled and the final *ionic equation* will be

$$Ag^+ + Cl^- \longrightarrow AgCl\downarrow$$

However for the sake of convenience the molecular equation is used often. This reaction is the basis for limit test for chlorides.

Another example will be the reaction between potassium sulphate and barium chloride solutions to form insoluble barium sulphate and potassium chloride. This reaction is the basis for limit test for sulphates.

$$K_2SO_4 + BaCl_2 \longrightarrow BaSO_4\downarrow + 2KCl$$
$$\text{(Molecular)}$$

$$2K^+ + SO_4^{2-} + Ba^{2+} + 2Cl^- \longrightarrow BaSO_4\downarrow + 2K^+ + 2Cl^-$$
$$\text{(Ionic)}$$

After cancelling ions present on both sides, the equation becomes

$$SO_4^{2-} + Ba^{2+} \longrightarrow BaSO_4\downarrow$$

So it appears that reactions between highly ionized compounds should be expressed only by way of ionic equations which are obviously more exact.

So are there any rules which govern the writing of chemical equations in the form of molecular or ionic equations?

(1) *Strong electrolytes,* which are completely soluble in water are expressed using *ionic symbols*, whereas *weak electrolytes* (which are not completely soluble and so are only *weakly ionized)* and covalent compounds are given in the molecular form.

(2) Electrolytes, which are insoluble in water, are given only in molecular form.

(3) The ionic charges also must be balanced on both sides of the equation, as is being done in the case of atoms.

6

V. BALANCING CHEMICAL EQUATIONS

A balanced equation should be written in such a way that it correctly represents the chemical reaction and also it is in accordance with the law of conservation of mass and the law of conservation of charge. The following methods are used for balancing chemical equations :-

(1) Balancing by inspection

(2) Partial equations method

(3) Balancing by oxidation number change

(4) Balancing by ion-electron method

We can use any one of the above methods depending on how simple or complicated the particular reaction is .

(1) Balancing by Inspection

(i)   First write the chemical equation in the unbalanced form.

(ii)   Then choose the atom which occurs at a minimum number of places and balance it. Afterwards, choose the atom occurring at maximum number of places for balancing in that order.

Example 1

Hydrogen sulphide is oxidized by sulphur dioxide to give sulphur and water. The reaction is represented as below :-

(a) The skeleton unbalanced equation will be

$$H_2S + SO_2 \longrightarrow S\downarrow + H_2O$$

(b) Balancing the above equation is done as below :-

(i) First multiply H_2O by 2 to make the oxygen atoms equal on both sides.

$$H_2S + SO_2 \longrightarrow S\downarrow + 2H_2O$$

7

(ii) Next multiply H_2S by 2 to make hydrogen atoms equal on both sides.

$$2H_2S + SO_2 \longrightarrow S\downarrow + 2H_2O$$

(iii) Finally multiply S by 3 to make the sulphur atoms equal on both sides.

$$2H_2S + SO_2 \longrightarrow 3S\downarrow + 2H_2O$$

This is the final balanced equation.

Example 2

Barium hydroxide is reacted with hydrochloric acid to form barium chloride and water. The unbalanced chemical equation is written as below :-

$$Ba(OH)_2 + HCl \longrightarrow BaCl_2 + H_2O$$

Balancing the above equation is done as below :-

(i) First multiply H_2O by 2 to make the oxygen atoms equal on both sides.

$$Ba(OH)_2 + HCl \longrightarrow BaCl_2 + 2H_2O$$

(ii) Then multiply HCl by 2 to make the chlorine atoms equal on both sides.

$$Ba(OH)_2 + 2HCl \longrightarrow BaCl_2 + 2H_2O$$

This is the final balanced equation. However since the reaction is ionic, the *ionic equation* can be written as below:

$$Ba(OH)_2 + 2HCl \longrightarrow BaCl_2 + 2H_2O$$

$$Ba^+ + 2OH^- + 2H^+ + 2Cl^- \longrightarrow Ba^+ + 2Cl^- + 2H_2O$$

Cancelling ions common on both sides, we get

$$2OH^- + 2H^+ \longrightarrow 2H_2O$$

or $\quad OH^- + H^+ \longrightarrow H_2O$

(2) Partial Equations Method

If the equations are found to be complicated, it will be difficult to balance them by Balancing by Inspection. In such cases, the partial equations method is found to be useful. In this method the chemical reaction is thought to proceed in two or more stages. Equations are written for these stages which are balanced by the method of balancing by inspection. Finally the equations for the various stages are added together. Any intermediate products formed are cancelled so that they do not appear in the final equation.

Example 1

The oxidation of hydrochloric acid to chlorine by manganese dioxide is thought to proceed in the following stages :-

$$MnO_2 + 2HCl \longrightarrow MnCl_2 + H_2O + O$$

$$2HCl + O \longrightarrow Cl_2 + H_2O$$

Combining both the equations, we get

$$MnO_2 + 4HCl \longrightarrow MnCl_2 + Cl_2 + 2H_2O$$

The equation at every stage is balanced by the Balancing by Inspection method. Nascent oxygen (intermediate product) is cancelled.

Example 2

The reaction of copper with sulphuric acid to form copper sulphate, sulphur dioxide and water is supposed to proceed through the following stages :-

$$Cu + H_2SO_4 \longrightarrow CuO + SO_2 + H_2O$$
$$CuO + H_2SO_4 \longrightarrow CuSO_4 + H_2O$$

Combining the above two equations we get

$$Cu + 2H_2SO_4 \longrightarrow CuSO_4 + SO_2 + 2H_2O$$

As usual the intermediate product (CuO) is cancelled and each stage is balanced by the method of Balancing by Inspection.

(3) Balancing by Oxidation Number Change

(a) Oxidation Numbers

Oxidation is a process in which any atom or ion loses electrons, whereas reduction is the reaction in which any atom or ion gains or acquires electrons. So oxidation may also be called as de-eletronation (meaning removal of electrons) and reduction may also be called as electronation (meaning gaining of electrons).

In the classic example of the conversion of the ferrous ion to the ferric ion, oxidation takes place.

$$Fe^{2+} \longrightarrow Fe^{3+} + 1 \text{ electron}$$

Similarly stannous ion is oxidised to stannic ion and manganate is oxidised to permanganate.

$$Sn^{2+} \longrightarrow Sn^{4+} + 2 \text{ electrons } (2e^-)$$

$$MnO_4^{2-} \longrightarrow MnO_4^- + 1 \text{ electron } (e^-)$$

Manganate   Permanganate
ion   ion

The following are the examples of reduction :-

(i) Formation of chloride ion from chlorine etc.,

$$Cl + e^- \longrightarrow Cl^-$$

$$Br + e^- \longrightarrow Br^-$$

$$I + e^- \longrightarrow I^-$$

(ii) Formation of mercurous ion from mercuric ion.

$$2Hg^{2+} + 2e^- \longrightarrow Hg_2^{2+}$$

Mercuric ion   Mercurous ion

$$Hg_2^{2+} + 2e^- \longrightarrow 2Hg$$

10

To follow these oxidation and reduction reactions, determination of oxidation number is necessary. Oxidation number is the formal charge which an atom or ion seems to have and to determine this charge, the electrons should be counted. The following rules may be observed in this connection :-

(i) *Atoms present in the elementary or uncombined state are given the oxidation number zero.*

(ii) *In neutral molecules the total of the oxidation numbers of all the atoms will be zero.*

(iii) *In the case of charged species such as complex ions the total of the oxidation numbers of all the atoms in the compelx ion is equal to the net charge on the ion.*

(iv) *Elements usually have different oxidation numbers in different compounds. However the oxidation number of fluorine is always −1. Oxidation number of hydrogen is usually +1 but in the case of metallic hydrides it has an oxidation number of −1.*

Using these rules we can calculate the oxidation number of an atom present in a molecule or complex ion.

Example

Calculate the oxidation number of Mn in the compounds (a) MnO (b) $KMnO_4$ and (c) K_2MnO_4.

Say the oxidation number of Mn = x

(a) In the case of MnO the oxidation number of oxygen = -2.

$$x - 2 = 0$$
$$\text{So } x = +2$$

Oxidation number of Mn in the compound MnO is +2.

(b) For $KMnO_4$, the total or sum of the oxidation numbers of various atoms will be

$$1 + x + 4\,(-2) = 1 + x - 8 = x - 7$$
$$\text{So } x - 7 = 0, \text{ we get } x = +7$$

11

So the oxidation number of Mn in $KMnO_4$ = +7.

(c) Sum of the oxidation numbers of the atoms present in K_2MnO_4

$$= 2(+1) + x + 4(-2)$$
$$= 2 + x - 8$$
$$= x - 6. \quad x - 6 = 0 = +6.$$

So the oxidation number of Mn in K_2MnO_4 is +6 .

Therefore *the oxidation number may be defined as the positive or negative charge an atom appears to have when electrons are counted. The oxidation state of an element is its oxidation number per atom. Oxidation and reduction take place in terms of oxidation numbers.*

(b) Balancing By Oxidation Number Change

The following rules should be followed :-

(i) Allot oxidation numbers to the atoms undergoing change.

(ii) Select the proper ratio of oxidising agent to the reducing agent so that the oxidation number change is balanced, ie, any increase in oxidation number is compensated by a decrease.

(iii) While balancing the oxygen atoms, add H_2O to the side found to be deficient in oxygen.

(iv) Similarly balance the hydrogen atoms by adding H^+ to the side found to be deficient in hydrogen atoms.

(v) If the reaction takes place in acidic solution, the equation is usually balanced. But in basic solution, it may be necessary to add on both sides enough number of OH^- to neutralise H^+.

(vi) Any repetition of any ion on both sides of the equation should be cancelled.

12

Example 1

Balance the reaction of oxidation of ammonia by cupric oxide. The products are copper, nitrogen and water.

Skeleton equation

$$\overset{+2}{\underset{\uparrow 2e^-}{Cu}}O + \overset{-3}{\underset{\downarrow 3e^-}{N}}H_3 \longrightarrow \overset{0}{Cu} + \overset{0}{N_2} + H_2O$$

Oxidation number of Cu in CuO is +2. It is changed to 0 when it becomes Cu (copper atom). So the cupric ion in CuO must gain two units of negative charge, ie, two electrons. This is indicated by the arrow going up with the two negative charges $2e^-$. The N atom in NH_3, which has 3 negative charges, must lose them to become N_2. We can indicate it by three negative charges going down, that is by the downward arrow with $3e^-$

The equation may now be partially balanced by multiplying CuO by 3 and NH_3 by 2. The equation now will be

$$3CuO + 2NH_3 \longrightarrow 3Cu + N_2 + H_2O$$

The gaining of electrons by the Cu and the losing of electrons by the N will now be equal. The same number of Cu and N atoms are provided on the right side also. The equation is still incomplete as the oxygen is not balanced.

By multiplying H_2O by 3, we can balance oxygen and also get the final balanced equation. The hydrogen atoms are already balanced.

$$3\ CuO + 2\ NH_3 \longrightarrow 3\ Cu + N_2 + 3H_2O$$

Example 2

Balance the reaction in which pot.manganate is oxidised to pot.permanganate.

13

Skeleton equation

$$\underset{\uparrow 2e^-}{\overset{+6}{K_2MnO_4}} + \underset{\uparrow 1e^-}{\overset{+6}{K_2MnO_4}} + H_2O \longrightarrow \overset{+4}{MnO_2} + \overset{+7}{KMnO_4} + KOH$$

Oxidation number changes from +6 in the first molecule of K_2MnO_4 to +4 in MnO_2. This can happen only if there is a $2e^-$ gain for K_2MnO_4. In the second molecule of K_2MnO_4, the oxidation number of Mn changes from +6 to +7 in $KMnO_4$. This involves a $1e^-$ loss.

For balancing these oxidation number changes, multiply the second molecule of K_2MnO_4 and also $KMnO_4$ by 2. This gives the $2e^-$ to the first molecule of K_2MnO_4.

$$K_2MnO_4 + 2K_2MnO_4 + H_2O \longrightarrow MnO_2 + 2KMnO_4 + KOH$$

For balancing the hydrogen and potassium atoms, multiply H_2O on the left by 2 and the KOH on the right by 4. The equation now becomes

$$K_2MnO_4 + 2K_2MnO_4 + 2H_2O \longrightarrow MnO_2 + 2KMnO_4 + 4KOH$$

The final balanced equation is obtained by adding the K_2MnO_4 molecules.

$$3K_2MnO_4 + 2H_2O \longrightarrow MnO_2 + 2KMnO_4 + 4KOH$$

(4) Balancing by Ion-Electron Method

This is also known as *Half–Reactions Method*. This is applied to oxidation–reduction reactions. The reaction is first divided into two half-reactions. In the first half-reaction, the oxidising agent gains electrons and gets reduced. In the second half - reaction, the reducing agent loses electron and gets oxidisied. Then the two half-reactions are balanced and added together. Electrons on the left and right side of the equation get cancelled out in the final equation.

After writing the half-reactions for both the oxidising agent and reducing agent, the following rules should be followed :-

14

(1) *Balance the atoms other than oxygen and hydrogen for each half-reaction by balancing the co-efficients, if required.*

(2) *The oxygen atoms on either side may be balanced by adding H_2O to the side deficient in oxygen.*

(3) *The hydrogen atoms on both sides may be balanced by adding H^+ ions to the side deficient in hydrogen.*

(4) *The charge on either side should be made equal by adding e^- (electron) to the side requiring it.*

(5) *Whenever the reaction takes place in basic solution, add enough OH^- to neutralise the H^+ and convert it into H_2O.*

(6) *The two balanced half-reactions may be added so that the electrons appearing on both sides cancel each other. For this purpose each half-reaction may be multiplied by a suitable number before adding.*

Example 1

Oxalic acid is oxidised by hydrogen peroxide to carbon dioxide and water.

The unbalanced reaction is

$$H_2C_2O_4 + H_2O_2 \longrightarrow CO_2 + H_2O$$

This is divided into two half-reactions. The first half-reaction for the oxidation of oxalic acid is

$$H_2C_2O_4 \longrightarrow CO_2$$

Balancing this reaction in the order of carbon-oxygen-hydrogen, we get

$$H_2C_2O_4 \longrightarrow 2CO_2 + 2H^+$$

Now the charge should be equalized.

$$H_2C_2O_4 \longrightarrow 2CO_2 + 2H^+ + 2e^- \quad .... \quad (1)$$

The second half-reaction for the reduction of H_2O_2 is

$$H_2O_2 \longrightarrow H_2O$$

Balancing this equation in the order of oxygen–hydrogen, we get

$$H_2O_2 + 2H^+ \longrightarrow 2H_2O$$

Now the charge is equalized.

$$H_2O_2 + 2H^+ + 2e^- \longrightarrow 2H_2O \quad .... \quad (2)$$

Let us now add equations (1) and (2)

$$H_2C_2O_4 + H_2O_2 \longrightarrow 2CO_2 + 2H_2O$$

This is the final balanced equation in which the charges on both sides are cancelled.

Example 2

Ferrous ions are oxidised to ferric ions by titration with dichromate in acid solution. This reaction may be divided into two half-reactions.

First Half - Reaction (Oxidation)

$$Fe^{2+} \longrightarrow Fe^{3+}$$

The charge may be equalized by adding an electron to the right side.

$$Fe^{2+} \longrightarrow Fe^{3+} + e^- (1) \quad .... \quad (1)$$

Second Half - Reaction (Reduction)

$$Cr_2O_7^{2-} \longrightarrow Cr^{3+}$$

16

In this reaction, the dichromate ion is **reduced to Cr^{3+}** ion Balancing the Cr, we get

$$Cr_2O_7^{2-} \longrightarrow 2\ Cr^{3+}$$

Next oxygen atoms are balanced. **For this add $7H_2O$ to the right** side.

$$Cr_2O_7^{2-} \longrightarrow 2\ Cr^{3+} + 7H_2O$$

Then balance the hydrogen atoms by adding $14H^+$ to the left side

$$Cr_2O_7^{2-} + 14\ H^+ \longrightarrow 2\ Cr^{3+} + 7H_2O$$

Now the charge is equalized by adding 6 electrons to the left side

$$Cr_2O_7^{2-} + 14\ H^+ + 6e^- \longrightarrow 2\ Cr^{3+} + 7H_2O \quad \dots\dots\dots\dots\dots (2)$$

Combining the two Half - Reactions

First multiply the half - reaction (1) by 6. **The equation now** becomes

$$6Fe^{2+} \longrightarrow 6Fe^{3+} + 6e^-$$

Combine the half - reactions (1) and (2) now.

$$6Fe^{2+} \longrightarrow 6Fe^{3+} + 6e^-$$

and $Cr_2O_7^{2-} + 14H + 6e^- \longrightarrow 2Cr^{3+} + 7H_2O$

Now the final equation will be

$$Cr_2O_7^{2-} + 6Fe^{2+} + 14H^+ \longrightarrow 2\ Cr^{3+} + 6Fe^{3+} + 7H_2O$$

The $6e^-$ present on both sides is cancelled.

CHAPTER 2
ATOMIC STRUCTURE

Even though John Dalton put forward the theory that matter was made up of very small indivisible particles known as atoms, it was later found that atoms themselves are made up of very small particles known as the fundamental particles. These subatomic particles are the *electron, proton* and the *neutron.*

Electron was found to have a negative charge. The ratio of charge to mass (*e/m*) of an electron was calculated by J.J. Thomson in 1897 using a special apparatus. It works out to -1.76×10^8 C per gram. The determination of charge on an electron was carried out by R.A. Millikan in 1908 using the well known Millikan's Oil-drop Experiment and found to be -1.60×10^{-19} coulombs. By using these two values, ie., *e* (charge) and *e/m* (charge to mass ratio), it is possible to calculate the mass of an electron as given below:—

$$\frac{e}{e/m} = \frac{1.60 \times 10^{-19}}{1.76 \times 10^8} = 9.1 \times 10^{-28} \text{ g.}$$

So the mass of an electron is 9.1×10^{-28} g. The mass of a single hydrogen atom has been found to be 1.67×10^{-24} g. From this we can calculate the mass of an electron relative to the mass of a hydrogen atom.

$$\frac{\text{mass of one atom of hydrogen}}{\text{mass of an electron}} = \frac{1.67 \times 10^{-24}}{9.1 \times 10^{-28}} = 1.835 \times 10^3 = 1835$$

This means that the hydrogen atom is 1835 times heavier than an electron, if the mass of an electron is taken as one unit.

Based on this reasoning, *an electron is a subatomic particle with a mass $\frac{1}{1835}$ th of a hydrogen atom and one unit of negative charge.*

The mass of a proton has been calculated as 1.672×10^{-24} g. The charge on the proton is equal and opposite to that of an electron, ie., proton carries a positive charge which is equal in magnitude to the charge on an electron, ie., $+1.60 \times 10^{-19}$ coulombs. The mass of a proton is considered to be one atomic mass unit. So *a proton is a subatomic particle with 1 amu and one unit of positive charge.*

The third subatomic particle to be discov red is neutron. Its mass is the same as that of a proton but it carries no charge. So a neutron is a subatomic particle with 1 amu but it has no charge.

Other subatomic particles subsequently discovered are *mesons, positrons, antiprotons, quarks, pions, gluons* etc., but the most important are the electrons, protons and neutrons.

All matter **has been** found to have the same atomic structure. An atom is **composed of a** very small dense, positively charged nucleus surrounded by sufficient number of negatively charged electrons in different orbits so that the atom is electrically neutral. Practically all the mass of the atom is in the nucleus since the electrons have only very negligible mass.

The nucleus contains protons and neutrons. *Atomic number (Z) of an element is equal to the number of protons present in the nucleus of the atom of the element.* Since atom is electrically neutral, the atomic number is also equal to the number of electrons around the nucleus which are also known as extranuclear or planetary electrons. Hydrogen's atomic number is 1 since it contains one proton in the nucleus. Helium's atomic number is 2 since it contains two protons in the nucleus.

Mass number (A) of an atom is **equal to the** mass of the total number of nucleons, that is protons **and neutrons** in the nucleus. Thus hydrogen has a mass number of 1 **and helium has** a mass number of 4 since it contains two **protons and two** neutrons in its nucleus. Since the uranium atom has 92 electrons, 92 protons and 146 neutrons, its atomic number is 92 and its mass number is 238 (ie., 92 protons +146 neutrons).

ATOMIC SPECTRA

When any element in the gaseous or vapour state is heated either in a high temperature flame or in a discharge tube, the atoms of the element are excited and emit light radiations of characteristic colours and particular wavelengths. Thus sodium salts give out a golden yellow colour when heated in the nonluminous part of the Bunsen flame, potassium salts a violet colour, strontium salts a characteristic red colour and the calcium salts a brick red colour etc. However these colours can be diffracted by a prism in a spectroscope and recorded on a photographic plate. The spectrum recorded on a photographic plate shows bright lines. Each line represents a specific wavelength of radiation emitted by the atoms of the element. These lines together are known as the *Line Spectrum* or *Atomic Emission Spectrum* of the element. Each line of these spectra is called a *spectral line*.

In the same way when white light is passed through the cool vapour of an element, some of the wavelengths is absorbed and the rest transmitted. These absorbed wavelengths are found to be missing, when the transmitted light is examined spectroscopically. The absorbed wavelengths form a series of dark lines in the spectrum. This is known as the *Absorption Spectrum or the Atomic Absorption Spectrum*. The wavelengths of the dark lines are found to match the bright lines of the emission spectrum. Light radiation is absorbed or emitted also in the infrared region (IR spectra) or in the ultraviolet region (UV spectra) of the electromagnetic radiation. Each element has its own characteristic spectra. So spectral analysis is a method of detecting or identifying the elements even when they are available in very small amounts.

ATOMIC SPECTRUM OF HYDROGEN

One can obtain the emission line spectrum of hydrogen by passing electricity through hydrogen gas contained in a discharge tube at low pressure. The emitted radiation is recorded on a photographic plate with the help of a spectroscope. This is the atomic emission spectrum of hydrogen.

As investigated by Balmer (1884), four prominent coloured lines were seen in the spectrum:—
1. a red line (wavelength 6563 Å)
2. a blue green line (wavelength 4861 Å)
3. a blue line (wavelength 4340 Å)
4. a violet line (wavelength 4102 Å)
This is known as the Balmer series.

20

Subsequent to the discovery of the **Balmer** series, four other spectral series were also discovered in the **ultraviolet and** infrared regions of the hydrogen spectrum. They are

1. Lyman series   ——— Ultraviolet region
2. Paschen series   ——— Infrared region
3. Brackett series   ——— Infrared region
4. Pfund series   ——— Infrared region

QUANTUM THEORY OF RADIATION

To explain the phenomenon of the spectral lines Max Planck in 1900 proposed that a hot body emits radiation not in continuous waves but in small units of waves, that is, radiation is produced in a discontinuous way by the hot body's molecules and each of these molecules is vibrating with a specific frequency which is increasing with rise in temperature. In effect he said that radiation was emitted in *pulses of energy* or *unit waves*. Each pulse of energy is known as a quantum.

The Quantum Theory of Electromagnetic Radiation is given below :—

1. *Atoms and molecules emit or absorb radiation in units of waves known as quanta or photons* (it was discovered by Einstein that light radiations also are emitted by excited atoms and molecules in quanta of energy called *photons*).

2. The energy of a quantum or photon is given by the equation

$$E = h\nu$$

Where ν is the frequency of the radiation and h is Planck's constant. The magnitude of a quantum or photon is directly proportional to the frequency of the radiation and indirectly proportional to its wavelength.

3. An atom or molecule emits or absorbs radiation either as one quantum of energy ($h\nu$) or any whole multiple of this unit, ie., in several quanta.

BOHR'S THEORY OF THE ATOM

According to the theory proposed by Bohr in 1913, electrons revolve around the nucleus in specific *circular orbits*. Each orbit is at a specific distance from the nucleus and the electrons in the orbits are endowed with a specific amount of energy. The orbits are numbered as 1, 2, 3, 4 etc., (or K, L, M, N etc.,) according to their distance from the nucleus.

Secondly electrons in these orbits do not lose energy. They are supposed to be in the lowest energy state or the ground state and the specific orbits are therefore known as *energy levels* or *stationary energy levels*.

Electrons can jump from one energy level to another energy level by absorbing energy. While an electron is in its specific orbit, it is in the ground state. But after it has absorbed energy, it jumps to a higher energy level. The absorption is always by a quantum or photon of energy and the electron is now said to be in the *excited state*.

Thirdly the angular momentum of an electron travelling around the nucleus in an orbit is an integral multiple of the Planck's constant divided by 2π. Angular momentum $= n\frac{h}{2\pi}$ where $n = 1, 2, 3$, etc., and h is Planck's constant. Giving values of 1, 2, 3 etc., for each orbit, we have angular momentums such as $\frac{h}{2\pi}, \frac{2h}{2\pi}, \frac{3h}{3\pi}, \frac{4h}{4\pi}$ etc. Here n is known as the *principal quantum number*.

EXPLANATION OF HYDROGEN SPECTRUM

Since the atomic number of hydrogen is 1, there is only one electron in the hydrogen atom and this electron is in the first orbit or energy level. When hydrogen gas is heated in a discharge tube, the electron absorbs energy and moves to higher energy levels such as 2, 3, 4, 5,6 etc., depending on the amount of energy absorbed. It then returns to the ground state (first orbit) by emitting the excess energy as photons. Thus Lyman series is produced, when the electron returns to the ground state (first orbit) from higher energy levels. Balmer series is produced, when the electron returns to the second orbit, Paschen, Brackett and Pfund series are produced, when it returns to the third, fourth and the fifth orbits respectively.

However the Bohr's theory was useful only in explaining the lines in the hydrogen atom. It could not explain the spectra of other atoms containing more than one electron. It also could not explain how molecules formed from atoms by chemical bonds.

SOMMERFELD'S MODIFICATION OF BOHR'S THEORY

On close examination, it was found that each spectral line consisted of several lines closely packed together. Bohr's theory could not explain this. Sommerfeld proposed that the electrons travelled in elliptical orbits instead of circular orbits as in Bohr's theory. There is a major axis and a minor axis in an ellipse, whereas a circle is a special ellipse with major axis and minor axis being equal. The angular momentum of an electron moving in an elliptical orbit has a particular value, that is

$$\text{angular momentum} = \frac{kh}{2\pi}$$

where k is known as the *azimuthal quantum number*. You may recall the *principal quantum number n* postulated in Bohr's theory. Both these quantum numbers are related to each other in the following way :-

$$\frac{n}{k} = \frac{\text{length of major axis}}{\text{length of minor axis}}$$

The values for k can be given as $n-1$, $n-2$, $n-3$, $n-4$, $n-5$ etc. The orbit is circular when $n = k$.

ELECTRONIC CONFIGURATIONS OF ATOMS

It has now been established that planetary or extranuclear electrons equal to the atomic number of the element are revolving around the nucleus in closed orbits. Langmuir put forward a theory in 1919 about the actual arrangement of these atoms in orbits.

LANGMUIR'S THEORY

According to this theory inert gases contain the most stable electronic configurations. The first inert gas in the periodic table *helium* contains two planetary electrons which are in the first orbit which is fully saturated. The next inert gas *neon* contains 10 planetary electrons. These are arranged as 2 in the first orbit and 8 in the second orbit fully saturating the two orbits. The next inert gas *argon* with 18 planetary electrons also is arranged as 2, 8, 8 in three orbits. For *krypton* (atomic number 36), the arrangement should be 2, 8, 18, 8. For *xenon* (atomic number 54), the arrangement is 2, 8, 18, 18, 8 and for *radon* with atomic number of 86, it is 2, 8, 18, 32, 18, 8. All the orbits are deemed to be saturated with these numbers of electrons. The other elements with different atomic numbers are having electronic arrangements with the outermost orbits being unsaturated. Langmuir's theory suffered from the defect that it failed to explain the physical and chemical properties of the higher elements completely.

BOHR-BURY SCHEME

This theory put forward by Bohr and Bury independently of each other in 1921 explained the physical and chemical properties of elements in a better way. The details of this scheme are

1. The maximum number of electrons which each orbit may contain may be given by the formula $2 \times n^2$ where n is the number of the orbit. According to this the first orbit contains $2 \times 1^2 = 2$, the second orbit $2 \times 2^2 = 8$, the third orbit $2 \times 3^2 - 18$, the fourth $2 \times 4^2 = 32$ etc.
2. The outermost orbit can contain only 8 electrons and the penultimate orbit (ie., the orbit next to the outermost) only 18.
3. A new orbit may begin to be formed even when the previous orbit is yet to the completed. A new orbit may also be formed after the outermost orbit has attained eight electrons.
4. The outermost orbit cannot contain more than 2 electrons and the penultimate one more than 9 electrons if the next inner orbit does not contain the maximum number of electrons as required under rule (1).

ZEEMAN EFFECT

Now we will revert back to the subject of emission spectrum and spectral lines. It was discovered by Zeeman in 1896 that *when the spectrum is subjected to or placed in a strong magnetic field,*

24

the spectral lines are split up into components. When viewed axially, it is seen that they split up symmetrically into two components, one having a shorter wavelength (higher frequency) and the other having longer wavelength (lower frequency) compared to the original spectral line which is no longer seen. However when viewed in a direction which is perpendicular to the applied magnetic field, the spectral lines are seen to split up into three components, the line in the middle having the same wavelength and frequency of the original line and the other two being the same as the two lines seen when viewed axially.

WAVE MECHANICAL APPROACH TO THE STRUCTURE OF THE ATOM

So far the discussion has been confined to the"mechanical theory" of matter which considered matter to be made up of discrete particles such as atoms, protons, neutrons, electrons etc. But this theory did not explain the nature of radiations like x-rays and light. So it was postulated that light or x-rays were made up of waves but this failed to explain the production of electrical energy or electrons by light falling on metal surfaces, ie., the photoelectric effect. So a via media was found by proposing that light radiation has the characteristics of both wave and particle.

Then the wave mechanical theory of matter followed. According to this, all matter in nature has both the properties of *particles* (discrete units) and also the properties of *waves* (continuity).

Electrons besides having the particulate nature possess wave nature also. This is proved by the fact that electrons get diffracted when they are sent through a crystal. *An orbital is defined as the most probable space in which the electron remains most of the time while it is in constant motion.*

QUANTUM NUMBERS

It has been found later that many single spectral lines actually consist of many close lines, when examined with highly sophisticated instruments, especially in the spectra of elements other than hydrogen. Secondly when placed in a magnetic field

25

(Zeeman effect) or in an electrical field (Stark effect), these spectral lines split up into different wavelengths.

To explain these phenomena, four different quantum numbers have been proposed and they seek to increase the number of possible 'orbits' where an electron can exist within an atom.

(1) Principal Quantum Number ('n')

Principal quantum number indicates the principal shell in which the electron exists. It is also known as the *major energy level* of the shell. It gives an idea about the average distance of the electron from the nucleus. It has positive integral values such as $n = 1, 2, 3$ etc., So far a maximum value of $n = 7$ only has been found though n can increase theoretically to infinity. The highest quantum number indicates the highest energy level and the lowest quantum number indicates the lowest energy level for the electron. Thus an electron with $n = 1$ has the lowest energy level. The energy levels or shells of electrons are designated by the letters K, L, M, N, O, P and Q corresponding to the n value of 1, 2, 3, 4, 5, 6, 7 respectively. As already stated the electrons in a shell are given by $2n^2$ (n = principal quantum number) and they all have the same energy level.

(2) Azimuthal Quantum Number ('l')

Azimuthal quantum number is also known by other names such as *secondary quantum number, subsidiary quantum number, orbital quantum number* and *angular quantum number*. It gives an idea about the spatial distribution of the electron cloud around the nucleus and also gives an idea about the angular momentum of the electron. By giving an idea about the spatial distribution of the electron, the shape of the electron is indicated. This quantum number has integral values from 0 to $n - 1$ for any principal quantum number n. Each is described as an Energy Sub-level or as a Sub-shell. These sub-shells are indicated by the letters s, p, d, f etc., The total of such sub-shells is equal to the value of the principal quantum number, ie., n. For example for $n = 1$, the value of l is 0, that is the first orbital s only. For $n = 2$, there are two possible values of l, that is $l = 0$ and $l = 2 - 1 = 1$. Here $l = 0$ represents the s orbital and $l = 1$ indicates p orbital. Similarly for $n = 3$ the possible values of l are 3, ie., $l = 0$ and $l = 3 - 1 = 2$, ie., 0 (s orbital), 1 (p orbital) and 2 (d orbital). For $n = 4$, the possible values of l are 4, ie., $l = 0$ and $l = 4 - 1 = 3$, ie., 0 (s orbital), 1 (p orbital), 2 (d orbital) and 3 (f orbital) and so on. While indicating a sub-shell, its principal quantum number also is given to identify the position as below:—

1s, 2s, 3s etc.,

2p, 3p, 4p etc.,

3d, 4d, 5d etc.,

4f and 5f

(3) Magnetic Quantum Number ('m_1')

This quantum number explains the Zeeman effect indicating why the spectral lines are splitting up in the presence of a magnetic or electrical field. Electrons may have the same principal quantum number n and azimuthal quantum number l but still behave differently. This is because the orientation or distribution of the electron cloud is different. For the value of azimuthal quantum number 'l', the magnetic quantum number may be between $+ l$ to $- l$ through zero with only integral values in between such as $+ l$, $(+ l - l)$, 0, $(- l + l)$, $- l$. Therefore, that for each value of l, the values of m_1, will be $(2l + 1)$. So when $l = 0$, $m_1 = 0$. It follows, therefore, that for each value of n (principal quantum number), there will be only one orientation if $l = 0$. This means that there is only s orbital. Since it has only one orientation, it must be spherical. So for each value of n, there is one spherically symmetric orbital 's'.

If $l = 1$ (p-orbital), m_1 will have three values $+ 1$, 0 and $- 1$. So there are three p-orbitals which differ only in their values for m_1, the magnetic quantum number. They are named as p_x, p_y, and p_z according to their axis of orientation. When there is no magnetic field, these orbitals possess equivalent energy and are said to be *three-fold degenerate or triply degenerate*. If an external magnetic field is applied, the energies vary depending upon their orientation, that is according to their magnetic quantum number. This explains the presence of many spectral lines under the influence of an external magnetic field. The p-orbitals are dumb-bell shaped and have two lobes.

(4) Spin Quantum Number ('s')

The spin quantum number has been postulated to give an idea about the spin of electrons about their axis. An electron can spin in two opposite directions, clockwise and anticlockwise. The values of 's' are equal and opposite. The two values are $+\frac{1}{2}$ and $-\frac{1}{2}$ depending upon the direction in which the electron spins or rotates on its own axis. These spins can also be denoted by upward and downward arrows such as $\uparrow\downarrow$. Thus two electrons spinning in the same direction or having the same spin quantum number are said to have *parallel spins*. Those having opposite spins are said to have *opposite spin* or *antiparallel spin or paired-up spin*. This spin of the electron clearly proves that it has a magnetic moment.

PAULI'S EXCLUSION PRINCIPLE

Wolfgang Pauli proposed a principle which sought to control the assignment of values of the four quantum numbers of an electron. According to this *"No two electrons in an atom can have the same identical quantum numbers"*.

Thus every electron is different from the other electrons in at least one quantum number. For example if two electrons have the same n, l and m_1, they will be different in s.

Thus the first shell has only one orbital because its n is 1. The two electrons ($2n^2$) in the first shell are arranged in the following way :—

n	l	m_1	s	
1	0	0	$+\dfrac{1}{2}$	First electron
1	0	0	$-\dfrac{1}{2}$	Second electron

Therefore only a maximum of only two electrons can be accommodated in any orbital. They must also have opposite spins. So the first shell ($n = 1$) should have necessarily only two electrons.

The second shell ($n = 2$) should have eight electrons ($2n^2$) distributed in one $1s$ orbital and three p orbitals as below:—

28

n	l	m_1	s		
				s orbital	
2	0	0	$+\frac{1}{2}$	First electron	} 2s orbital
2	0	0	$-\frac{1}{2}$	Second electron	
				p-orbital	
2	1	+1	$+\frac{1}{2}$	First electron	} $2p_x$ orbital
2	1	+1	$-\frac{1}{2}$	Second electron	
2	1	−1	$+\frac{1}{2}$	First electron	} $2p_y$ orbital
2	1	−1	$-\frac{1}{2}$	Second electron	
2	1	0	$+\frac{1}{2}$	First electron	} $2p_z$ orbital
2	1	0	$-\frac{1}{2}$	Second electron	

Therefore the total number of electrons that can be accommadated by the second shell is 8 ($2n^2$). It can be shown in a similar way that the third shell can accommadate 18 electrons and the fourth shell 32 electrons.

From the above table it is clear that the s subshell or sublevel can accommadate upto 2 electrons and the p sublevel upto six electrons. Similarly it can be shown that the d subshell may contain upto 10 and the f subshell upto 14 electrons. Therefore Pauli's exclusion principle is very useful in giving an idea about the maximum number of electrons accommadated in any shell.

ARRANGEMENT OF ELECTRONS IN ORBITALS

When the periodic table is examined, it is found that one electron is added every time when we move from one atom to another. The distribution of electrons in orbitals in atoms is governed by the *Hund's Rule of Maximum Multiplicity*. Hund's Rule states that *electrons are distributed among orbitals of a subshell in such a way as to give the maximum number of unpaired electrons which have the same direction of spin.*

In accordance with this rule, the first electron is in the first orbital (1s1). The second electron also goes to the first orbital (1s2). But both the electrons have different spin quantum numbers, ie. +1/2 and - 1/2. The third electron enters the first orbital of the next shell (1s2 2s1). The fourth electron also enters this orbital (1s2 2s2). The 5th electron enters the second orbital of the shell. This is the px orbital of the p subshell. So the arrangement now is 1s2 2s2 $2p_x1$. The 6th electron does not enter the p_x but enters the p_y orbital. So now the arrangement is 1s2 2s2 $2p_x1$ $2p_y1$. The 7th electron also enters only the p_z orbital and the distribution now is 1s2 2s2 $2p_x1$ $2p_y1$ $2p_z1$. The 8th electron enters the vacant position in the $2p_x$ orbital and the arrangement now becomes 1s2 2s2 $2p_x2$ $2p_y1$ $2p_z1$. The 9th electron enters the $2p_y$ orbital and the distribution now becomes 1s2 2s2 $2p_x2$ $2p_y2$ $2p_z1$. The 10th electron enters the $2p_z$ orbital to give the arrangement of 1s2 2s2 $2p_x2$ $2p_y2$ $2p_z2$.

So it can be seen that electrons partially fill up the three *p* orbitals and only after the three *p* orbitals get one electron each, the electrons begin to pair up. This is because when several orbitals of equal energy (degenerate orbitals) are available, electrons prefer to occupy separate orbitals rather than getting paired in the same orbital. Such electrons have the same spin quantum number. It has been found that half-filled orbitals possess better stability. The electronic configurations of the elements are mostly on the expected lines but there are many anomalies as can be seen by examining the Table 1 on pages 31 and 32.

Table 1

Ground state electronic configurations of the elements

Atomic number and symbol	1 s	2 s	2 p	3 s	3 p	3 d	4 s	4 p	4 d	4 f	5 s	5 p	5 d	5 f	6 s	6 p	6 d	6 f	7 s
1 H	1																		
2 He	2																		
3 Li	2	1																	
4 Be	2	2																	
5 B	2	2	1																
6 C	2	2	2																
7 N	2	2	3																
8 O	2	2	4																
9 F	2	2	5																
10 Ne	2	2	6																
11 Na	2	2	6	1															
12 Mg	2	2	6	2															
13 Al	2	2	6	2	1														
14 Si	2	2	6	2	2														
15 P	2	2	6	2	3														
16 S	2	2	6	2	4														
17 Cl	2	2	6	2	5														
18 A	2	2	6	2	6														
19 K	2	2	6	2	6		1												
20 Ca	2	2	6	2	6		2												
21 Sc	2	2	6	2	6	1	2												
22 Ti	2	2	6	2	6	2	2												
23 V	2	2	6	2	6	3	2												
24 Cr	2	2	6	2	6	5	1												
25 Mn	2	2	6	2	6	5	2												
26 Fe	2	2	6	2	6	6	2												
27 Co	2	2	6	2	6	7	2												
28 Ni	2	2	6	2	6	8	2												
29 Cu	2	2	6	2	6	10	1												
30 Zn	2	2	6	2	6	10	2												
31 Ga	2	2	6	2	6	10	2	1											
32 Ge	2	2	6	2	6	10	2	2											
33 As	2	2	6	2	6	10	2	3											
34 Se	2	2	6	2	6	10	2	4											
35 Br	2	2	6	2	6	10	2	5											
36 Kr	2	2	6	2	6	10	2	6											
37 Rb	2	2	6	2	6	10	2	6			1								
38 Sr	2	2	6	2	6	10	2	6			2								
39 Y	2	2	6	2	6	10	2	6	1		2								
40 Zr	2	2	6	2	6	10	2	6	2		2								
41 Nb	2	2	6	2	6	10	2	6	4		1								
42 Mo	2	2	6	2	6	10	2	6	5		1								
43 Tc	2	2	6	2	6	10	2	6	6		1								
44 Ru	2	2	6	2	6	10	2	6	7		1								
45 Rh	2	2	6	2	6	10	2	6	8		1								
46 Pd	2	2	6	2	6	10	2	6	10										
47 Ag	2	2	6	2	6	10	2	6	10		1								
48 Cd	2	2	6	2	6	10	2	6	10		2								
49 In	2	2	6	2	6	10	2	6	10		2	1							
50 Sn	2	2	6	2	6	10	2	6	10		2	2							
51 Sb	2	2	6	2	6	10	2	6	10		2	3							
52 Te	2	2	6	2	6	10	2	6	10		2	4							

Ground state electronic configurations of the elements (cont.)

Atomic number and symbol	1 s	2 s	2 p	3 s	3 p	3 d	4 s	4 p	4 d	4 f	5 s	5 p	5 d	5 f	6 s	6 p	6 d	6 f	7 s
53 I	2	2	6	2	6	10	2	6	10		2	5							
54 Xe	2	2	6	2	6	10	2	6	10		2	6							
55 Cs	2	2	6	2	6	10	2	6	10		2	6			1				
56 Ba	2	2	6	2	6	10	2	6	10		2	6			2				
57 La	2	2	6	2	6	10	2	6	10		2	6	1		2				
58 Ce	2	2	6	2	6	10	2	6	10	1	2	6	1		2				
59 Pr	2	2	6	2	6	10	2	6	10	2	2	6	1		2				
60 Nd	2	2	6	2	6	10	2	6	10	3	2	6	1		2				
61 Pm	2	2	6	2	6	10	2	6	10	4	2	6	1		2				
62 Sm	2	2	6	2	6	10	2	6	10	5	2	6	1		2				
63 Eu	2	2	6	2	6	10	2	6	10	6	2	6	1		2				
64 Gd	2	2	6	2	6	10	2	6	10	7	2	6	1		2				
65 Tb	2	2	6	2	6	10	2	6	10	8	2	6	1		2				
66 Dy	2	2	6	2	6	10	2	6	10	9	2	6	1		2				
67 Ho	2	2	6	2	6	10	2	6	10	10	2	6	1		2				
68 Er	2	2	6	2	6	10	2	6	10	11	2	6	1		2				
69 Tm	2	2	6	2	6	10	2	6	10	12	2	6	1		2				
70 Yb	2	2	6	2	6	10	2	6	10	13	2	6	1		2				
71 Lu	2	2	6	2	6	10	2	6	10	14	2	6	1		2				
72 Hf	2	2	6	2	6	10	2	6	10	14	2	6	2		2				
73 Ta	2	2	6	2	6	10	2	6	10	14	2	6	3		2				
74 W	2	2	6	2	6	10	2	6	10	14	2	6	4		2				
75 Re	2	2	6	2	6	10	2	6	10	14	2	6	5		2				
76 Os	2	2	6	2	6	10	2	6	10	14	2	6	6		2				
77 Ir	2	2	6	2	6	10	2	6	10	14	2	6	7		2				
78 Pt	2	2	6	2	6	10	2	6	10	14	2	6	9		1				
79 Au	2	2	6	2	6	10	2	6	10	14	2	6	10		1				
80 Hg	2	2	6	2	6	10	2	6	10	14	2	6	10		2				
81 Tl	2	2	6	2	6	10	2	6	10	14	2	6	10		2	1			
82 Pb	2	2	6	2	6	10	2	6	10	14	2	6	10		2	2			
83 Bi	2	2	6	2	6	10	2	6	10	14	2	6	10		2	3			
84 Po	2	2	6	2	6	10	2	6	10	14	2	6	10		2	4			
85 At	2	2	6	2	6	10	2	6	10	14	2	6	10		2	5			
86 Rn	2	2	6	2	6	10	2	6	10	14	2	6	10		2	6			
87 Fr	2	2	6	2	6	10	2	6	10	14	2	6	10		2	6			1
88 Ra	2	2	6	2	6	10	2	6	10	14	2	6	10		2	6			2
89 Ac	2	2	6	2	6	10	2	6	10	14	2	6	10		2	6	1		2
90 Th	2	2	6	2	6	10	2	6	10	14	2	6	10		2	6	2		2
91 Pa	2	2	6	2	6	10	2	6	10	14	2	6	10		2	6	3		2
92 U	2	2	6	2	6	10	2	6	10	14	2	6	10	3	2	6	1		2
93 Np	2	2	6	2	6	10	2	6	10	14	2	6	10	4	2	6	1		2
94 Pu	2	2	6	2	6	10	2	6	10	14	2	6	10	5	2	6	1		2
95 Am	2	2	6	2	6	10	2	6	10	14	2	6	10	6	2	6	1		2
96 Cm	2	2	6	2	6	10	2	6	10	14	2	6	10	7	2	6	1		2
97 Bk	2	2	6	2	6	10	2	6	10	14	2	6	10	8	2	6	1		2
98 Cf	2	2	6	2	6	10	2	6	10	14	2	6	10	9	2	6	1		2
99 Es	2	2	6	2	6	10	2	6	10	14	2	6	10	10	2	6	1		2
100 Fm	2	2	6	2	6	10	2	6	10	14	2	6	10	11	2	6	1		2
101 Md	2	2	6	2	6	10	2	6	10	14	2	6	10	12	2	6	1		2
102 No	2	2	6	2	6	10	2	6	10	14	2	6	10	13	2	6	1		2

CHAPTER 3

ELECTRONIC THEORY OF VALENCY

In olden days valency was described as the *combining capacity of elements*. It means the capacity of an element to combine with another element or elements to form compounds,. The valency of an element is defined as *the number of hydrogen atoms or twice the number of oxygen atoms with which one atom of any element may combine*.

Thus to form hydrogen chloride (HCl), one atom of chlorine is combining with one atom of hydrogen. So the valency of chlorine is 1. One atom of nitrogen combines with three atoms of hydrogen to form one molecule of ammonia (NH_3). Therefore the valency of nitrogen is 3. Similarly one atom of magnesium combines with one atom of oxygen to form one molecule of magnesium oxide (MgO). So the valency of magnesium is 2.

However this theory could not explain the formation of certain compounds and the variable valencies of some elements. For example the valency of sulphur is 2 when one atom of sulphur combines with two atoms of hydrogen to form one molecule of hydrogen sulphide (H_2S). However its valency seems to be 4 when it comines with two atoms of oxygen to form one molecule of sulphur dioxide (SO_2). Similaryly carbon forms compounds such as C_2H_2 (acetylene), C_2H_4 (ethylene) and C_2H_6 (ethane) etc. From these examples it appears that carbon has valencies 1, 2 and 3, whereas it is known that carbon is tetravalent in all compounds. So this concept of valency is no longer tenable and it is better to describe valency as *the number of bonds formed by an atom of an element to form one molecule of a compound*. To explain this concept more fully the electronic theory of valency was proposed by Kossel and Lewis.

According to this theory, the electrons in the outermost orbit of an atom are the valency electrons and they only take part in chemical bonding. So these electrons are called as *bonding electrons*.

For stability of the atom as a whole, the electrons in the outermost shell should be eight or two (as in the case of helium). This octet of eight electrons is present in the outermost shell of inert gases or rare gases as given below:—

Inert Gas	Atomic Number	Electronic Orbits					
		1st (K)	2nd (L)	3rd (M)	4th (N)	5th (O)	6th (P)
Helium	2	2					
Neon	10	2	8				
Argon	18	2	8	8			
Krypton	36	2	8	18	8		
Xenon	54	2	8	18	18	8	
Radon	86	2	8	18	32	18	8

It is clear that the outermost orbit of these inert gases contains eight electrons except helium which alone contains two electrons. So they are completely stable. This is known as the *Octet Theory*. The atoms of elements other than the inert gases have incomplete outermost shells and so are unstable. They naturally try to complete the octet and become stable. Therefore they try to combine with the atoms of other elements to acquire this stable octet and in the process gain, lose or share electrons. It has been found that atoms of elements enter into three types of linkages and they are:—

1. Electrovalent Bond (Ionic Bond)
2. Covalent Bond
3. Co-ordinate Covalent Bond

1. ELECTROVALENT BOND

This type of chemical bonding is produced by the transfer of electron(s) from one atom to another atom. For example atom A has one electron in its outermost or valence shell and atom B has seven electrons in the valence shell. Both the atoms try to acquire octets to complete their outermost shells so that they will acquire the electronic configuration of the inert gas nearest to them and become stable. So A transfers one electron to B (its penultimate shell with 8 electrons now becomes the outermost shell) and both acquire the stable octet. Since A has lost one electron (which is negatively charged), it becomes the positive ion (catic) and since B has gained one electron, it becomes the negative ion (anion). The reaction is given below:—

$$A_x + \cdot \ddot{\underset{\cdot\cdot}{B}} : \;=\; A \dot{\underset{\cdot\cdot}{x}} \ddot{\underset{\cdot\cdot}{B}} : \quad \text{or} \quad A^+ B^-$$

Both the anion and cation in the molecule are held together strongly by forces of electrostatic attraction. In this reaction there is a net lowering of energy resulting in the formation of a stable molecule.

Examples of Electrovalent or Ionic Compounds

a) Formation of Sodium Chloride

Sodium with atomic number 11 has electronic configuration of 2, 8, 1 whereas chlorine (atomic number 17) has the electronic configuration of 2, 8, 7. So chlorine lacks one electron in its valency shell to complete the octet. Therefore sodium transfers its single electron to chlorine and gets the stable configuration of neon (2, 8). Chlorine by accepting the electron from sodium gets the stable configuration of the inert gas argon (2, 8, 8).

$$\underset{2,\,8,\,1}{Na_x} + \underset{2,\,8,\,7}{\cdot \ddot{\underset{\cdot\cdot}{Cl}} :} = \underset{2,\,8}{Na} \underset{2,\,8,\,8}{\dot{x} \ddot{\underset{\cdot\cdot}{Cl}} :} \quad \text{or} \quad Na^+ Cl^-$$

Both the cations and the anions attract each other because of the electrostatic attraction. This attraction is present in all directions. So in the crystal there is an alternate cation and anion arrangement.

b) Formation of Magnesium Chloride

Magnesium (atomic No.12) has the electronic configuration of 2,8,2. So it has two electrons in its valence shell. Chlorine has seven electrons in its valence shell as we have already seen in the above example of the formation of sodium chloride. So magnesium transfers the two electrons in its valence shell to two atoms of chlorine resulting in the formation of magnesium chloride ($MgCl_2$). Both magnesium and chlorine get the stable octet.

$$Mg_x^x \begin{matrix} 2,8,7 \\ \cdot \ddot{\underset{\cdot\cdot}{Cl}}: \\ \cdot \ddot{\underset{\cdot\cdot}{Cl}}: \\ 2,8,7 \end{matrix} \quad = \quad Mg \begin{matrix} 2,8,8 \\ \{\overset{\cdot\cdot}{\underset{\cdot\cdot}{x Cl}}:\} \\ \{\overset{\cdot\cdot}{\underset{\cdot\cdot}{x Cl}}:\} \\ 2,8,8 \end{matrix} \quad or \quad Mg^{2+}Cl_2^{2-}$$

$2, 8, 2$ $2, 8$

b) Formation of Magnesium Oxide

As we have already seen, magnesium has two electrons in its valence shell. Oxygen (atomic No. 8) has the electronic configuration of 2, 6. So magnesium transfers its two electrons to oxygen and both acquire the stable octet.

$$Mg_x^x + \ddot{\underset{\cdot\cdot}{O}}: = Mg_x^x \ddot{\underset{\cdot\cdot}{O}}: \quad or \quad Mg^{2+}O^{2-}$$

$\quad 2,8,2 \quad 2,6 \qquad 2,8 \; 2,8$

Other examples of electrovalent compounds are K_2S, CaS, Al_2O_3, KCl, $CaCl_2$ etc.

Properties of Electrovalent Compounds

1. Because of the strong electrostatic attraction between anion and cation, electrovalent compounds are solids at room temperature.

2. Since the ions in the electrovalent compounds are held strongly in the crystal lattice, a lot of kinetic energy is required to overcome the electrostatic attraction and make them mobile. So electrovalent compounds have high melting points. They are also hard and brittle due to the same reason.

3. When they are dissolved in a polar liquid such as water, the cations and anions are dragged by the water molecules. These ions are now surrounded by the water molecules and solvated. So electrovalent compounds are soluble in water. By the same reason they are also insoluble in organic solvents.

4. When electrovalent compounds are melted or dissolved in water, the ions acquire freedom of movement and are able to conduct electricity.

5. Since electrovalent compounds are formed by ionic bonds involving electrostatic attraction, they are non-rigid and non-directional. So they do not exhibit any type of space isomerism.

2. COVALENT BOND

The theory of electrovalency could not explain the formation of organic compounds which do not ionize. Also it could not explain the formation of molecules such as H_2, Cl_2, O_2 etc. Therefore it was suggested by G.N. Lewis that atoms could share electrons and thereby achieve stable duplets or octets. For this purpose both the atoms should have almost equal electronegativity.

Some Examples of Covalent Compounds

(a) Formation of Hydrogen Molecule, H_2

Hydrogen molecule is composed of two atoms of hydrogen. Each atom has one electron. So the two hydrogens share the electrons, complete the duplet (2) and acquire the stable configuration of the inert gas helium.

$$H^x + .H = H^x H \text{ or } H—H$$

The covalent bond due to the shared pair of electrons is indicated by a dash or continuous line (—) between the two atoms.

(b) Formation of Chlorine Molecule, Cl_2

As we already know, each chlorine atom has the electronic configuration of 2, 8,7. One valence electron each in the outermost shell of each is shared and both the chlorine atoms acquire the stable octet and form of the chlorine molecule.

$$\overset{x\,x}{\underset{x\,x}{^x_xCl^x}} + \cdot\overset{..}{\underset{..}{Cl}}: = \overset{x\,x}{^x_xCl^x}\overset{..}{\underset{..}{Cl}}: \text{ or } Cl—Cl$$

2, 8, 7   2, 8, 7

37

In the above two examples only one electron pair is shared. So the bond between them is designated as single bond. However there are instances of atoms sharing more than one pair of electrons to complete the octet as given below:-

(c) Formation of Water, H_2O

We know already that one atom of oxygen combines with two atoms of hydrogen to form water. Oxygen atom has the electronic configuration of 2,6, whereas hydrogen has the configuration of 1.

$$ H^{\bullet} + {}_{x}^{xx}O_{x}^{xx} + {}^{\bullet}H \ = \ H {}_{x}^{xx}O {}_{x}^{xx} H \ \text{ or } \ H—O—H $$

Here the two hydrogen atoms get the stable duplet whereas the oxygen atom gets the stable octet.

(d) Formation of Ammonia

Nitrogen atom has the configuration of 2, 5. So to acquire the stable octet, it must get another 3 electrons. So it combines with three hydrogen atoms which have each one electron for sharing with the nitrogen atom.

$$ H^{\bullet} + {}_{x}^{xx}N_{x}^{x} + {}^{\bullet}H \ = \ H {}_{x}^{xx}N {}_{x \bullet}^{x} H \ \text{ or } \ H—N—H $$
$$ \qquad\quad \overset{x}{\underset{H}{+}} \qquad\qquad\qquad\ H \qquad\qquad\quad | $$
$$ \qquad\qquad\qquad\qquad\qquad\qquad\qquad\qquad\qquad\ H $$

(e) Formation of Methane, CH_4

In the formation of organic compounds, covalency plays a large part. Thus carbon, which has the electronic configuration of 2,4 and thus requires four more electrons to complete the octet, combines with four hydrogen atoms leading to the formation of methane.

38

$$H. + \overset{\overset{\textstyle H}{\textstyle \cdot}}{\underset{\underset{\textstyle H}{\textstyle +\cdot}}{\overset{\times}{C}}}{}^{\times} + .H = H{\overset{\overset{\cdot\times}{}}{\underset{\underset{\textstyle H}{\times\cdot}}{\overset{\times}{C}}}}^{\times}H \quad \text{or} \quad H-\underset{\underset{\textstyle H}{|}}{\overset{\overset{\textstyle H}{|}}{C}}-H$$

Sometimes it may be necessary for two atoms to share more than one pair of electrons, say two or three pairs of electrons between the same atoms to complete the octet. Examples are given below:—

(f) Formation of Oxygen Molecule, O_2

The two oxygen atoms here have the configuration of 2, 8, 6. So they can share two pairs of electron between themselves, that is, each contributing two electrons to the union thereby both completing the octet.

$$\underset{2,6}{\overset{\times\times}{\underset{\times}{\overset{\times}{O}}}\overset{\times}{}} + \underset{2,6}{\overset{\cdot\cdot}{:\overset{\cdot\cdot}{O}:}} = \underset{2,8}{\overset{\times\times}{\underset{\times}{\overset{\times}{O}}}\overset{\times}{}}\underset{2,8}{:\overset{\cdot\cdot}{O}:} \quad \text{or} \quad O = O$$

Thus two links are formed between the two oxygen atoms making up the oxygen molecule. This is known as a *double bond*.

(g) Formation of Nitrogen Molecule, N_2.

Each nitrogen atom has the configuration of 2, 5. So two nitrogen atoms join together to complete the octet as below:—

$$\overset{\times}{\underset{\times}{N}}{}^{\times}_{\times} + :N: = \overset{\times}{\underset{\times}{N}}{}^{\times}_{\times}:N: \quad \text{or} \quad N \equiv N$$

The bond that is established between the nitrogen atoms is a *triple bond.*

Properties Of Covalent Compounds

(a) Since only weak intermolecular forces (van der Waals forces) are present between the molecules, the covalent compounds are usually gases, liquids or soft solids at room temperature.

(b) For the same reason they also have low melting points in the case of solids and low boiling points in the case of liquids.

(c) Since there is no electrostatic force holding the atoms in the molecules, the crystals can be easily broken. So they are not hard and brittle like electrovalent compounds.

(d) Covalent compounds are soluble in nonpolar liquids such as organic solvents. The weak intermolecular forces of the covalent compounds are easily overcome by the kinetic energy of the solvent molecules. However, some covalent compounds such as alcohols and amines dissolve in water due to hydrogen-bonding.

(e) Since covalent compounds are rigid and directional, the atoms in the molecules can be arranged in various ways in space. So covalent compounds exhibit stereoisomerism.

(f) Since the covalent compounds do not ionize and form ions, they do not conduct electricity both in solution and in the molten condition.

(g) Covalent compounds undergo slow molecular reactions since there are no ions to undergo fast ionic reactions.

3. COORDINATE COVALENT BOND

This type of bond links apparently saturated compounds to electronegative atoms. In a covalent bond, each of the two atoms contributes one electron so that the two electrons can be shared in common by both the atoms. But in a coordinate covalent bond both the electrons are contributed by one of the atoms to be shared in common by both the atoms. The compound which contains a coordinate bond is known as a *coordinate compound*.

If one atom A (having completed the octet) has an unshared pair of electrons (also known as *lone pair*) and another atom B is short of the stable octet by two electrons, then A transfers the lone

40

pair of electrons to B and both the atoms share the two electrons in common. In the process atom B gets the stable octet. Atom A which has donated the lone pair is known as the *donor* and atom B which has accepted the same in known as the *acceptor.*

$$A_x^{\bullet} + \overset{\bullet\bullet}{\underset{\bullet\bullet}{B}}: = A_x^{\bullet} \overset{\bullet\bullet}{\underset{\bullet\bullet}{B}}: \text{ or } A \rightarrow B$$

Donor   Acceptor   Coordinate Compound

The coordinate linkage connecting A and B is denoted by an arrow ($\rightarrow$) pointing from A to B and indicating that the lone pair has been transferred from A to B.

The molecule of iron which contains the donor atom is known as a ligand.

Some Examples of Coordinate Covalent Compounds

a) Formation of Ammonium Ion, NH_4^+

In ammonia molecule, the central nitrogen atom is linked to three hydrogen atoms (refer under covalent bond). Still the nitrogen has one unshared pair or lone pair of electrons. The hydrogen ion (H^+) coming from an acid has no electron, so the nitrogen in the ammonia molecule transfers its lone pair to the hydrogen in forming the ammonium ion.

$$H\text{---}\underset{\overset{|}{H}}{\overset{\overset{H}{|}}{N}}: + H^+ = H\text{---}\underset{\overset{|}{H}}{\overset{\overset{H}{|}}{N}} \rightarrow H^+ \text{ or } \left[H\text{---}\underset{\overset{|}{H}}{\overset{\overset{H}{|}}{N}}\text{---}H \right]^+$$

Ammonia Hydrogen ion   Ammonium ion

41

b) Formation of Hydronium Ion, H_3O^+

In water, oxygen atom is linked to two hydrgen atoms through two covalent bonds. However there are two lone pairs of electrons in the oxygen atom. It transfers or donates one lone pair to the hydrogen ion (H^+) to form the hydronium ion.

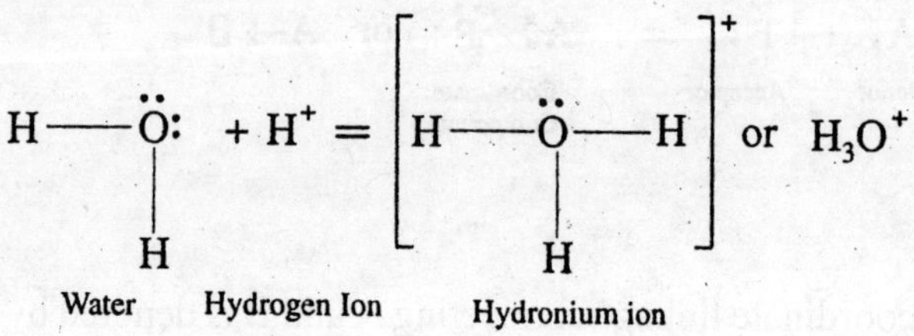

$$H — \overset{..}{O}: + H^+ = \left[H — \overset{..}{O} — H \right]^+ \text{ or } H_3O^+$$

Water	Hydrogen Ion	Hydronium ion

c) Formation of Nitro Compound

Nitromethane, CH_3NO_2, is formed only through a coordinate covalent linkage. First one nitrogen atom, one oxygen atom and the methyl radical get linked through covalent bonds to form a nitroso compound.

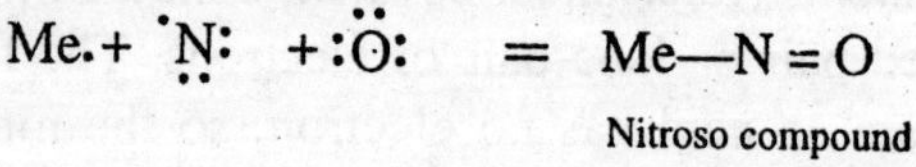

$$Me. + \; \overset{.}{N}: + : \overset{..}{O}: \; = \; Me — N = O$$

Nitroso compound

It may be noted here that in the nitroso compound the nitrogen has completed its octet but still has a lone pair of electrons. It donates the same to another oxygen atom to form the nitromethane.

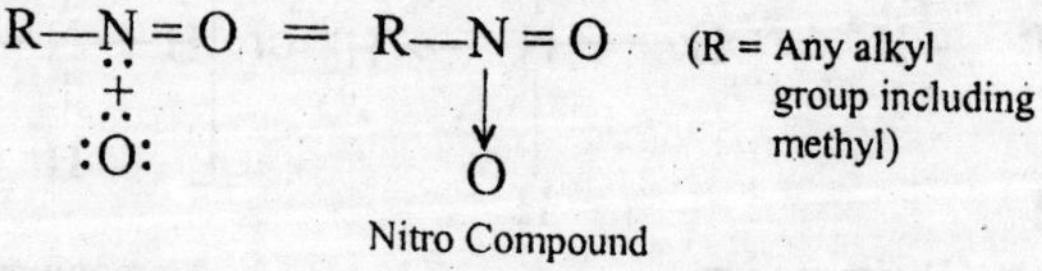

$$R — \underset{\overset{+}{:\overset{..}{O}:}}{N} = O \;\; = \;\; R — N = O$$

(R = Any alkyl group including methyl)

Nitro Compound

d) Formation of Sulphur Dioxide and Sulphur Trioxide

Sulphur has six electrons in the valence shell and completes its octet by forming two covalent bonds with an oxygen atom resulting in the formation of the compound SO. In this compound the sulphur atom has two lone pairs of electrons. It shares one lone pair with another oxygen atom to from SO_2. The sulphur in SO_2 shares the other lone pair with yet another oxygen atom to form SO_3.

$$:\overset{..}{\underset{..}{O}}: \;+\; \overset{xx}{\underset{x}{x}S\overset{x}{x} \;=\; :\overset{..}{O}:\overset{xx}{x}S\overset{x}{x} \quad \text{or} \quad O{=}S$$

$$O{=}\overset{xx}{S}\overset{x}{x} + \;:\overset{..}{O}: \;=\; O{=}\overset{xx}{S}\overset{x}{x}:\overset{..}{O}: \quad \text{or } O{=}S{=}O \quad \text{or} \quad SO_2$$

$$\qquad\qquad\qquad\qquad O \qquad\qquad\text{Sulphur dioxide}$$
$$\qquad\qquad\qquad\qquad \uparrow$$
$$O{=}\overset{xx}{S}{=}O \;+\; \overset{..}{O}: \;=\; O{=}S{=}O \quad \text{or} \quad SO_3$$
$$\qquad\qquad\qquad\qquad\text{Sulphur trioxide}$$

Formation of Sulphate, SO_4^{2-}

First metallic atoms such as two sodium atoms transfer their electrons to the sulphur atom to complete the octet through electrovalent linkage.

$$\begin{matrix} Na^{\cdot} \\ + \\ Na. \end{matrix} \quad \overset{xx}{\underset{xx}{S}}\overset{x}{x} \;=\; \begin{matrix} Na^+ \\ \\ Na^+ \end{matrix} \left[\, :\overset{xx}{\underset{xx}{S}}\overset{x}{x} \,\right]^{2-}$$

Then four oxygen atoms, each of which has six electrons in the valence shell, combine with the sulphur atom to form the sulphate ion. Thus sulphur contributes four lone pairs to the four oxygen atoms to complete their octets.

(Please see the next page for the figure)

43

$$\left[\begin{array}{c} \ddot{\underset{\ddot{}}{O}} \\ \ddot{:}\ddot{\underset{\ddot{}}{O}}\overset{xx}{S}\overset{xx}{\underset{\ddot{}}{O}}\ddot{:} \\ \ddot{\underset{\ddot{}}{O}}\ddot{:} \end{array}\right]^{2-} \quad \text{or} \quad \left[\begin{array}{c} O \\ \uparrow \\ O \leftarrow S \rightarrow O \\ \downarrow \\ O \end{array}\right]^{2-}$$

Sulphate ion

f) Formation of Ozone, O_3

Oxygen molecule is produced by the linkage of two oxygen atoms through two covalent bonds (i.e., a double bond). Each oxygen atom has two unshared pairs of electrons. When one of these lone pairs is donated to another oxygen atom, ozone is formed.

$$\overset{xx}{\underset{x}{O}} = \overset{xx}{\underset{x}{O}} \; + \; \overset{..}{\underset{.}{O}} \; = \; \underset{\text{Ozone}}{O = O \rightarrow O}$$

Properties of Coordinate Covalent Compounds

1. The coordinate covalent compounds do not dissociate when placed in water or melted.

2. They are insolube in water but soluble in organic solvents just like the covalent compounds.

3. Thier melting points and boiling points are relatively higher than those of the covalent compounds but lower than those of the electrovalent compounds.

4. Like the covalent compounds, these are also rigid and directional. So these compounds also exhibit space isomerism.

4. POLAR COVALENT BONDS

In the hydrogen molecule (H_2) there is covalent bond between the two hydrogen atoms. Each atom contributes one elec-

44

tron to the bond and both the electrons are equally shared by both the atoms. Since both the nuclei are identical , the two electrons making up the covalent bond are equally attracted by both the nuclei.

However when two different atoms are linked by a covalent bond as in HF (hydrogen fluoride), the electron pair is not shared equally. The nucleus of fluorine (F) has a greater attraction for the electrons compared to the nucleus of hydrogen. So the electrons find themselves nearer the nucleus of fluorine. Because of this a polarity is developed in the molecule. Hydrogen atom develops a partial positive charge and the fluorine atom develops a partial negative charge. Such a type of bond is known as a *polar covalent bond.*

$$H \overset{\delta^+}{\underline{\quad\vdots\quad}} \overset{\delta^-}{F} \quad \text{or} \quad H \overset{+\longrightarrow}{\underline{\quad\quad}} F$$

A molecule such as the HF having partial positive and negative charges separated by a distance is called a *dipole.* This dipole is indicated by an arrow flowing from positive to negative end with a crossed tail at the positive end.

Since all dissimilar atoms have different attractions for the electrons, all covalent bonds between unlike atoms are polar to some extent. *The greater the difference in electronegativity between the two atoms, the greater will be the polarity.* In the above example, the electronegativity of fluorine is 4 and that of hydrogen is 2.1. So the molecule HF has a strong dipole, since the difference in electronegativities is large.

Other Examples of Polar Covalent Bond

a. Hydrogen Chloride, HCl

$$H \overset{\delta^+}{\underline{\quad\vdots\quad}} \overset{\delta^-}{Cl} \quad \text{or} \quad H \overset{+\longrightarrow}{\underline{\quad\quad}} Cl$$

45

b. Water, H₂O

Water molecule (H_2O) has one oxygen atom linked to two hydrogen atoms through covalent bonds. The electronegativity of oxygen is 3.5 and that of hydrogen is 2.1. Thus both the bonds are polar.

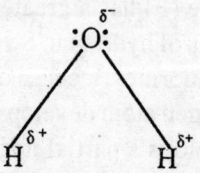

c. Ammonia, NH₃

Ammonia has three N—H bonds. Nitrogen has an electronegativity of 3 and hydrogen has the electronegativity of 2.1. Thus all three N—H bonds are polar.

5. HYDROGEN BONDING

In the above examples given for polar covalent bonds, a strong dipole results since the shared electron pair is pulled closer to one atom which may be either F, Cl, O or N. As the hydrogen atom at the positive end of the dipole has nearly lost the electron pair it exerts a strong electrostatic attraction on the nearest lone pair of electrons available with another electronegative atom in a nearby molecule.

$$:X \overset{\delta^-}{\text{——}} H \overset{\delta^+}{+} :X \overset{\delta^-}{\text{——}} H = X—H\text{------}X—H$$

$$(X = F, Cl, O \text{ or } N)$$

The broken line is known as *a hydrogen bond*. For hydrogen bonding to take place, the conditions to be fulfilled are that the molecules must have polar bonds and the electronegative atom should have an unshared electron pair. Only elements such as oxygen, nitrogen or fluorine because of their small atomic size and high electronegativity can form hydrogen bonds. Hydrogen bond is a weak bond, weaker than a normal covalent bond. Hydrogen bonding results in the formation of *'associated molecules'*. These compounds have high melting points and high boiling points.

Examples of Hydrogen Bonding

a. Hydrogen Fluoride, HF

Since the electronegativity of fluorine is the highest of all elements, the crystals of hydrogen fluoride contain long chains of H-F molecules. In this every hydrogen atom is covalently linked to one fluorine atom and linked to another fluorine attom also through hydrogen bonding. The bonding is through p-orbitals of the fluorine atom containing a lone electron pair.

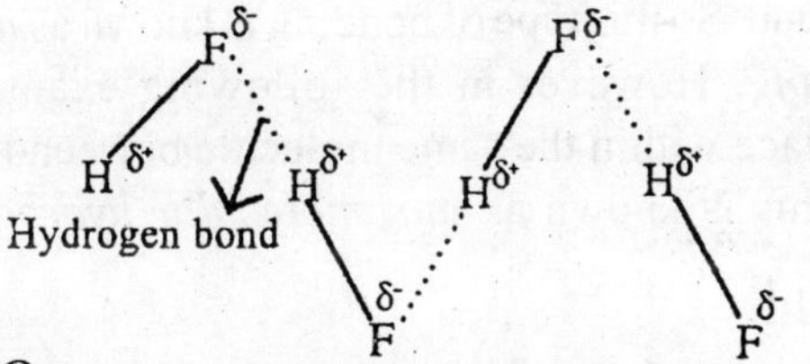

Hydrogen bond

B. Water, H$_2$O

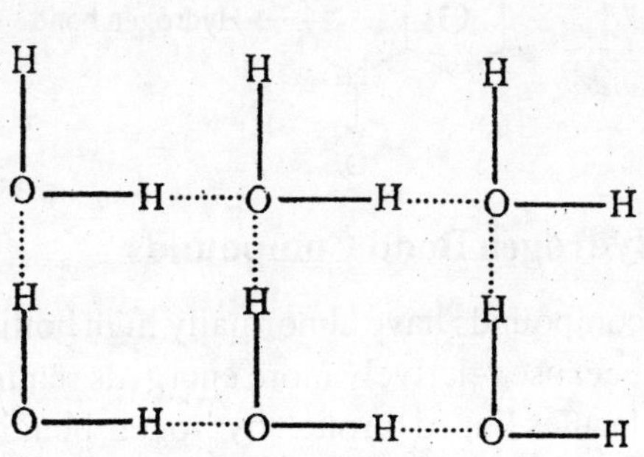

47

In water each hydrogen atom in a water molecule is bonded to one oxygen atom through a covalent bond and also linked to another oxygen atom of another water molecule through hydrogen bonding. Thus large chains or clusters of water molecules are formed. These are known as 'associated molecules'.

c. Ammonia, NH₃

In the molecule of ammonia, the highly electronegative nitrogen atom is linked to three hydrogen atoms through covalent bonds. Therefore each hydrogen atom can form hydrogen bonds with the nitrogen atoms of neighbouring molecules.

The above hydrogen bonds are formed between molecules of the same compound. So this type of bonding is known as *intermolecular hydrogen bonding*. However in the following example hydrogen bonding takes place within the same molecule beween the --OH and --NO₂ groups. This is known as *intramolecular hydrogen bonding*.

d. 2-Nitrophenol

Properties of Hydrogen Bond Compounds

1. These compounds have abnormally high boiling and melting points because relatively more energy is required to separate the molecules linked through hydrogen bonding.

2. These compounds are very soluble in water as they form hydrogen bonds with water. eg., methanol, ammonia etc.

3. The crystals of these compounds are three dimensional because of the hydrogen bonds which are directional and very strong.

VARIABLE VALENCIES

Some elements have more than one valency. For example copper has Cu^{1+} and Cu^{2+} ions indicating two types of valency. Similarly iron forms Fe^{2+} and Fe^{3+} ions (ie, ferrous and ferric ions). This is because since some of the electrons in the d orbital of these atoms have energy nearly equal to that of the outermost electrons, they are also able to participate in the chemical bonding. Thus these elements have more than one valency.

CHAPTER 4
THE PERIODIC TABLE

Now about 106 elements are known to us and it is difficult to study the chemistry of all the elements individually and their many compounds. The study becomes simpler if we can find a way to classify them into groups of elements having similar properties. The periodic table, as we know it today, evolved out of the attempts of many chemists to classify the elements in the nineteenth and the twentieth centuries. Since the elements are classified into sections known as periods, the whole table is known as a periodic table. The following is the evolution of the periodic table:—

1. Dobereiner's Triads (1829): Dobereiner classified elements into groups of three and called them *triads*. The elements which Dobereiner classified into triads had similar properties and also the average of the atomic weights of the first and the third elements in the triad was the atomic weight of the second element as given below:—

a. Lithium   Sodium   Potassium
   $(A = 7)$ $(A = 23)$ $(A = 39)$

Atomic weight of sodium $= \dfrac{7 + 39}{2} = 23$

b. Chlorine   Bromine   Iodine
   $(A = 35.5)$ $(A = 80)$ $(A = 127)$

Atomic weight of bromine $= \dfrac{35.5 + 127}{2} = 81.25$

However this scheme fell through since only a limited number of elements could be classified into such triads.

2. Newland's Law of Octaves (1863): Newland arranged elements in groups of eight in the order of their increasing atomic weights and observed that *the eighth element starting from a given element is almost a repetition of the first element in properties*. He called it the *Law of Octaves*.

However the main defects of this kind of arrangement were :-

1. Not all elements could be classified like this.

2. After the discovery of the noble gases it was the ninth elements (not the eighth element) which rese~ ᵇled the first one.

3. Lothar Meyer's Graph (1869) : Lothar Meyer prepared a graph of atomic volumes of the elements against their atomic weights. Atomic volume is nothing but the atomic weight divided by its density. In this graph some similar elements (such as the alkah metals) occupied the peaks, some others occupied the ascending parts of the curve (the halogens) and some others occupied the descending portions of the curve (the alkaline earth metals). This arrangement also suffered from the defect that it was not uniformly applicable to all the elements.

4. Mendeleeff's Periodic Table (1869) : Mendeleeff constructed a table of elements in which the elements were arranged in the order of their increasing atomic weights. He also used all the physical and chemical properties of the elements for the arrangement and this resulted in a table in which elements with similar physical and chemical properties occurred at regular intervals in a predictable manner. He also utilised the similarities of the properties of the compounds formed by the elements for the classification. He also ignored the order of atomic weights of the elements sometimes when the elements could not be fitted in their proper places in the periodic table as per their chemical properties. He also left some gaps for some missing elements and predicted the properties of those missing elements with a high degree of accuracy. Gallium and germanium were discovered like this later and their properties almost exactly matched the properties predicted by Mendeleeff. However the noble gases were not discovered at that time and Mendeleeff could not include them in his periodic table. Mendeleeff stated the periodic law as *"the properties of the elements as well as the formulae and properties of their compounds, are a periodic function of their atomic weights"*

Uses of Mendeleeff's Periodic Table

a. Prediction of New Elements : As stated already, Mendeleeff left some vacant spaces in his periodic table stating that he was leaving the gaps for the elements yet to be discovered. His predicitions proved to be correct and many elements were discovered later. Examples are gallium and germanium.

b. Correction of Doubtful Atomic Weights : The atomic weight of beryllium was believed to be 13.5. So on this basis it could find a place only between carbon (at.wt. = 12) and nitrogen (at. wt. = 14). Actually it should be placed between lithium and carbon only. So its atomic weight was revised to 9 so that it could occupy its proper place between lithium and carbon.

Defects in Mendeleef's Periodic Table

a. Position of hydrogen : Hydrogen resembles both the alkali metals and the halogens and its position in the periodic table is ambiguous since it can be placed both in the I and VII groups.

b. Separation of similar elements : Certain elements (eg : gold and platinum) which are similar in properties were found to be placed in different groups.

c. Dissimilar elements grouped together : Copper, silver and gold which had similar properties were found to be grouped with dissimilar elements like the alkali metals.

d. Lanthanides and actinides : A group of 15 elements known as lanthanides (or rare earths) are placed together in one position in the sixth period of the table. Similarly another group of 15 elements called actinides also are placed in one position in the seventh period of the table.

e. Some elements anomalously placed : Argon with the atomic weight of 39.9 comes before potassim (at. wt.=39.1). Similarly tellurium (at.wt.=127.6) comes before iodine (at.wt.=126.9).

f. Position of isotopes : The isotopes of the different elements have not been taken into account in the table.

5. Modern Periodic Table

Moseley changed the basic classification of elements from atomic weights to atomic numbers. Immediately the last two defects pointed out in the Mendeleeff's periodic table, viz, anomalously placed elements and the position of isotopes disappeared. The elements occupied their correct positions according to their atomic numbers without any anomaly and the problem of giving positions to isotopes of any element disappeared since even though they differed in atomic weight they had the same atomic number.

Amongst the many modifications suggested, Bohr's long table is the most convenient and easiest. It is given on page 54.

The table consists of seven horizontally arranged units known as 'periods'. Except the first (which starts with hydrogen), every other period starts with an alkali metal. For example the second period starts with lithium (Li), the third with sodium (Na), the fourth with potassium (K), the fifth with rubidium (Rb), the sixth with caecium (Cs) and the seventh with francium (Fr). Similarly except the seventh period, each period ends with an inert gas or noble gas. Thus the first period ends with helium (He), the second with neon (Ne), the third with argon (A), the fourth with krypton (Kr), the fifth with xenon (Xe) and the sixth with radon (Rn). The seventh period is incomplete.

The first period contains 2 elements, the second and third 8 elements each, the fourth and the fifth 18 elements each and the sixth contains 32 elements. Apart from the first period which contains 2 elements, the second and third containing 8 elements each are known as *short periods* The fourth, fifth and the sixth periods are known as *long periods.* The seventh period is an incomplete period of 18 elements which are radioactive. The elements in the two short periods (ie., the second and the third) are known as *typical elements.*

Each long period is divided into two series, that is, the even and the odd. The even series begins with an alkali metal and ends with a group of three transitional elements. The total no. of elements is 10. In the sixth period, however, there are 24 elements due to the inclusion of the rare earths. The odd series each starts with a coinage metal (ie., copper, silver and gold) and ends with an inert gas. Totally there are eight elements in each odd series. Elements in even series are considered to belong to *a* sub-groups and the elements in the odd series to *b* sub-groups.

In the sixth period, which is a very long period, after lanthanum (La), there are 14 elements grouped together. They resemble

53

MODERN PERIODIC TABLE (*Extended Form*)

Group → Period ↓	IA	IIA	IIIA	IVA	VA	VIA	VIIA	VIII			IB	IIB	IIIB	IVB	VB	VIB	VIIB	0
1	H 1																	He 2
2	Li 3	Be 4											B 5	C 6	N 7	O 8	F 9	Ne 10
3	Na 11	Mg 12											Al 13	Si 14	P 15	S 16	Cl 17	A 18
4	K 19	Ca 20	Sc 21	Ti 22	V 23	Cr 24	Mn 25	Fe 26	Co 27	Ni 28	Cu 29	Zn 30	Ga 31	Ge 32	As 33	Se 34	Br 35	Kr 36
5	Rb 37	Sr 38	Y 39	Zr 40	Nb 41	Mo 42	Tc 43	Ru 44	Rh 45	Pd 46	Ag 47	Cd 48	In 49	Sn 50	Sb 51	Te 52	I 53	Xe 54
6	Cs 35	Ba 56	La* 57	Hf 72	Ta 73	W 74	Re 75	Os 76	Ir 77	Pt 78	Au 79	Hg 80	Tl 81	Pb 82	Bi 83	Po 84	At 85	Rn 86
7	Fr 87	Ra 88	Ac** 89	Ku 104	Ha 105							Eka-mer-cury 112						

Active metals · Transition Metals · Cu-Zn Group · Metalloids and Non-metals

* Lanthanide Elements	Ce 58	Pr 59	Nd 60	Pm 61	Sm 62	Eu 63	Gd 64	Tb 65	Dy 66	Ho 67	Er 68	Tm 69	Yb 70	Lu 71
** Actinide Series	Th 90	Pa 91	U 92	Np 93	Pu 94	Am 95	Cm 96	Bk 97	Cf 98	Es 99	Fm 100	Md 101	No 102	Lr 103

54

lanthanum and also each other so closely that all the fifteen (including lanthanum) are assigned to one position in the table. These are known as the *rare earths or lanthanides or lanthanon elements*. Similarly uranium and 14 other elements which are radioactive are grouped together in one position in the seventh period. These elements are known as *actinides or actinons*. In this connection elements with atomic numbers 93 to 105 are only synthetic elements discovered during atomic research.

In this table, there are 16 vertical columns which are known as groups. They are numbered from I to VIII (ie., Ia and Ib, IIa and IIb etc) and O. The elements in the *a* sub-group mentioned above are coming under the *a* series (ie., Ia, IIa etc. upto VIIa). Similarly, the elements in the *b* sub-group are coming under the *b* series (ie. Ib, IIb etc. upto VIIb). In addition to these, the other groups are group VIII and group O. Elements of the *a* sub-groups are known as *normal elements*. Elements of the *b* sub-groups and group VIII are known as *transitional elements*. Elements of the O group are inert gases and show little reactivity.

Gradation of properties of elements can be seen as we examine the groups. Elements in the same group have a common valency which is equal to the number of the group. However the inert gases do not have any valency. Elements in the same sub-group resemble each other in physical and chemical properties closely. However the *a* sub-group elements do not resemble the *b* sub-group elements even though the group number is the same. The elements in the sub-groups which resemble each other closely mainly in chemical properties are said to constitute a family. For example, the halogen family consists of fluorine, chlorine, bromine, iodine and astatine. Progressive gradation of properties is visible in each family as we move from the top downwards. This is because the size of the atom increases with increase in atomic number and this makes the electrons in the outermost orbit to be progressively less strongly held. The first member of a family is found to be usually abnormal in some aspects. For example lithium is different from other alkali metals in some respects.

The *a* sub-group elements are metals. The *b* sub-group elements are different. The elements of the first five groups on the left side of the thick separating line are metals. The others in other *b* sub-groups on the right of the separating line are metalloids (that is, elements intermediate between metals and non-metals) and non-metals. Elements from top to bottom of the table in the groups show increased electropositivity which decreases from left to right along the periods. As a result of this, electropositivity of an element is the same as that of an element in the following period and group since the two effects (increase from top downwards for the group and decrease from left to right for the period) compensate each other. This is known as a *"diagonal relationship"*. Many such pairs having almost the same electropositivity can be seen. Examples are lithium and magnesium, beryllium and aluminium and boron and silicon.

PERIODIC TABLE AND ELECTRONIC CONFIGURATIONS OF ELEMENTS

It has been found that there is a close relationship between the electronic configurations of the atoms of the elements and the periodic table. A particular type of configuration is seen with each set of elements which means that this configuration only is responsible for the similarity in the physical and chemical properties of these groups of elements. If we go through the electronic configurations of these groups of elements, we are able to notice a particular type of configuration in each element belonging to a particular group. These details are outlined below:—

a. Elements which finish with ns^1: In these elements the outermost shell contains one electron in the s sub-shell invariably. n is the number of the outermost shell. These elements with their atomic numbers given in brackets are H(1), Li(3), Na(11), K(19), Rb(37), Cs(55) and Fr(87). Their detailed electronic configurations are given below:—

H $1s^1$
Li $1s^2, 2s^1$
Na $1s^2, 2s^2, 2p^6, 3s^1$
K $1s^2, 2s^2, 2p^6, 3s^2, 3p^6, 4s^1$
Rb $1s^2, 2s^2, 2p^o, 3s^2, 3p^6, 3d^{10}, 4s^2, 4p^6, 5s^1$

Cs $1s^2, 2s^2, 2p^6, 3s^2, 3p^6, 3d^{10}, 4s^2, 4p^6, 4d^{10}, 5s^2, 5p^6, 6s^1$

Fr $1s^2, 2s^2, 2p^6, 3s^2, 3p^6, 3d^{10}, 4s^2, 4p^6, 4d^{10}, 4f^{14},$
$5s^2, 5p^6, 5d^{10}, 6s^2, 6p^6, 7s^1$

It may be noticed that the outermost shell of all the elements contains one electron in the s sub-shell. This accounts for the gradation in physical properties seen with them and also for the similar chemical properties. When they react with other elements, they lose this s^1 electron and become electropositive. Because of this their valency is 1. They usually form ionic compounds. These are known as the *alkali metals*.

b. Elements which finish with ns^2. In these elements the outer-most shell contains 2 electrons in the s sub-shell. These elements are Be(4), Mg(12), Ca(20), Sr(38), Ba(56), and Ra(88). These are known as the *alkaline earth elements*.

Be $1s^2, 2s^2$

Mg $1s^2, 2s^2, 2p^6, 3s^2$

Ca $1s^2, 2s^2, 2p^6, 3s^2, 3p^6, 4s^2$

Sr $1s^2, 2s^2, 2p^6, 3s^2, 3p^6, 3d^{10}, 4s^2, 4p^6, 5s^2$ etc.

The alkali metals and the alkaline earth elements are together known as *s-block elements*.

c. Similarly for the following elements the electronic configurations will be - after ns^2 it is np^1 to np^5 (n is the number of the shell):-

1. B, Al, Ga, In, Ti ———— ns^2, np^1 Boron family
2. C, Si, Ge, Sn, Pb ———— ns^2, np^2 Carbon family
3. N, P, As, Sb, Bi ————ns^2, np^3 Nitrogen family
4. O, S, Se, Te, Po ———— ns^2, np^4 Oxygen family
5. F, Cl, Br, I, At ———— ns^2, np^5 Halogen family

d. The elements in this group are noble gases or rare gases. They have the electronic configuration of ns^2, np^6 except in the case of helium which has the electronic configuration of $1s^2$ only.

He $1s^2$
Ne, A, Kr, Xe and Rn — ns^2, np^6

Elements classified under c and d are known as *p-block elements*.

e. Transition Elements (d-block Elements): In the first series of transition elements (Z = 21 to 30), the incoming electron goes to the 3d sub-shell instead of occupying the 4p sub-shell.

Sc	$3d^1, 4s^2$
Ti	$3d^2, 4s^2$
V	$3d^3, 4s^2$
Cr	$3d^5, 4s^1$
Mn	$3d^5, 4s^2$
Fe	$3d^6, 4s^2$
Co	$3d^7, 4s^2$
Ni	$3d^8, 4s^2$
Cu	$3d^{10}, 4s^1$
Zn	$3d^{10}, 4s^2$

The electrons choose to create the 3d orbital instead of occupying the 4p orbital since the 3d orbital has less energy associated with it. The same reason is responsible for one of the 4s electrons shifting to 3d (see Cr and Cu above).

In the second series of transition elements with atomic numbers 39 to 48, the incoming electron occupies the 4d sub-shell instead of going to 5p.

Y	$4d^1, 5s^2$
Zr	$4d^2, 5s^2$
Nb	$4d^4, 5s^1$
Mo	$4d^5, 5s^1$
Tc	$4d^6, 5s^1$
Ru	$4d^7, 5s^1$
Rh	$4d^8, 5s^1$
Pd	$4d^{10}$
Ag	$4d^{10}, 5s^1$
Cd	$4d^{10}, 5s^2$

In the third series of transition elements (Z = 57 and 72 to 80), the incoming electron occupies the 5d sub-shell instead of going to the 6p. In position 57, lanthanon and 14 other elements occupy the same place since they have the same chemical properties. These are known as *rare earths*. In the lanthanides (Z = 58 to 71) the incoming electrons occupy 4f sub-shell in preference to 5d or 6p sub-shells.

In the actinides also (Z = 90 to 103), the electrons occupy the 5f sub-shell in preference to 6d or 7p sub-shells. Therefore both the lanthanides and actinides are together known as *f-block elements*. These are also known as *inner transition elements*.

The long form of the periodic table of the elements with their atomic numbers and ground state electronic configurations is given on page 60. This is a modification of the modern periodic table already given. In this table also there are seven periods but the groups are numbered from 1 to 18. Group 1 contains the alkali metals, group 2 the alkaline earth elements, groups 3 to 12 the transition elements, groups 13 to 17 metalloids and non-metals and finally group 18 contains the rare gases or noble gases.

PERIODIC TRENDS IN PROPERTIES

We have studied so far about various types of elements such as s-block elements, p-block elements, d-block elements and f-block elements. From this we understand that there is a regular periodic repetition of the same type of electronic configuration in these elements as the charge on the nucleus (and therefore the number of electrons around the nucleus) increases. This is responsible for the regular variations in the chemical properties of these elements and outlined below are the variations in some of these properties :-

1. IONIZATION ENERGY

The ionization energy is defined as the energy required to remove an electron from an atom in the gaseous state in the ground state. In other words, energy is required for removing an electron from the atom. After the electron is removed, a gasous ion is formed.

$$M (g) + IE \longrightarrow M^+(g) + e^-$$

MODERN PERIODIC TABLE (according to electronic configuration)

Representative elements

d-transition elements

f-inner transition elements

Noble gases — GROUP 18

Representative elements (Groups 1 and 2)

Period	GROUP 1	GROUP 2
1	H $1s^1$	
2	3 Li $2s^1$	4 Be $2s^2$
3	11 Na $3s^1$	12 Mg $3s^2$
4	19 K $4s^1$	20 Ca $4s^2$
5	37 Rb $5s^1$	38 Sr $5s^2$
6	55 Cs $6s^1$	56 Ba $6s^2$
7	87 Fr $7s^1$	88 Ra $7s^2$

d-transition elements (GROUP NUMBER 3–12)

Group	3	4	5	6	7	8	9	10	11	12
	21 Sc $3d^1 4s^2$	22 Ti $3d^2 4s^2$	23 V $3d^3 4s^2$	24 Cr $3d^5 4s^1$	25 Mn $3d^5 4s^2$	26 Fe $3d^6 4s^2$	27 Co $3d^7 4s^2$	28 Ni $3d^8 4s^2$	29 Cu $3d^{10} 4s^1$	30 Zn $3d^{10} 4s^2$
	39 Y $4d^1 5s^2$	40 Zr $4d^2 5s^2$	41 Nb $4d^4 5s^1$	42 Mo $4d^5 5s^1$	43 Tc $4d^5 5s^2$	44 Ru $4d^7 5s^1$	45 Rh $4d^8 5s^1$	46 Pd $4d^{10}$	47 Ag $4d^{10} 5s^1$	48 Cd $4d^{10} 5s^2$
	57 La* $5d^1 6s^2$	72 Hf $4f^{14} 5d^2 6s^2$	73 Ta $5d^3 6s^2$	74 W $5d^4 6s^2$	75 Re $5d^5 6s^2$	76 Os $5d^6 6s^2$	77 Ir $5d^7 6s^2$	78 Pt $5d^9 6s^1$	79 Au $5d^{10} 6s^1$	80 Hg $5d^{10} 6s^2$
	89 Ac** $6d^1 7s^2$									

Representative elements (GROUP NUMBER 13–18)

Group	13	14	15	16	17	18
						2 He $1s^2$
	5 B $2s^2 2p^1$	6 C $2s^2 2p^2$	7 N $2s^2 2p^3$	8 O $2s^2 2p^4$	9 F $2s^2 2p^5$	10 Ne $2s^2 2p^6$
	13 Al $3s^2 3p^1$	14 Si $3s^2 3p^2$	15 P $3s^2 3p^3$	16 S $3s^2 3p^4$	17 Cl $3s^2 3p^5$	18 Ar $3s^2 3p^6$
	31 Ga $4s^2 4p^1$	32 Ge $4s^2 4p^2$	33 As $4s^2 4p^3$	34 Se $4s^2 4p^4$	35 Br $4s^2 4p^5$	36 Kr $4s^2 4p^6$
	49 In $5s^2 5p^1$	50 Sn $5s^2 5p^2$	51 Sb $5s^2 5p^3$	52 Te $5s^2 5p^4$	53 I $5s^2 5p^5$	54 Xe $5s^2 5p^6$
	81 Tl $6s^2 6p^1$	82 Pb $6s^2 6p^2$	83 Bi $6s^2 6p^3$	84 Po $6s^2 6p^4$	85 At $6s^2 6p^5$	86 Rn $6s^2 6p^6$

f-inner transition elements

* Lanthanides $4f^n 5d^{0-1} 6s^2$

58 Ce $4f^1 5d^1 6s^2$	59 Pl $4f^3 5d^0 6s^2$	60 Nd $4f^4 5d^0 6s^2$	61 Pm $4f^5 5d^0 6s^2$	62 Sm $4f^6 5d^0 6s^2$	63 Eu $4f^7 5d^0 6s^2$	64 Gd $4f^7 5d^1 6s^2$	65 Tb $4f^9 5d^0 6s^2$	66 Dy $4f^{10} 5d^0 6s^2$	67 Ho $4f^{11} 5d^0 6s^2$	68 Er $4f^{12} 5d^0 6s^2$	69 Tm $4f^{13} 5d^0 6s^2$	70 Yb $4f^{14} 5d^0 6s^2$	71 Lu $4f^{14} 5d^1 6s^2$

** Actinides $5f^n 6d^{0-1} 7s^2$

90 Th $5f^0 6d^2 7s^2$	91 Pa $5f^2 6d^1 7s^2$	92 U $5f^3 6d^1 7s^2$	93 Np $5f^4 6d^1 7s^2$	94 Pu $5f^6 6d^0 7s^2$	95 Am $5f^7 6d^0 7s^2$	96 Cm $5f^7 6d^1 7s^2$	97 Bk $5f^9 6d^0 7s^2$	98 Cf $5f^{10} 6d^0 7s^2$	99 Es $5f^{11} 6d^0 7s^2$	100 Fm $5f^{12} 6d^0 7s^2$	101 Md $5f^{13} 6d^0 7s^2$	102 No $5f^{14} 6d^0 7s^2$	103 Lr $5f^{14} 6d^1 7s^2$

Long form of the Periodic Table of the Elements with their atomic number and ground state electronic configurations.

The ionization energy is expressed in units of kj mol^{-1} More ionization energy is required to remove a second electron because it is more difficult to remove an electron from a positively charged ion than from a neutral atom. The same is the case for the removal of the third electron.

Ionization energy depends on the following factors :-

a. **Nuclear Charge** : As the nuclear charge increases, the pull on the electrons by the nucleus becomes more and more ionization energy is required to remove the electrons from the atoms. As the nuclear charge increases in the elements from left to right in a period in the periodic table, *the ionization energy increases from left to right in a period.*

b. **Principal Quantum Number** *(n)* : Principal quantum number indicates the distance at which the electron is located from the nucleus. It means that the higher the value of *n,* the longer will be the distance of the electron from the nucleus, that is, away from the positive charge of the nucleus and so that much easier for it to be removed. This results in a lowering of ionization energy. *The value of n increases as we move down a group leading to a decrease in ionization energy.*

c. **Shielding Effect :** In addition to the valence electron in the outermost shell there are other electrons closer to the nucleus in the other orbits and they reduce the pull of the nucleus on the valence electron by their own negative charge. This is known as shielding effect. Because of this, ionization energy will decrease. So the more number of inner electrons present between the valence electron and the nucleus, the more the ionizatin energy will decrease.

However the noble gases have high ionization energy because of their closed electron shells. Therefore they exhibit extremely low chemical reactivity. In contrast, the alkali metals are highly reactive because of their low ionization energies. Generally the ionization energy decreases as we move down the column of a group. This is due to the shileding effect of the inner electrons.

d. **Azimuthal Quantum Number** *(l)*: When electrons are added one by one to build up an atom, they prefer to occupy the sub-shells with lower energy, if they are vacant. For a given value of *n,* the

61

probability of finding the electron near the nucleus decreases in the following order as the value of l increases:—

$$s > p > d > f$$

Consequently the electron entering the s sub-shell finds itself nearer the nucleus than the electrons in the other sub-shells and therefore is subject to the attraction or pull of the nucleus more than the others. Therefore the ionization energy of s electron is greater than that of p electron which itself has more IE than d electron and so on.

2. ELECTRON AFFINITY

An atom's chemical properties are determined by its tendency to pick up another electron. This is known as electron affinity. The more electron affinity a given atom has, the more electropositive it is considered to be. Generally electron affinity increases with atomic number as we move from left to right along a period. Electron affinity decreases as we descend the groups. However there are a few exceptions due to various factors.

3. VALENCY

The number of valence electrons is found to increase from 1 to 8 if we move from left to right along a period. These valence electrons are in the outermost orbital(s). The number of valence electrons remains the same as we move down a group.

In each short period the valency increases from 1 to 4 and then falls again to one. Rare gases do not have any valency. As an example the valencies of the elements of the second group are given below:—

Group	1	2	13	14	15	16	17
Valency	1	2	3	4	3	2	1
Chlorides	LiCl	$BeCl_2$	BCl_3	CCl_4	NCl_3	Cl_2O	ClF

4. PROPERTIES OF COMPOUNDS

Even the compounds formed by the elements exhibit regular gradation of properties with a few exceptions. For example the basicity of the alkaline earth hydroxides increases as we move down the group (group 2). $Be(OH)_2$ is amphoteric, $Mg(OH)_2$ is a weak base. $Ca(OH)_2$ and $Sr(OH)_2$ are moderately strong bases and $Ba(OH)_2$ is quite strong. The solubilities of these hydroxides also exhibit regular gradation in that the solubility increases from $Mg(OH)_2$ to $Ba(OH)_2$, that is from 0 g per litre to 38 g per litre. The solubilities of the sulphates of these compounds, however, decrease as we go down the group. Magnesium sulphate is very soluble in water, calcium sulphate is slightly soluble and $SrSO_4$ and $BaSO_4$ are practically insoluble in water.

CHAPTER 5
RADIOACTIVITY AND RADIOISOTOPES

RADIOACTIVITY : The atoms of heavy elements such as uranium and thorium are unstable. In their nuclei the neutron to proton ratio is high. Only nuclei which have almost the same number of neutrons and protons are stable. So the nucleus of elements like uranium-235 throws out or emits some particles such as the alpha particles or beta particles and also gives out some radiation like the γ-rays in order to attain stability. This is known as *radioactivity*. In this process the nucleus of the heavy element breaks of its own accord to form a smaller atomic nucleus of another element. The spontaneous breaking down of the unstable atoms is known as radioactive disintegration or radioactive decay.

Types of Radiations : The radiations emitted due to radioactivity are of three types. They can be easily separated by passing them between oppositely charged plates.

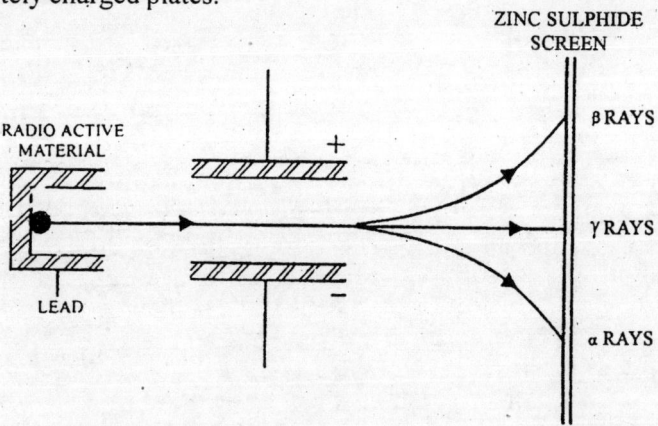

The radiation which bends towards the negatively charged plate must itself be positively charged and is known as alpha rays. That whic bends towards the positively charged plate is obviously negatively charged itself and is known as beta rays. The third one

64

which does not bend towards either the positively charged plate or the negatively charged plate but passes straight through is uncharged and is known as gamma rays.

Alpha Rays : Alpha rays consist of streams of alpha particles. They have two positive charges and a mass of 4 amu (atomic mass units). So they are helium nuclei and may be represented as $_2^4\alpha$ or $_2^4He$.

They have very high velocity equal to about one-tenth ($\frac{1}{10}$) of that of light. However their penetrating power through matter is very low. They can be stopped even by a sheet of paper. They have the capacity to cause intense ionisation in the molecules of gases through which they pass. This means that alpha rays, because of their positive charge and relatively high velocity, break off electrons in gas molecules and produce ion-pairs (that is, electrons and positively charged ions).

Beta rays : Beta rays consist of streams of electrons. They have very small mass and a negative charge of one. A beta particle may be represented as $_{-1}^0\beta$ or $_{-1}^0e$. They move with a velocity equal to that of light. They are very much more penetrating than alpha rays. They can be stopped only by an 1 cm thick aluminium sheet. They produce weak ionisation in gases through which they pass. This is because of their small mass.

Gamma rays : Gamma rays do not consist of particles. They are radiation of wave form shorter than x-rays. They are usually emitted along with alpha rays or beta rays. They have neither mass nor charge and may be represented as $_0^0\gamma$. Gamma rays also move with the velocity of light and have the highest penetrating power. They can be stopped only by a 5 cm thick sheet of lead or concrete of many metres thickness. However they are very weak ionisers.

DETECTION AND MEASUREMENT OF RADIO ACTIVITY

There are several methods for detecting and measuring radioactive radiation. These are:

1. Cloud chamber method.

2. Ionisation chamber method.
3. Geiger-Muller counter method.
4. Scintillation counter method.

For our purpose the last two are important.

Geiger – Muller Counter

This consists of a cylindrical metal tube serving as the cathode and a central wire inside the tube serving as the anode (see figure). Argon gas is filled in the tube at a reduced pressure of 0.1 atmosphere.

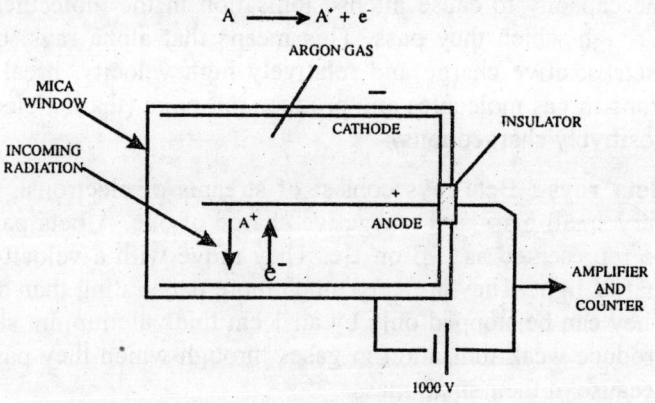

A potential difference of about 1000 volts is applied across the two electrodes. The argon gas is ionised whenever any alpha or beta particle enters the tube through the mica window. The positively charged argon ions, formed due to the ionisation of the gas, are attracted to the cathode and the negatively charged electrons to the anode. Thus an electrical pulse flows between the electrodes whenever one alpha or beta particle enters the tube. The electrical pulses are counted in an automatic counter. The intensity of the radioactivity of any radioactive material can be found out by finding the number of pulses per minute.

Scintillation Counter

Scintillation means a flash of light. In this counter the radioactive substance mounted on a wire emits alpha particles. Each alpha particle strikes a zinc sulphide screen and gives a flash. The flashes produced per second can be counted to find out the intensity of radiation.

In the 'well-type' scintillation counter, instead of the zinc sulphide screen a crystal of sodium iodide m· ·ed with a little thallium iodide is used. The sample of the radioactive substance is kept in a 'well' cut in the crystal. The radiation from the radioactive substance strikes the crystal wall and produces flashes. These scintillations fall on a photoelectric cell which converts the light energy into electrical energy for each flash. These are counted in a counter, even upto one million scintillations per second. This counter can be used for counting either alpha or beta particles.

ISOTOPES, ISOBARS AND RADIOISOTOPES

Some of the atoms of an element are found to be different from other atoms. These different atoms contain equal number of protons like the other atoms but have a different number of neutrons. This means that they have the same atomic number but different mass number. This is called an isotope of the element which may have two or more isotopes occurring together.

Isotopes occur in nature and an element may be considered to be a mixture of isotopes, However the isotopes occur mixed in the same proportion always. Thus the atomic weight is always the same because it is the average weight of all the atoms in the isotopic mixture.

Symbolic Representation of Isotopes

As per international usage, the symbol of the element is given accompanied by the mass number of the isotope at the head and the atomic number at the bottom on the left side of the symbol. It is not necessary to mention the atomic number always as it is the same for all isotopes of an element. In the alternative one may give the name of the element followed by the mass number of the isotope on the right side with a hyphen (-) in between

Examples : $^{12}_{6}C$ or ^{12}C or Carbon-12 (Carbon twelve)

$^{13}_{6}C$ or ^{13}C or Carbon-13 (Carbon thirteen)

$^{14}_6C$ or ^{14}C or Carbon-14(Carbon fourteen)

Other Examples of Isotopes

1. Isotopes of Hydrogen - ^1H Protium
(Z =1) - ^2H—— Deuterium or D
-^3H—— Tritium or T

2. Isotopes of Oxygen - ^{16}O, ^{17}O and ^{18}O
(Z = 8)

3. Isotopes of Chlorine - ^{35}Cl, ^{37}Cl and ^{39}Cl
(Z = 17)

4. Isotopes of Iron - ^{54}Fe and ^{56}Fe

5. Isotopes of Bromine - ^{79}Br and ^{81}Br
(Z = 35)

All the isotopes of an element follow the same chemical reactions. Therefore isotopes are chemically identical. They differ only in their physical properties. However even if the isotopes undergo the same chemical reactions. the reaction rates of individual isotopes are different. An isotope which exhibits radioactivity is known as a *radioisotope*. The various atomic species are known as *nuclides*.

Isobars : These are atoms which have the same mass numbers but different atomic numbers. It must be clearly understood that in the case of isotopes, they are different atoms of the *same* element with different mass numbers. In the case of isobars they are atoms with the same mass numbers of *different* elements, their only similarity being in having the same mass number but having different atomic numbers. Examples of isobars are given below :-

1. $^{40}_{18}Ar$ $^{40}_{19}K$, and $^{40}_{20}Ca$

2. $^{235}_{92}U$, $^{235}_{93}Np$, and $^{235}_{94}Pu$

BIOLOGICAL EFFECTS OF RADIATION

Humans may at times be exposed to radiation from various sources such as cosmic rays, x-rays (in diagnostic procedures), monazite sands of Kerala containing radioactive thorium etc. Abnormally we may be exposed to the intense radiation due to the testing and explosion (as in Hiroshima and Nagasaki in 1945) of fission bombs (atom bombs) and radiation due to leakage from nuclear reactors such as the Chernobyl nuclear disaster in Russia in which the radiation was carried to many parts of Europe from Russia as a fallout.

Therefore in this context there is need to study the biological effects of radiation. The radiations that can produce damage are alpha particles, beta particles, protons, neutrons, gamma rays and x-rays. They do so by ionization and excitement of molecules in cells. One theory says that they ionize the water present in the cells to the extent of 80% and produce free radicals. These free radicals are highly unstable and very reactive. They react with each other and also with organic molecules in the cells producing a variety of secondary chemical substances such as peroxides which are very injurious to the cell. The DNA in the cell is particularly sensitive and is damaged, destroying the cell. There is also inhibition of mitosis or cell division.

The damage caused by radiation may be divided into two types

1. Somatic effects, affecting the various parts of the body.

2. Genetic effects, affecting the reproduction and heredity.

The initial symptoms in humans are severe nausea, vomiting and prostration. After a few hours diarrhoea comes on due to ulceration of the gut with bleeding. Red cells, lymphocytes, blood platelets and granulocytes are found to be reduced in number, leading to anaemia etc. Antibody production is decreased and the body resistance comes down promoting infection. Death will follow after 2 to 3 weeks after a heavy dose of radiation.

Delayed Effects of Radiation

Continuous exposure to low level radiation can give rise to delayed effects of radiation. The hair greys quickly and other de generative changes take place leading to premature aging. Several types of cancer are induced. These include cancer of the skin, lung cancer, leukaemia, Hodgkin's disease etc. Large doses of radiation may inactivate the gonads causing sterility. Radiation exposure also produces chromosomal damage leading to mutations and consequent decreased fertility.

ARTIFICIAL RADIOACTIVITY

Artificial radioactivity can be brought about by bombarding a suitable element with neutrons. Slow neutrons are very effective. This disturbs the nucleus which becomes unstable. To regain stability it starts disintegrating and emits some rays, thus becoming radioactive.

The radioactive isotopes of certain elements have been used as *tracers* in various types of investigastions. The stable element and a little of its radioactive isotope are mixed and converted to the required compounds. The compounds are now said to be *labelled*. The stable and the radioactive isotopes go through all physical and chemical changes in the same ratio. Thus the compound can be etimated by simply measuring the radioactivity of the active isotope. Biochemical and physiological properties of certain compounds can be studied like this. For this a mixture of stable and radioisotopes is fed to an animal. It may be distributed to several parts of the body or concentrated to one particular part of the body. Thus sodium radioiodide is absorbed mainly by the thyroid gland.

Important artificial radionuclides used in medicine are cobalt-60 (used like radium in the treatment of cancer), phosphorus-32 (used in blood studies) and iodine-131 (used in the diagnosis and treatment of thyroid disease).

MEDICAL USES OF RADIOISOTOPES

1.Radiation Sterilization: Thermolabile (heat sensitive) drugs such as penicillin may be sterilized by radiation from radionuclides. All microorganisms and their spores are killed within seconds and the drug becomes *sterile*. Gamma rays from radioisotopes are used for this purpose in addition to high speed electrons.

2. Radio Therapy: Here the aim is to destroy the diseased tissue without destroying healthy tissue. Gamma radiation, being the most penetrating, is used for destroying deep-seated tumours. Both external and internal therapy are used. X-radiation can only be used for external therapy. In internal therapy the radionuclide is placed in a natural or surgical cavity of the body or injected into the tissue. Sometime, there is selective uptake by a diseased organ. Gamma-emitter iodine-131 is given orally and is taken up by the thyroid. Sources with a short half-life such as iodine-131 and gold-198 can be left in the body permanently but sources such as radium-226 with a long half-life must be removed after the treatment is over.

However artificial γ-emitters such as cobalt-60 and iridium-192 are now available and they have many advantages. Apart from being cheap, they are chemically inert and their disintegration products are harmless.

3. Radio Diagnosis : Many materials which are opaque to visible light are transparent to x-rays and gamma rays.

The function of a particular organ may be studied by following or 'tracing' the manner in which it secretes or removes a particular radio-isotope eg. iodine (given in the form of sodium radioiodide) is taken up by the thyroid gland. This can be easily followed by a radiation detector. Another use of iodine-131 is in the form of di-iodofluorescein used to map out a brain tumour before surgery.

Storage of Radio Isotopes : It is necessary to protect people from the harmful radiations emitted by the radioisotopes since we earlier studied about the harmful biological effects caused by the radiations. For this purpose the radioisotopes should be kept in remote places in the general store where people should not be allowed to go. The radioisotopes emitting gamma rays should be kept in lead containers of suitable thickness, as gamma rays are most penetrating. Alpha and beta ray emitters should be kept in thick glass containers, as alpha and beta rays are not as penetrating as gamma rays. The area where the radioactive materials are kept should be monitored regularly for radioactivity and any untoward increase in radiation should be detected in time and remedial measures taken.

Precautions in the Use of Radioisotopes: The following precautions should be observed while handling the radio isotopes:

71

1. Glass apparatus and other equipment should be tested for radioactivity before use.
2. Rubber gloves should be used while handling radioactive materials.
3. Absorbent paper should be used while handling radioactive liquids so that any liquid spilled may be absorbed by the paper and the paper thrown out.
4. Pipettes should not be used for withdrawing or transferrring radioactive liquids.

Half-Life Period : The rate of disintegration of radioactive element is independent of temperature, pressure or its state of chemical combination. The time required for the disappearance of one half of the original amount of the radioactive substance is called its Half-Life period.

UNITS OF RADIOACTIVITY

The unit of radioactivity is the curie (Ci). It is the weight of any radioactive substance undergoing the same number of disintegrations as 1 g of radium, which is 3.7×10^{10} disintegrations per second. It is also known as a becquerel (Bq). Therefore 1 curie is equal to 3.7 $\times 10^{10}$ becquerels. Curie is a large unit; so in its place smaller units such as millicuries and microcuries are used frequently. One millicurie is one-thousandth(1/1000th) of a curie and therefore represents 3.7 $\times$ 10^7 disintergrations per second or becquerels. Like wise one microcurie is one thousandth [1/1000] of a millicurie and so represents 3.7×10^4 disintegrations per second or becquerels. It is stressed that the weight of any radio-active substance with a radio-activity of one curie need not be 1 g as in the case of radium but may be different.

RADIO PHARMACEUTICALS IN MEDICAL PRACTICE

The following are some of the radiopharmaceuticals official in B.P.:-

1. FERRIC CITRATE (^{59}Fe) INJECTION

This is a sterile solution containing (^{59}Fe) iron in the ferric state. It also contains 1 per cent of sodium citrate and also enough sodium chloride to make the solution isotonic with bood serum. Neutron irradiation of iron-58 produces the radioactive isotope iron-59. Its half-life is 44.6 days only. The iron-58 selected for radiation should be sufficiently low in the content of iron-54. Otherwise the radioactive isotope iron-55 may also be produced. Since it has a half-life of 2.7 years, its presence in this injection is not desirable. Therefore a limit of 2 per cent is prescribed on the content of iron-55 in the total activity. Hence before the iron-58 is irradiated to get radioactive iron-59, any iron-54 present along with iron-58 is electromagnetically separated so that the product will be able to comply with the provision of the content of iron-55 not to exceed 2 per cent of total activity. Radioactive isotope ^{59}Fe is capable of emitting both beta particles and gamma rays. It is sterlised by Heating in an Autoclave. The following are the official standards that the injection is required to comply with:

Description: A clear, colourless or faintly orange-brown solution.

Tests for Identity

a. It has already been indicated that it emits gamma rays. Therefore the gamma ray spectrum of the injection should be compared with the gamma ray spectrum of an already standardised iron-59 solution. The two must be identical. Further the principal energies of the gamma rays should be 1.10 and 1.29 MeV (million electron volts). The activity of the injection also decays with a half-life of 44.6 days.

b. When the injection is boiled with mercuric sulphate solution and potassium permanganate is added, the potassium permanganate is decolourised and a white precipitate is produced. This is a general test for citrates.

pH: 6 to 8.

Radionuclidic Purity : The gamma ray spectrum of the injection is compared with the gamma ray spectrum of a standardised iron-59 solution. There should be no significant difference indicating that the injection contains only the required iron-59 isotope. In short this is a test for isotopic purity (refer also the first Test for Identity). If any iron-55 is present, it may not be detected by this test.

Total Iron : The amount of iron present is limited by this test. In this test a volume of the injection equivalent to 10 microcuries is subjected to the limit test for iron and required to comply with it.

Sterility : Since this a parenteral preparation, it must comply with the test for sterility. However the B.P. states that the preparation may be released for use before completion of the test. Because of the radioactive nature of the preparation, it is not always possible to wait for final results of the test for sterility for use of the batch.

Standard : The content of iron-59 should be between 90 and 110 per cent of what is stated on the label on the particular date stated on the label. The specific activity is not less than 1 microcurie per mg of iron (37 megabecquerels) on the date stated on the label.

Assay : It is assayed for its activity by detection of its gamma radiation in a scintillation counter and comparing it with the activity of a standardised iron-59 solution.

Use : In the investigation of blood disorders.

2. SODIUM IODIDE (^{131}I) SOLUTION

This solution is suitable for oral administration and it contains iodine-131 in the form of sodium iodide. Sodium thiosulphate or other suitable reducing agent is also present. By irradiating tellurium with neutrons, we can obtain the radioactive isotope of iodine, iodine-131 which is converted to sodium radioiodide.

Description : It is a clear, colourless solution. It has a half-life of 8.06 days and emits both beta particles and gamma rays.

Test for Identity : The gamma ray spectrum of this solution is compared with the gamma ray spectrum of a standardised iodine-131 solution. There should be no significant difference. Further the principal gamma-photon has an energy of 0.36 MeV.

pH : 7 to 10

Radionuclidic Purity : The gamma ray spectrum measured in a suitable instrument, is compared with the gamma ray spectrum of a standardised iodine-131 solution. There should be no significant difference.

This test is meant to ensure the absence of isotopes other than sodium [^{131}I] iodide.

Radiochemical Purity : This test is meant to ensure that all the radioactivity is present only in the iodide ion and not because of the presence of some other iodine-containing compound such as the iodate. It is done by paper chromatography. In this it should be proved that the radioactive part of the paper chromatogram coincides with the position of the iodide ion. It should also be proved that the position corresponding to the iodate ion has no radioactivity.

Standard : The content of iodine-131 activity should be between 90 and 100 per cent of that stated on the label at the time and hour stated on the label. The specific activity is not less than 5 mCi per microgram or 185 MBq [megabecquerals] per microgram of iodine at the date and hour stated on the label.

Assay: By using a suitable counter, the activity is compared with the activity of a standardised iodine-131 solution. It should have the iodine-131 activity and specific activity as prescribed.

Use : Used for the diagnosis and treatment of disorders of the thyroid gland.

3. SODIUM PHOSPHATE (^{32}P) INJECTION

This is the sterile solution of disodium and monosodium orthophosphates in isotonic saline. Phosphorus-32 is produced by the neutron irradiation of sulphur and is a radioactive isotope of phosphorus. It emits only beta particles with an energy of 1.71 MeV. It has a half-life of 14.3 days. The injection should comply with the general requirements for all injections and in addition should comply with the following also:-

Description: A clear, colourless solution.

Tests for Identity : The beta ray spectrum or the beta ray absorption curve of the injection is measured and compared with that of a phosphorus-32 solution obtained under the same conditions. There should be no significant difference. The beta radiation has also an energy of 1.71 MeV.

pH : Beween 6 and 8.

Radionuclidic Purity : This is to prove that the radio activity in the solution comes only from the radioisotope phosphorus-32 and not from any other radioisotope. For this purpose the beta-ray spectrum or the beta-ray absorption curve is measured and compared with that of a standardised phosphorus-32 solution obtained under the same conditions. There should be no significant difference.

Radiochemical Purity : This test is designed to prove that all the radioactivity resides in the phosphate ion and not in any other ion such as the phosphite. For this purpose the solution is first diluted to an activity of about 20,000 counts per minute. This dilution is then subjected to paper chromatography separately along with inactive orthophosphoric acid. The position of the inactive phosphoric acid is determined by spraying perchloric acid and ammonium molybdate solutions and then exposing to hydrogen sulphide when a blue colour develops. The radioactive spot is then located by using a suitable instrument and measured. Not less than 95 per cent of the total radioactivity should be present in the spot corresponding to the orthophosphoric acid.

Total phosphate : The amount of phosphate present is limited by diluting the solution with water and treating with ammonium metavanadate, ammonium molybdate and perchloric acid solutions. The colour produced after diluting to the specified volume is compared with the colour produced in a standard solution prepared at the same time and under the same conditions and containing a definite amount of orthophosphate. The colour in the test solution should not be more intense than the colour in the standard solution.

Sterility : The test for sterility is done. However the preparation may be released for use before the completion of the test.

Standard : The content of phosphorus-32 activity is between 90 and 110 per cent of that stated on the label at the date and hour stated on the label. The specific activity is not less than 0.3 mCi (11.1 MBq) per mg of orthophosphate ion.

Assay : The activity is determined by comparing with a standardised phosphorus-32 solution by using a suitable instrument.

Use : Used in the treatment of polycythaemia vera (increase in the number of red blood cells in the blood due to stimulation of the bone marrow due to less oxygen at high altitudes or due to respiratory disease).

4. CYANOCOBALAMIN (^{58}Co) SOLUTION

This is a solution of vitamin B_{12} or cyanocobalamin with the cobalt atom present in its structure as the cobalt-58 isotope. It is prepared by the growth of appropriate microorganisms on a medium containing cobalt (II) [^{58}Co] ion. It is permitted to contain a stabiliser and antimicrobial preservative. Cobalt-58 is a radioactive isotope of cobalt which is prepared by the neutron irradiation of nickel. It is stipulated that not less than 90% of the cobalt-58 present in this preparation should be in the form of cyanocobalamin. Cobalt-58 has a half-life of 70.8 days and it emits beta plus (β^+) rays and also gamma radiation. These gamma-photons have energies of 0.511 MeV and 0.811 MeV. This preparation should comply with the following standards given in the B.P. :-

Description : This is a clear, colourless or slightly pink solution.

Identification

1. The gamma ray spectrum of this solution may be measured in a suitable instrument. This may be compared with the gamma ray spectrum of an already standardised cobalt-58 solution. There should be no significant difference. Secondly the gamma-photons emitted by this solution should have energies of 0.511 MeV and 0.811 MeV.

2. The solution may be subjected to a special chromatographic analytical technique known as *liquid chromatography*. In particular the retention time (the time taken by the cyanocobalamin containing the cobalt-58 isotope to go through the chromatographic column and emerge) is determined. This is compared with the retention time given by a reference standard sample of cyanocobalamin (^{58}Co) solution which is also similarly treated. Both should be the same.

Acidity : pH 4.0 to 6.0

Radionuclidic Purity : This is to prove that the radioactivity present in this solution comes only from the radioisotope cobalt-58 and not from any other radioisotope such as cobalt-57 and cobalt-60 which may also be present in some quantity. For this purpose the gamma ray spectrum of this solution is determined in a suitable instrument suitably calibrated for the measurement of cobalt-57, cobalt-58 and cobalt-60. The energies of the gamma-photons emitted by these isotopes are diffferent. Thus cobalt-57 emits gamma-photons with energy of 0.122 MeV. The gamma-photons emitted by cobalt-60 have energies of 1.173 and 1.332 MeV.

So by measuring the energies of the gamma-photons emitted by the solution, it is possible ot determine the amounts of the extraneous radioisotopic impurities. It is stipulated that no more than 1% of the total radioactivity is due to cobalt-60 and not more than 2% of the total radioactivity is due to cobalt-57, cobalt-60 and other radionuclidic impurities. The reason for fixing such low limits is that these other radioisotopes have longer half-life periods. So their presence is not desirable in this solution of cyanocobalamin containing cobalt-58 which has a half-life of only 70.8 days. Cobalt-57 has a half-life of 271 days whereas the half-life of cobalt-60 is 5.27 years.

Radiochemical Purity : This test is designed to prove that all the radioactivity in this solution resides only in cyanocobalamin containing cobalt-58 and not in any other substance containing cobalt-58.

For this purpose (as mentioned in test 2 under Identification above), the solution may be subjected to a special chromatographic analytical technique known as *liquid chromatography*. The retention time (the time taken by the cyanocobalamin containing cobalt-58 to go through the chromatographic column and emerge) is measured. Using this it will be possible for us to determine the percentage of cobalt-58 present as cyanocobalamin. This is also compared with the retention time given by a reference standard sample of cyanocobalamin (^{58}Co) solution which is also similarly treated.

Assay : The activity of this solution should be determined by using a suitable counter and compared with the activity of a standardised cobalt-58 solution.

Storage : This solution should be stored at a temperature of 2 to 8°C and protected from light.

Barium sulphate is used as the radio-opaque contrast medium.

1. BARIUM SULPHATE, $BaSO_4$

Preparation : It is prepared by treating a cold, dilute solution of any soluble barium salt such as barium chloride with dilute sulphuric acid.

$$BaCl_2 + H_2SO_4 = BaSO_4\downarrow + 2HCl$$

The precipitate is filtered, washed with water till free from chloride and dried.

Physical and Chemical Properties

Barium sulphate is a fine, heavy, white powder free from gritty particles. It is odourless and tasteless. It is insoluble in water and organic solvents and also in dilute acids and alkalis. It is soluble in concentrated sulphuric acid.

Since barium sulphate is practically insoluble, it is not reactive chemically. However it can be fused with one or both of the alkali carbonates such as sodium carbonate and potassium carbonate.

$$BaSO_4 + Na_2CO_3 = Na_2SO_4 + BaCO_3$$

The barium carbonate may be neutralised by any acid to yield a soluble barium salt and the mixture now answers tests for barium. The filtrate after removal of the barium carbonate in the above reaction also answers the reactions of sulphate.

$$BaCO_3 + 2HCl = BaCl_2 + CO_2\uparrow + H_2O$$

It is official in I.P.

Official Tests for Identity

1. A small quantity of the sample is boiled with sod. carbonate solution, filtered and the filtrate acidified with dilute hydrochloric acid. It now answers the reactions of sulphate (see Chapter 22).

79

2. The residue obtained in (1) above is washed with water and treated with dilute hydrochloric acid. It is filtered and dilute sulphuric acid is added. A white precipitate is formed and it is insoluble in dilute hydrochloric acid (refer Physical and Chemical Properties).

Tests for Purity

1. Acidity or alkalinity
2. Phosphate
3. Arsenic
4. Heavy metals
5. Sulphide
6. Acid - soluble substances
7. Soluble barium salts
8. Bulkiness

Phosphate is detected by the usual ammonium molybate test. A hot nitric acid extract of the substance is mixed with ammonium molybdate solution. No yellow precipitate is produced.

Sulphide is tested by boiling the substance with dilute hydrochloric acid. Lead acetate paper is exposed to the vapour coming out. The paper should not darken. Any sulphide present is converted into hydrogen sulphide which will darken the lead acetate paper by forming lead sulphide.

Soluble barium salts are tested by digesting the residue obtained in the test for acid soluble substances with water and filtering through a filter paper moistened with diluted hydrochloric acid. Dilute sulphuric acid is added to the filtrate and set aside for 30 minutes. No turbidity is produced. See the caution at the end.

The test for *bulkiness* is done by suspending the substance in water in a 50 ml graduated cylinder and shaking for five minutes. The substance should not settle below the 15 ml mark indicating that the sample has sufficient bulkiness.

Standard : Barium sulphate contains between 97.5 per cent and 100.5 per cent of $BaSO_4$.

Storage : Since barium sulphate is very stable, it is enough if it is stored in well-closed containers.

Medicinal and Pharmaceutical Use : *Diagnostic aid (radio opaque medium).* It is used in the form of a suspension orally or rarely as a rectal injection.

Caution : I.P. prescribes tests for sulphide and soluble barium salts which are very poisonous. Therefore if these salts are present, such a sample of barium sulphate should not be used as it will kill the patient.

2. BARIUM SULPHATE FOR SUSPENSION, I.P. (BARIUM MEAL)

This is specially prepared barium sulphate for use as barium meal for oral administration prior to mapping out the gut by x-rays, It is a dry mixture containing in addition to barium sulphate suitable flavour, colours, preservatives and suspending and dispersing agents.

Official Tests for Identity : Some as for Barium Sulphate.

Tests for Purity :

1. *pH* (in place of acidity or alkalinity in the case of Barium Sulphate). pH should be between 4 and 8.

2. *Soluble barium compounds* - Same as for Barium Sulphate.

3. *Water stability :* A suspension in water is mixed thoroughly and allowed to stand for 24 hours. The supernatant liquid is decanted. The volume of sediment is not greater than a specified value.

4. *Acid stability :* Done in the same way as for (3) but taking hydrochloric acid along with water. In this case also the volume of sediment should not exceed a particular value.

   These two tests indicate that the sample has good stability in both water and acid and is able to leave a compact sediment.

Standard : It contains not less than 90% of $BaSO_4$.

Storage & Medicinal Use : Same as for Barium Sulphate.

CHAPTER 6
COORDINATION COMPOUNDS

Coordination compounds widely occur in the mineral, plant and animal worlds. In a coordination compound there is a central metal ion surrounded by oppositely charged ions or neutral molecules. These ions or neutral molecules are known as *ligands*. Combination of the ligands with the central metal ion occurs by the donation of a pair of electrons by each ligand to the central metal atom, that is through the formation of dative or coordinate covalent bonds. The number of such ligands surrounding the central metal ion is the *coordination number* of the metal ion. The coordination numbers most commonly encountered are 4 and 6. The group containing the metal and its ligands may carry a positive or negative charge. Then it is known as a *complex ion*.

Some examples of coordination compounds are given below:—

a) **Hydrates of salts :**

$CuSO_4, 5H_2O$

$MgSO_4, 7H_2O$

$Na_2CO_3, 10H_2O$

$CaCl_2, 6H_2O$

b) **Cyano complexes :**

$K_4 Fe (CN)_6$

c) **Complex halides :**

K_2HgI_4

K_2PtCl_6

d) **Ammine complexes :**

$CoCl_3 \cdot 6NH_3$

$CoCl_3 \cdot 5NH_3 \cdot H_2O$

$CoCl_3 \cdot 4NH_3$

$[Ni(NH_3)_6] \, Cl_2$

e) Complexes involving anions such as sulphate (SO_4), nitrate (NO_3), oxalate ($^-OOC{-}COO^-$) ions.

Werner did pioneering work in unravelling the mysteries of coordination chemistry. He proposed a theory to explain the nature of bonding in these coordination compounds. It may be stated briefly as below:—

Metals have two types of valencies. One is known as the primary valency and the other is known as the secondary valency. The linkage due to secondary valency is nonionizable, whereas the linkage due to primary valency is able to ionize. Since the metal is electropositive, the primary valencies are satisfied by negative ions or anions and the secondary valencies are satisfied by negative or neutral groups. While the primary valencies are rigid and non-directional in space, the secondary valencies are directed or oriented in space. Because of this, isomerisms such as optical isomerism and geometrical isomerism are seen in coordination compounds. Other isomerisms encountered are ionization isomerism, coordination isomerism and linkage isomerism.

Properties of Coordination Compounds

The transition metals are capable of forming coordination compounds. The coordination compounds of transition metals are usually coloured and are able to absorb strongly in the visible region of the electromagnetic radiation. The wavelength of maximum absorption (γ_{max}) of the coordination compound often gives information about the metal ion and the type of combination it has undergone to form the coordination compound, the nature of the ligand, the coordination number of the metal ion etc. Some coordination compounds are paramagnetic. The number of ions present in any coordination compound can be found out by finding out the conductivity of its solution. It is customary to write the groups which are linked to the metal ion directly in square brackets (these are nonionizable) and the ionizable groups outside the brackets. For example in the compound $[Co(NH_3)_5Cl] \, Cl_2$, only two chlorine atoms are precipitated by silver nitrate. So these two chlorine atoms only are ionizable and so they are placed outside the square brackets. The other single chlorine atom is linked in such a way to the cobalt atom that it is considered to be nonionizable along with the five ammonia molecules.

Classification of Ligands

As already stated, ligands are negative ions or neutral molecules which are able to donate pairs of electrons to the metal atom. In the complex ferrocyanide ion, the ligands are the cyanide ions and the iron is the central metal ion. Similarly in $Ag(NH_3)_2^{2+}$, NH_3 molecules are the ligands and Ag^+ is the central metal ion.

Ligands may be classified into monodentate or unidentate and polydentate such as bidentate, tridentate, tetradentate etc. Where a ligand has only one point of attachment to the central metal ion, it is known as an *unidentate* or *monodentate ligand*. Examples of unidentate ligands are anions such as Cl^-, Br^-, I^-, $CH_3 COO^-$, CN^-, SCN^- and neutral molecules such as water (H_2O), ammonia (NH_3) and pyridine.

When a single ligand occupies two or more coordination positions on the same central metal ion, it is called a polydentate ligand. Usually a closed ring is formed when a polydentate ligand combines with a metal and the stability of the complex is found to be high because of the formation of the ring. When a single ligand has two coordination positions, it is known as a *bidentate ligand*. Examples of bidentate ligands are ions such as oxalato ($^-OOC–COO^-$) and glycinate ($H_2N–CH_2–COO^-$) and molecules such as ethylenediamine (en, $H_2N–CH_2–CH_2–NH_2$) and 2,2'-dipyridyl(dipy). Other bidentate ligands are acetylacetonate ion, 1,10-phenanthroline and dimethylglyoxime. When a single ligand has three coordination positions available, it is known as a *tridentate ligand*. Examples of *tridentate ligands* are diethylenetriamine ($H_2N–CH_2–CH_2–NH–CH_2–CH_2–NH_2$) and 2,2',2''–terpyridine (terpy). Examples of *tetradentate ligands* are triethylenetetramine ($H_2NCH_2CH_2NHCH_2CH_2NHCH_2CH_2NH_2$) and ethylenediaminetriacetate ion [$^-OOCCH_2NH CH_2CH_2N(CH_2COO^-)_2$] Ethylenediamine tetraacetate ion,

$$\text{}^-OOCH_2C \diagdown \quad \diagup CH_2COO^-$$
$$ NCH_2CH_2N$$
$$\text{}^-OOCH_2C \diagup \quad \diagdown CH_2COO^-$$

is the example for a *hexadentate ligand*. This ligand is most important for pharmacy students because the disodium salt of ethylenediamine-tetraacetic acid (disodium edetate, EDTA, sodium edetate) is the titrant extensively used in complexometric analysis for the assay of various metallic ions such as calcium, magnesium, aluminium etc.

The total number of ligands which are directly attached to the central metal atom is known as the coordination number of that complex. Some of the coordination numbers commonly met with in complexes are 2, 3, 4 and 6. A particular metal may have different coordination numbers in different complexes. Thus platinum has a coordination number of 4 in $[PtCl_4]^2$ and a coordination number of 6 in $[PtCl_6]^4$.

Nomenclature of Coordination Compounds

The following rules outlined by the IUPAC (International Union of Pure and Applied Chemists) are adopted for naming the coordination compounds.

1. *Outside the square brackets, cation is named first and then the anion. Example--$K_3[Fe(CN)_6]$ -- potassium hexacyanoferrate.*

2. *Names of the ligands are given first. Then the name of the central metal atom. For example see once again $K_3[Fe(CN)_6]$.*

3. *While naming the complex anions, the name of the metal atom ends in - ate. In neutral or cationic complexes, the name of the central metal atom is retained as such. Examples are $K_3I[Fe(CN)_6]$- potassium hexacyanoferrate and chloropentammine cobalt (III) chloride - $[CoCl(NH_3)_5]Cl_2$.*

4. *The numerical prefixes mono, di, tri, tetra etc. are used to give the number of the ligands in the complex. However the prefix mono is not usually used. Example is $K_3[Al(C_2O_4)_3]$ - potassium trioxalatoaluminate (III).*

5. The oxidation number of the central metal atom is given by a Roman numeral in parentheses or square brackets after the name of the complex. If the oxidation number is zero, it is given as O. Examples are $[Co(NH_3)_6]Cl_3$ – hexa- mmine cobalt (III) chloride, $CoCl(NH_3)_5]Cl_2$ – chloropentam-minecobalt(III) chloride, $K_3[Fe(CN)_6]$ – potassium hex-acyanoferrate(III) and $K_3[Fe(C_2O_4)_3]$–potassium trioxa-latoferrate (III).

6. Neutral ligands are named as the molecules are named. Example is $NH_2CH_2CH_2NH_2$ (ethylenediamine). Negative ligands are named with the suffix 'o' after the name. Examples for this are Cl^- – chloro, Br^- – bromo, I^- – iodo, CN^- – cyano, SO_4^{2-} – sulphato, CH_3COO^- – acetato, OH^- - hydroxo, $C_2O_4^-$ – oxalato and SCN^- – thiocyanato. The names of the positive ligands (which we come across very rarely) end with the suffix-ium. Example is NH_2NH_2 – hy-drazinium.

Water and ammonia are given special names when they function as ligands. Water is known as aquo and ammonia is known as ammine (please note the double m).

Structures of Some Coordination Compounds

Cobalt forms different complexes with ammonia and chloride ion. The details of these complexes are given below:—

Formula of the complex	Cation	Anion	Total no of ions in the complex
$[Co(NH_3)_6]Cl_3$	$[Co(NH_3)_6]^{2+}$	$3Cl^-$	4
$[Co(NH_3)_5Cl]Cl_2$	$[Co(NH_3)_5Cl]^{2+}$	$2Cl^-$	3
$[Co(NH_3)_4Cl_2]Cl$	$[Co(NH_3)_4Cl_2]^+$	Cl^-	2
$[Co(NH_3)_3Cl_3]$	No cation	No anion	0

It can be seen in the above structures that the secondary valencies of cobalt are satisfied by ammonia molecules and the primary valencies are satisfied by chlorine. Except for the first complex (in which chlorine satisfies only the primary valencies), in all other complexes chlorine is required to satisfy both the secondary and primary valencies. In the last complex chlorine satisfies only the secondary valencies. Because of this there is no ionizable chlorine in the complex. The structures of the complexes can be depicted as below:—

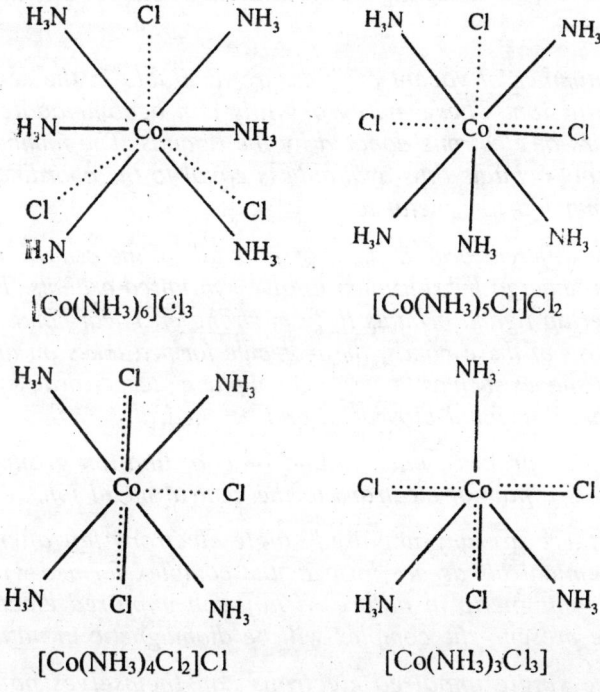

From the above structures it is seen that chlorine satisfies both the primary and secondary valencies. Where it is playing this role, the chlorine atom does not ionize. Only where it satisfies primary valency only, it is able to ionize. The primary valencies are denoted by broken lines and the secondary valencies by continuous lines.

PAULING'S VALENCE BOND THEORY

The formation of coordination compounds can also be explained by the application of the modern concept of valence bond theory. This is based on the fact that majority of the complexes are formed by the transition metals which have their d orbitals incomplete. Since the d orbitals of the penultimate (last but one) shell have almost the same energy as the *s* and *p* orbitals of the outermost shell, they also participate in hybridization along with the *s* and *p* orbitals of the outermost shell.

Briefly stated, the following are the important points in the valence bond theory :--

1. *A number of vacant orbitals are available in the central metal ion. These empty orbitals can accommadate the pairs of electrons donated by the ligands. The number of empty orbitals thus available is equal to the coordination number of the metal ion.*

2. *The different orbitals (s, p or d or all) of the central metal ion undergo hybridization to give hybridized orbitals. These overlap ligand orbitals to form strong chemical bonds. Because of these bonds, the molecule formed takes on different shapes such as linear, trigonal planar, tetrahedral, square planar, trigonal bipyramid and octahedral.*

3. *In this process, each ligand or coordination group donates a pair of electrons to the central metal ion.*

4. *If there are any unpaired single electrons left after the chemical bonds are formed, the complex formed will be paramagnetic in nature. If no such unpaired electrons are present, the complex will be diamagnetic in nature.*

5. *The single unpaired electrons can themselves pair up (against the Hund's rule of maximum multiplicity) when subjected to the influence of a strong ligand.*

6. *The other electrons in the central metal ion present in the inner orbitals do not take part in the chemical bonding.*

Given below are some examples of complex formation based on the above principles :--

1. Formation of the Complex $Cr(NH_3)_6^{3+}$ Cation

The following is the route of chemical combination for the formation of this complex cation :--

Cr (atom)

3d   4s

[↑] [↑] [↑] [↑] [↑]   [↑]

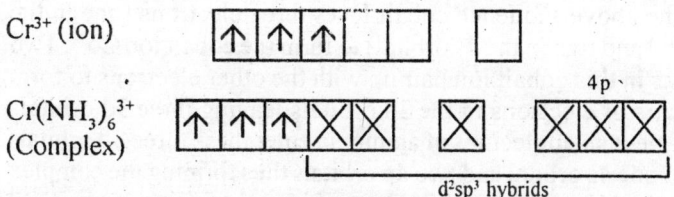

Cr^{3+} (ion)

Cr(NH$_3$)$_6^{3+}$
(Complex)

4p

d^{2}sp^3 hybrids

Chromium atom (Cr. Z=24) has the electronic configuration of $1s^2 2s^2$ $2p^6 3s^2 3p^6 3d^5 4s^1$. Chemical combination takes place through the $3d^5$ $4s^1$ electrons as given above. Under the influence of the ligand, Cr atom forms the Cr^{3+} ion by losing the outermost three electrons (two in the $3d^5$ orbital and one in the 4s orbital). Now there are two empty 3d orbitals and one 4s orbital. The six pairs of electrons donated by the six molecules of ammonia enter these vacant orbitals and also three 4p orbitals thus completing the chemical combination for the formation of the Cr(NH$_3$)$_6^{3+}$ complex cation. This results in an octahedral configuration of ligands around the metal ion and the complex is also paramagnetic as there are three unpaired electrons present.

2. Formation of Co(NH$_3$)$_6^{3+}$ Complex Cation

Cobalt (Z=27) has the electronic configuration $1s^2 2s^2 2p^6 3s^2 3p^6$ $3d^7 4s^2$. Cobalt is different from chromium in the sense that its ion does not have any vacant 3d orbital. So the vacant 3d orbitals have to be created by the pairing up of electrons in the 3d orbitals when the complex cation is formed as below :

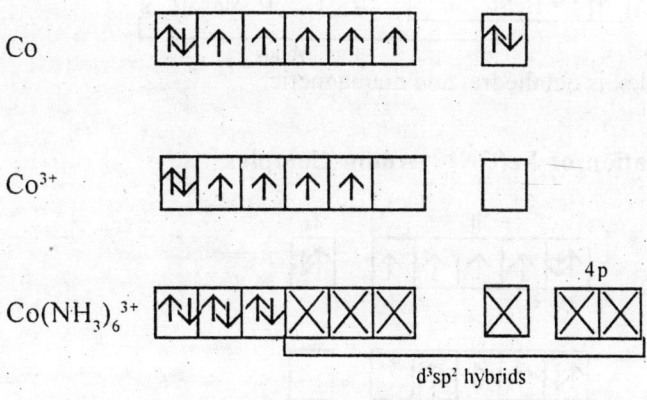

Co

Co^{3+}

Co(NH$_3$)$_6^{3+}$

4p

d^{3}sp^2 hybrids

89

In the above sequence cobalt loses three electrons (one in the 3d orbital and two in the 4s orbital) to form the cobalt ion Co^{3+}. Two electrons in this cobalt ion pair up with the other electrons to form three pairs of electrons in the 3d orbitals leaving three 3d orbitals vacant. Next six molecules of ammonia enter these three 3d orbitals and also one 4s orbital and two 4p orbitals thus forming the complex cation which is octahedral in shape. Since there are no unpaired electrons, the molecule is diamagnetic.

3. Formation of $Fe(CN)_6^{4+}$ Anion Complex

As we know already, iron atom (Fe) ionises to form ferrous (Fe^{2+}) and ferric (Fe^{3+}) ions. This complex is a ferrous complex.

Fe has the electronic configuration (Z=26) of $1s^2\ 2s^2\ 2p^6\ 3s^2\ 3p^6\ 3d^6\ 4s^2$.

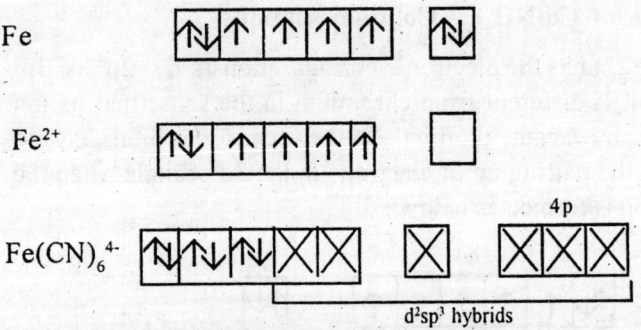

The complex is octahedral and diamagnetic.

4. Formation of $Fe(CN)_6^{3-}$ Anion Complex

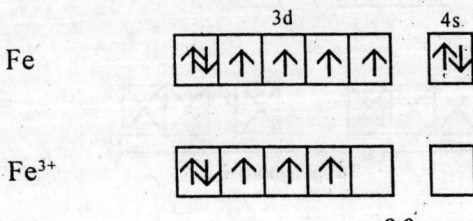

90

Fe (CN)$_6^{3-}$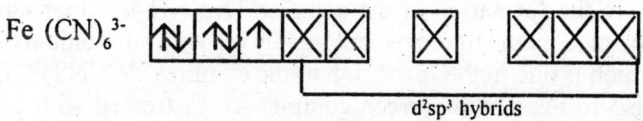

d²sp³ hybrids

This complex is also octahedral in shape but paramagnetic in nature because of the presence of one unpaired electron.

5. Formation of Complex Ion Cu(CN)$_4^{3-}$

Copper (Cu) has the ground state electronic configurartion $1s^2\, 2s^2\, 2p^6\, 3s^2\, 3p^6\, 3d^{10}\, 4s^1$ (Z = 29).

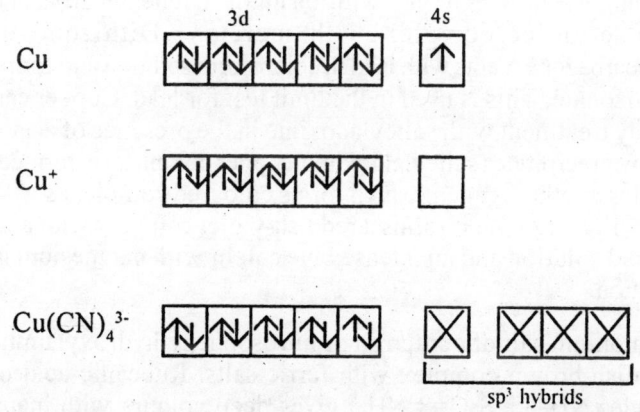

This complex has a tetrahedral shape. The ligands use 4s and 4p orbitals only as the 3d orbitals are already completely filled with paired electrons.

Applications of Coordination Compounds

Many of the coordination compounds formed by metals are complexes with high stability. They are usually strongly coloured and do not ionize being sparingly soluble in many solvents. So they are useful in qualitative, volumetric, gravimetric and colorimetric analyses.

Examples in Qualitative Analysis : In group analysis silver is detected in the I group by the easy dissolution of its chloride in am-

91

monia due to the formation of the complex $[Ag(NH_3)_2]^+$. Ferric iron (Fe^{3+}) is detected by the blood red colour it gives with ammonium thiocyanate which is due to the formation of the complex $Fe(CNS)^{2+}$. Ferric iron also forms a stable green complex when treated with 8-hydroxy-7-iodoquinoline-5-sulphonic acid in the presence of acetic acid. Similarly nickel is detected by the rose red colour it gives with dimethylglyoxime. It is due to the formation of the complex $Ni(DMG)_2$. Like dimethylglyoxime many organic reagents react with metals to give highly coloured complexes.

Uranyl zinc acetate acts as a precipitant for sodium, the complex that is formed being $[NaZn(UO)_2)_3]$ $(CH_3COO)_9$, $9H_2O$. Thiourea forms an orange-yellow complex with bismuth. Diphenylcarbazone forms a rose-violet complex with mercury. Dithizone or diphenylthiocarbazone reacts with lead in chloroform solution and forms red lead dithizonate. This is used in the limit test for lead. Copper can be detected by treatment with salicyladoxime in the presence of acetic acid. A yellow precipitate (salicylaldoxime-copper complex) is formed. Quinalizarin is another reagent which forms coloured complexes with many metals. For example it forms a reddish-violet complex with aluminium in acid solution and an intense blue colour with magnesium in alkaline solution.

The ammonium salt of cupferron or nitrosophenylhydroxylamine forms a reddish-brown complex with ferric salts. Rubeanic acid or dithiooxamide (NH_2 C=S–C=S–NH_2) gives deep colours with many metals. Cobalt can be detected by several reagents due to the formation of complexes. For example the disulphonic acid derivative of 1-nitroso-2-naphthol forms a coloured compound with even traces of cobalt.

Gravimetric Analysis : The antimalarial proguanil is assayed in the I.P. by drying and weighing of the complex it forms with copper.

Volumetric Analysis : In volumetric analysis many complexes formed by metals are used as indicators. Ferroin is one such. It is the complex formed by ferrous iron with 1, 10-phenanthroline. Ferroin is deep red and is easily oxidized to a blue colour in which ferrous iron is oxidized to ferric iron. So it is used as an indicator in redox titrations such as titrations using ceric ammonium sulphate (an oxidizing agent) as the titrant (refer assay of acetomenadione).

Aminopolycarboxylic acids are very good chelating agents. Chelation is the process in which the ligands combine with the metal forming a ring compound. Formation of 5 or 6 – membered rings confers good stability on the complex and this is known as chelation. If the ligand or chelating agent is able to form a complex which is water-soluble, it is known as a sequestering agent. Ethylenediaminetetraacetic acid is one such sequestering agent which forms water-soluble complexes or chelates with many metals such as calcium, magnesium, aluminium etc. Its disodium salt is known as the EDTA or disodium edetate or just sodium edetate. Its solution in water is used as the titrant in the volumetric analysis of many metals such as calcium and magnesium. This is known as complexometric analysis.

Colorimetric Analysis: Many limit tests and tests for purity are based on colorimetric procedures through the formation of coordination complexes. In the limit test for iron, ferrous iron reacts with thioglycollic acid to form the coordination compound ferrous thioglycollate. Ferric iron is also detected by this test since it is reduced by the thioglycollic acid to ferrous iron.

Other Applications: EDTA is also used in agriculture for regulating the concentration of certain metal ions in the soil. Since plants require minute amounts of certain metals for growth, EDTA-metal chelates can be mixed with the soil to release the metals required in small quantities over a long period.

Hard water containing calcium and magnesium salts is unsuitable for use in boilers in industry as it forms scales in the boilers. It cannot be used for washing purpose also if soap is used for washing. However EDTA is used for removing the boiler scales. EDTA is also used as an antidote in medicine for heavy metal poisoning such as poisoning by lead. The lead is complexed and removed by EDTA which is used as its calcium disodium salt. Recently cisplatin, a complex of platinum $[PtCl_2(NH_3)_2]$, has been found to be useful as an anticancer agent.

Biological Role of Coordination Compounds

Many biological processes involve the formation of coordination compounds. Many coordinate linkages are made and broken during a biological process. Many enzymes operate through the formation of intermediate compounds involving coordinate linkages with metals like zinc. Vitamin B_{12} (cyanocobalamin), haemoglobin and chlorophyll play an important role in living organisms and they are all coordination compounds. They belong to a class of compounds known as metalloporphyrins. Metalloporphyrins are complex compounds in which a metal ion is at the centre of a ring of four nitrogen atoms which are part of four pyrrole rings constituting a porphyrin group. The central metal ion in haemoglobin is iron, that in cyanocobalamin is cobalt and the metal in chlorophyll is magnesium.

Haemoglobin is actually a conjugated protein carrying four prosthetic groups. It contains four atoms of iron and has a molecular weight of about 67, 000. In haemoglobin the iron is in the ferrous (Fe^{2+}) state. This ferrous ion can form coordinate linkages with ligands like O_2, CO, CN^-. The Fe^{2+} ion contains four unpaired electrons and it is able to take up four molecules of oxygen as given below :--

$$Hb + O_2 \rightleftharpoons HbO_2$$

$$HbO_2 + O_2 \rightleftharpoons Hb(O_2)_2$$

$$Hb(O_2)_2 + O_2 \rightleftharpoons Hb(O_2)_3$$

$$Hb(O_2)_3 + O_2 \rightleftharpoons Hb(O_2)_4$$

Thus haemoglobin can function as an efficient carrier of oxygen from the lungs to the various parts of the body. However carbon monoxide (CO) and cyanide ion (CN^-) also can combine with haemoglobin. Since they are stronger field ligands than oxygen, they form complexes which are more stable than the complex formed by oxygen. So this explains how and why they are able to act as poisons.

Vitamin B_{12} is a compound with a large complex molecule. It contains a cobalt atom in the centre coordinated to four nitrogen atoms which are themselves part of pyrrole molecules forming part of a metalloporphyrin molecule. It occurs only in animals and microorganisms and not in plants. Deficiency of this vitamin gives rise to a particular form of anaemia.

Chlorophyll is the green pigment in the leaves of plants and it is essential for photosynthesis. Chlorophyll initiates the process of photosynthesis by absorbing the energy from sunlight. Actually chlorophyll is a mixture of four pigments of which chlorophyll *a* and chlorophyll *b* are organic complexes containing magnesium bonded to four heterocyclic nitrogens forming part of a porphyrin.

Dimercaprol and D-Penicillamine

Dimercaprol (or BAL or British Anti-Lewisite) is a sulphur analogue of glycerol and is structurally 2,3-dimercaptopropanol. In the trihydric alcohol glycerol there are three hydroxyl groups. But in dimercaprol, two of these hydroxyl groups are converted into —SH groups (thiol or mercapto groups).

$$
\begin{array}{ll}
CH_2OH & \qquad CH_2SH \\
| & \qquad | \\
CHOH & \qquad CHSH \\
| & \qquad | \\
CH_2OH & \qquad CH_2OH \\
\text{Glycerol} & \qquad \text{Dimercaprol}
\end{array}
$$

This was introduced in the second world war as an antidote by the British to the war gas *lewisite* which was an arsenical. Since it contains the thiol (—SH) groups, it combines with the arsenic and so prevents or reverses the effect of arsenic on thiol-containing enzymes. Its reaction with sodium arsenite is given below:—

$$
NaOAs = O + \begin{array}{l} HS-CH_2 \\ | \\ HS-CH \\ | \\ HO-CH_2 \end{array} \rightleftharpoons NaOAs \begin{array}{l} S-CH_2 \\ | \\ S-CH \\ | \\ HO-CH_2 \end{array}
$$

Cyclic thio-arsenite

Dimercaprol forms poorly dissociating complexes also with mercury and cadmium ions. Actually dimercaprol is useful in the treatment of acute poisoning due to arsenic, mercury, gold, antimony, bismuth and thallium. It is given by injection. The injection is a sterile solution of dimercaprol in a mixture of benzyl benzoate and arachis oil.

D-Penicillamine is chemically β, β-dimethylcysteine. It is derived from the sulphur-containing aminoacid cysteine and is a monothiol. It is prepared by the alkaline hydrolysis of benzylpenicillin.

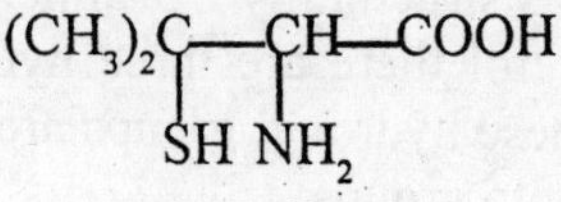

$$(CH_3)_2C—CH—COOH$$
$$\quad\quad\quad SH\quad NH_2$$

D-Penicillamine

It readily chelates with heavy metals such as mercury, copper and lead. It is used in the treatment of Wilson's disease in which the copper content of the liver, brain and other tissues is grossly increased. It is also used in the treatment of heavy metal poisoning such as acute lead poisoning and acute mercury poisoning. D-Penicillamine is also used in the treatment of rheumatoid arthritis.

1, 10 - PHENANTHROLINE

1, 10 - phenanthroline is a complexing agent which forms stable, highly coloured complexes with a metal in two oxidation states with a suitable oxidation - reduction potential. So 1, 10-phenanthroline-metal complex can be used as an oxidation - reduction indicator. 1,10- orthophenanthroline has the following structure :-

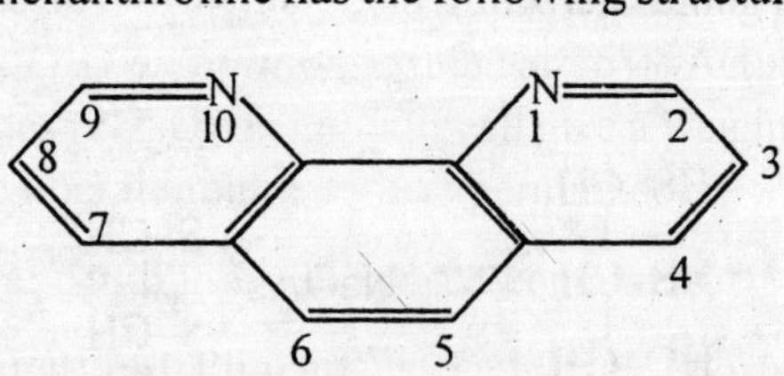

or $C_{12}H_8N_2$

It forms complexes with metals like iron, copper and zinc. Three molecules of 1, 10-phenanthroline dissolve easily in solutions of ferrous salts and combine with one ferrous ion to give the 1, 10-phenanthroline-ferrous complex known as *ferroin* which is intensely red in colour. It has the following structure :-

96

It is oxidised to the pale blue ferric compound by any oxidising agent such as ceric ammonium sulphate or nitrate. Since the colour change is very striking, ferroin is used as an indicator in redox titrations such as the assays of ascorbic acid tablets, ferrous gluconate tablets. acetomenadione tablets etc., At the end point ferroin is converted to the pale blue ferric complex.

$$[Fe(C_{12}H_8N_2)_3]^{2+} \rightleftharpoons [Fe(C_{12}H_8N_2)_3]^{3+} + e^-$$

Deep red   Pale blue

EDTA

It has already been stated that aminopolycarboxylic acids are very good complexing agents. They complex metals and fix them in unionisable combination in 5-or 6-membered rings which are quite stable. Ethylene diaminetetraacetic acid is one such. Its structure is given below :-

It forms water -soluble complexes knowns as chelates with metals like Cu^{2+} and Mg^{2+}

Disodium salt of ethylene diaminetetraacetic acid is a white, water - soluble dihydrate which can be used as a primary standard. It is known as EDTA or disodium edetate or sodium edetate. It is used in complexometric analysis as a titrant. It is non-specific in action and can be used for the estimation of the alkaline earths and transition elements. It is simply known as Na_2H_2Y and it ionises in solution as H_2Y^{2-} which reacts quantitatively with many cations such as Ca^{2+} and Mg^{2+}, forming complexes. Other applications of EDTA may be found in the text.

97

CHAPTER 7
PHARMACOPOEIAS AND
PHARMACOPOEIAL MONOGRAPHS

Pharmacopoeias are officially published books of standards for drugs and medicinal chemicals usually with directions for making preparations from them and many other relevant details. Many countries are now publishing pharmacopoeias of their own and by this they are able to control the standards of the drugs produced in their countries and also the standards of the drugs imported into their countries and ensure the health of their people.

The British Pharmacopoeia (B.P.) was one of the first to be published. The first British Pharmacopoeia was published in 1864. Other pharmacopoeias are the Pharmacopoeia of the United States of America (U.S.P.), European Pharmacopoeia, Pharmacopoeia Internationalis (International Pharmacopoeia published by W.H.O.) etc.

The first Indian Pharmacopoeia (I.P.) was published in 1955.and the second appeared in 1966. The third I.P. was published in 1985. The next I.P. was published in 1996. The latest I.P. was published in 2014. Companion volumes published to some of the pharmacopoeias are British Pharmaceutical Codex (B.P.C.), British National Formulary (B.N.F.), National Formulary of the United States of America (N.F.) etc.

A drug or a medicinal chemical included in a pharmacopoeia is termed as *official* and the sections dealing with official drugs, preparations and substances are known as *"monographs"*.The monographs may give some or all of the following details in the order given:-

1. Main Title:- This is the approved name of the drug or preparation.

2. Subsidiary Title:- Here the other names or synonyms (excluding brand names) currently in use for the drug are also given.

3. (i) Chemical formula (if known and where applicable).

   (ii) Molecular weight (if applicable and available).

   (iii) Systematic chemical name (if available).

   (iv) A general statement on some possible meth d of preparation or a detailed procedure.

   (v) Quantitative standards of purity or strength (for e.g. Ascorbic Acid contains not less than 98% of $C_6H_8O_6$).

4. Description: (a statement concerning the external characters such as appearance, odour and taste).

5. Solubility: A statement on the extent of solubility of the drug in various solvents, which may be general (e.g. readily soluble in water) or specific (e.g. soluble in 20 parts of alcohol, 95%).

6. Identification: Here tests for identifying the drug to find out whether the sample is that particular drug as claimed are given. Specific tests are given. Sometimes non-specific tests such as boiling point are also given.

7. Tests for Purity: These are tests for specific impurities which may be present in the drug due to various reasons. By these tests we can find out whether the impurities present are within the limits permitted or not. In addition to specific tests for impurities, non-specific tests such as melting point, distillation range, weight per ml, specific gravity etc. also may be given under this heading. The specific tests for impurities are the limit tests.

8. Method of Assay: Wherever possible, a method of assay is given. By this it will be possible to find out whether the sample contains the prescribed amount of the active ingredient (refer 3(v) above).

9. (i) Methods of Storage: It is necessary that drugs and pharmaceutical preparations should be stored under proper storage conditions so that physical and chemical changes may not take place during storage. Usually instructions such as "use a sealed container" (to prevent atmospheric effects)," "use containers free from alkalinity" (for some injections in which the active ingredients are affected by alkali released from the containers), "store in a cool place" "protect from heat", (to prevent effects of temperature) are given.

(ii) Labelling: Specific instructions are given for labelling the containers as well as the cartons. These are meant to ensure that correct and necessary details are displayed on the label (such as the main title, quantity or strength, dose, method of storage, expiry date, any caution about its use etc.)

10. Preparation(s): This applies to drugs which are converted into formulations before use (e.g.: Ascorbic Acid Tablets, Atropine Eye Ointment etc.)

11. Action and use: A brief account only of the actions and uses is given.

12. Dose(s): This is given only for substances meant for systemic use.

A substance which complies with all the provisions given in the monograph is said to be **standard**. If it fails in even one while complying with the others, it is said to be **sub-standard**. In the I.P. 1996, it is enough if the substance complies with the provisions given under the term **'standards'** which does not include Description, Solubility etc.

Appendices: These give details of general tests (such as Limit Test for Iron), methods of quantitative analysis (such as Determination of Acid Value), biological assays (such as Assay of Penicillin) and other processes mentioned in the monographs. Standard for materials and solutions employed in tests or assays are also given in one of the appendices.

CHAPTER 8

IMPURITIES AND LIMIT TESTS

1. IMPURITIES IN PHARMACOPOEIAL SUBSTANCES

Chemical purity means freedom from all foreign materials. It is not possible to obtain an absolutely pure compound and even analytically pure samples contain minute traces of other substances which are called as impurities. Purification of chemicals is expensive and therefore purifying a substance to a much higher degree than is necessary for the purpose for which it is intended to be used will increase its cost too much.

However it is possible at a comparatively less cost to mass produce certain substances in a high state of purity. Refined sugar contains more than 99.9 per cent of sucrose. Similarly 'vacuum salt' made by purification of rock salt, contains more than 99.9 per cent of sodium chloride.

The Different Types of Impurities Commonly Occurring in Drugs

1. Impurities which have a toxic effect and cause unpleasant reactions in the body when present beyond certain limits, e.g. lead and arsenic.

2. Impurities which, though otherwise harmless, are present in such proportions that is not desirable. The presence of sodium bromide in the more expensive potassium bromide is not likely to cause harm to the patient. However medicinal quality potassium bromide should contain only potassium bromide and not contain large quantities of sodium bromide.

3. Impurities which lessen the keeping properties of the substances. For example a small amount of moisture may cause many substances to be easily oxidised or to undergo hydrolysis.

4. Impurities which render the substance incompatible with other substances.

5. Impurities which cause technical difficulties in the use of the substance, for example presence of potassium iodate in a sample or potassium iodide. Such a sample will liberate iodine on being mixed with a mineral acid due to the interaction of both the substances.

6. Impurities which impart a different odour or colour to the main substance and so are not desirable. Sodium salicylate is often discoloured due to phenolic impurities. Sodium chloride becomes damp due to the presence of traces of deliquescent magnesium salts.

Generally medicinal compounds should not only be free from undue amounts of toxic and undesirable substances but should also be of a reasonably pure quality. Those impurities, such as lead and arsenic which have deleterious effects, should not be present in amounts likely to be harmful. Very low limits are fixed for such impurities. Similarly very low limits are fixed for the other types of impurities also stated above for the reasons mentioned. However if the impurity is harmless and is at the same time difficult to remove, the limits may be fixed even as high as 5–10%.

Sources of Impurities in Pharmacopoeial Substances

Impurities in pharmacopoeial substances may be due to the following sources:

(a) Raw Materials Used in Manufacture

A good example is the presence of tin, lead, silver, copper, cobalt and gold in bismuth salts. These metals occur along with bismuth in bismuth ores. Rock salt contains small amounts of calcium sulphate and magnesium chloride, so that sodium chloride prepared from this source will almost certainly contain traces of calcium and magnesium compounds.

(b) The Method of Manufacture

Contamination by reagents and solvents at various stages of the manufacturing process may give rise to impurities as given below:—

102

(i) Reagents Employed in the Process

Lead as an impurity may result from the sulphuric acid used as reagent, especially if it has been prepared by the lead chamber process. Soluble alkali may be an impurity in calcium carbonate if the calcium carbonate is made by reacting calcium chloride and sodium carbonate and not properly washed.

(ii) Reagents Added to Remove Other Impurities

Potassium bromide is liable to contain traces of barium which is added in the course of the manufacturing process to remove excess sulphate.

(iii) Solvents

Water is the solvent easily available and cheap and is used in the manufacture of inorganic chemicals. This can give rise to trace impurities such as sodium, calcium, magnesium, carbonate, chloride and sulphate ions. These difficulties do not arise in the use of Purified Water (distilled or demineralised water).

(iv) The Reaction Vessels

The vessels used in the manufacturing process are made of metals like copper, iron, aluminium, zinc, nickel and tin though these days many of these metals are replaced by stainless steel. The above metals are introduced as impurities due to the solvent action of the raw materials on the material of the plant. Glass vessels may give rise to traces of alkali, though this is unlikely if the vessels are made of neutral glass.

(c) Atmospheric Contaminants

Atmospheric contamination may take place through dust, sulphur dioxide, hydrogen sulphide etc. Carbon dioxide and water vapour are possible contaminants of substances which are affected by their action.

(d) Decomposition of the Product During Storage

Many chemical substances undergo changes due to careless storage. Ferrous sulphate is slowly changed into insoluble ferric oxide by air and moisture. Solution of potassium hydroxide absorbs carbon dioxide on exposure to air and exerts a solvent action on lead glass. Therefore it should be stored in well-stoppered bottles of green glass which is lead-free. There are certain precautions regarding storage and if they are observed, decomposition and deterioration of substances could be brought down if not totally eliminated. All chemicals should be stored in tightly closed containers made of dark glass and extremes of temperatures should be avoided. Sunlight affects many chemicals. For example bismuth carbonate turns black on exposure to sunlight for a long period. Such chemicals should be stored in a dark place preferably.

(e) Deliberate Adulteration with Spurious or Useless Materials

This is still a common occurence in some parts of the country where the Drugs and Cosmetics Act has not yet been properly enforced. Therefore one has to be vigilant and purchase drugs only from reputed manufacturers.

2. LIMIT TESTS

Limit tests are quantitative or semi-quantitative tests which are designed to detect and limit small quantities of impurities which are likely to be present in the substance. They may be of three types :—

(a) Tests in Which There is no Visible Reaction

It may be stated that on testing as prescribed there shall be no colour, opalescence or precipitate, whichever is relevant. Such negative tests only indicate the absence of an undesirably large amount of the impurity.

(b) Comparison Methods

These tests require a standard containing a definite amount of impurity to be set up at the same time and under the same conditions of the test experiment. In this way, it is possible to compare the amount of the impurity in the substance with a standard of known concentration and find out whether the impurity is within or excess of the limit prescribed. This is the basis of the official limit tests for chloride, sulphate, iron etc.

(c) Quantitative determinations

Here the amount of the impurity present is actually determined and compared with the numerical limit given in the pharmacopoeia.

Examples are :--

1. Limits of soluble matter

2. Limits of insoluble matter

3. Limits of non-volatile matter

4. Limits of moisture and volatile matter

5. Limits of residue on ignition

6. Loss on ignition

7. Ash values.

However we will limit our discussion to the comparison methods only. These limit tests involve simple comparisons of opalescence, turbidity or colour with standards prescribed in the pharmacopoeias. The variations in the permissible limits for the various substances are obtained by taking varying quantities of the substance under test. In these limit tests the extent of opalescence, turbidity or colour produced is influenced by the presence of other impurities present in the substance and also by variations in time and method of performance of tests and hence the pharmacopoeias do not prescribe numercial values for these tests.

LIMIT TESTS FOR ACID RADICAL IMPURITIES

A. LIMIT TEST FOR CHLORIDES (I.P. 1996)

Principle: The limit test for chlorides is based on the well known reaction between silver nitrate and soluble chlorides forming precipitate of silver chloride which is insoluble in dilute nitric acid. The test solution becomes turbid, the extent of turbidity depending upon the amount of silver chloride produced which in turn depends upon the amount of chloride present in the test substance. The opalescence or turbidity so obtained is compared with the opalescence obtained in a standard solution containing a known quantity of chloride. The test is done in Nessler glasses, the same volume of dilute nitric acid is used in both the cases and both are diluted to the same volume. The standard turbidity is produced from the amount of chloride which is prescribed as the limit for chloride impurity in the test substance. If the turbidity from the sample is less than the standard turbidity, the sample passes the limit test. If it is more, it fails the limit test. The solutions must be viewed transversely against a black background.

$$Cl^- + AgNO_3 = AgCl \downarrow + NO_3^-$$

Practical Details : A specified weight of the substance (accurately weighed) is dissolved in water or the solution is prepared by special treatment as given in the monograph in a Nessler cylinder. 10 ml of dilute nitric acid is added to the solution and the volume is made up to 50 ml with water (distilled or purified water only). 1 ml of silver nitrate is then added and the solution is stirred and set aside for *5 minutes*.

Standard opalescence is likewise obtained by taking 10 ml of Chloride Standard Solution (25 ppm Cl) and 10 ml of dilute nitric acid in a Nessler cylinder, making upto 50 ml with water (distilled or purified water only) and adding 1 ml of 0.1 M silver nitrate solution. It is also stirred well and set aside for *five minutes*, protected from light.

As already stated, when viewed transversely preferably against a dark background, the opalescence in the test solution should not be more intense than the opalescence in the standard solution. Then only the sample passes the test. Otherwise it fails.

Certain points may be noted :--

1. Certain substances have to be specially treated for a solution to be made which can be used in the test. The procedure for this is given in the individual monograph.

2. It must be stressed that the standard must be *accurately* prepared. Otherwise the test will not be reliable. Therefore it is necessary that *exactly 10 ml of Chloride Standard Solution* (25 ppm Cl) should be taken as the source for chloride.

3. The total quantity at the conclusion of the test in each Nessler cylinder is 51 ml and not 50 ml.

B. LIMIT TEST FOR SULPHATES (I.P. 1996)

Principle: This is based on the reaction between barium chloride and soluble sulphates in the presence of dilute hydrochloric acid. An opalescence is produced by the precipitation of barium sulphate in a fine state of division. This is compared with the opalescence produced in a standard containing a known quanitity of sulphate and similarly treated. The test substance passes the limit test if the opalescence in it is less intense than that in the standard. If the opalescence is found to be more, then it fails the test. The barium sulphate reagent used contains barium chloride, sulphate-free alcohol and a small amount of potassium sulphate and is made *in situ*. The addition of potassium sulphate increases the sensitivity of the test. The ionic concentration in the reagent is so adjusted that the solubility product of barium sulphate is exceeded. Barium sulphate present in the reagent in a small quantity acts as a seeding agent for precipitation of barium sulphate if sulphate is present in the substance under test. Alcohol prevents supersaturation and a more uniform turbidlity is formed.

$$SO_4^{2-} + BaCl_2 = BaSO_4 \downarrow + 2Cl^-$$

Practical Details: A specified quantity of 25% w/v barium chloride solution is mixed with a specified quantity of Ethanolic Sulphate Standard Solution (10 ppm SO_4) in a Nessler cylinder. The latter contains alcohol and a definite quantity of potasium sulphate. Thus barium sulphate reagent is made *in situ*. To this a solution of the substance in water (containing a specified quantity) prepared as mentioned in the monograph or solution is prepared by dissolving the substance in water and 5M acetic acid. Then it is diluted to the mark. A standard is prepared by taking a definite volume of Sulphate Standard Solution (10 ppm SO_4) and treating it in the same manner. Both the solutions are stirred well and allowed to stand for five minutes.

As already stated, when viewed transversely against a black background the opalescence in the test should not be greater than the opalescence in the standard. Then only the sample passes the test. Otherwise it fails.

Certain points may be noted :-

1. This is the same as in the case of limit test for chlorides.

2. The standard must be accurately prepared. Otherwise the test will not be reliable. Exactly 15 ml of Sulphate Standard Solution (10 ppm SO_4) should be taken as the source for sulphate.

LIMIT TESTS FOR BASIC RADICAL (OR METALLIC) IMPURITIES

A. LIMIT TEST FOR IRON (I.P.1996)

Principle : This depends upon the reaction of iron with thioglycollic acid in the presence of citric acid and ammonia when a pale pink to deep reddish purple colour is produced. Citric acid forms a complex with iron and prevents its precipitarion by ammonia. The colour produced is due to the formation of a ferrous compound with thioglycollic acid (which is a coordination compound). This is stable in the absence of air and fades when exposed to air due to oxidation. The original state of oxidation is immaterial as thioglycollic acid is a reducing agent and reduces ferric iron to ferrous. Only because of this advantage this test has been selected as the limit test, since other tests such as the ammonium thiocyanate test give reaction with only one type of iron like the ferric. The thioglycollic acid test is also considered to be more sensitive. Ferrous thioglycollate is colourless in acid or neutral solutions. The colour develops only in the presence of alkali. The reactions are given below :-

$$2Fe^{3+} + 2CH_2SH.COOH \rightarrow 2Fe^{2+} + \begin{matrix} S.CH_2COOH \\ | \\ S.CH_2COOH \end{matrix} + 2H^+$$

Ferric iron Thioglycollic acid Ferrous iron

$$2Fe^{2+} + 2CH_2SH.COOH \rightarrow$$

Ferrous Thioglycollate
(Coordination Compound)

108

Practical Details: A solution of the specified quantity of test substance is prepared in a Nessler cylinder. 2 ml of a 20% solution of iron-free citric acid and 0.1 ml of thioglycollic acid are added. The solution is then mixed and made alkaline with iron-free ammonia solution, diluted to 50 ml with water, stirred well and allowed to stand for five minutes. The colour obtained is compared with the standard colour, prepared similarly in a Nessler cylinder by taking 2 ml of Iron Standard Solution and similarly treating it and making up to 50 ml with water. The intensity of the colour in the test solution should be less than that in the standard so that it may be declared to have passed the test. If it is more, it fails the test.

Certain points may be noted :—

1. A colour and not a turbidity or opalescence develops.

2. The colours in the test and the standard should be compared immediately after the five minutes allowed for full development of the colour is over. If there is any delay, the colour fades due to oxidation and the test becomes unreliable.

B. LIMIT TEST FOR HEAVY METALS (I.P. 1996)

Principle: Many heavy metals, such as lead, iron, copper, nickel, cobalt, bismuth etc. may occur as impurities in official substances. So their quantity is limited by inclusion of a limit test for heavy metals. The test is based on the reaction between hydrogen sulphide and many heavy metals resulting in the formation of their sulphides which may have colours varying from dark brown to black. Since so many metals are sought to be tested for, fixing of a standard for comparison is difficult. However a standard solution containing a definite quantity of lead nitrate is chosen for the purpose. The quantity is stated as the heavy metals limit and is expressed as parts of lead (by weight) per million parts of the substance. The usual limit for heavy metals in I.P. is 20 p.p.m. The sulphides formed in the test are distributed in colloidal state and produce brownish solutions.

There are four methods prescribed in the I.P. depending upon the type of metals involved. Method A is used for substances, which give clear, colourless solutions, when the test solution is prepared as given in the individual monograph. Method B is used for substances which do not give clear, colourless solutions. It is also used for substances which interfere with the precipitation of the contaminating heavy metals as their sulphides. Method C is used for substances which give clear, colourless solutions when they are dissolved in sodium hydroxide solution. While the precipitation of the metallic sulphides is carried out in methods A and B under moderately acid conditions, it is done in Method C in alkaline conditions. It is therefore, obvious that optimum conditions are being provided for the metals to be precipitated as their sulphides. Method D is used for certain substances in which other impurities or the drug intself may interfere with the usual sulphide test.

Method A

Two solutions are prepared.

1. Standard solution: 1 ml of Standard Lead Solution (20 ppm Pb) is diluted with water to 25 ml in a 50 ml Nessler cylinder. The pH is adjusted to a value between 3 and 4 by the addition of either dilute acetic acid Sp or dilute ammonia solution Sp. The solution is then diluted to 35 ml with water and mixed.

2. Test solution : The specified quantity of the substance is made into a solution of 25 ml in a 50 ml Nessler cylinder as prescribed in the individual monograph. Then it is adjusted to a pH between 3 and 4 by the addition of either dilute acetic acid Sp or dilute ammonia solution Sp. The solution is then diluted to 35 ml with water and mixed.

Procedure : To both the solutions 10 ml of freshly prepared hydrogen sulphide solution are added, mixed and diluted with water to 50 ml. They are allowed to stand for five minutes and viewed downwards over a white surface. The colour produced in the test solution should not be more intense than the colour produced in the standard solution. Then only the sample passes the test. Otherwise it fails.

Method B

Two solutions are prepared as in Method A.

1. Standard solution: It is prepared in the same way as in Method A.

2. Test solution: Since the substances coming under this category may contain a lot of organic matter, the sample is taken in a crucible and the organic matter is destroyed by addition of nitric and sulphuric acids and ignition at 500 to 600°C. in a muffle furnace. Then the residue is digested with hydrochloric acid. It is evaporated to dryness and the residue digested with hydrochloric acid and hot water. Then ammonia is added till it is alkaline to litmus and adjusted with dilute acetic acid to a pH of 3 to 4. It is then filtered. The filtrate and washings are taken in a Nessler cylinder, diluted with water to 35 ml and mixed.

This extract contains the heavy metals present in the substance.

Procedure: It is the same as under Method A.

Method C

Two solutions are prepared as under Method A.

1. Standard solution: 1ml of Standard Lead Solution (20 ppm Pb) and 15 ml of sodium hydroxide solution are taken in a 50 ml Nessler cylinder, diluted with water to 50 ml and mixed.

2. Test solution: The test solution is prepared as given in the individual monograph in a 50 ml Nessler cylinder. 20 ml of water and 5 ml of sodium hydroxide solution are added. It is diluted to 50 ml and mixed.

Procedure: To both the solutions are added 5 drops of sodium sulphide solution. Each solution is mixed and allowed to stand for five minutes. When viewed downwards over a white surface, the colour produced in the test solution should not be more intense than the colour produced in the standard solution.

All the reagents used in the tests should be free from heavy metals which is indicated by the suffix Sp.

Method D

This method is applied to certain substances in which other impurities may interfere in the usual sulphide test. In this method the heavy metals are allowed to react with thioacetamide at a pH of 3.5 producing a brown colour. Two solutions are prepared as under Method A.

1. Standard Solution: 10 ml of either Lead Standard Solution (1 ppm Pb) or Lead Standard Solution (2 ppm Pb) as given in the monograph are pipetted into a small Nessler cylinder.

2. Test Solution: It is prepared as directed in the individual monograph and 12 ml are pipetted into a small Nessler cylinder.

Procedure: To the cylinder containing the standard solution are added 2 ml of the test solution and mixed. 2 ml of acetate buffer of pH 3.5 and 1.2 ml of thioacetamide reagent are added to each of the cylinders, mixed and allowed to stand for 2 minutes.

When viewed downwards over a white surface, the colour produced in the test solution should not be more intense than that produced in the standard solution.

C. QUANTITATIVE TEST FOR LEAD

Lead is one of the most undesirable and dangerous impurities in medicinal substances. The primary sources of lead in chemicals are the sulphuric acid used in manufacture and the use of lead or lead-lined apparatus. Lead may also be absorbed from lead glass, when some chemicals are stored in bottles made of such glass. For example potassium carbonate kept in a badly stoppered bottle becomes moist and absorbs lead from the glass container and hence its lead content increases.

Quantitative Test for Lead in B.P.

The test depends upon the formation of a brownish colouration when sodium sulphide is added to dilute solutions of lead salts, the intensity of the colouration varying with the quantity of lead present. Traces of other metals, particularly copper and iron, interfere with the test since they also yield dark precipitates or colouration with sodium sulphide (refer the Limit Test for Heavy Metals). Addition of ammonia and potassium cyanide before the addition of sodium sulphide, by formation of complex cyanides, prevents their precipitation as sulphides. So under these conditions lead alone is precipitated. By this test it possible to find out not only whether the lead impurity present in the substance under test is within the prescribed limit but also the exact amount of the impurity.

The apparatus consists of two Nessler cylinders, which should be made of clear, lead free glass with 50 ml position clearly marked. The special reagents used are labelled PbT. With the exception of the standard lead solutions, these reagents must be lead-free.

Two standard solutions of the substance are prepared.

1. a *primary solution* containing a definite quantity of the substance.

2. an *auxiliary solution* containing a definite but much smaller quantity of the substance.

To the *auxiliary solution* only a definite volume of a standard very dilute solution of lead nitrate is added. To both the solutions are added excess of ammonia and potassium cyanide. Any difference in colour between both solutions should be adjusted by adding dilute solution of burnt sugar. The two solutions are diluted to 50 ml. Then sodium sulphide is added to both the solutions and stirred. The colour developed in the primary should be less than the colour developed in auxiliary. Then only the substance contains lead within the limit.

Limit Test for Lead in I.P. (I.P. 1996)

This is known as the Diphenylthiocarbazone Test.

Diphenylthiocarbazone or dithizone dissolves in chloroform and the solution is green in colour. It has the ability to extract lead as a complex from substances containing lead as impurity, if the substance is dissolved in water and made alkaline.

The solution of the sample is prepared as directed in the monograph and transferred to a separator. Some of the metals other than lead particularly iron are complexed by the addition of ammonium citrate solution Sp and hydroxylamine hydrochloride solution Sp. The solution is then made just alkaline by the addition

113

of strong ammonia solution. Other metals are kept complexed by the addition of potassium cyanide.

This solution is then extracted with dithizone in chloroform repeatedly. Lead dithizonate is red in colour and the resultant colour (along with the green colour of unchanged dithizone) is a shade violet. Extraction is continued till the dithizone extraction solution remains green. This indicates that all lead has been extracted.

Nitric acid is added to the combined extract which converts all the lead dithizonate into lead nitrate. It is again extracted with dithizone extraction solution. The colour of the extract is not a deeper shade of violet than that of a standard solution made with required quantity of lead solution similarly treated.

The double extraction is intended to ensure that only lead is extracted and all other metals are excluded. All reagents used with the exception of lead standard solution should be lead free and are marked as Sp.

$$C_6H_5-N=NCS-NH-NH-C_6H_5$$
Dithizone

Dithizone–Lead Complex

D. LIMIT TEST FOR ARSENIC (I.P. 1996)

Principle : The substance (which is supposed to contain the arsenic impurity) is dissolved in hydrochloric acid or an aqueous solution or extract is acidified. The arsenic present in the substance is converted to either arsenious acid (if the arsenic is trivalent) or arsenic acid (if the arsenic is pentavalent). Then it is further treated with a reducing agent such as stannous chloride or sulphurous acid. All the arsenic acid present is reduced to arsenious acid. In the I.P.

stannated hydrochloric acid (i.e stannous chloride mixed with hydrochloric acid) is added to the substance.

$$H_3AsO_4 \rightarrow H_3AsO_3$$

Arsenic acid   Arsenious acid

The arsenious acid is further reduced to arsine (arsenious hydride, AsH_3) by nascent hydrogen which is produced by the action of granulated zinc on hydrochloric acid.

$$H_3AsO_4 + 3H_2 = AsH_3 + 3H_2O$$

Arsine

When arsine comes into contact with dry paper saturated with mercuric chloride, it produces a yellow or brown stain.

$$2AsH_3 + HgCl_2 = Hg(AsH_2)_2 + 2HCl$$

Yellow or brown stain

The intensity of the stain is compared by daylight with a standard stain which is similarly prepared but taking a specified quantity of standard dilute arsenic solution in place of the substance. If the test stain is less in intensity than the standard stain, the sample passes the test. Otherwise it fails. This test is a modified Gutzeit test.

Practical Details

A. Apparatus : The apparatus consists of a wide-mouthed glass bottle or conical flask fitted with a rubber bung or ground glass stopper. A glass tube of specified dimensions is passed through the rubber bung. The internal diameter of the tube (5 mm) is important and should be uniform throughout. The tube is open at the upper end but tapers to a small diameter at the lower end. Near the lower end a hole is present at the side to allow any condensed moisture to escape.

The tube is first lightly packed with cotton wool saturated with lead acetate and dried. This is to trap any hydrogen sulphide which may be formed during the reaction if any sulphur impurity is

115

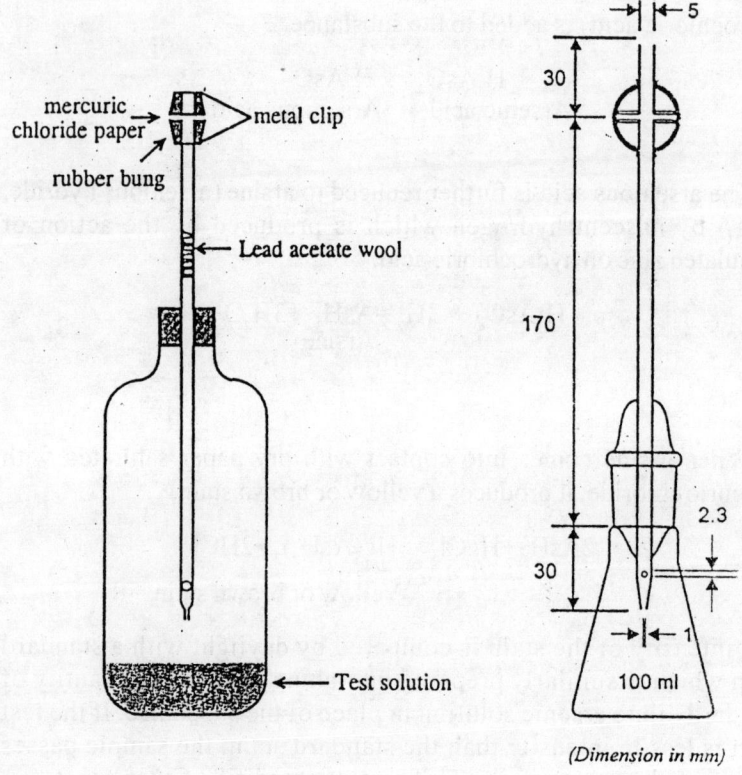

Labels in figure:
- mercuric chloride paper
- metal clip
- rubber bung
- Lead acetate wool
- Test solution
- 30
- 170
- 30
- 5
- 2.3
- 1
- 100 ml
- *(Dimension in mm)*

Apparatus for Limit Test for Arsenic

present in the substance. If this not done, the hydrogen sulphide will affect the mercuric chloride paper.

The mercuric chloride paper is fixed at the upper end of the tube between two rubber bungs by means of a spring clip. The two rubber bungs contain the tube in two parts and the mercuric chloride paper is correctly positioned between them. All the reagents are designated as AsT.Except Dilute Arsenic Solution they should be arsenic-free (see figure).

B. Procedure: The solution of the substance to be examined is prepared as given in the monograph. Potassium iodide and arsenic-free zinc are added and the bottle is closed immediately with the cork carrying the attachments. It is immersed in a water bath at a temperature such that uniform evolution of gas is maintained. The reaction is allowed to go on for forty minutes. A standard is also simultaneously done taking dilute solution of arsenic (specified quantity) in place of the substance and treating it similarly. The mercuric chloride paper in the test is removed and compared by daylight with the standard stain. The standard stains fade on keeping and should be freshly prepared.

For modified procedures in respect of the limit tests for certain substances see the Practical Section.

CHAPTER 9

GASTROINTESTINAL AGENTS AND RELATED COMPOUNDS

I. ACIDIFIERS

In patients suffering from achlorhydria, there is deficient secretion of hydrochloric acid in the stomach. In such cases, acidifiers are useful in providing the necessary acidity for the proper digestion of food. Systemic acidifiers are those which, when given usually by injection, act by reducing the alkali reserve in the body and so are useful in reducing metabolic alkalosis.

1. HYDROCHLORIC ACID, HCl

Hydrochloric acid is prepared by dissolving hydrogen chloride gas in water.

Preparation of Hydrogen Chloride

1. Hydrogen chloride may be made by reacting sodium chloride (common salt) with sulphuric acid. The reaction takes place in two steps.

$$NaCl + H_2SO_4 = NaHSO_4 + HCl$$
$$\text{Sodium bisulphate}$$

$$NaHSO_4 + NaCl = Na_2SO_4 + HCl$$
$$\text{Sodium sulphate}$$
$$\text{(salt cake)}$$

The hydrogen chloride obtained in the first step above known as the 'pan acid' is comparatively more pure whereas the hydrogen chloride obtained in the second step along with the salt cake is less pure and is known as 'muriatic acid' of commerce. Muriatic acid is a yellow liquid.

2. In this method the hydrogen and chlorine obtained in the electrolysis of sodium chloride in the manufacture of caustic soda

117

are burnt preferably using quartz bunsen burners.

$$H_2 + Cl_2 = 2HCl$$

100% pure hydrogen chloride is formed in this method.

Physical and Chemical Properties

Hydrogen chloride is a colourless gas with an acrid irritating odour and an acid taste. It is heavier than air and is very soluble in water. About 460 ml of the gas dissolve in 1 ml of water at 20°C at 760 mm pressure.

Hydrochloric Acid, I.P. is an aqueous solution of hydrogen chloride in water. It contains between 35 per cent and 38 per cent w/w of HCl. It is a clear, colourless, fuming liquid with a pungent taste.

Hydrochloric acid combines directly with alkalis such as ammonia and sodium hydroxide. These are known as neutralization reactions.

$$NH_3 + HCl = NH_4Cl$$
$$NaOH + HCl = NaCl + H_2O$$

It also reacts with metals to form the corresponding chlorides.

$$2Na + 2HCl = 2NaCl + H_2\uparrow$$

It releases carbon dioxide from carbonates and bicarbonates.

$$Na_2CO_3 + 2HCl = 2NaCl + H_2CO_3$$
$$\text{Carbonic acid}$$

$$H_2CO_3 = H_2O + CO_2\uparrow$$
$$NaHCO_3 + HCl = NaCl + CO_2\uparrow + H_2O$$

There is another type of neutralisation reaction. It gives a curdy white precipitate with silver nitrate.

$$AgNO_3 + HCl = AgCl + HNO_3$$

The silver chloride precipitate is photosensitive and becomes slightly pink on exposure to light. It is very sparingly soluble in water.

Hydrochloric acid produces sulphur dioxide on reaction with a sulphite.

$$Na_2SO_3 + 2HCl = 2NaCl + H_2SO_3$$
Sulphurous acid
$$H_2SO_3 = SO_2\uparrow + H_2O$$

It produces hydrogen sulphide with sodium sulphide and decomposes sodium thiosulphate to precipitate sulphur.

$$Na_2S + 2HCl = 2NaCl + H_2S\uparrow$$

$$Na_2S_2O_3 + 2HCl = 2NaCl + SO_2\uparrow + S\downarrow + H_2O$$

It is offical in I.P

Official Tests for Identity

1. When a sample is neutralised and diluted with water, it gives the reactions of chlorides (see Chapter 18).

2. When the sample is added to pot. permanganate, chlorine is evolved.

Non-official Tests for Identity

1. When the sample is added to silver nitrate solution, a white, curdy precipitate of silver chloride is formed. It is insoluble in nitric acid but soluble in ammonia solution. In ammonia it forms the soluble diammino-silver chloride, $Ag(NH_3)_2Cl$.

2. It gives with ammonia thick white fumes (formation of ammonium chloride).

3. Chlorine is produced when hydrochloric acid is heated with manganese dioxide.

Tests for Purity

1. Arsenic
2. Heavy metals
3. Bromide and iodide

119

4. Sulphite
5. Sulphate
6. Free Chlorine
7. Residue on evaporation

Bromide and iodide are tested by dissolving the sample in water and adding chlorinated lime solution and chloroform. The chloroform layer should not become brown or violet. If bromide is present, it is decomposed by the chlorine from the chlorinated lime and the liberated bromine dissolves in the chloroform colouring it brown. Similarly the liberated iodine from any iodide present colours the chloroform layer violet.

Sulphite is detected by adding barium chloride solution and a dilute solution of iodine. Sulphite is oxidised to sulphate and iodine is decolourised. The colour of the iodine should not be completely discharged.

Sulphate is tested by neutralising the acid with sodium bicarbonate and evaporating to dryness. The residue, dissolved in water, complies with the limit test for sulphates.

Free chlorine can be detected by adding to a diluted solution potassium iodide and chloroform. The chloroform layer should not become violet.

Standard : Hydrochloric Acid is an aqueous solution of hydrogen chloride gas (HCl) in water. It contains not less than 35% w/w and not more than 38% w/w of HCl.

Assay : An accurately weighed sample of the acid is diluted with water and titrated with 1M sodium hydroxide using methyl red solution as the indicator. End point is the appearance of a faint yellow colour.

Storage : Hydrogen chloride gas volatilises from Hydrochloric Acid when exposed to atmosphere till a constant boiling mixture of 20.24% boiling at 110^0C is formed. Therefore Hydrochloric Acid should be stored in glass-stoppered containers securely closed at a temperature not exceeding 30°C.

Medicinal and Pharmaceutical Uses

Pharmaceutical Aid (Acidifying Agent).

Hydrochloric is used in cases of *achlorhydria* (lack of hydrochloric acid in the gastric juice) in the form of Dilute Hydrochloric Acid, I.P.

It is also used in the manufacture of glucose from corn starch, for extracting glue (gelatin) from bones and as a reagent in the laboratory.

2. DILUTE HYDROCHLORIC ACID, HCl

Preparation: Dilute hydrochloric acid is prepared from Hydrochloric Acid by diluting 274 g of the acid with 726 g of purified water.

Physical and Chemical Properties

Dilute hydrochloric acid is a clear, colourless liquid with an acid taste. Its chemical properties are the same as those given under Hydrochloic Acid. It is official in I.P.

Official Tests for Identity

Complies with the tests given under Hydrochloric Acid.

Standard: Dilute Hydrochloric Acid contains not less than 9.5 per cent w/w and not more than 10.5 per cent w/w of HCl.

Storage: It should be kept in a stoppered container of glass or other inert material and stored at a temperature not exceeding 30°C.

Assay: Refer Hydrochloric Acid.

Medicinal and Pharmaceutical Uses: *Acidifier.* Dilute hydrochloric acid is administered orally to treat achlorhydria (lack of hydrochloric acid in the gastric juice). The dose is 0.6 to 8 ml. It is also used as a reagent in the laboratory.

3. SODIUM PHOSPHATE, $Na_2HPO_4 \cdot 12H_2O$.

Sodium phosphate is disodium hydrogen phosphate or secondary sodium orthophosphate.

Preparation : (1) Sodium phosphate is prepared by adding sodium carbonate to boiling phosphoric acid solution until the mixture is slightly alkaline to litmus and crystallizing the product.

$$Na_2CO_3 + H_3PO_4 = Na_2HPO_4 + CO_2\uparrow + H_2O$$

(2) It is also made from calcium phosphate by reacting with the correct amount of sulphuric acid. Monobasic calcium phosphate is formed along with calcium sulphate.

$$Ca_3(PO_4)_2 + 2H_2SO_4 = Ca(H_2PO_4)_2 + 2CaSO_4$$

Boiling water is added to the mixture which is filtered. The filtrate is treated with sodium carbonate. Sodium phosphate is formed in solution along with a precipitate of dibasic calcium phosphate which is filtered off. The filtrate is concentrated and cooled. Sodium phosphate crystallizes out.

$$Ca(H_2PO_4)_2 + Na_2CO_3 = CaHPO_4 + Na_2HPO_4 + CO_2\uparrow + H_2O$$

Physical and Chemical Properties

Sodium phosphate occurs as colourless, monoclinic prisms containing 12 molecules of water of crystallization. It is odourless and has a not unpleasant saline taste. When crystallized from water at a temperature above 35^0C. it has seven molecules of water. It strongly effloresces in warm, dry air, losing finally 5 molecules of water of crystallization. It is freely soluble in water and practically insoluble in alcohol.

When heated at 40^0C, it becomes a colourless liquid. On further heating, it becomes anhydrous at 100^0C and at 300^0C it is converted into sodium pyrophosphate.

$$2Na_2HPO_4 \overset{\Delta}{=} Na_4P_2O_7 + H_2O$$
Sodium
pyrophosphate

Aqueous solution of sodium phosphate is alkaline to litmus and phenolphthalein. This is because sodium phosphate is hydrolysed in solution and the alkalinity is due to the hydroxyl ion formed.

$$Na_2HPO_4 \rightleftarrows 2Na^+ + HPO_4^{2-}$$
Monohydrogen
phosphate ion

$$HPO_4^{2-} + H_2O \rightleftarrows H_2PO_4^- + OH^-$$

Sodium phosphate combines with barium, ferric and lead salts to form the corresponding insoluble phosphates.

$$Na_2HPO_4 + BaCl_2 \rightleftarrows 2NaCl + BaHPO_4\downarrow$$

$$Na_2HPO_4 + FeCl_3 \rightleftarrows FePO_4\downarrow + 2NaCl + HCl$$

$$2Na_2HPO_4 + 3Pb(CH_3COO)_2 = Pb_3(PO_4)_2 + 2CH_3COOH + 4CH_3COONa$$

Sodium phosphate, dissolved in nitric acid and treated with an excess of ammonium molybdate solution, precipitates yellow ammonium phosphomolybate.

$$12(NH_4)_2 MoO_4 + Na_2HPO_4 + 23HNO_3 = (NH_4)_3PO_4.12MoO_3$$
Ammonium   Ammonium
molybdate   phosphomolybdate
$$21NH_4NO_3 + 2NaNO_3 + 12H_2O$$

It is official in I.P.

Official Tests for Identity : An aqueous solution of the substance gives the reactions of sodium and of phosphates. See Chapter 18.

Tests for Purity

1. Clarity and colour of solution
2. Arsenic
3. Heavy metals
4. Iron
5. Chloride
6. Sulphate

7. Reducing substances
8. Sodium dihydrogen phosphate
9. Water

Reducing substances are tested by adding a dilute solution of potassium permanganate and heating on a water bath for five minutes. The red colour should not be completely discharged.

Sodium dihydrogen phosphate is limited by finding out its content during the assay.

Water: The content of water should be between 57 and 61% w/w and it is determined by aquametry using the Karl Fischer reagent.

Standard : Sodium phosphate contains between 98 and 101% of Na_2HPO_4, calculated with reference to the anhydrous substance.

Assay : It is done by potentiometric titration. The substance is dissolved in water. 1M hydrochloric acid is added and the solution is titrated with 1M sodium hydroxide to the first inflection and then till the second inflection is reached. The percentage content of Na_2HPO_4 is found out by using the formula given in the I.P.

Storage : Since the salt is strongly efflorescent, store in tightly closed containers.

Medicinal and Pharmaceutical Uses

Systemic acidifier and buffering agent. It is also a saline laxative and cathartic.

4. AMMONIUM CHLORIDE, NH_4Cl

Preparation : Ammonium chloride is made by reacting hydrochloric acid with ammonia. The solution is evaporated to dryness:

$$NH_3 + HCl = NH_4Cl$$

The product is purified by recrystallization or by sublimation.

Physical and Chemical Properties: Crude ammonium chloride or *sal ammoniac* consists of tough, fibrous, crystalline masses. The

124

pure substance is a white, crystalline powder. It is odourless with a saline taste. It is freely soluble in water.

When heated, ammonium chloride volatilises. It is considered to decompose into ammonia and hydrochloric acid but the components reunite when cooled. This phenomenon can be seen when ammonium chloride is heated in a test tube. Ammonia and hydrochloric acid formed at the bottom due to the decomposition of ammonium chloride reunite at the top of the test tube to form a white deposit.

$$NH_4Cl \rightleftharpoons NH_3 + HCl$$

Due to this dissociation, ammonium chloride is used as a flux in soldering for removing the film of oxide from the surface of the metal. The HCl formed converts the metallic oxide into chloride which, being volatile, is driven of easily at the high temperature. Even though ammonium chloride solution is neutral when freshly prepared, it becomes slightly acid on standing due to hydrolysis.

It is official in I.P.

Official Tests for Identity

Gives the reactions characteristic of ammonium salts and of chlorides (refer Chapter 18).

Tests for Purity

1. Arsenic
2. Heavy metals
3. Iron
4. Sulphate
5. Thiocyanate
6. Sulphated ash
7. Loss on drying
8. Calcium

Thiocyanate is tested by adding hydrochloric acid and ferric chloride solution. No red colour (due to the formation of ferric thiocyanate) is produced.

125

Loss on drying is determined by drying the sample in an oven at 105°C. (Actually when heated, ammonium chloride volatilises. So it is better to find out the loss on drying by drying the sample for a few hours in a desiccator containing concentrated sulphuric acid as the drying agent).

Standard: Contains not less than 99.5 per cent of NH_4Cl calculated with reference to the substance dried over silica gel for four hours.

Storage: Since ammonium chloride is slightly hygroscopic, it is stored in a well closed container.

Assay: I.P.'96 gives the following method:

Formaldehyde, previously neutralised to phenolphthalein, is added to a solution of the substance. It fixes the ammonia in ammonium chloride as hexamine. The liberated hydrochloric acid is titrated against 0.1M sodium hydroxide, using phenolphthalein as indicator.

A modified Volhard's method was used in I.P. '66. A solution of the substance, acidified with nitric acid, is shaken with a measured volume of N/10 silver nitrate, nitrobenzene being previously added. Nitrobenzene is added to coagulate the precipitate of silver chloride, so that it will not interfere with the titration later of excess of silver nitrate which is determined by titration with N/10 ammonium thiocyanate, using ferric ammonium sulphate as indicator.

$$AgNO_3 + NH_4Cl = AgCl + NH_4NO_3$$

$$AgNO_3 + NH_4SCN = AgSCN + NH_4NO_3$$
$$\text{Ammonium} \quad \text{Silver}$$
$$\text{thiocyanate} \quad \text{thiocyanate}$$

The following is the reaction taking place at the end point when red ferric thiocyanate is formed (by reaction of ammonium thiocyanate with the indicator ferric ammonium sulphate).

$$FeNH_4(SO_4)_2 + 3NH_4SCN = Fe(SCN)_3 + 2(NH4)_2SO_4$$

Ferric ammonium   Ammonium   Ferric   Ammonium
   sulphate   thiocyanate thiocyanate   sulphate

Medicinal and Pharmacutical Uses: *Expectorant, diuretic and systemic acidifier.*

II. ANTACIDS

Antacids are drugs used to neutralize the hydrochloric acid secreted in the stomach in the gastric juice. They raise the pH of the gastric contents to above 3.5 and give symptomatic relief of pain (in gastric and duodenal ulcers) by lowering the acidity and consequently relieving the muscle spasm. They do this by acting as weak bases.

An *ideal antacid* should not have any side effects other than its main action of neuralizing the gastric acid. For example it should not have a constipating or laxative effect. It should not cause, if absorbed, systemic alkalosis (in this condition the pH of the body fluids and tissues is high). It should not cause precipitation of phosphate in the gastrointestinal tract and depletion of phosphorus in the body..It should not also interfere with the absorption of other drugs such as tetracycline from the gut. It should not also delay the absorption of drugs which are weak acids or speed up the absorption of basic drugs. This happens when the pH of the gastric contents is raised.

In the case of antacids, the *acid neutralizing capacity* is important. This may be determined by allowing the antacid to remain in contact with hydrochloric acid at 37°C in a thermostatically controlled bath and measuring the pH at successive time intervals. Finally the concentration of the acid is increased further and the neutralizing capacity of the antacid is found out by determining acid by titration with 0.1 M sodium hydroxide after one hour.

CLASSIFICATION OF ANTACIDS

Antacids are divided into:

127

1. Non-systemic Antacids: These, as stated above, directly neutralize the acid in the stomach and give relief in gastric and duodenal ulcers.

a) Aluminium hydroxide gel
b) Dried aluminium hydroxide gel
c) Aluminium phosphate
d) Magnesium hydroxide
e) Magnesium trisilicate
f) Light and heavy magnesium carbonate
g) Magaldrate
h) Calcium carbonate
i) Bismuth subcarbonate

2. Systemic Antacids: These may be absorbed from the gut into the blood circulation and cause alkalosis. So they may also called as systemic alkalisers when they are used by injection to relieve acidosis in the blood, especially in diabetic coma.

1. Sodium bicarbonate
2. Potassium citrate

COMBINATIONS OF ANTACIDS

There are three complications usually seen when antacids are used. First, many antacids exert an action on the bowel. For example some have a mild laxative effect (eg. magnesium hydroxide) and some are constipating (eg. aluminium hydroxide). Secondly if the cation (the metallic ion) is absorbed, systemic alkalosis (a condition in which the alkalinity of body fluids and tissues is abnormally high) may be produced (eg. sodium bicarbonate). Calcium ions may produce hypercalcaemia (the presence in the blood of an abnormally high concentration of calcium). Magnesium and aluminium cause precipitation of phosphate in the gastrointestinal tract and depletion of phosphorus. Finally antacids may affect the absorption of other drugs which may be administered along with antacids such as antichlolinergics and antibiotics. These drugs may be adsorbed by the antacids. Antacids may also alter the pH of the gastric contents thereby delaying the absorption of weak acids and speeding the absorption of basic drugs.

If dyspepsia (indigestion) leading to gas formation in the gut is present, use of a drug like methylpolysiloxane (dimethicone or simethicone) is necessary. Therefore because of the defects associated with the antacids as discussed in the previous paragraph, it is apparent that it is wiser to use a combination of antacids so that the defects can be minimized. For example magnesium hydroxide and aluminium hydroxide may be combined to balance the constipating effect of the latter with the laxative effect of the former. On this basis the following combinations are in regular clinical use:

1. Magnesium and aluminium hydroxides (Magaldrate)

2. Magnesium and aluminium hydroxides, dimethicone (Dioval Forte Tabs)

3. Magnesium and aluminium hydroxides, methylpolysiloxane (Gelusil MPS)

4. Aluminium hydroxide gel, magnesium trisilicate (Gelusil)

5. Aluminium hydroxide gel, magnesium hydroxide, magnesium trisilicate (Gelusil M)

6. Mag. hydroxide, dried alu.hydroxide gel, methylpolysiloxane, sod.carboxymethyl cellulose (Digene gel).

The chemistry of the various antacids is discussed below:-

1. SODIUM BICARBONATE, $NaHCO_3$

Preparation : Sodium bicarbonate may be made by the ammonia soda process for sodium carbonate. However this does not give medicinal grade sodium bicarbonate. Therefore to obtain medicinal grade sodium bicarbonate the sample is heated to get sodium carbonate. The sodium carbonate is dissolved in water and carbon dioxide is passed through it. Sodium bicarbonate is precipitated and it is washed and dried.

129

$$Na_2CO_3 + CO_2 + H_2O = 2NaHCO_3$$

Physical Properties : Sodium bicarbonate is a white, odourless, crystalline, monoclinic powder. It is stable in dry air but in moist air it slowly decomposes to sodium carbonate, carbon dioxide and water. It is soluble 1 in 10 in water. It is insoluble in alcohol.

Chemical Properties

1. When heated dry or in solution in water, it loses water and carbon dioxide and forms the normal carbonate.

$$2NaHCO_3 = Na_2CO_3 + H_2O + CO_2\uparrow$$

2. Carbon dioxide is again liberated when it is treated with any acid :

$$NaHCO_3 + HCl = NaCl + CO_2\uparrow + H_2O$$

3. Aqueous solutions of sodium bicarbonate are slightly alkaline, as the bicarbonate ion is hydrolysed in solution.

$$HCO_3^- + H_2O = H_2CO_3 + OH^-$$

However it is so slightly alkaline that it just turns phenol-phthalein faintly red. This distinguishes sodium bicarbonate from sodium carbonate. It is official in I.P.

Official Tests for Identity

1. Gives the reactions characteristic of sodium and of bicarbonates (See Chapter 18).

2. To a solution of the substance in carbon dioxide-free water, phenolphtalein solution is added. A pale pink colour is produced (due to the alkalinity of sodium bicarbonate). On heating, a gas (CO_2) is evolved. The solution becomes red (due to the formation of sodium carbonate).

Tests for Purity

1. Clarity and colour of solution.

2. *Carbonate :* pH of a freshly prepared solution in carbondioxide-free water should be not more than 8.6. With this pH limit a maximum of 2% of sodium carbonate is allowed.

3. Calcium
4. Arsenic.
5. Heavy metals.
6. Chloride.
7. Sulphate.

Calcium is detected by boiling a solution of the sample for 5 minutes. The solution should be clear. If calcium is present, calcium carbonate will be precipitated during boiling.

Assay : An acccurately weighed quantity of the sample is dissolved in carbon dioxide-free water and titrated with 1M hydrochloric acid using methyl orange as indicator.

$$HCl + NaHCO_3 = NaCl + CO_2\uparrow + H_2O$$

Storage : Since it slowly decomposes when exposed to moist air, store it in a well - closed container.

Medicinal Uses

Sodium bicarbonate may be used as an *antacid*. Since it quickly neutralizes the gastric acid, the stomach secretes more acid to maintain the acid pH. This is what is known as 'rebound acidity' and this may even lead to peptic ulcer. However sodium bicarbonate can be used as a good antacid, if used in controlled doses.

Sodium bicarbonate may also be given by injection to relieve acidosis in the blood, especially in diabetic coma. So it is *a systemic alkaliser*. It is also an *electrolyte replenisher*.

2. POTASSIUM CITRATE, $K_3C_6H_5O_7.H_2O.$

Preparation : Potassium citrate is prepared in the same way as sodium citrate by neutralizing a solution of citric acid with either potassium carbonate or potassium bicarbonate. The effervescence is allowed to subside and the solution is evaporated to crystallization.

$$3KHCO_3 + H_3C_6H_5O_7.H_2O = K_3C_6H_5O_7.H_2O + 3CO_2\uparrow + 3H_2O$$

Physical and Chemical Properties

Potassium citrate occurs as transparent crystals or as a white granular powder. It is odourless and has a cooling, saline taste. It is hygroscopic and very soluble in water.

When heated, potassium citrate begins to lose water at $100^{\circ}C$ and becomes anhydrous at about $200^{\circ}C$. On further strong heating, it carbonizes and evolves non-inflammable gases having a pungent, acrid odour. It leaves a residue of carbon and potassium carbonate which can be tested by adding dilute acid (effervescence).

$$2K_3C_6H_5O_7.H_2O + 9O_2 = 3K_2CO_3 + 9CO_2\uparrow + 6H_2O$$

It is official in I.P.

Official Tests for Identity

An aqueous solution gives the reactions of potassium and of citrates. See Chapter 18.

Tests for Purity

1. Acidity or alkalinity
2. Arsenic
3. Heavy metals
4. Sodium
5. Chloride
6. Sulphate
7. Oxalate
8. Readily carbonisable substances
9. Water

Readily carbonisable substances are tested by adding to the sample concentrated sulphuric acid and heating on a water bath at $90^{\circ}C$ for one hour. The colour of the solution is compared with a standard coloured solution coloured by using ferric chloride, copper sulphate and cobalt chloride solutions and dilute hydrochloric acid. If the impurities are present, they will be charred and carbonised by the concentrated sulphuric acid.

Standard : Potassium citrate contains between 99 and 101 percent of $K_3C_6H_5O_7.H_2O$, calcuated with reference to the anhydrous substance.

Assay : This is a non - aqueous titration. An accurately weighed quantity is dissolved in glacial acetic acid by warming to 50^0C, cooled and titrated with 0.1N perchloric acid using 1 - naphtholbenzein as indicator. A blank titration also is done.

Storage : Since it is hygroscopic it must be stored in a tightly closed or airtight container.

Medicinal and Pharmaceutical Uses : *Systemic alkalizer,. diuretic, expectorant and diaphoretic.*

3. ALUMINIUM HYDROXIDE GEL, Al(OH)₃

According to I.P., Aluminium Hydroxide Gel is an aqueous suspension of hydrated aluminium oxide together with varying quantities of basic aluminium carbonate and bicarbonate. It may contain glycerin, sorbitol, sucrose or saccharin as sweetening agent and peppermint oil or other flavours. It may also contain suitable antimicrobial agents. 0.5% sodium benzoate or benzoic acid may be used as preservative.

Preparation: For preparing this a hot solution of potash alum is. added slowly to a hot solution of sodium carbonate and not vice versa. The precipitate of aluminium hydroxide is washed thoroughly with hot water till it is free from sulphate. The gel is then adjusted to the required volume with distilled water.

$$3Na_2CO_3 + 2KAl(SO_4)_2 + 3H_2O = 3Na_2SO_4 + K_2SO_4$$
$$\text{Potash alum} \qquad + 2Al(OH)_3\downarrow + 3CO_2\uparrow$$

If sodium carbonate solution is added to potash alum solution, then it is difficult to wash out the sulphate completely. Due to adsorption by aluminium hydroxide, some carbonate may be present.

133

Physical and Chemical Properties

Aluminium hydroxide gel is a white viscous suspension which is translucent (that is, allows the light to pass through partially). Small amounts of clear liquid may separate from this on standing. It is insolule in water and readily soluble in acids and alkalis.

It is amphoteric in nature. It affects both blue litmus and red litmus. Heated strongly, it decomposes into aluminium oxide and water. It reacts with hydrochloric acid to form aluminium chloride.

$$Al(OH)_3 + 3HCl = AlCl_3 + 3H_2O$$

So aluminium hydroxide gel is able to neutralize the acid in the stomach and is a good antacid. It is official in I.P. There is a test for neutralizing capacity prescribed in the I.P.

Official Tests for Identity

A solution in dilute hydrochloric acid gives the reactions of aluminium (see Chapter 18).

Tests for Purity
1. pH
2. Arsenic
3. Heavy metals
4. Chloride
5. Sulphate
6. Neutralizing capacity
7. Microbial limits

pH should be between 5.5 and 8.

Neutralizing capacity is determined by allowing the gel to remain in contact with 0.1M hydrochloric acid at 37°C in a thermostatically controlled bath and measuring the pH at successive time intervals. Finally the concentration of the acid is increased further and the neutralizing capacity of the gel is found out by finding the remaining acid by titration with 0.1M sodium hydroxide after one hour.

Since this is an orally administered preparation, the total *microbial content* should not exceed 100 per ml. In this also *E.coli* should be absent. This is to avoid dangers due to microbial contamination especially dangerous bacteria like *E.coli*.

Standard: It contains between 3.5 per cent and 4.4 per cent w/w of Al_2O_3.

Assay: An accurately weighed quantity of the gel is dissolved in concentrated hydrochloric acid by warming and diluted with water. To an aliquot a known excess of 0.05M sodium edetate is added and the mixture is neutralized with 1M sodium hydroxide using methyl red as indicator. This neutral mixture is warmed on a water bath for half an hour to ensure complexation of aluminium by sodium edetate. Hexamine is added and it is back titrated with 0.05M lead nitrate using xylenol orange as indicator.

This is a complexometric titration and the sodium edetate is allowed to complex aluminium under conditions under which metals such as calcium and magnesium do not interfere. The excess of sodium edetate left after complexation of aluminium is over is back titrated with 0.05M lead nitrate solution. Hexamine is added to raise the pH to the alkaline side to facilitate the complexometric titration of the excess of EDTA with 0.05M lead nitrate.

Storage: Store in tightly closed containers in a cool place and avoid freezing.

Medicinal and Pharmaceutical Use: *Antacid.* It is used as an antacid and protective in treating peptic ulcers. It is also used in cases of acute hyperacidity.

4. DRIED ALUMINIUM HYDROXIDE GEL

Properties: It is a white, light, amorphous powder containing some aggregates and is odourless and tasteless. It consists largely of hydrated aluminium oxide and varying small quantities of basic aluminium carbonate and bicarbonate. It is insoluble in water and in alcohol but soluble in dilute mineral acids and in excess of caustic alkali solutions.

Official Tests for Identity

A solution of the substance in dilute hydrochloric acid gives the reactions of aluminium. See Chapter 18.

Tests for Purity

1. pH
2. Arsenic
3. Heavy metals
4. Chloride
5. Sulphate
6. Neutralizing capacity
7. Microbial limits

pH is determined on a 4 per cent w/v suspension of the substance in carbon dioxide-free water. It should be not more than 10.

All the other tests for purity are carried out in the same way as for aluminium hydroxide gel.

It contains not less than 47 per cent and not more than 60 per cent of Al_2O_3.

Assay: Same as for aluminium hydroxide gel.

Storage: Store in tightly-closed containers.

Medicinal Use: *Antacid.*

5. ALUMINIUM PHOSPHATE, $AlPO_4$

It consists mainly of about 80% of hydrated aluminium orthophosphate.

Preparation

A solution of dried dibasic sodium phosphate in water is added slowly to solution of aluminium chloride and aluminium phosphate is formed along with sodium chloride and hydrochloric acid.

$$AlCl_3.6H_2O + Na_2HPO_4 = AlPO_4\downarrow + 2NaCl + HCl + 6H_2O$$

The hydrochloric acid formed is neutralized by adding diluted ammonia.

$$HCl + NH_4OH = NH_4Cl + H_2O$$

The mixture is then filtered and washed with water to free it from soluble salts such as sodium chloride and ammonium chloride. Then sufficient water is added to get a gel with a concentration of about 4% of aluminum phosphate. Alternatively all the water is removed and the product is dried under suitable conditions to get the dried aluminium phosphate.

Physical and Chemical Properties

Dried aluminium phosphate is a white amorphous powder containing some friable aggregates. It is practically insoluble in water and alcohol but is readily soluble in mineral acids. It is insoluble in solutions of alkali hydroxides.

Aluminium phosphate answers all the reactions of the aluminium ion and the phosphate radical. For this it must be dissolved in nitric acid (for testing for phosphate) and in hydrochloric acid (for testing for aluminium).

Tests for Identity

(1) A solution of aluminium phosphate in hydrochloric acid gives the reactions of aluminium. (See Chapter 18).

(2) A solution of aluminium phosphate in nitric acid gives the reactions of phosphates (see Chapter 18).

Medicinal Use: *Antacid.*

Aluminium phosphate gel, which contains about 4% of aluminium phosphate, is normally used as the antacid. Sweetening agents such as glycerin, sugar or saccharin may be added to make he gel more palatable and oil of peppermint to give a nice flavour.

Dried aluminium phosphate tablets (500 mg) are also available flavoured with peppermint. Sodium benzoate or benzoic acid (0.5%) is usually added to the gel to serve as a preservative.

Aluminium phosphate is a slow-acting antacid. It is better than aluminium hydroxide gel in the sense that it does not interfere with the absorption of phosphates from the intestine.

6. MAGNESIUM HYDROXIDE, Mg(OH)$_2$

Preparation: Milk of magnesia is evaporated to dryness carefully. Preparation of milk of magnesia is given next to this.

Properties: Magnesium hydroxide is a bulky, white powder without odour. It is practically insoluble in water and in alcohol. It dissolves in dilute acids. It is official in I.P.

Official Tests for Identity

The substance is dissolved in dilute nitric acid and neutralised with dilute sodium hydroxide. The resulting solution gives the reactions of magnesium salts. See Chapter 18.

Tests for Purity

1. Colour of Solution
2. Arsenic
3. Heavy metals
4. Chloride
5. Sulphate
6. Calcium
7. Iron
8. Soluble substances; substances insoluble in acetic acid
9. Loss on ignition

Standard: It contains not less than 95 per cent and not more than 100.5 per cent of Mg(OH)$_2$.

Assay: This is a complexmetric assay. The sample is dissolved in dilute hydrochloric acid and diluted to a definite volume with water To an aliquot the buffer strong ammonia-ammonium chloride solution is added and it is titrated with 0.05M disodium edetate, using mordant black II mixture as indicator.

Storage: Store in well-closed containers

Medicinal Use: *Antacid and osmotic laxative.*

7. MAGNESIUM HYDROXIDE ORAL SUSPENSION

(Magnesium hydroxide mixture, milk of magnesia, cream of magnesia)

Preparation: Milk of magnesia is prepared by the following method:

Ingredients : Light magnesium oxide
Magnesium sulphate
Sodium hydroxide
Purified water, sufficient

Light magnesium oxide is mixed with a solution of sodium hydroxide to form a smooth cream and purified water is added to further dilute it. This suspension is then poured into a solution of magnesium sulphate with continuous stirring. Magnesium hydroxide is precipitated. It is allowed to settle down, the supernatant liquid is decanted and the residue is washed with purified water on a calico strainer till the filtrate gives only a slight reaction for sulphates. The precipitate is then mixed with sufficient purified water to produce the required volume.

In this preparation, the magnesium oxide is hydrated to form magnesium hydroxide. In addition, magnesium hydroxide is also formed by reaction between magnesium sulphate and sodium hydroxide.

$$MgO + H_2O = Mg(OH)_2$$
$$MgSO_4 + 2NaOH = Mg(OH)_2 + Na_2SO_4$$

139

These two methods combine to give a precipitate which is easily distributed and the preparation also has such consistency as to be easily pourable.

Properties: It is a white, uniform suspension which does not separate readily on standing. It is official in I.P.

Official Tests for Identity: A solution of the milk of magnesia in hydrochloric acid gives the reactions of magnesium. See Chapter 18.

Tests for Purity

1. Sulphate
2. Microbial limits
3. Soluble alkalis
4. Soluble salts
5. Heavy metals

As far as *microbial limits* are concerned, the total microbial count should not exceed 1000 per ml and 1 ml of the mixture should also be free from *E. coli*. Since this is an orally administered preparation, these microbial limits are prescribed from the point of view of safety.

To determine *soluble alkalies*, the mixture is filtered and the filtrate is diluted and titrated with 0.05M sulphuric acid, using methyl red as indicator. This limit test has been prescribed to ensure proper washing of the precipitate to eliminate the presence of excess of sodium hydroxide.

Soluble salts are also determined by taking the filtrate and adding sulphuic acid. It is then evaporated to dryness on a water bath and ignited gently to constant weight. This limit test has also been prescribed to ensure proper washing of the precipitate in order to remove the soluble bye product, that is sodium sulphate completely.

Standard: Milk of magnesia contains between 7 percent and 8.: percent w/w of hydrated magnesium oxide, calculated as $Mg(OH)_2$.

Assay: It is by a back titration. A weighed quantity of the mixture is treated with a known volume of 0.5M sulphuric acid and the excess of acid is back-titrated with 1M sodium hydroxide, using methyl orange as indicator.

$$Mg(OH)_2 + H_2SO_4 = MgSO_4 + 2H_2O$$
$$H_2SO_4 + 2NaOH = Na_2SO_4 + 2H_2O$$

Medicinal Use: *Antacid and Laxative*

8. MAGALDRATE, $Al_5Mg_{10}(OH)_{31}(SO_4)_2, xH_2O$

Magaldrate is a product of chemical combination of aluminium hydroxide and magnesium hydroxide along with the sulphates of aluminium and magnesium. It contains a variable amount of water of hydration and corresponds to the formula given above.

Properties: It is a white or almost white, crystalline powder which is without odour. It is practically insoluble in water and alcohol. It is soluble in dilute mineral acids. It is official in I.P.

Official Tests for Identity

1. The substance is dissolved in dilute hydrochloric acid and heated to boiling. It is neutralized with dilute ammonia, boiled and filtered. The filtrate gives the reactions of magnesium salts. See Chapter 18.

2. The precipitate obtained in test (1) is washed with hot ammonium chloride solution and dissolved in dilute hydrochloric acid. The solution gives the reactions of aluminium salts. See Chapter 18.

Tests for Purity

1. Arsenic
2. Heavy metals

3. Soluble chloride
4. Soluble sulphate
5. Sodium
6. Aluminium hydroxide
7. Magnesium hydroxide
8. Sulphate
9. Loss on drying
10. Microbial limits

For *souble chloride*, a hot aqueous extract of the substance is titrated with 0.1M silver nitrate solution using potassium chromate solution as the indicator.

For *souble sulphate*, the aqueous extract is taken in a Nessler cylinder, dilute hydrochloric acid and barium chloride solution are added and diluted to the mark. Any turbidity, produced is not greater than that produced by treating one ml of 0.01M sulphuric acid in the same manner.

Sodium is limited by estimating its amount by flame photometry. *Aluminium hydroxide* is limited by a complexometric titration. For this purpose the substance is dissolved in dilute hydrochloric acid and mixed with a known excess of 0.05M disodium edetate. Aluminium is complexed by the EDTA. The excess of EDTA is found out by titrating the solution with 0.05M zinc sulphate after adding acetic acid-ammonium acetate buffer, ethanol(95%) amd dithizone solution. Dithizone acts as the indicator and the end point is marked by the appearance of a bright rose-pink colour. A blank titration is also done without taking the substance.

Magnesium hydroxide is limited by another complexometric titration in which the sample is dissolved in dilute hydrochloric acid, ammonium chloride, triethanolamine, ammonia-ammonium chloride buffer and eriochrome black T solution indicator are added and titrated with 0.05M disodium edetate. A blank titration without the substance is also done. End point is the appearance of a blue colour. Triethanolamine and ammonia-ammonium chloride buffer raise the pH to 10 at which complexation of magnesium by the EDTA can take place. Triethanolamine also masks the other metal aluminium.

Microbial limits: Since this substance is to be formulated into an oral suspension, it is required to be free from *Escherichia coli.*

Standard: Magaldrate contains not less than 90 per cent and no more than 105 per cent of $Al_5Mg_{10}(OH)_{31}(SO_4)_2$, calculated with reference to the dried substance.

Assay: The sample is dissolved in a known volume of 1M hydrochloric acid and stirred well until a clear solution is obtained The excess of acid is titrated with 1M sodium hydroxide to a pH o 3. The end point is determined potentiometrically.

Storage: Store in well-closed containers.

Medicinal Use: *Antacid.* Magaldrate is used in the form o magaldrate oral suspension and magaldrate tablets.

MAGNESIUM CARBONATE

Magnesium carbonate occurs in two forms, that is, heav magnesium carbonate and light magnesium carbonate. They are bot hydrated basic magnesium carbonates and differ only in the conten of water of hydration (the heavy variety having $4H_2O$ and the ligh one with $3H_2O$) and in the bulk density.

9. HEAVY MAGNESIUM CARBONATE, $3MgCO_3$ $Mg(OH)_2$, $4H_2O$

Preparation: Crystalline magnesium sulphate (125 parts) and crystalline sodium carbonate (150 parts), each dissolved in 250 parts

143

of boiling water, are mixed together and evaporated to dryness. The residue is digested with boiling water for half an hour. The precipitate of heavy magnesium carbonate is collected on a calico filter, washed till sulphate is fully removed and dried in a water-oven.

$$4MgSO_4.7H_2O + 4Na_2CO_3.10H_2O = 3MgCO_3.Mg(OH)_2.4H_2O$$
$$+ 4Na_2SO_4 + CO_2\uparrow + 63H_2O$$

Physical and Chemical Properties

Heavy magnesium carbonate is a white, granular powder without odour and taste. It is practically insoluble in water and in alcohol. It is soluble in dilute acids with effervescence. 15 g of heavy magnesium carbonate occupy a volume of about 30 ml. It is stable in air.

Because of its insolubility in most solvents, it is quite inert chemically. When heavy magnesium carbonate is treated with dilute hydrochloric acid, carbon dioxide is evolved.

$$3MgCO_3.Mg(OH)_2.4H_2O + 8HCl = 4MgCl_2 + 3CO_2\uparrow$$
$$+ 9H_2O$$

When heated to redness, it loses carbon dioxide and water and leaves a residue of heavy magnesium oxide.

$$3MgCO_3.Mg(OH)_2.4H_2O = 4MgO + 3CO_2\uparrow + 5H_2O.$$

By heating in solution with sodium bicarbonate, the normal carbonate ($MgCO_3$) is formed. It is official in I.P.

Official Tests for Identity

A solution in dilute nitric acid gives the reactions of magnesium and of carbonates (see Chapter 18).

Non-official Test for Identity

When magnesium carbonate is treated with dilute hydrochloric acid, carbon dioxide is evolved.

Tests for Purity

1. Arsenic
2. Calcium
3. Copper
4. Iron
5. Heavy metals
6. Chloride
7. Sulphate
8. Soluble substances
9. Substances insoluble in acetic acid.

Calcium is determined by precipitating it as calcium oxalate by adding ammonium oxalate. The opalescence produced is compared with that of a standard calcium solution similarly treated.

Copper is limited by dissolving the substance in hydrochloric acid and making alkaline with dilute ammonia solution. No blue colour is produced.

Standard: It contains the equivalent of not less than 40 per cent and not more than 45 per cent of MgO.

Assay: This is also a complexometric assay. First an accurately weighed quantity of the substance is dissolved in dilute hydrochloric acid.

Ammonia-ammonium chloride buffer is added and the mixture is titrated with M/20 disodium ethylenediaminetetraacetate (EDTA or disodium salt of ethylenediamine tetraacetic acid or sodium edetate) using mordant black as indicator.

The buffer of strong ammonia-ammonium chloride solution is added to raise and maintain the pH of the solution at 10, because at this pH only complexation takes place. Magnesium is fixed as unionisable magnesium-EDTA complex by the EDTA. No blank titration is necessary as in the case of calcium assay. The end point

145

is the appearance of blue colour. The complexation of magnesium by EDTA is given below:

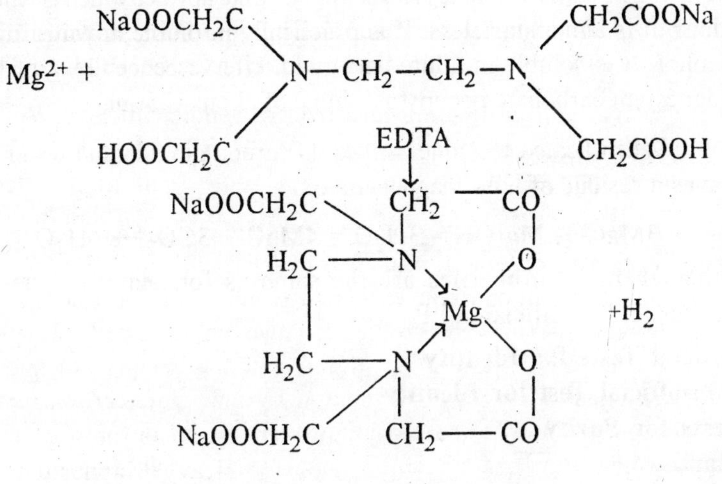
NaOOCH2C
CH2COONa
Mg2+ +
N—CH2—CH2—N
HOOCH2C
CH2COOH
EDTA
NaOOCH2C
CH2
CO
H2C
N
O
Mg
+H2
H2C
N
O
NaOOCH2C
CH2
CO

Magnesium - EDTA Complex

Storage : Store in well-closed containers.

Medicinal and Pharmaceutical Uses

Antacid and osmotic laxative. It is used as a clarifying or filtering agent for alkaline solutions (eg : Tolu Syrup). It is also used as an abrasive in some tooth powders.

10. LIGHT MAGNESIUM CARBONATE, $3MgCO_3$. $Mg(OH)_2$. $3H_2O$

Preparation: Crystalline magnesium sulphate (125 parts) and crystalline sodium carbonate (150 parts) are dissolved separately in 1000 ml cold water each and mixed. Then the solution is boiled for fifteen minutes. The precipitate of light magnesium carbonate is collected on a calico filter, washed free from sulphate and dried in a water-oven.

$$4MgSO_4.7H_2O + 4Na_2CO_3.10H_2O = 3MgCO_3.Mg(OH)_2.3H_2O + 4Na_2SO_4 + CO_2\uparrow + 64H_2O$$

Physical and Chemical Properties

Light magnesium carbonate is a very light, white powder which is without odour. It is almost tasteless. It is practically insoluble in water and in alcohol. It is soluble in dilute acids with effervescence. 15 g of light magnesium carbonate occupy a volume of about 125 ml.

When heated to redness, it loses carbon dioxide and water and leaves a residue of light magnesium oxide.

$$3MgCO_3.Mg(OH)_2.3H_2O = 4MgO + 3CO_2\uparrow + 4H_2O$$

Other chemical properties are the same as for heavy magnesium carbonate. It is official in I.P.

Official Tests for Identity	
Non-official Test for Identity	
Tests for Purity	Same as for
Standard	Heavy Magnesium
Assay	Carnbonate
Storage	
Medicinal and Pharmaceutical uses	

11. MAGNESIUM TRISILICATE, $2MgO, 3SiO_2, xH_2O$

Preparation: Magnesium trisilicate is prepared by slowly running a solution of magnesium sulphate into a solution of sodium silicate. The precipitated magnesium trisilicate is washed free from sulphate, dried and powdered.

Physical and Chemical Properties: Magnesium trisilicate is a fine, white, colourless and tasteless powder. It is free from grittiness and is slightly hygroscopic. It is practically insoluble in water.

Magnesium trisilicate when treated with any acid such as dilute hydrochloric acid forms magnesium chloride and gelatinous trisilicic acid.

$$Mg_2Si_3O_8 + 4HCl = 2MgCl_2 + H_4Si_3O_8$$
(or $2MgO, 3SiO_2$)   Trisilicic acid
Magnesium trisilicate

147

The same reaction takes place when magnesium trisilicate comes into contact with hydrochloric acid in the stomach. It is estimated that one gram of magnesium trisilicate neutralizes about 155 ml of 0.1N hydrochloric acid. A gelatinous mass which is formed covers and protects the ulcer tissue for several hours. The I.P. gives a test for acid absorption which is a measure of its acid neutralising capacity.

Offical Tests for Identity: (1). Gives the reactions of silicates. See chapter 18. (2). The sample is heated with nitric acid to boiling. filtered, filtrate diluted with water and neutralised with dilute sodium hydroxide solution. The solution gives reactions of magnesium salts. See Chapter 18.

Tests for Purity

1. Arsenic
2. Heavy metals
3. Chloride
4. Sulphate
5. Acid absorption
6. Alkalinity
7. Water soluble salts
8. Loss on ignition

For determining *alkalinity*, an aqueous extract of the substance is titrated with 0.1M hydrochloric acid using phenolphthalein. Again for determining *water soluble salts*, an aqueous extract is prepared, evaporated to dryness, ignited at 900°C and the residue weighed. *Loss on ignition* is determined by igniting at 900°C to constant weight. Since magnesium trisilicate contains varying proportions of water, the limit given is between 17 and 34 per cent.

Acid absorption can be determined by suspending the sample in 0.1M hydrochloric acid and allowing to stand in a water bath at 37°C for 2 hours shaking frequently. Bromophenol solution is added to an aliquot of the supernatant liquid and it is titrated with 0.1M sodium hydroxide until a blue colour is produced. By this way we can find out the amount of 0.1M hydrochloric acid still left unneutralised.

Standard: Magnesium trisilicate contains not less than 29 per cent of MgO and not less than 65 per cent of SiO_2, both calculated with reference to the ignited substance.

Assay: Assay is done for both MgO and SiO_2 contents.

For MgO: The sample is mixed with water and heated on a water bath for 15 minutes. It is cooled, filtered and the combined filtrate and washings diluted to a particular volume. An aliquot is taken and neutralised with sodium hydroxide solution. Ammonia buffer and mordant black II indicator are added, warmed to 40°C and titrated with 0.05M EDTA. End point is the change of colour from violet to blue. Magnesium is estimated by complexometric analysis.

For SiO_2: This is a gravimetric assay. The sample is decomposed by treatment with dilute sulphuric acid and heating on a water bath for 1½ hours with frequent shaking. Then it is cooled and filtered. The precipitate is washed with hot water till it is free from sulphuric acid as shown by testing the filtrate with barium chloride solution and dilute hydrochloric acid. The filter paper containing the silicic acid is heated and ignited in a platinum crucible at 1000°C to constant weight. The residue is SiO_2 and it is weighed.

Storage: Since it is slightly hygroscopic, store in a well closed container.

Medicinal and Pharmaceutical Uses

Good antacid. It does not produce any rebound acidity like sodium bicarbonate. It does not interfere with peptic digestion.

12. CALCIUM CARBONATE, $CaCO_3$

Preparation: Calcium carbonate is prepared by passing carbon dioxide through lime water (calcium hydroxide solution).

$$Ca(OH)_2 + CO_2 = CaCO_3\downarrow + H_2O$$

However calcium carbonate is usually prepared by mixing boiling sodium carbonate and calcium chloride solutions and the resulting precipitate is allowed to subside.

$$CaCl_2 + Na_2CO_3 = CaCO_3\downarrow + 2NaCl$$

The precipitated calcium carbonate is collected on a calico filter, washed with boiling water till it is free from chloride and dried.

Physical and Chemical Properties

Calcium carbonate is a fine, white, microcrystalline powder which is odourless and tasteless. It is practically insoluble in water but slightly soluble in water containing carbon dioxide or any ammonium salt. This is because it forms the bicarbonate with carbon dioxide and the bicarbonate is slightly soluble in water. Excepting annonium bicarbonate and carbonate, all the other ammonium salts are acidic and give effervescence with calcium carbonate.

$$CaCO_3 + CO_2 + H_2O = Ca(HCO_3)_2$$
Calcium bicarbonate

$$CaCO_3 + 2NH_4Cl = CaCl_2 + 2NH_3 + H_2O + CO_2\uparrow$$

It is insoluble in alcohol but soluble in most acids with effervescence.

$$CaCO_3 + 2HCl = CaCl_2 + CO_2\uparrow + H_2O$$

It is stable in air. It is official in I.P.

Calcium carbonate is the most abudant calcium salt occurring in nature. It occurs as chalk, limestone, marble, calcite and aragonite. It is amorphous in chalk whereas it is in irregular crystls in limestone. It is crystalline in marble, calcite and aragonite.Calcite occurs as hexagonal crystals and aragonite as rhombic crystals.

Official Tests for Identity

A solution of the substance in acetic acid, which is boiled, gives the reactions of calcium and of carbonates. See Chater 18.

Tests for Purity
1. Substances insoluble in acetic acid
2. Magnesium and alkali metals
3. Barium
4. Iron
5. Arsenic
6. Heavy metals

7. Chloride
8. Sulphide
9. Loss on drying

Substances insoluble in acetic acid are determined by allowing the sample to react with acetic acid till effervescence ceases. Then the solution is boiled, cooled, diluted and filtered through a sintered glass filter. The residue is washed repeatedly with hot water, dried at 100°C for 1 hour and weighed.

For *magnesium and alkali metals*, the sample of calcium carbonate is removed as calcium oxalate by dissolving in dilute hydrochloric acid, then adding dilute ammonia and a little acetic acid, heating the solution and adding ammonium oxalate solution. The precipitated calcium oxalate is filtered off. To the filtrate dilute sulphuric acid is added, converting magnesium and alkali metals, if any, to their sulphates. It is evaporated to dryness and weighed.

Barium is detected by dissolving in boiling dilute acetic acid and adding calcium sulphate solution. The solution should remain clear. If barium is present, it will be precipitated as barium sulphate.

Standard: Calcium carbonate is precipitated calcium carbonate. It is also known as precipitated chalk. It contains not less than 98 per cent of $CaCO_3$ and not more than 100.5 per cent calculated with reference to the dried substance.

Assay: It is assayed by complexometry. The sample is dissolved in dilute hydrochloric acid and titrated against 0.05M EDTA. Towards the end of the titration, sodium hydroxide solution and the indicator calcon mixture are added and the titration is continued till the change of colour from pink to full blue takes place at the end point. Calcon mixture consists of calcon (mordant black) and freshly ignited anhydrous sodium sulphate. It gives a purple-red colour with calcium ions in alkaline solution.

Storage: Since it is stable in air, it may be stored in a well closed container.

151

Medicinal and Pharmaceutical Uses

Antacid. Precipitated chalk is used as a dentifrice (tooth powder). Prepared chalk (made by the process of elutriation) is usually used in preference to precipitated chalk as an antacid. Because of its mild, non-irritating nature, it is also used in the treatment of some forms of diarrhoea.

Limestone is used in the manufacture of cement, lime, washing soda and glass.

13. BISMUTH SUBCARBONATE

Bismuth subcarbonate is also known as bismuth carbonate. It is a basic salt of variable composition.

Preparation: For preparing bismuth subcarbonate an acid solution of bismuth nitrate is added with constant stirring to a warm solution of sodium carbonate. The precipitated bismuth subcarbonate is washed with a small quantity of cold water to remove the nitrate and dried at a temperature below 60°C. The precipitate should not be washed repeatedly with water as the subcarbonate will be decomposed and bismuth hydroxide will be formed.

$$4Bi(NO_3)_3 + 6Na_2CO_3 + H_2O = [(BiO)_2CO_3]_2.H_2O +$$
$$\underset{\text{Bismuth subcarbonate}}{}$$
$$12NaNO_3 + 4CO_2\uparrow$$

The bismuth nitrate itself may be prepared by dissolving metallic bismuth in 50 per cent nitric acid. The solution is evaporated to a low volume.

$$2Bi + 8HNO_3 = 2Bi(NO_3)_3 + 2NO + 4H_2O$$

Physical and Chemical Properties

Bismuth subcarbonate is a white or nearly white, tasteless and odourless powder. It is slowly affected by light. It is practically insoluble in water, ethanol and ether. It dissolves with copious effervescence in mineral acids. It is stable in air but when exposed to air containing traces of hydrogen sulphide, it darkens slowly.

When it is strongly heated, it decomposes into yellow bismuth trioxide, carbon dioxide and water. This was the basis of its assay in the past.

$$[(BiO)_2CO_3]_2. \ H_2O \triangleq 2Bi_2O_3 + 2CO_2\uparrow + H_2O$$

If the solution obtained after dissolving it in hydrochloric acid (or nitric acid) is diluted with water, a white precipitate of bismuth oxychloride is produced.

$$BiCl_3 + 4H_2O = Bi(OH)_2Cl + 2H_3O^+ + 2Cl^-$$

When hydrogen sulphide is passed though a hydrochloric acid solution of a bismuth salt, a brownish-black precipitate of bismuth sulphide is produced.

$$2BiCl_3 + 3H_2S = Bi_2S_3\downarrow + 3HCl$$

This brownish-black precipitate of bismuth sulphide is soluble in a warm mixture of water and nitric acid. It is official in I.P.

Official Tests for Identity

1. Gives the reactions of bismuth. See Chapter 18.

2. When the substance is dissolved in dilute acetic acid, carbon dioxide is produced. This gas is passed through a solution of barium hydroxide and a white precipitate (of barium carbonate) is produced. It dissolves on adding dilute hydrochloric acid.

Tests for Purity

1. Clarity and colour of solution
2. Alkalis and alkaline earth metals
3. Arsenic
4. Copper
5. Lead
6. Silver
7. Chloride
8. Loss on drying.

Alkalis and alkaline-earth metals are determined by first precipitating the bismuth as bismuth sulphide which is filtered off. The filtrate is evaporated to dryness and the residue treated with concentrated sulphuric acid to convert the alkalis and alkaline-earth metals into their nonvolatile sulphates. The residue is ignited, cooled and weighed. Sodium carbonate, resulting from incomplete washing in the method of preparation is the main impurity in this category.

Arsenic, copper, lead and silver may result as impurities from the ores used for extracting bismuth which may be used in the preparation of bismuth subcarbonate. *Copper* is detected by adding to a nitric acid solution of the substance ammonia, filtering and adding to the filtrate solution of sodium diethyldithiocarbamate. Any colour produced is compared with a standard solution of copper similarly treated. *Lead* is determined by atomic absorption spectrophotometry. *Silver* is limited by precipitation as silver chloride and the opalescence produced is compared with a silver standard solution similarly treated.

Standard: Bismuth Subcarbonate contains not less than 80 per cent and not more than 82.5 per cent of Bi, calculated with reference to the dried substance.

Assay: Bismuth subcarbonate is assayed by a complexometric method. It is dissolved in nitric acid, diluted with water and titrated with 0.1M disodium edetate using xylenol orange a indicator. The colour change at the end point is from pinkish violet to lemon yellow.

Storage: Since it may discoloured by the hydrogen sulphide in the atmosphere and since it is also affected by light, store it in well closed containers protected from light.

Medicinal Use: *Antacid.* It can also be used as a *protective, mild astringent, antiseptic and dusting powder.*

SILICONE POLYMERS

Compounds that are formed as a result of the bonding of silicon, oxygen and carbon by condensation are known as silicones. One of the building blocks of silicones is dimethyldihydroxysilane, $(CH_3)_2 Si (OH)_2$.

Two dimethyldihydroxysilane molecules undergo condensation with elimination of a molecule of water. Repeated condensation of the

154

molecules results in the formation of macro molecules (big molecules) or polymers. These are known as *silicones*. The Si-O-Si linkage in these molecules is very strong.

$$\underset{HO}{\overset{CH_3\ \ CH_3}{\underset{Si}{\diagdown\diagup}}}\underset{O}{\overset{CH_3\ \ CH_3}{\underset{Si}{\diagdown\diagup}}}\underset{O}{\overset{CH_3\ \ CH_3}{\underset{Si}{\diagdown\diagup}}}\underset{O}{\overset{CH_3\ \ CH_3}{\underset{Si}{\diagdown\diagup}}}\underset{O}{\overset{CH_3\ \ CH_3}{\underset{Si}{\diagdown\diagup}}}O$$

The general formula of silicones may be given as $[(CH_3)_2SiO\text{-}]n$. Silicones obtained by starting with dimethyldihydroxysilane are known as *silicones oils*.

The silicones are stable even at very high and very low temperatures and are water repellent. Silicones are used for making water-proof cloth and lubricants which do not freeze even at very low temperatures. Activated dimethicone is official in I.P.

ACTIVATED DIMETHICONE

Activated dimethicone is activated polydimethylsiloxane. It is also known as simethicone. It has the formula $(CH_3)_2Si - [OSi(CH_3)_2] - CH_3$.

Preparation: It is prepared by the hydrolysis and polycondensation of dichlorodimethylsilane, $(CH_3)_2SiCl_2$ and chlorotrimethylsilane, $(CH_3)_3Si\,Cl$.

Properties: It is a translucent (partly opaque and partly transparent), grey, viscous liquid. It is amost odourless and tasteless. It is insoluble in water and in methyl alcohol but soluble in organic solvents such as CCl_4, chloroform and ether. It is official in I.P.

Official Test for Identity: The sample is treated with carbon tetrachloride and dilute hydrochloric acid and shaken well for five minutes. The lower layer is shaken with anhydrous sodium sulphate to remove any water. The mixture is centrifuged till a clear supernatant liquid is obtained. The infra-red absorption spectrum of the resulting solution exhibits maxima at the same wavelengths as in the spectrum of a solution of polydimethylsiloxane R.S. (Reference Standard).

Activated dimethicone is a mixture of polydimethylsiloxane and silicon dioxide. The polydimethylsiloxane dissolves in carbon tetra chloride and hydrochloric acid, whereas silicon dioxide is insoluble. The lower layer (containing polydimethylsiloxane) is dried with anhydrous Sodium sulphate and centrifuged to get a clear liquid. The IR spectrum of this solution is compared with the IR spectrum of a solution obtained in the same way from dimethicone RS.

2. The sample is ignited in a platinum crucible along with conc. sulphuric acid to destroy the polydimethylsiloxane. The residue gives the reactions of silicates. See Chapter 18.

Tests for Purity

1. Acidity
2. Heavy metals
3. Defoaming activity

For determining *acidity*, an accurately weighed quantity is dissolved in a mixture of alcohol and ether which has been previously neutralised using bromothymol blue solution and titrated against 0.01M sodium hydroxide. Not more than a specified volume of 0.01M sodium hydroxide is required to change the colour of the solution to blue.

Dimethicone is a defoaming agent which means it reduces foaming. To determine the *defoaming activity*, an accurately weighed quantity is dissolved in 2-methylpropanol and a specified volume of this solution is added to a 1% solution of octoxinol. This is shaken in an automatic shaker for 10 seconds. Then the time required for the foam (that has been formed from octoxinol) to collapse is found out. It should not be more than 15 seconds.

Standard: It contains not less than 90 per cent of polydimethylsiloxane, $[(CH_3)_2SiO-]n$ and not more than 7 per cent of silicon dioxide.

Assay: Assay is done for both polydimethylsiloxane and silicon dioxide.

For *polydimethylsiloxane*, an accurately weighed quantity is dissolved in carbon tetrachloride, dilute hydrochloric acid added and shaken for five minutes. The lower layer containing polydimethylsiloxane is dried with anhydrous sodium sulphate and centrifuged to get a clear supernatant liquid. The absorbance of this liquid at 7.9 µm is measured in an infrared spectrophotometer. The absorbance obtained from a blank using the solvent carbon tetrachloride etc. and going through the same procedure is also found out and deducted from the above. The final absorbance is compared with the absorbance at 7.9 µm obatained from a sample of dimethicone RS. From the declared content of polydimethylsiloxane in dimethicone RS, the content of the same in the test sample is calculated.

For *silicon dioxide,* the sample is placed in a tared, sintered-glass filtering crucible and washed with carbon tetrachloride first and n-hexane next to remove the polydimethylsiloxane. The filtrate (containing polydimethylsiloxane) is discarded. The filtering crucible is heated in a muffle furnace initially and ignited strongly at 550°C in an atmosphere of nitrogen to destroy any organic matter. Then the filtering crucible (containing only silicon dioxide) is cooled in a desiccator and weighed.

Storage: Store in tighty closed containers.

Medicinal and Pharmaceutical Uses

Protective and Defoaming Agent. Dimethicone is used for preparing dimethicone cream (formerly official in B.P.C.). This cream is used to protect the skin against colostomy and other discharges and to prevent bed sores and napkin-rash. (Colostomy is an operation to make an artificial opening so that the colon opens on to the anterior abdominal wall. This operation is done when there is an obstruction in the colon). *Dimethicone is also included in antacid mixtures to treat cases of flatulence.*

III. PROTECTIVES AND ADSORBENTS

Protectives and adsorbents are drugs which adsorb intestinal toxins, bacteria etc. and also give a protective coating to the inflamed mucosal walls.

1. HEAVY KAOLIN, $Al_2O_3, 2SiO_2, 2H_2O$

Kaolin is a native, hydrated aluminium silicate, powdered and freed from gritty particles by elutriation. It is insoluble in water, in cold dilute acids and in solutions of alkali hydroxides. It may contain a suitable dispersing agent.

Preparation:

Kaolin occurs in special types of clay known as *kaolinite*, *dickite* and *nacrite*. Heavy kaolin is prepared from these by a process of elutriation.

Kaolin consists mainly of hydrated aluminium silicate, Al_2O_3. $2SiO_2, 2H_2O$ with traces of magnesium, calcium and iron.

It is used in the preparation of kaolin poultice.

It is official in I.P. Tests for adsorption power and swelling power are prescribed in the I.P.

Properties: Heavy kaolin is a purified, natural, hydrated aluminium silicate of variable composition. It is a fine, white or greyish-white, soft powder without odour. It is practically insoluble in water and organic solvents. It is not soluble in mineral acids and in alkali hydroxide solutions.

Official Tests for Identity

1. Gives the reactions of silicates. See Chapter 18.

2. A small quantity of the sample is heated in a metal crucible with solid potassium nitrate and anhydrous sodium carbonate till the mixture is melted and cooled. The residue is extracted with boiling water, filtered and washed with water. The residue is dissolved in hydrochloric acid and filtered. To the filtrate sodium hydroxide solution and ammonium chloride solution are added. A gelatinous, white precipitate is produced.

The heavy kaolin is decomposed by heating with potassium nitrate and sodium carbonate. Finally the aluminium in the substance is converted to a white, gelatinous precipitate of aluminium hydroxide.

Tests for Purity

1. Acidity or alkalinity
2. Arsenic
3. Heavy metals
4. Chloride
5. Sulphate
6. Substances soluble in mineral acids
7. Organic impurities
8. Adsorption power
9. Swelling power
10. Loss on ignition

Organic impurities are determined by heating the sample to redness in a calcination tube. The residue should be only slightly more coloured than the original sample.

Adsorption power is found out by shaking the sample with a solution of methylene blue and allowing to settle. It is centrifuged and the supernatant liquid is diluted with water to a definite volume. The solution is not more intensely coloured than a standard solution of methylene blue. If the adsorption power of the sample is good, most of the dye would have been adsorbed by it and the colour of the solution will be less intense than that of the standard solution.

Swelling power is determined by triturating the sample with water. The mixture should not flow. The sample should have enough swelling power to absorb all the water and swell making it difficult for the mixture to flow. *Loss on ignition* is fixed at 15%. Actually the loss of the water molecules ($2H_2O$) on ignition will give a weight loss of about 14% only. A more liberal limit of 15% is permitted.

Storage: Store in well - closed containers.

Medicinal and Pharmaceutical Use: *Pharmaceutical aid. Anti-inflammatory and counter irritant* (Kaolin Poultice, I.P.'66 contains 50.5 per cent of heavy kaolin).

2. LIGHT KAOLIN, Al$_2$O$_3$, 2SiO$_2$, 2H$_2$O

Preparation: Light kaolin is a native, hydrated aluminium silicate and it is prepared by freeing it from most of its impurities and gritty particles by a process of elutriation and drying.

Properties: Light kaolin is a light, white powder. It does not contain any gritty particles. It is odourless and almost tasteless and is unctuous (oily or greasy) to touch. It is practically insoluble in water and mineral acids.

Light kaolin is chemically inert since it is insoluble in all the common solvents. It is official in I.P. There are tests for coarse particles and fine particles prescribed in the I.P. to ensure that the official compound will contain only the fine particles. This is necessary in view of the fact that light kaolin is used as an antidiarrhoeal agent and presence of coarse particles will harm the inflamed mucosal surface of the gut in diarrhoea.

Official Tests for Identity

1. Coarse particles
2. Fine particles
3. Arsenic
4. Heavy metals
5. Chloride
6. Soluble matter
7. Loss on drying
8. Loss on ignition

Coarse particles should not be present in the substance for the reasons mentioned under properties. It is determined by preparing a suspension of the sample in a solution of sodium pyrophosphate and withdrawing after 5 minutes an aliquot of the suspension below 5 cm. This is repeated again and again adding water till a definite volume has been collected. The remainder is evaporated to dryness on a water bath and the residue dried at 105°C and weighed. The remainder of the suspension contains the coarse particles.

Fine particles are determined by preparing a suspension of the sample in water, withdrawing a definite volume, evaporating to dryness and drying to constant weight at 105°C. The remainder of the suspension is allowed to stand for four hours, a second similar volume is withdrawn from a depth below 5 cm, evaporating to dryness and drying to constant weight at 105°C. The weight of the residue from the second portion is not less than 70% of the weight of the residue from the first portion.

Soluble matter is determined by boiling the sample with 0.2M hydrochloric acid and evaporating a definite volume of the filtrate to dryness. The residue is ignited at 600°C and weighed.

Loss on drying should be below 1.5% but *loss on ignition* is permitted upto 15% (see under Heavy Kaolin).

Storage: Store in well-closed containers.

Medicinal Uses: *Adsorbent (in the treatment of diarrhoea).* It is used both for its adsorptive property and also for its ability to coat the mucosa. It is used in diarrhoea due to food poisoning or due to bacteria. It provides relief by adsorbing gases, toxins and bacteria.

3. ACTIVATED CHARCOAL, C

Preparation: This is prepared by igniting any carbonaceous matter such as coal or wood in the presence of a limited amount of air and allowing it to burn well for some time. Then the air is completely cut off.

It is 'activated' (which means that its adsorptive power is increased) by heating it to a high temperature in a stream of gas, either carbon dioxide or steam with or without the addition of some inorganic salts.

Alternatively, raw vegetable material may be treated with a solution of zinc chloride or phosphoric acid and ignited to get the activated charcoal. The inorganic matter is removed by washing.

All the above treatments increase the activity by forcing apart the adsorptive planes of hexagons in the structure of charcoal.

Properties: Charcoal is a light, black powder which is free from grittiness and odour. It is practically insoluble in all the usual solvents. It is official in I.P.

Official Tests for Identity

1. Heat to redness. It burns slowly without a flame.

2. It complies with the *test for adsorbing power* (given under Tests for Purity)

Tests for Purity

1. Acidity or alkalinity
2. Acid-soluble substances
3. Ethanol-soluble substances
4. Alkali-soluble coloured matter
5. Chloride
6. Sulphate
7. Sulphide
8. Uncarbonised constituents
9. Copper
10. Lead
11. Zinc
12. Sulphated ash
13. Loss on drying
14. Adsorbing Power

Acidity and alkalinity are determined by preparing a hot, aqueous extract of the sample and filtering it. To a specific volume of the filtrate bromothymol blue solution (indicator) and a specific volume of 0.02M sodium hydroxide are added. The solution should be blue and not more than the specified volume of 0.02M hydrochloric acid is required to change the colour to yellow.

For *acid-soluble substances*, a hot, aqueous extract of the sample using hydrochloric acid is evaporated to dryness and weighed.

Similarly, *ethanol-soluble substances* are also found out by preparing an ethanolic extract, evaporating to dryness and weighing.

An alkaline extract of the sample in the hot condition is filtered and the colour is compared with the colour of a reference solution GYS_4 (greenish yellow). The colour of the sample is not more intensely coloured. This test is for determining *alkali-soluble coloured matter*.

Since activated charcoal is obtained from natural sources, *sulphide* may be present in small quantities. This is detected and controlled by treating with hydrochloric acid. The fumes evolved should not turn lead acetate paper brown (due to the evolved hydrogen sulphide).

Uncarbonised constituents are those from the natural sources not converted into charcoal. An alkaline extract of the sample is filtered and the filtrate should be colourless.

Copper, Lead and Zinc are determined by atomic absorption spectrophotometry.

A determination of *sulphated ash* screens out any inorganic materials accompanying activated charcoal.

Loss on drying should not be more than 15%.

Adsorbing power of the sample should be not less than 40% of its own weight of phenazone. To find out the adsorbing power, a 1% solution of phenazone is added to the sample, shaken and filtered. To the filtrate containing the amount of phenazone not adsorbed by charcoal, potassium bromide and hydrochloric acid are added and the mixture titrated with potassium bromate solution. A blank is also done taking only phenazone solution. From these the percentage of phenazone adsorbed by the charcoal is calculated.

Storage: Store in a tightly-closed container.

Medicinal and Pharmaceutical Uses: *Adsorbent.* Charcoal is of great value in the purification of chemicals and the adsorption of gases.

4. BISMUTH SUBCARBONATE

See earlier in this Chapter under "Antacids".

IV. SALINE CATHARTICS

Saline cathartics are also called as osmotic laxatives. They are not much absorbed in the gastrointestinal tract and exert an osmotic effect leading to the retention of large quantity of water and consequently increasing the bulk of the intestinal contents. This stimulates the intestinal motor activity leading to evacuation of the bowels.

1. MAGNESIUM HYDROXIDE, $Mg(OH)_2$

See earlier in this Chapter under "Antacids".

2. MAGNESIUM SULPHATE, $MgSO_4.7H_2O$ (EPSOM SALTS)

Preparation: It may be prepared by any one of the following methods:

By neutralizing hot, dilute sulphuric acid with magensium oxide or magnesium carbonate.

$$MgO + H_2SO_4 = MgSO_4 + H_2O$$

Physical Properties and Chemical Properties

Magnesium sulphate occurs in small, colourless, needle-like crystals or rhombic prisms without odour and with a cooling saline and bitter taste. It is efflorescent in warm, dry air. When gently heated, it readily loses some of its water of hydration. It becomes completely anhydrous at 200°C. Magnesium sulphate crystallizes from cold water in needles ($MgSO_4.7H_2O$). With many other sulphates, magnesium sulphate forms double salts. They are isomorphous with one other. These double salts have the general formula $M_2SO_4, MgSO_4, 6H_2O$ where M represents sodium, potassium, ammonium, etc. It is soluble 1 in 1 water and sparingly soluble in alcohol. It dissolves slowly in 1 part of glycerin. It loses 51.1 per cent of its weight when dried. This is due to the loss of all water molecules.

Aqueous solution of magnesium sulphate is neutral to litmus. All the reactions of magnesium and sulphate are answered. Magnesium is precipitated as magnesium ammonium phosphate by the addition of ammonium phosphate in the presence of ammonia. The magnesium ammonium phosphate precipitate ($MgNH_4PO_4$) may be collected, dried and ignited when magnesium pyrophosphate is formed.

$$2MgNH_4PO_4 = Mg_2P_2O_7 + 2NH_3 + H_2O$$
$$\text{Magnesium}$$
$$\text{pyrophosphate}$$

This was the previous gravimetric assay method for magnesium sulphate. The magnesium pyrophosphate is collected, dried and weighed. It is official in I.P.

Official Tests for Identity: Gives reactions characteristic of magnesium and of sulphates. See Chapter 18.

Tests for Purity

1. Clarity and colour of solution
2. Acidity or alkalinity
3. Arsenic
4. Iron
5. Heavy metals
6. Chloride
7. Sulphide
8. Loss on drying : The substance is dried to constant weight at 110°-120°C for 1 hour and drying at 400°C. It loses about 48 to 52 per cent of its weight. All the water molecules are lost.

Standard: Contains not less than 99.0 per cent and not more than the equivalent of 100.5 per cent of $MgSO_4$ calculated with reference to the dried substance (please note that the content is given in terms of the anhydrous substance).

B.P. and I.P. Assay: This is a volumetric method and a complexometric assay.

It is assayed by titration of the substance against M/20 sodium edetate (disodium salt of ethylenediaminetetraacetic acid) using mordant black mixture, as indicator. A mixture of strong ammonia and ammonium chloride is used as the buffer. The end point is the appearance of blue colour. See heavy magnesium carbonate in this Chapter for equation and other details.

Storage: It is efflorescent, so store in a well-closed container.

Medicinal Use: *Cathartic (drastic purgative). Osmotic laxative.*

This salt is very widely used as a saline cathartic. Neither the sulphate nor the magnesium ion is readily absorbed. Therefore water is retained in the intestine. Because of this the quantity and fluidity of the intestinal contents are increased. This mechanically stimulates peristalsis and the bowels are emptied. It is also used in the treatment of electrolyte deficiency.

3. MAGNESIUM CARBONATE

See in this Chapter earlier under "ANTACIDS".

4. SODIUM PHOSPHATE

See in this Chapter earlier under "ACIDIFIERS".

CHAPTER 10
TOPICAL AGENTS

Topical means pertaining to a particular locality or place or simply it means 'local'. Therefore the drugs dealt with in this chapter may be substances which are applied directly on the skin or mucous membrane or any other surface.

A. PROTECTIVES

Protectives are substances which are applied over the skin for protecting it from irritation, injury, inflammation etc. They are used in the form of dusting powder etc.

1. TALC (FRENCH CHALK, PURIFIED TALC, TALCUM), $3MgO,4SiO_2,H_2O$.

Preparation: Purified talc is made by boiling very finely powdered talc with water containing about 2 per cent of hydrochloric acid. The insoluble matter is allowed to settle down and the supernatant liquid is removed. This process is repeated again with more dilute hydrochloric acid. Iron and other soluble impurities are removed by thorough washing with water and the substance is dried at 100°C.

Properties: Talc is a very fine white or greyish white crystalline powder. It is unctuous sticking readily to the skin. It is also known as *soapstone* because it is very soft and greasy to touch like the soap. The specific gravity is 2.6 to 2.8.

Talc is without odour and taste and is insoluble in water. It is insoluble also in dilute acids and alkali hydroxides. Talc is not a good adsorbent. Because of this property talc can be used for clarifying solutions of alkaloids, dyes etc.

Chemically talc is hydrated magnesium silicate with the formula $3MgO, 4SiO_2, H_2O$. It may be considered as a salt of dimetasilicic acid $Mg_3H_2 (Si_2O_6)_2$. It should contain about 31 per cent of MgO and 63.5

per cent of SiO_2 according to this formula but usually there are wide variations.

Talc is an inert magnesium polysilicate not affected by acid or bases and so is useful as filtering aid and diluent. On fusing with sodium and potassium carbonates, the magnesium part is converted into magnesium carbonate which can be treated with dilute hydrochloric acid to bring it into solution. The silica remains insoluble. This property is used in the official test for identity for talc in the I.P.

Official Tests for Identity

1. The talc is fused with sodium carbonate and potassium nitrate in a platinum crucible. The mass is extracted with water and hydrochloric acid is added until the effervescence ceases. Evaporate the mixture to dryness. The silicic acid formed is converted on dehydration into silica which is insoluble in water. It is mixed with a little water and filtered. The filtrate contains magnesium chloride which is identified by conversion into magnesium ammonium phosphate by adding ammonium chloride, ammonia and sodium phosphate.

2. It gives the reactions of silicates. See Chapter 18.

3. When examined under a microscope, the sample shows irregular plates less than 50 millimicrons in length. The particles are not much stained by solution of methylene blue in ethanol.

Tests for Purity

1. Acidity or alkalinity
2. Water-soluble substances
3. Acid-soluble substances
4. Iron
5. Carbonates
6. Loss on drying
7. Organic compounds.
8. Chloride

Storage: Talc is an inert substance not affected by acids or bases or other chemicals. So store in a well closed container.

Medicinal and Pharmaceutical Uses: *Pharmaceutical aid (dusting powder).* It is used as a filtering and distributing medium in the preparation of aromatic waters etc. It is the main ingredient in talcum powders and dusting powders.

2. ZINC OXIDE, ZnO

Preparation

1. Zinc oxide is prepared on a large scale by burning zinc metal in a current of air:

$$Zn + O_2 = 2ZnO$$

2. In this method, zinc carbonate is prepared first by reacting zinc sulphate with a boiling solution of sodium carbonate. The precipitated basic carbonate of zinc is collected, washed to remove sulphate, dried and finally gently ignited. It loses carbon dioxide and water, leaving zinc oxide as the residue.

$$2ZnCO_3.2Zn(OH)_2 \triangleq 4ZnO + 2CO_2 + 2H_2O$$

Basic zinc carbonate.

Properties: Zinc oxide is a very fine white or yellowish white amorphous powder without gritty particles. It is tasteless and odourless. It gradually absorbs carbon dioxide from the air and is converted into a basic carbonate. It is insoluble in water and alcohol but is soluble in dilute acids, ammonia, ammonium carbonate and alkali hydroxides. Low commercial grades may contain arsenic and lead as impurities and therefore are unsuitable for medicinal use.

As already stated, it readily dissolves in acids, ammonia and ammonium carbonate solution, it forms zinc chloride with hydrochloric acid and the corresponding zinc ammonium salt with ammonia and ammonium carbonate.

$$ZnO + 2HCl = ZnCl_2 + H_2O$$

$$ZnO + 4NH_4OH = Zn(NH_3)_4 (OH)_2 + 3H_2O$$

$$ZnO + 2(NH_4)_2CO_3 = Zn(NH_3)_4(OH)_2 + 2CO_2\uparrow + H_2O$$

It is official in I.P.

Official Tests for Identity

   1. When strongly heated, zinc oxide gets a yellow colour which disappears on cooling.

   2. A solution in dilute hydrochloric acid gives the reactions characteristc of zinc (see Chapter 18).

Tests for Purity

   1. Alkalinity
   2. Carbonates and substances insoluble in acids.
   3. Arsenic
   4. Iron
   5. Lead
   6. Loss on ignition

Carbonates and substances insoluble in acids are limited by suspending the sample in water and adding dilute hydrochloric acid. No efferversence occurs and the solution is not more opalescent than an opalescence standard in I.P.

Lead is limited by adding glacial acetic acid and potassium chromate solution. The solution remains clear. If lead is present, it will be precipitated as yellow lead chromate. Zinc chromate will not be precipitated as it is soluble.

Standard: Contains not less than 99 per cent and not more than the equivalent of 100.5 per cent of ZnO, calculated with reference to the substance ignited to constant weight.

Assay: The sample is dissolved in 2M acetic acid and diluted with water. Xylenol orange triturate (indicator) and sufficient hexamine to produce violet pink colour are added. A further quantity of hexamine is added and titrated with 0.1M disodium edetate until the solution becomes yellow.

In this complexometric titration hexamine is added to raise the pH to the alkaline side and the zinc oxide converted to zinc acetate by dissolving in acetic acid is titrated with 0.1M disodium edetate using xylenol orange as indicator. Zinc is complexed by the disodium edetate and the indicator changes colour from violet-pink to yellow at the end point.

Storage: Since it absorbs carbon dioxide from the air, store in a well-closed container.

Medicinal Use: *Astringent and topical protective.* Zinc oxide is a mild antiseptic and astringent. In the form of zinc oxide ointment or dusting powder, it is used in the treatment of eczema, ring worm, pruritus and psoriasis. It is also widely used in the manufacture of plasters.

3. CALAMINE

According to B.P., calamine is basic zinc carbonate suitably coloured with ferric oxide. According to the I.P., calamine is zinc oxide coloured with ferric oxide. It is an amorphous, reddish brown powder and the colour depends on the variety and amount of ferric oxide present and the method by which it is incorporated. It is practically insoluble in water and completely insoluble in mineral acids. Since there is a possibility of adulteration with dyes, there are tests for water soluble dyes and alcohol soluble dyes.

Official Tests for Identity (I.P.)
1. A specified quantity is shaken with dilute hydrochloric acid and filtered. The filtrate gives the reactions of zinc (see Chapter 18).
2. A little quantity is mixed with dilute hydrochloric acid, heated to boiling and filtered. To the filtrate is added ammonium thiocyanate solution. A reddish colour is produced. This is due to the formation of ferric thiocyanate by the ferric oxide used for colouring calamine.

Tests for Purity (I.P.)
1. Acid-insoluble substances
2. Alkaline substances
3. Arsenic
4. Calcium

171

5. Lead
6. Water-soluble dyes
7. Alcohol-soluble dyes
8. Loss on ignition

Calcium is detected by precipitation as calcium oxalate. The solution should remain clear.

Lead is detected by precipitation as lead chromate. The solution should remain clear for five minutes.

For *water-soluble dyes*, an alcoholic extract of the sample is filtered and the filtrate should be colourless. The original dye used to colour the calamine is insoluble in both water and alcohol.

Loss on ignition should be not more than 2 per cent. This indicates that the calamine of I.P. consists mainly of zinc oxide only.

Standard: Contains between 98 and 100.5 per cent of ZnO, calculated with reference to the ignited substance.

Assay: Assay is by back titration and involves acidimetry-alkalimetry. See assay for zinc oxide.

Storage: Store in well closed containers.

Medicinal and Pharmaceutical Uses: *Topical protective.* Widely used in lotions, ointments and dusting powders as a soothing agent. It is used in sunburn, eczema and urticaria and some other skin conditions. Calamine lotion (Lotio Calaminae) is very popular.

4. ZINC STEARATE, $(C_{17}H_{35}COO)_2Zn$

Zinc stearate is mixture of zinc salts obtained from commercial stearic acid which itself is prepared from the hydrolysis of fats. It consists mainly of variable proportions of zinc stearate and zinc palmitate.

Preparation: Stearic acid is added slowly with constant stirring to a hot solution of sodium carbonate. Then the mixture is cooled and zinc acetate or zinc sulphate is added to the sodium stearate formed. Zinc stearate is precipitated. It is collected, washed and dried.

$$Na_2CO_3 + 2C_{17}H_{35}COOH = 2C_{17}H_{35}COONa + CO_2\uparrow$$
$$+ H_2O$$
$$2C_{17}H_{35}COONa + ZnSO_4 = (C_{17}H_{35}COO)_2Zn + Na_2SO_4$$

Physical and Chemical Properties

Zinc stearate is a fine, white, bulky powder, free from grittiness with a faint but characteristic odour. It is unctuous to touch and readily sticks to the skin. It is practically insoluble in water.

When it is heated at a high temperature, it fuses and gives fumes which are inflammable and smell of burning fat. A residue of zinc oxide is left behind. It is decomposed by hot mineral acids with liberation of stearic and palmitic acids.

$$(C_{17}H_{35}COO)_2Zn + 2HCl = 2C_{17}H_{35}COOH + ZnCl_2$$
Stearic acid

It is official in I.P.

Official Test for Identity

The sample is decomposed by heating with nitric acid and the stearic acid is extracted with ether. The ether is evaporated to dryness and the freezing point of the residue should be not lower than 53°C. The aqueous layer after neutralisation with sodium hydroxide solution gives the reactions of zinc. See Chapter 18.

Since zinc stearate is a mixture of zinc salts of stearic and other acids, mainly palmitic acid, it is possible that the freezing point may be lower than 53°C, if it contains more of other acids. So this test is to control the amount of other fatty acid salts of zinc other than zinc stearate present in the sample.

Tests for Purity
1. Acidity or alkalinity
2. Alkalis and alkaline earths
3. Chloride
4. Arsenic
5. Heavy metals
6. Sulphate

Alkalis and alkaline earths are limited by dissolving the sample in hydrochloric acid and adding dilute ammonia solution (to make the solution just alkaline) and ammonium sulphide solution to precipitate zinc as zinc sulphide completely. Filter and to the filtrate is added concentrated sulphuric acid to convert the alkalis and alkaline earths to their nonvolatile sulphates. It is evaporated to dryness and ignited to constant weight.

Standard: Zinc stearate contains between 10 and 12 per cent of Zn.

Assay: It is assayed by the method described under zinc oxide after preliminary decomposition of the sample with dilute sulphuric acid and filtration of the resulting fatty acids.

Storage: Store in well closed containers.

Medicinal and Pharmaceutical Uses

Dusting Powder. Since zinc stearate is a mild antiseptic and astringent, it is used in the form of dusting powder or ointment in several skin conditions. Sometimes it is used as a solid diluent.

5. TITANIUM DIOXIDE, TiO_2

Titanium dioxide occurs in nature in the minerals *rutile, brookite and ilmenite.* Magnetic iron ores usually contain titanium.

Preparation: Titanium dioxide is prepared by heating ilmenite $FeTiO_3$ with hydrogen chloride and chlorine.

$$2FeTiO_3 + 4HCl + Cl_2 = 2FeCl_3 + 2TiO_2 + 2H_2O.$$

Physical and Chemical Properties

Titanium dioxide is a white or almost white amorphous infusible powder. It is odourless and tasteless. It is insoluble in water and in dilute mineral acids. It is slowly soluble in hot concentrated sulphuric acid. Because of the high refractive index (2.7), titanium dioxide has great opacity.

It dissolves in hydrofluoric acid also. It is reduced to titanium metal when it is heated with carbon, calcium, sodium or magnesium

Titanium dioxide in dilute sulphuric acid reacts with hydrogen peroxide and gives an orange red colour. This is due to the formation of titanium peroxide and this test is used as a test for identity for titanium dioxide.

It is official in I.P.

Official Tests for Identity

1. A small quantity is dissolved in concentrated sulphuric acid containing a little sodium sulphate with the aid of heat and diluted. To this solution is added strong hydrogen peroxide solution. An orange-red colour is produced.

2. To another quantity of solution obtained in (1), granulated zinc is added. A violet-blue colour is produced after forty five minutes.

3. When strongly heated, it becomes pale yellow. The colour is discharged on cooling.

Tests for Purity

1. Clarity and colour of solution
2. Acidity or alkalinity
3. Water-soluble substances
4. Arsenic
5. Barium
6. Heavy metals
7. Iron

Standard: Contains not less than 98 per cent of TiO_2, calculated with reference to the dried substance.

Assay: Titanium dioxide is assayed by dissolving it in sulphuric acid with the aid of anhydrous sodium sulphate to form a soluble double salt of titanium and sodium. The titanium sulphate solution is then passed through a reducing column containing zinc amalgam so that the titanic sulphate is reduced to titanous sulphate. The titanous sulphate is oxidized back to titanic sulphate by running the solution into ferric ammonium sulphate solution. The ferrous sulphate formed in this reaction by the reduction of ferric ammonium sulphate is titrated with 0.1M ceric ammonium nitrate using ferroin sulphate as indicator..

175

$$TiO_2 + 2H_2SO_4 + Na_2SO_4 = Ti(SO_4)_2.Na_2SO_4 + H_2O$$
Titanium sodium sulphate

$$2Ti(SO_4)_2 + H_2 = Ti_2(SO_4)_3 + H_2SO_4$$
Titanic sulphate   Titanous sulphate

$$Ti_2(SO_4)_3 + 2FeNH_4(SO_4)_2 = 2Ti(SO_4)_2 + (NH_4)_2SO_4 + 2FeSO_4$$
Ferric ammonium   Titanic sulphate
sulphate

$$2FeSO_4 + H_2SO_4 + O = Fe_2(SO_4)_3 + H_2O$$

Cerric ammonium nitrate oxidizes ferrous sulphate to ferric sulphate.

Storage: Store in well closed containers made of glass or any metal other than aluminium.

Medicinal and Pharmaceutical Uses

Pharmaceutical Aid and Topical Protective. Since it spreads well, it is used as a white pigment in paints. Because of its high refractive index it is used in sun-tan preparations.

6. THE KAOLINS

See Chapter 9.

7. SILICONE POLYMERS - DIMETHICONE

See Chapter 9.

B. ASTRINGENTS

An astringent is a drug which makes the cells shrink by precipitating proteins from their surfaces. They are used in lotions to harden and protect the skin and to reduce bleeding from minor abrasions. Other preparations in which they are used are antiperspirant preparations, mouth washes, eye drops, throat lozenges etc.

1. ALUM (POTASH ALUM, ALUMINIUM POTASSIUM SULPHATE), KAl (SO$_4$)$_2$, 12H$_2$O

Alum is either potash alum or ammonia alum. An alum is a double salt of a trivalent element and an univalent element with 12 molecules of water of hydration. The trivalent elements are ususaly iron, aluminium, chromium, manganese etc. and the univalent elements may be sodium, potassium, or ammonium. Alum of the pharmacopeia (official in I.P. 1966 and B.P. 1988) is potash alum, i.e., double salt of aluminium sulphate and potassium sulphate with 12 molecules of water of hydration.

Preparation: Potash alum is prepared by adding a hot, concentrated solution of potassium sulphate to a hot solution of an equivalent quantity of aluminium sulphate. The solution is cooled and the alum crystallizes out. By crystallizing slowly it is possible to get large, regular, octahedral crystals.

$$Al_2(SO_4)_3.18 H_2O + K_2SO_4 \longrightarrow 2KAl(SO_4)_2.12H_2O + 6H_2O$$
$$\text{Potash alum}$$

Physical and Chemical Properties

Alum occurs as large, octahedral, colourless crystals or in small crystals or as a white powder. It is without odour and has a sweetish, strongly astringent taste. Alum is soluble in cold water but more soluble in hot water. Alum is transparent but it is sometimes opaque on the surface due to traces of basic salt being formed. When basic salt is present, alum will not give a clear solution. When alum is heated, it melts at 92°C and loses all the water of hydration at 200°C leaving a white residue known as burnt alum containing anhydrous aluminium and potassium sulphates.

Official Tests for Identity

1. A solution in water gives the reactions characteristic of aluminium and sulphates (see Chapter 18).

2. A small quantity of a solution in water is treated with sodium bicarbonate and filtered. The filtrate gives the reactions of potassium (see Chapter 18).

Tests for Purity
1. Arsenic
2. Heavy metals
3. Iron
4. Zinc
5. Ammonium salts

The testing for *Zinc* is done by precipitating it as zinc ferrocyandie by treatment with potassium ferrocyanide in the presence of dilute hydrochloric acid and ammonium chloride. Any opalescence produced is compared with that produced in a solution of zinc sulphate similarly treated.

The presence of *ammonium salts* is tested by treating a solution of the sample in ammonia-free water with alkaine potassium mercuri-iodide solution (Nessler's reagent) and any colour produced should not be deeper than that produced in a solution of ammonium chloride treated in the same way.

Standard: Alum contains not less than 99.5 per cent of $KAl(SO_4)_2.12H_2O$.

Storage: Alum should be stored in a well-closed container.

Assay: Assay is done by adding to a solution of the sample, accurately weighed, ammonium chloride solution and making it alkaline by adding dilute ammonia solution in the presence of methyl red till a distinct yellow colour is obtained. The mixture is boiled and filtered, Aluminium hydroxide is precipitated. It is filtered and washed with ammonium nitrate solution to remove chloride. The precipitate is dried to constant weight at more than 120°C and the residue of Al_2O_3 is weighed. Each g of residue is equivalent to a particular weight of $KAl(SO_4)_2.12H_2O$.

Medicinal and Pharmaceutical Uses

Astringent. Alum precipitates proteins and protects and hardens the skin. It is used to prepare styptic pencil used for stopping the bleeding in small cuts.

Since alum precipitates proteins, this property is made use of in preparing certain biological preparations such as alum precipitated tetanus toxoid and alum precipitated diphtheria toxoid.

2. ZINC CHLORIDE, $ZnCl_2$

Preparation: Zinc metal or zinc oxide or zinc carbonate is treated with hydrochloric acid to form the zinc chloride.

$$ZnO + 2HCl = ZnCl_2 + H_2O$$

Physical and Chemical Properties

Zinc chloride occurs as white or nearly white, crystalline powder or granules. It is also available as fused sticks or pencils. It is odourless and very deliquescent. It is very soluble in water and freely soluble in alcohol. The solutions are slightly turbid due to the formation of the carbonate. They become clear on the addition of dilute hydrochloric acid. At 290°C zinc chloride fuses to a clear liquid. At about 750°C a part of it is volatilized. The rest is decomposed and leaves a residue of zinc oxide.

Aqueous solution of zinc chloride is acid to litmus due to hydrolysis. Zinc chloride forms auto-complex halides. Auto-complex halides are salts in which the same metal is attached to both anion and cation.

$$2ZnCl_2 \rightleftarrows Zn(ZnCl_4)$$

It is official in I.P.

Official Tests for Identity

1. A solution in very dilute hydrochloric acid gives the reactions of zinc (see Chapter 18).

2. A solution in very dilute nitric acid gives the reactions of chlorides (see Chapter 18).

Tests for Purity

1. pH
2. Ammonium salts
3. Aluminium, calcium, heavy metals, iron and magnesium
4. Sulphate
5. Oxychloride

pH should be between 4.6 and 6 for an aqueous solution of the sample. It is slightly acid and affects litmus but it is alkaline to methyl orange.

Aluminium, calcium, heavy metals, iron and magnesium are limited first by adding to an acidified solution of the sample strong ammonia

179

solution and shaking. The solution should be clear and colourless. If aluminium, calcium, iron and magnesium are present, they would have formed their insoluble hydroxides and the solution would be turbid. Then disodium hydrogen phosphate solution is added. The solution should remain clear. Some of these metals, if they are present, will form the corresponding phosphates. Then sodium sulphide solution is added. A white precipitate is produced and the supernatant liquid remains colourless. White zinc sulphide is produced. If heavy metals are present, they will form their corresponding dark brown to black sulphides and the supernatant liquid will be coloured.

Ammonium salts are detected by adding 1M sodium hydroxide solution to an aqueous solution of the sample until the precipitate first formed (of zinc hydroxide) is redissolved. The solution is warmed. There should be no perceptible odour of ammonia.

Oxychloride may be formed, when zinc chloride is dissloved in water, due to hydrolysis. The oxychloride, $Zn(OH)Cl$, is precipitated when alcohol is added to the aqueous solution and the solution turns cloudy. It becomes clear once again after hydrochloric acid is added. The opalescence after the addition of water to the sample should not be more than the opalescence in a standard in the I.P.

Standard: Zinc chloride contains not less than 95 per cent and not more than 100.5 per cent of $ZnCl_2$.

Assay: This is a complexometric assay. The sample is dissolved in water, solid ammonium chloride and strong ammonia-ammonium chloride solution are added and titrated with 0.05M EDTA, using eriochrome black T as indicator. End point is the appearance of a deep blue colour.

Storage: Since it is very deliquescent, store in tightly closed non-metallic containers.

Medicinal and Pharmaceutical Uses: Zinc chloride is used in mouth washes for its antiseptic and astringent properties. It is also used for preparing zinc insulins.

3. ZINC SULPHATE, $ZnSO_4.7H_2O$

Preparation: It is prepared by boiling a slight excess of metallic zinc with dilute sulphuric acid.

$$Zn + H_2SO_4 = ZnSO_4 + H_2\uparrow$$

The liquid is filtered and evaporated to crystallization.

Properties: Zinc sulphate occurs as colourless, transparent crystals, or as a crystalline powder. It is odourless and has an astringent, metallic taste. It is efflorescent in dry air. It is easily soluble in water, insoluble in alcohol and soluble in glycerin. It combines with potassium and ammonium sulphates to form double salts. $M_2SO_4, ZnSO_4, 6H_2O$. Aqueous solution of zinc sulphate is slightly acidic.

It is official in I.P.

Official Tests for Identity: Gives the reactions characteristic of zinc, and of sulphates (refer Chapter 18).

Tests for Purity

1. Clarity and colour of solution
2. pH
3. Arsenic
4. Iron
5. Chloride

pH of an aqueous solution should be between 4.4 and 5.6. Solution of zinc sulphate is acidic due to hydrolysis of zinc sulphate.

Standard: Contains not less than 99.0 per cent and not more than 104 percent of $ZnSO_4, 7H_2O$

Assay: The weighed substance is dissolved in 2M acetic acid and diluted with water. Xylenol orange triturate (indicator) and hexamine (to raise the pH) are added to produce violet-pink colour. More hexamine is added and the solution is titrated with 0.1M disodium edetate until the colour changes to yellow.

Storage: Since it is efflorescent, store in a well-closed, non-metallic container.

Medicinal use: *Emetic (induces vomiting) and astringent.*

C. ANTIMICROBIALS

Antimicrobials are drugs which destroy the microoganisms. They can be divided into disinfectants and antiseptics. *A disinfectant or germicide* is a chemical which destroys microorganisms by killing them. Spores of the microorganisms are not usually killed by disinfectants. Disinfectants can also be more specifically called as *bactericides, fungicides, virucides, amoebicides* etc. depending on whether they are able to kill bacteria, fungi, viruses, amoebae etc. respectively. They can be used for the (external) sterilization of instruments, articles, surfaces, rooms etc. Sterilization is the total elimination of all kinds of microorganisms including their spores and the product thus obtained is said to be sterile. An *antiseptic* is a substance which eliminates the microorganisms by inhibiting their growth. They can be safely applied to the skin or mucous membrane to prevent sepsis.

1. HYDROGEN PEROXIDE, H_2O_2

Hydrogen peroxide was discovered by L.J. Thenard in 1818 and he designated it as "oxygenated water". Hydrogen peroxide solution is official in I.P. as Hydrogen Peroxide Solution (100 Vols) and Hydrogen Peroxide Solution (20 Vols).

Preparation

The methods for commercial manufacture may be divided into two groups:-

(a) the non-electrolytic and (b) the electrolytic

(A) The Non-electrolytic Methods

1. Barium peroxide is made into a thin cream with water. It is added slowly with constant stirring to dilute sulphuric acid which should be kept cooled in ice:

$$BaO_2 + H_2SO_4 = BaSO_4\downarrow + H_2O_2$$

2. Hydrogen peroxide can also be made by decomposing barium peroxide with phosphoric acid, or by passing carbon dioxide through a suspension of barium peroxide in water :

$$3BaO_2 . 8H_2O + 2H_3PO_4 = Ba_3(PO_4)_2\downarrow + 3H_2O_2 + 24H_2O$$

182

3. Another method is by decomposition of sodium peroxide with sulphuric acid at a low temperature ($-2°C$). Most of the sodium sulphate produced is crystallised as the decahydrate, $Na_2SO_4, 10H_2O$ and the hydrogen peroxide is subsequently distilled under 20 mm. pressure:

$$Na_2O_2 + H_2SO_4 = H_2O_2 + Na_2SO_4$$

(b) The Electrolytic Methods

1. Hydrogen peroxide is prepared by electrolysis of sulphuric acid to peroxydisulphuric acid which is hydrolysed to give the product. In this electrolysis, sulphuric acid is oxidised to peroxydisulphuric acid ($H_2S_2O_8$):

$$2H_2SO_4 = H_2S_2O_8 + H_2$$

Peroxydisulphuric acid, when heated, forms peroxysulphuric acid, H_2SO_5, (Caro's acid):

$$H_2S_2O_8 + H_2O \triangleq H_2SO_5 + H_2SO_4$$

The peroxysulphuric acid is then hydrolysed by further heating to give hydrogen peroxide.

$$H_2SO_5 + H_2O = H_2O_2 + H_2SO_4$$

2. By a modification of this method, a solution of ammonium sulphate and sulphuric acid is electrolysed to form ammonium peroxydisulphate:

$$(NH_4)_2SO_4 + H_2SO_4 = 2NH_4HSO_4$$
$$2NH_4HSO_4 = (NH_4)_2S_2O_8 + H_2$$

Hydrogen peroxide may be distilled directly from the ammonium peroxydisulphate solution:

$$(NH_4)_2S_2O_8 + 2H_2O = 2NH_4HSO_4 + H_2O_2$$

All these procedures, both non-electrolytic and electrolytic, produce a solution of hydrogen peroxide which may be concentrated by distillation under reduced pressure to produce a concentration of even upto 90 per cent H_2O_2.

183

Physical and Chemical Properties

Hydrogen peroxide is stable in solutions of high purity. However, it decomposes rapidly in alkaline solutions or under catalytic influence such as copper, iron or manganese ions.

$$2H_2O_2 = 2H_2O + O_2\uparrow$$

When pure, hydrogen peroxide decomposes very slowly. Its stability is increased by making it slightly acid (eg. by adding sulphuric or phosphoric acid) and also by adding very small quantities of preservatives or stabilizers such as boric acid, urea, acetanilide or hexamine (not more than 0.05 per cent).

Hydrogen peroxide in aqueous solution ionizes to give the peroxide ion.

$$H_2O_2 \rightleftarrows 2H^+ + O_2^{2-}$$

Potassium permangante in acid solution is rapidly reduced..Here hydrogen peroxide acts as a reducing agent.

$$2KMnO_4 + 3H_2SO_4 + 5H_2O_2 = K_2SO_4 + 2MnSO_4 + 8H_2O + 5O_2\uparrow$$

Oxygen is always produced when hydrogen peroxide functions as a reducing agent.

The official solution is 27 per cent w/v i.e., it is 100 volumes hydrogen peroxide which means it will give 100 times its volume of oxygen on heating. A more dilute solution is also official i.e., a 6% w/v solution which gives 20 times its volume of oxygen on heating.

It is official in I.P.

Official Tests for Identity

1. A small quantity decolourises acidified potassium permanganate with evolution of gas.
2. To a small quantity mixed with dilute sulphuric acid, add potassium chromate and solvent ether. The ethereal layer is coloured blue (the blue colour is due to a perchromic acid which is more soluble in ether). This test is capable of detecting hydrogen peroxide as dilute as 0.0015%.

Tests for Purity
1. Acidity
2. Organic Stabilisers
3. Non-volatile matter

Acidity is determined by titrating an aliquot with 0.1M sodium hydroxide using methyl red as indicator.

Organic stabilisers are required to be present in a quantity not exceeding 0.05 per cent w/v. To find out whether these organic stabilisers are present within or excess of the limit prescribed, the hydrogen peroxide solution is extracted with chloroform (which extracts the organic stabilisers), chloroform is removed by evaporation at a low temperature (25ºC) and the residue is dried in a desiccator and weighed.

Non-volatile matter is determined by evaporating the solution on a water bath, drying the residue at 105ºC and weighing.

Standard: Hydrogen peroxide solution (100 vols) contains not less than 26 per cent and not more than 28 per cent w/w of H_2O_2, corresponding to about 100 times its volume of available oxygen.

Hydrogen peroxide solution (20 vols) contains not less than 5 per cent and not more than 7 per cent w/w of H_2O_2, corresponding to about 20 times its volume of available oxygen.

Assay: It is acidified with dilute sulphuric acid and titrated against N/10 potassium permanaganate.

$$2KMnO_4 + 3H_2SO_4 + 5H_2O_2 = K_2SO_4 + 2MnSO_4 + 8H_2O + 5O_2\uparrow$$
$$\text{or } O + H_2O_2 = H_2O + O_2\uparrow$$

Storage: Hydrogen peroxide solution should be stored only in a glass-stoppered bottle and cork, rubber or metal should not be used for storing it, as it will attack them. Plastic-protected metal caps may be used as stoppers. Store in light-resistant containers in a cool place. It should not be stored for long periods.

Medicinal and Pharmaceutical Use: *As an antiseptic and topical anti-infective.* It is especially useful in cleaning wounds, particularly where pus is present.

2. POTASSIUM PERMANGANATE, $KMnO_4$.

Preparation: Manganese dioxide is fused with excess of potassium hydroxide in the presence of a free supply of air, or in the presence of an oxidizing agent such as potassium chlorate.

$$6KOH + 3MnO_2 + KClO_3 = 3K_2MnO_4 + KCl + 3H_2O$$

Manganese   Potassium   Potassium
dioxide   chlorate   manganate

The green residue consisting of potassium manganate is extracted with water. From this potassium permanaganate is made by any one of the following three methods :

1. By passing carbon dioxide. Two-thirds of the manganate are converted into potassium permanganate while the one-third is precipitated as manganese dioxide.

$$6K_2MnO_4 + 2CO_2 = 2KMnO_4 + MnO_2 + 2K_2CO_3$$

2. All the manganate may be converted into permanaganate by passing chlorine through the solution:

$$2K_2MnO_4 + Cl_2 = 2KMnO_4 + 2KCl$$

3. By electrolysing a warm solution of the managanate.

$$2K_2MnO_4 + 2H_2O = KMnO_4 + 2KOH + H_2\uparrow$$

The solution obtained by any one of the above methods is filtered and concentrated until potassium permanganate separates as crystals.

Physical Properties: Potassium permanganate occurs in the form of slender, dark purple, monoclinic prisms, almost opaque by transmitted light and having a blue metallic lustre by reflected light. It has a solubility of 1 in 15 in water. It is reduced by alcohol.

Chemical Properties: Potassium permanganate is a very *powerful* oxidizing agent when dry and also in solution. Explosions may occur when it comes into contact with organic or other readily oxidizable material such as cork or charcoal. When mixed with glycerin, it burns.

Potassium permanganate acts as an oxidizing agent because it is able to produce nascent oxygen in solution.

$$2KMnO_4 + 3H_2SO_4 = K_2SO_4 + 2MnSO_4 + 3H_2O + 5(O)$$
(acid solution)

$$2KMnO_4 + H_2O = 2MnO_2 + 2KOH + 3(O)$$
(alkaline or neutral solution)

1. Hydrogen peroxide decolourises acidified potassium permanganate :

$$2KMnO_4 + 3H_2SO_4 + 5H_2O_2 = K_2SO_4 + 2MnSO_4 + 8H_2O + 5O_2\uparrow$$

2. It is also decolourised by oxalic acid in sulphuric acid in the hot condition:

$$\underset{\text{Oxalic acid}}{5H_2C_2O_4 . 2H_2O} + 2KMnO_4 + 3H_2SO_4 = K_2SO_4 + 2MnSO_4 + 18H_2O + 10CO_2\uparrow$$

3. On heating potassium permanganate at 240°C very pure oxygen is evolved, and a black powdery residue of potassium manganate and manganese dioxide is left.

$$2KMnO_4 \triangleq \underset{\substack{\text{Potassium} \\ \text{manganate}}}{K_2MnO_4} + MnO_2 + O_2$$

When a little water is added to the residue, potassium permanganate is reformed along with potassium hydroxide.

$$3K_2MnO_4 + 2H_2O = 2KMnO_4 + MnO_2 + 4KOH$$

4. Iodine is liberated from potassium iodide by an acid solution of potassium permanganate.

$$2KMnO_4 + 10KI + 8H_2SO_4 = 6K_2SO_4 + 2MnSO_4 + 5I_2 + 8H_2O$$

5. Ferrous salts are oxidised to ferric salts by acidified permanganate.

$$2KMnO_4 + 10FeSO_4 + 8H_2SO_4 = K_2SO_4 + 2MnSO_4 + 5Fe_2(SO_4)_3 + 8H_2O$$

It is official in I.P.

Official Tests for Identity

1. A solution in water, acidified with sulphuric acid and heated to 70°C, is decolourised by solution of hydrogen peroxide.

2. On strong heating, it evolves oxygen and leaves a black residue. On adding water to the residue potassium hydroxide solution is formed (reaction No. 3 above). This, after neutralisation with hydrochloric acid, gives the reactions characteristic of potassium. See Chapter 18.

Tests for Purity

1. Chloride and sulphate
2. Water-insoluble matter.
3. Colour of solution.

The first test for purity is for *chloride and sulphate*. The sample is dissolved in boiling water and heated on a water bath. Alcohol is added till the solution becomes colourless. It is filtered. Aliquots are taken from the filtrate and the limit tests for chloride and sulphate are applied. The permanganate is reduced with alcohol before the limit tests are done.

$$2KMnO_4 + 3CH_3CH_2OH = 2KOH + 2MnO_2 + 3CH_3CHO + 2H_2O$$

The filtration is to remove the precipitated manganese dioxide.

Standard: Potassium Permanganate contains not less than 99 percent and not more than 100.5 per cent of $KMnO_4$.

Assay (I.P.'96): The assay is based on the oxidizing action of potassium permanganate on potassium iodide or rather on hydrogen iodide which is oxidized to iodine. The liberated iodine is titrated with sodium thiosulphate solution using starch as the indicator towards the end of the titration.

An accurately weighed quantity of the sample is dissolved in a definite quantity of water to make up to a particular volume. To an aliquot solid potassium iodide and 2M hydrochloric acid are added and titrated with 0.1M sodium thiosulphate using starch solution as indicator.

$$2KMnO_4 + 10KI + 8H_2SO_4 = 6K_2SO_4 + 2MnSO_4 + 5I_2 + 8H_2O$$

Assay (I.P.'85): By titration against 0.1N oxalic acid. The oxalic acid is acidified with sulphuric acid and kept at 70°C throughout the titration. If the temperature is not maintained at 70°C, the reaction will be slow (refer reaction 2 above.)

In short, the reaction is

$$2KMnO_4 = 5(O)$$
$$5(O) + 5(COOH)_2 = 10CO_2 + 5H_2O$$

The permangante should be taken in the burette and the end-point is appearance of a pale pink colour.

Storage: Store in a well-closed container.

Medicinal Use: As *anti-infective* (i.e. as disinfectant). Its action is due to the liberation of oxygen which oxidizes the protein of the bacteria and kills them. Used as a mouthwash and gargle.

3. BLEACHING POWDER OR CHLORINATED LIME, Ca(OCl)Cl

Chlorinated Lime is official in I.P. 1966.

Preparation: Slaked lime is spread upon shelves in a box-like container and subjected to the action of chlorine gas which is introduced at the top of the chamber and flows through the contents. The temperature is maintained below 25°C so that formation of calcium chlorate is brought down. When the absorption of chlorine is complete, which may take about 12 to 24 hours, powdered lime is sent into the chamber so that any excess chlorine may be absorbed.

$$Ca(OH_2) + Cl_2 = Ca(OCl)Cl + H_2O$$

Physical and Chemical Properties

Bleaching powder is a white or grayish white granular powder having a pronounced odour of chlorine. it is considered as consisting of "calcium chlorohypochlorite", $Ca(OCl)Cl, H_2O$, which is intermediate between calcium chloride, $CaCl_2$ and calcium hypochlorite, $Ca(OCl)_2$. It has varying amounts of calcium hydroxide and moisture. Although it becomes moist on exposure to air, it is not deliquescent. When it is exposed to the air, it is slowly decomposed.

$$Ca(OCl)Cl + CO_2 + H_2O = CaCO_3 + HCl + HOCl$$
$$HOCl + HCl = Cl_2\uparrow + H_2O$$

So It is necessary that chlorinated lime is stored only in tightly stoppered bottles. Bleaching powder is used toilets, latrines etc.because chlorine is produced as given in the above equations and sterilizes the places. It is used mainly for its disinfecting properties and as a bleaching agent.

Official Tests for Identity

1. When hydrochloric acid is added to bleaching powder, chlorine is copiouly evolved.
2. Gives the reactions characteristic of calcium and of chlorides (see Chapter 18).

Standard: Chlorinated lime is required to contain not less than 30% w/w of available chlorine.

Storage: Refer the reaction with carbon dioxide and moisture. Because of this it must be stored in a tightly stoppered container.

Assay: An aqueous suspension of the substance is first treated with excess of potassium iodide and acetic acid. Acetic acid, like other acids liberates chlorine from chlorinated lime as given below:-

$$Ca(OCl)Cl + 2CH_3COOH = (CH_3COO)_2Ca + HOCl + HCl$$
$$HOCl + HCl = Cl_2\uparrow + H_2O$$

The liberated chlorine displaces an equivalent amount of iodine from potassium iodide,

$$2KI + Cl_2 = 2KCl + I_2$$

The iodine is titrated with 0.1 N sodium thiosulphate using starch mucilage as indicator.

$$Na_2S_2O_3 + I_2 = Na_2S_4O_6 + 2NaI$$

Medicinal and Pharmaceutical Uses: *Disinfectant.* Please see Properies.

4. IODINE

Iodine is widely distributed in the form of iodides in sea water and sea weeds. Chile salt petre contains $NaIO_3$ and the iodine content in Chile salt petre is about 0.2%. Iodine itself and solutions of iodine are official and they are discussed below:-

Preparation: Iodine is mostly obtained from sea weeds, Chile salt petre mother liquors and various brines.

A. From Sea Weeds: Most sea weeds contain iodine, the largest content (0.5 per cent) in the stem of *Laminaria digitata*. Others such as *Fucus vesiculosis* usually contain much less.

Dried sea weed is burnt and the ash or kelp is extracted with water. The extract is concentrated and the less soluble salts such as the sulphates and chlorides of sodium and potassium crystallize and are filtered out. Next sulphuric acid is added and this results in the decomposition of sulphides and thiosulphates with consequent precipitation of sulphur which is removed. The sulphuric acid also converts the iodides and bromides into sulphates. Hydrogen iodide and hydtrogen bromide are produced and remain in solution. Then any of the two following procedures may be used:-

1. The acid solution which now contains the freely soluble iodides with only small proportions of bromides and chlorides is treated with the correct proportion of chlorine and iodine is precipitated.

$$2HI + Cl_2 = I_2 + 2HCl \qquad \text{or}$$

191

2. The acid solution is warmed in a still and manganese dioxide is added from time to time. The liberated iodine volatilises and is condensed in suitable receivers.

$$2HI + MnO_2 + H_2SO_4 = MnSO_4 + 2H_2O + I_2$$

Iodine obtained by either of these methods may contain iodine chloride, ICl, and iodine bromide, IBr. The iodine from these is liberated by sublimation with a small quantity of potassium iodide:

$$ICl + KI = KCl + I_2$$
$$IBr + KI = KBr + I_2$$

This treatment also removes iodine cyanide which is usually present.

B. From Chile Salt Petre: Crude chile salt petre contains about 0.2 per cent of iodine chiefly in the form of sodium iodate, $NaIO_3$. The mother liquor remaining after the crystallization of sodium nitrate from solution of caliche (crude chile salt petre) is treated with sodium bisulphite:-

$$2NaIO_3 + 5NaHSO_3 = Na_2SO_4 + 3NaHSO_4 + I_2 + H_2O$$

Alternatively the mother liquor is mixed with a stream of sulphur dioxide to liberate the iodine.

$$2NaIO_3 + 4H_2O + 5SO_2 = Na_2SO_4 + 4H_2SO_4 + I_2$$

In both the cases the precipitated iodine is collected and purified by sublimation.

Physical and Chemical Properties

Iodine is a greyish black solid, having a metallic lustre and a characteristic penetrating odour. It crystallizes in large rhombic plates or granules, It is appreciably volatile at ordinary temperatures and should be stored in bottles with glass stoppers. This is because the vapour attacks both cork and rubber. It melts at 114°C but sublimes at temperatures below its melting point. It gives off a violet-coloured vapour which is one of the heaviest known gases, 8.8 times as heavy as air. The liquid boils at 183°C. It has a specific gravity of 4.93 and is the heaviest nonmetallic element.

Iodine is only very slightly soluble in water, but is more soluble in alcohol. It dissolves easily in ether, chloroform and carbon disulphide. It also dissolves in solutions of potassium iodide forming the compound KI_3.

$$KI + I_2 \rightleftharpoons KI_3$$

The I_3^- ion is formed by the union of I_2 and an iodide ion (I^-) which is attracted to the iodine molecule by a coordinate covalent bond. Solutions of iodine in chloroform, carbon disulphide and liquid paraffin are violet in colour, i.e. the natural colour of iodine vapour, indicating that the iodine exists as such in solution. However solutions in water, alcohol and aqueous iodides are reddish brown in colour, the reason being probably the chemical combination of iodine with the solvent (refer solution of iodine in potassium iodide given above).

Iodine gives with mucilage of starch a deep blue colour. The blue colour disappears on warming but reappears on cooling. This is a very characteristic and sensitive reaction.

Iodine functions as an oxidizing agent. Many reducing agents are oxidised by it and sodium thiosulphate is the most important of them.

$$2Na_2S_2O_3 + I_2 = 2NaI + Na_2S_4O_6$$
Sodium thiosulphate

Ferrous chloride, hydrogen sulphide and sulphurous acid are also oxidised.

$$2FeCl_2 + I_2 + 2HCl = 2HI + 2FeCl_3$$
Ferrous   Ferric
chloride   chloride

$$H_2S + I_2 = 2HI + S\downarrow$$

$$H_2SO_3 + I_2 + H_2O = 2HI + H_2SO_4$$
Sulphurous   Sulphuric
acid   acid

193

Iodine functions also as reducing agent in the presence of strong oxidising agents like nitric acid which oxidizes it to iodic acid.

$$I_2 + 10HNO_3 = 2HIO_3 + 10NO_2 + 4H_2O$$
Iodic acid

With alkalis, iodine gives the corresponding iodi.' s and iodates on heating.

$$3I_2 + 6NaOH \triangleq 5NaI + NaIO_3 + 3H_2O$$

Iodine reacts with iron to convert it to ferrous iodide.

$$Fe + I_2 = FeI_2$$

Iodine is official in I.P.

Tests for Identity

Official

1. When gently heated in a test tube, it gives off violet coloured vapours which condense forming a bluish black crystalline sublimate at the top of the test tube.

2. With solution of starch, a deep blue colour is produced which disappears on boiling and reappears on cooling.

Non-Official

Iodine is easily reduced by many reducing agents, especially sodium thiosulphate. Iodine is decolourised when a solution of sodium thiosulphate is added to it.

Tests for Purity

1. Bromides and chlorides
2. Non-volatile matter

Bromides and chlorides are tested by treating the sample in aqueous solution with a little zinc powder which reduces the iodine. Then dilute ammonia and silver nitrate solution are added. The precipitate is filtered off and the filtrate is acidified with nitric acid. The opalescence produced should not be more than the standard opalescence in the limit test for chlorides.

If chloride and bromide are present, the corresponding silver chloride is freely soluble and the corresponding silver bromide is appreciably soluble in ammonia. The filtrate containing these will deposit them again as precipitates if it is treated with nitric acid in which both silver chloride and bromide are insoluble.

Standard: Iodine contains between 99.5 per cent and 100.5 per cent of I.

Assay: Since iodine is volatile, it is weighed in a stoppered bottle. An accurately weighed quantity is dissolved in a solution of potassium iodide and slightly acidified with dil. acetic acid. It is titrated against 0.1M sodium thiosulphate using starch mucilage as indicator.

$$2Na_2S_2O_3 + I_2 = Na_2S_4O_6 + 2NaI$$

Storage: It is appreciably volatile at ordinary temperatures and should be stored in well closed bottles fitted with glass stoppers or well waxed stoppers.

Medicinal and Pharmaceutical Uses

Disinfectant. Iodine is an effective disinfectant. It acts by oxidizing the protoplasm of organisms. In the presence of organic matter is action is very much reduced.

Iodine when administered orally will be converted to inorganic iodide ion in the gastro-intestinal tract. Its systemic effect is therefore the same as that of a corresponding quantity of inorganic iodide.

Pharmaceutically iodine preparations are usually externally used as antiseptics or internally as a source of iodine for the thyroid gland.

5. THE IODINE SOLUTIONS

There are three iodine solutions official in I.P.' 66.

1. Strong Iodine Solution.
2. Weak Iodine Solution.
3. Aqueous Iodine Solution.

195

Strong Iodine Solution contains 10% w/v of iodine whereas the content of iodine in Weak Iodine Solution is 2 per cent w/v. The content of iodine in Aqueous Iodine Solution is between these two, viz. 5 per cent w/v. Naturally the amount of potassium iodide in Aqueous Iodine Solution which contains no alcohol is relatively more than in the other two solutions which contain alcohol.

Aqueous Iodine Solution

Also known as Lugol's solution. This is the only official solution of iodine which contains no alcohol. It contains 5.0 per cent w/v of iodine and 10.0 per cent w/v of potassium iodide. In making this solution. potassium iodide may be replaced by sodium iodide.

Assay: A 25 per cent v/v dilution is prepared with water.

For iodine: An aliquot is taken and titrated with 0.1N sodium thiosulphate solution.

For potassium iodide: An aliquot is diluted with water and strongly acidified with hydrochloric acid. It is then titrated with 0.05M(M/20) potassium iodate. At first iodine is released but as the titration is continued, the iodine also reacts with the titrant potassium iodate. Since starch will be hydrolysed by the high concentration of the acid, it cannot be used as an indicator. So cholorform is used as an indicator and the end point is the disappearance of the violet colour in the chloroform layer. In the B.P. method, amaranth is used as the indicator, and the end point is the change of colour from red to pale yellow.

Initially the hydriodic acid (HI) from potassium iodide and the iodic acid (HIO_3) from potassium iodate (KIO_3) react to release iodine.

$$5HI + HIO_3 = 3I_2 + 3H_2O$$

On further addition of the potassium iodate, the iodine is converted into iodine monochloride

$$5HI + 2I_2 + HIO_3 = 5ICl + 3H_2O$$

A high concentration of hydrochloric acid is necessary for these reactions to take place and the reactions may be summarized as given below:-

$$KIO_3 + 2KI + 6HCl = 3KCl + 3ICl + 3H_2O$$
$$KIO_3 + 2I_2 + 6HCl = KCl + 5ICl + 3H_2O$$

While calculating the content of potassium iodide, allowance must be made for the amount of free iodine already present in the Aqueous Iodine Solution.

Strong Iodine Solution

This contains 10.0 per cent w/v of iodine and 6.0 per cent w/v of potassium iodide. Iodine is dissolved in a mixture of potassium iodide solution and alcohol 90 per cent. Potassium iodide may be replaced by sodium iodide.

Assay: For this purpose a 25% v/v dilution with alcohol 90 per cent is prepared.

For iodine: 20 ml is titrated against 0.1N sodium thiosulphate using starch mucilage as indicator.

For potassium iodide: 10 ml of the solution is diluted with water, hydrochloric acid and potassium cyanide are added and titrated with M/20 potassium iodate until the dark brown solution becomes pale yellow. Then solution of starch is added and the titration is continued until the blue colour is discharged.

Here the potassium iodate obviously reacts with both the potassium iodide and free iodine. The reactions are given below :

$$KIO_3 + 2KI + 3KCN + 6HCl = 6KCl + 3ICN + 3H_2O$$
$$KIO_3 + 2I_2 + 6HCl = KCl + 5ICl + 3H_2O$$

The volume of M/20 iodate used in reacting with the potassium iodide only is given by subtracting from the total volume half the volume of 0.1N thiosulphate. Since the concentration of acid is low, starch can be conveniently used as an indicator.

Weak Iodine Solution

This is also known as Iodine Tincture. This contains 2 per cent of iodine and 2.5 per cent of potassium iodide. It is also assayed in the same way as Strong Solution of Iodine. Potassium iodide may be replaced by sodium iodide.

Assay: For iodide and for potassium iodide as for Strong Solution of Iodine.

Storage: as for iodine.

Medicinal Use: Aqueous Iodine Solution is used as a *source of iodine* and used internally in cases of thyroid deficiency. The *alcoholic solutions* are used as *antiseptics and disinfectants*. Even though the potassium iodide in them is enough to keep the iodine in solution, the alcohol facilitates the antiseptic action by dissolving the cutaneous fat and enabling the iodine to exert its disinfectant action more effectively.

6. POVIDONE - IODINE (P.V.P. - IODINE)

Povidone-iodine belongs to the class of indophores. These are large organic molecules which carry loosely bound iodine. This iodine is liberated slowly at the site of application. The most popular of the indophores is povidone-iodine which is a complex produced by the interaction of iodine and polyvinyl pyrrolidone. This complex contains about 9-12 per cent of available iodine.

Properties: Povidone-iodine is a yellowish brown amorphous powder with a characteristic odour. It is slightly hygroscopic. It is soluble in water and alcohol. The aqueous solution is acidic to litmus. The solution is transparent and reddish brown and it has a faint iodine odour. As the solution is diluted more and more, the free iodine content increases and it becomes more powerfully disinfectant. Therefore povidone-iodine solution should be well diluted before use. It is official in I.P.

Tests for Identity

1. A solution of the sample is added to a diluted solution of starch. A deep blue colour is produced.

2. A solution of the sample is dried over a glass plate at room temperature. The dry, brown film formed dissolves readily in water.

Tests for Purity

1. Heavy metals
2. Nitrogen
3. Iodide
4. Sulphated ash
5. Loss on drying

Nitrogen is determined by the Method for Determination of Nitrogen given in the I.P.

Inorganic *iodide* should be present only upto 6.6%. This is found out by taking a solution of the sample and treating with sodium bisulphite solution till the iodine colour is discharged. To the sodium iodide formed, excess of 0.1M silver nitrate and nitric acid are added. The excess of silver nitrate (left after the formation of silver iodide) is backtitrated with 0.1M ammonium thiocyanate using ferric alum as indicator. From the volume obtained, the percentage of free iodine obtained in the assay is subtracted to give the percentage of iodide.

Loss on drying is prescribed (not more than 8%), since povidone-iodine is slightly hygroscopic.

Standard: Povidone-iodine contains available iodine between 9 and 12 per cent, calculated with reference to the dried substance.

Storage: Sine it is slightly hygroscopic and also because it contains volatile free iodine, store in tightly-closed, light-resistant containers.

Assay: Assay is by simple titration with 0.1M sodium thiosulphate using starch solution added towards the end of the titration. For this the sample is dissolved in a large quantity of water and shaken in a mechanical shaker for about one hour to get complete release of iodine.

Medicinal Use: *Disinfectant.* The advantages of povidone-iodine are that it is nonirritating, nontoxic and nonstaining and also exerts prolonged germicidal action. It is used against bacteria and fungi mainly, that is in diseases such as boils, burns, ulcers, furunculosis (occurrence of several boils at the same time and also repeated appearance of boils in the skin over a period of weeks or months), otitis externa (inflammation of the skin of the external ear), tinea (ringworm) and vaginitis (inflammation of the vagina due to *trichomonas*, a parasitic flagellate protozoan organism or *monilia*, a type of fungi now known as *candida).* It is also used for surgical scrubbing and disinfection of instruments and endoscope. Povidone-iodine solution is generally used for disinfection of skin, mouth and throat. It is used as a solution, scrub solution, mouth wash, cream, ointment, vaginal pessary and also as an aerosol spray. Its another advantage is that it is easily washable from the skin.

Some Branded Preparations of Povidone-Iodine

1. BETADINE - 5% mouth wash, 10% solution, 7.5% surgical scrub solution, 5% ointment and cream and 10% paint.
2. PIODIN - 5% solution and 5% ointment.

A 5% aerosol spray with freon as propellant is also available.

7. BORIC ACID, H_3BO_3

Preparation: Boric acid occurs in volcanic jets of steam. The steam is condensed and cooled. Crude boric acid crystallizes out. It is purified by recrystallization.

Native borates may also be decomposed with a mineral acid.

$$2Na_2B_4O_7 + H_2SO_4 + 5H_2O = Na_2SO_4 + 4H_3BO_3$$

The boric acid is allowed to crystallize after filtration. It is collected by filtration, washed free from soluble sulphate and dried.

Physical and Chemical Properties: Boric acid occurs in three forms:-
1. Transparent, smooth, pearly scales
2. Triclinic crystals
3. A white, bulky powder

These forms are stable in air. The scale and the crystalline form can be used for preparing solutions. The powder can be used in dusting powders and ointments.

Boric acid is soluble 1 in 25 in water and in 4 parts of glycerol. It volatilizes appreciably from aqueous solutions at 60°C and above.

Orthoboric acid is a weak acid. It is a tribasic acid and cannot be titrated with standard alkali directly. However when mixed with glycerol or mannitol, a stronger monobasic acid is formed which can be titrated with alkali directly (refer assay) using phenolphthalein as indicator. Orthoboric acid turns litmus a dull claret red. Only the alkali borates such as sodium borate or borax are soluble in water. Their solutions have a strong basic reaction.

When orthoboric acid is heated at 100°C or slightly above, it is converted to metaboric acid by loss of a molecule of water.

$$H_3BO_3 \xrightarrow[100°C]{\Delta} HBO_2 + H_2O$$
Metaboric acid

Further heating to approximately 160°C results in the formation of tetraboric acid called as pyroboric acid:

$$4HBO_2 \xrightarrow{\Delta} H_2B_4O_7 + H_2O$$
Pyroboric acid

Still further heating converts the residue to boron trioxide, a glass-like solid:

$$H_2B_4O_7 \xrightarrow{\Delta} 2B_2O_3 + H_2O$$

Boron trioxide dissolves in water to form orthoboric acid:

$$3H_2O + B_2O_3 \longrightarrow 2H_3BO_3$$

The borates are salts of neither H_3BO_3 or HBO_2 but mainly of $H_2B_4O_7$. A solution of boric acid in water contains only a minute amount of $H_2B_4O_7$ but when neutralised with a base and concentrated, the more crystalline salt $Na_2B_4O_7$ will be formed.

It is official in I.P.

Official Tests for Identity

1. Dissolve the sample in a mixture of methyl alcohol and concentrated sulphuric acid. Ignite the solution. The flame burns with a green border. This is due to the formation of methyl borate.

2. Dissolve the sample in boiling water and cool. The solution is faintly acid.

Non-Official Tests for Identity

1. Acidify a 5 per cent w/v solution with hydrochloric acid, moisten a piece of turmeric paper with this solution and dry. The colour of the paper becomes pink or brownish red. Pour dilute ammonia solution or solution of sodium hydroxide on the paper. The colour changes to blue or greenish black.

2. Ignite in a procelain dish a solution in alcohol. It burns and the flame is tinged green. This is due to the formation of volatile ethyl borate.

Tests for Purity

1. Clarity and colour of solution
2. Solubility in ethanol
3. pH
4. Sulphate
5. Arsenic
6. Heavy metals
7. Loss on drying.

Clarity and colour of solution and solubility in ethanol are tested by dissolving the sample in boiling water and boiling ethanol (95%) respectively. The solutions should be colourless and clear or at the most only slightly opalescent. These are tests to exclude metallic borates and insoluble impurities generally.

Standard: Contains between 99.5 per cent and 100.5 per cent of H_3BO_3 calculated with reference to the dried substance.

Storage: The substance is quite stable in air. So there is no special storage condition other than the following:

Store in a well closed container.

Assay: An accurately weighed quantity of the sample is dissolved in a mixture of water and glycerol previously neutralised to phenolphthalein and titrated with 1M sodium hydroxide using phenolphthalein as indicator. A permanent pale pink colour is the end point.

As already stated since boric acid is a weak acid, it cannot be titrated with alkali directly. Glycerol combines with boric acid to form a monobasic acid known as glyceryl boric acid which is strong enough to be directly titrated with 1M sodium hydroxide and give a satisfactory end point.

Glycerol   Boric acid   Glyceryl boric acid

Other polyhydric alcohols such as glycols and mannitol produce a similar result :

Mannitol   Mannityl boric acid

Medicinal or Pharmaceutical Use: *Pharmaceutical aid and local anti-infective.*

8. SILVER NITRATE, $AgNO_3$

Preparation: Silver nitrate is prepared by dissolving metallic silver in hot, slightly concentrated nitric acid.

$$Ag + 2HNO_3 = AgNO_3 + NO_2\uparrow + H_2O$$

The solution is filtered through glass wool and set aside in a dark, dust proof room to crystallize. It is recrystallized from water.

Physical and Chemical Properties

Silver nitrate occurs as colourless or white rhombic or tabular crystals without odour and with a bitter, caustic, metallic taste. It is very soluble in water and sparingly soluble in alcohol. It is not affected by light, when pure. But when it comes into contact with any organic matter such as skin, it is reduced to metallic silver which is grey or greyish black in colour and leaves a stain. The best way to remove this stain is to paint it with tincture of iodine or any iodine solution and remove the iodine with a solution of sodium thiosulphate. When it is heated at 209°C, it melts to a slight, yellow liquid without decomposition. However, on further heating, it slowly decomposes with evolution of oxides of nitrogen, leaving a residue of metallic silver. Aqueous solution of silver nitrate is neutral to litmus. Silver nitrate is photosensitive (affected by light).

On heating it gives metallic silver and nitrogen dioxide.

$$2AgNO_3 = 2Ag + 2NO_2 + O_2$$

With ammonia, it forms a complex known as silver diammino nitrate. The solution is known as ammoniacal silver nitrate and it is prepared by adding strong ammonia solution to silver nitrate solution till the black precipitate formed is dissolved.

$$AgNO_3 + 2NH_3 = Ag\,(NH_3)_2NO_3$$
$$\text{Silver diammino nitrate}$$

Further it answers the chemical reactions of silver and of the nitrate ion. Silver nitrate is official in I.P.

Official Tests for Identity

Gives the reactions of silver and of nitrates (see Chapter 18).

Non-Official Test for Identity

This test is for the nitrate ion. A dilute solution is mixed with a drop of diphenylamine and the mixture is added on a layer of concentrated sulphuric acid in a test tube. A blue colour is formed at the junction of the two layers.

Tests for Purity

 1. Acidity or alkalinity
 2. Clarity and colour of solution
 3. Aluminium, bismuth, copper and lead
 4. Foreign salts.

Acidity or alkalinity is limited by adding to a 4% w/v solution of the sample bromocresol green solution. The solution should have a blue colour. Then to another quantity of the solution phenol red solution is added. The colour of the solution should now be yellow. This testing ensures a pH of 5.2 to 6.8 for the substance.

Foreign salts should not be more than 0.3% and are determined by adding to an aqueous solution of the sample 2M hydrochloric acid and heating on a water bath. The silver chloride is filtered off and the filtrate is evaporated to dryness. The residue is dried at 105°C and weighed.

Aluminium, bismuth, copper and lead are tested by adding to an aqueous solution excess of dilute ammonia solution. The mixture remains clear and colourless. Aluminium, bismuth, copper and lead, if present, are precipitated as their hydroxides whereas silver nitrate remains dissolved (see above). If copper is present, it will produce a blue solution due to the formation of cuoxam.

Standard: Silver nitrate contains not less than 99.5 per cent and not more than 100.5 per cent of $AgNO_3$.

Assay: An accurately weighed quantity is dissolved in water and nitric acid is added. It is titrated with 0.1M ammonium thiocyanate, using ferric ammonium sulphate as indicator. End point is the appearance of a red colour due to the formation of ferric thiocyanate.

$$AgNO_3 + NH_4SCN = AgSCN + NH_4NO_3$$

Storage: Since silver nitrate is affected by light, store in tightly closed, light resistant (amber glass) containers.

Medicinal and Pharmaceutical Uses

Local Anti-infective: It is used in the form of eye drops for instillation in the eyes of newborn babies to guard against *Ophthalmia neonatorum.* Toughened silver nitrate (Lunar Caustic) containing about 95 per cent of silver nitrate is used for removing warts etc.

Ammonical silver nitrate is used as a reagent in the laboratory. Silver nitrate, besides its use in volumetric analysis, is also used for preparing silver halides used in photography and in silvering of mirrors.

9. SELENIUM SULPHIDE, SeS$_2$

Preparation: It is prepared by adding selenious acid solution to aluminium chloride solution saturated with hydrogen sulphide which is continuously passed. Actually the reaction is between selenious acid and hydrogen sulphide only and aluminium chloride only acts as a coagulant precipitating the selenious sulphide. The precipitate is filtered, washed with water and dried.

$$H_2SeO_3 + 2H_2S = SeS_2 + 3H_2O$$

Selenious	Selenious
acid	sulphide

Physical and Chemical Properties

Selenium sulphide is a bright orange to reddish brown powder with a faint odour of hydrogen sulphide. It is practically insoluble in water but dissolves in nitric acid forming selenious acid and sulphuric acid.

$$SeS_2 + 16HNO_3 = H_2SeO_3 + 2H_2SO_4 + 16NO_2 + 5H_2O$$

By adding urea, the excess of nitric acid is converted into urea nitrate. Urea also eliminates any nitrous acid present.

$$2HNO_2 + CO(NH_2)_2 = CO_2 + 2N_2 + 3H_2O$$
$$\text{Urea}$$

Potassium iodide may now be added and the selenious acid oxidises potassium iodide to iodine, itself getting reduced to selenium. So initially a yellow to orange colour is produced and this darkens rapidly on standing. This is the basis of the identification test for selenium sulphide. A modification of this test in which fuming nitric acid is used is the basis for the assay. Selenium sulphide is official in B.P.

Official Tests for Identity

1. A small quantity is boiled with concentrated nitric acid, diluted with water and filtered. To the filtrate is added urea. It is boiled and cooled. Potassium iodide solution is added. A yellow to orange colour, which darkens rapidly on standing, is produced (see Properties).

2. The coloured solution obtained in (1) above is allowed to stand for 10 minutes and filtered through kieselguhr. The filtrate gives the reactions of sulphates. This is due to the presence of sulphuric acid.

Standard: Selenium sulphide contains not less than 52 per cent and not more than 55 per cent of Se.

Tests for Purity

The only test for purity prescribed is for soluble selenium compounds only. This is limited by a spectrophotometric test.

Assay: The sample is treated with fuming nitric acid and heated on a water bath. To the selenious acid formed are added potassium iodide and chloroform.

$$H_2SeO_3 + 4HI = 2I_2 + Se + 3H_2O$$

The liberated iodine is titrated with 0.02M sodium thiosulphate using starch as indicator towards the end of the titration. The end point is the discharge of blue colour completely from the aqueous layer.

Storage: Store in a well - closed container.

Medicinal Use: Used in the treatment of dandruff and seborrhoeic dermatitis of the scalp. It is available as Selsun Cream (0.5%) and Selsun suspension (a 2.5% shampoo). In these preparations, selenium sulphide is non - irritant and is not absorbed significantly.

10. ZINC UNDECENOATE (ZINC UNDECYLENATE), $[CH_2 = CH.(CH_2)_8COO]_2Zn$

Preparation: Destructive distillation or pyrolysis of castor oil gives the unsaturated acid, 10-undecenoic acid along with the saturated aldehyde heptanal.

10-undecenoic acid is added slowly with constant stirring to a hot solution of sodium carbonate. Then the mixture is cooled and zinc acetate or zinc sulphate is added to the sodium undecenoate formed. Zinc undecylenate is precipitated. It is collected, washed and dried.

$$Na_2CO_3 + 2CH_2 = CH.(CH_2)_8COOH = 2CH_2 = CH.(CH_2)_8COONa$$
$$\text{10-Undecenoic acid} \qquad\qquad \text{Sodium undecenoate}$$
$$CO_2 + H_2O$$

$$2CH_2 = CH.(CH_2)_8COONa + ZnSO_4 = [CH_2 = CH.(CH_2)_8COO]_2Zn$$
$$+ Na_2SO_4$$

Properties: Zinc undecylenate or zinc undecenoate is a fine, white or pale yellowish-white powder. It is practically insoluble in water and in alcohol.

On addition of acid, it is decomposed to form undecenoic acid. Sine it is an unsaturated acid, it decolourises potassium permanganate solution. It is official in I.P.

Official Tests for Identity

1. The sample is acidified with dilute sulphuric acid and extracted with solvent ether. The extract is evaporated to remove ether and the colour of the potassium permanganate solution added to it is discharged.

The undecenoic acid, precipitated by the acid, extracted into ether and evaporated to dryness, decolourises the potassium permanganate. It also melts at 67°C.

2. The aqueous layer gives the reactions of zinc. See Chapter 18.

3. The substance melts between 115°C and 121°C.

Tests for Purity

1. Degree of unsaturation.
2. Alkalinity
3. Alkalis and alkaline earths
4. Sulphate
5. Loss on drying

Degree of unsaturation is determined by dissolving the sample in hydrochloric and glacial acetic acids and titrating with 0.05M bromine, using ethoxychrysoidine hydrochloride solution as indicator added towards the end of the titration.

Alkalis and alkaline earths - see zinc stearate (this Chapter).

Standard: It contains between 98 and 102 per cent of $C_{22}H_{38}O_4Zn$, calculated with reference to the dried substance.

Assay: Same as for zinc sulphate.

Storage: Store in well-closed light-resistant containers.

Medicinal Use: *Antifungal (topical).*

11. SODIUM ANTIMONY GLUCONATE

This is also known as *sodium stibogluconate* and is a pentavalent compound.

Preparation: This is made by allowing sodium hydroxide to act on a mixture of antimony pentachloride and gluconic acid solution. It has a variable composition.

Properties: It is a white, amorphous powder which is practically without odour. It is very soluble in water and practically insoluble in alcohol and ether. When hydrogen sulphide is passed through a solution of sodium antimony gluconate, an orange precipitate of antimony sulphide, Sb_2S_3, is formed only after some time and not immediately. This is because hydrogen sulphide has to reduce the pentavalent sodium antimony gluconate to the trivalent compound which reacts with hydrogen sulphide to give the orange antimony sulphide. It is official in I.P. 1985.

Official Tests for Identity

1. When the substance is heated, it chars without melting and emits an odour of burnt sugar. The residue gives the reactions of antimony and of sodium. See Chapter 18. The charring and the emission of the odour of burnt sugar are due to gluconic acid.

2. A 10 per cent w/v solution of the substance is dextrorotatory.

Tests for Purity

1. Stability of solution
2. pH
3. Chloride
4. Arsenic
5. Heavy metals
6. Calcium
7. Trivalent antimony
8. Loss on drying

Stability of solution is found out by heating an aqueous solution of the substance in an autoclave at 115°C for thirty minutes. The resulting solution should be almost colourless. *pH* should be between 5 and 6 determined on the solution obtained in the test for stability of solution.

Chloride is limited by adding to a 5% solution of the substance dilute nitric acid and silver nitrate solution. No immediate precipitate is produced.

210

Heavy metals are limited by dissolving the substance and adding sodium sulphide solution. The solution should remain clear. If heavy metals (or even trivalent antimony) are present, the sulphides of these metals will be precipitated.

Calcium is limited by adding to an aqueous solution of the substance dilute ammonia solution and ammonium oxalate solution. The solution should remain clear. If calcium is present, then white calcium oxalate will be precipitated.

Trivalent antimony is detected by acidifying an aqueous solution of the substance with dilute acetic acid and adding iodine and starch solutions. A blue colour should develop. If trivalent antimony is present, iodine will be used up for oxidising it to the pentavalent state, iodine itself getting converted to HI. So no blue colour will be formed with starch. Sodium antimony gluconate itself, being in the pentavalent state, is not affected by iodine. So the development of blue colour indicates the absence of trivalent antimony.

Standard: It contains not less than 30 per cent and not more than 34 per cent of total antimony, calculated with reference to the dried substance.

Assay: An accurately weighed quantity of the substance is heated with concentrated nitric and sulphuric acids. Then it is cooled, ammonium sulphate is added and again heated. It is again thoroughly cooled, tartaric acid and potassium iodide are added and the solution is gently boiled, until free iodine is expelled. It is cooled, made just alkaline with sodium hydroxide solution and made just acid with dilute sulphuric acid. Then excess of sodium bicarbonate is added and titrated with 0.05N iodine (N/20) using starch solution as the indicator.

The assay is for the determination of total antimony. The substance is fully oxidised by heating with concentrated nitric and sulphuric acids. After the nitric acid is expelled, tartaric acid is added to prevent subsequent precipitation of antimony trioxide when sodium bicarbonate is added. The antimony, which is now in the pentavalent state, is reduced to the trivalent state by adding potassium iodide. Then after basification with sodium hydroxide and acidification with dilute

211

sulphuric acid, sodium bicarbonate is added and titrated with 0.05N iodine solution. Iodine oxidises the trivalent antimony to the pentavalent state.

$$Sb_2O_3 + 2H_2O + 2I_2 \rightleftharpoons Sb_2O_5 + 4HI$$

Since this is a reversible reaction, sodium bicarbonate is added to neutralise the HI and prevent the backward reaction.

Storage: Store in well-closed containers.

Medicinal Use: *Antiprotozoal. Systemic leishmaniacidal.*

CHAPTER 11
CONSUMER DENTAL PRODUCTS

Consumer dental products include dentifrices (tooth powders, tooth pastes and liquid dentifrices), mouth washes and rinses, toothache drops, denture adhesives and denture cleaners. The compounds considered below may be used for preparation of one or more of the above classes of dental products and some of them like sodium fluoride are also used for toughening the tooth enamel against dental caries.

I. ANTICARIES AGENTS

Indigenous bacterial flora in the mouth are supposed to cause dental caries or tooth decay. They act on the remnants of food materials especially the sugars left on or between the teeth releasing acids during the process. The dissolution of minerals in the dental enamel and also dentin by these acids produces caries lesions or *cavities* in the teeth. The fluoride ion is thought to bond with the dental enamel and make it tough against dental caries. Fluoridation (adding fluoride to water supply) is the most effective way for prevention of dental caries in a population. Topical fluorides such as those present in tooth pastes, mouth washes and gels are generally less effective than systemic fluorides such as fluoride in water supply.

1. SODIUM FLUORIDE, NaF

Preparation: Sodium fluoride is made by adding sodium carbonate to hydrofluoric acid. It can also be prepared by reacting calcium fluoride with sodium carbonate.

$$2HF + Na_2CO_3 = 2NaF + H_2O + CO_2\uparrow$$
$$CaF_2 + Na_2CO_3 = 2NaF + CaCO_3\downarrow$$

Physical and Chemical Properties

It occurs either as a white powder or as colourless crystals. It is soluble (1 in 25) in water but is practically insoluble in alcohol. When a mineral acid is added, hydrofluoric acid is produced.

$$NaF + HCl = NaCl + HF$$
$$\text{Hydrofluoric}$$
$$\text{acid.}$$

Hydrofluoric acid tends to corrode glass and damages tissues leading to painful, slow-healing burns. Since sodium fluoride is the salt of a weak acid and a strong base, it hydrolyzes in aqueous solution to give an alkaline reaction.

$$NaF + H_2O = HF + NaOH$$

It forms stable complexes with ferric compounds.

$$FeCl_3 + 6NaF = Na_3FeF_6 + 3NaCl$$

This reaction was the basis of an assay method for sodium fluoride. In this method a neutralized solution of sodium fluoride in a strong saline solution was titrated with a freshly prepared and standardized ferric chloride solution. Potassium thiocyanate was used as the indicator. End point is the appearance of a red colour (ferric thiocyanate). Sodium fluoride gives a yellow colour (due to the formation of a complex) with a zirconyl-alizarin red lake (which itself is formed by zirconyl nitrate with alizarin red). It is official in I.P.

Official Tests for Identity

1. To an aqueous solution of the substance in carbon dioxide-free water, calcium chloride is added. A gelatinous white precipitate (of calcium fluoride) is produced. It dissolves on adding ferric chloride solution.

2. To a mixture of alizarin red S solution and zirconyl nitrate solution is added the substance and mixed. The colour changes to yellow.

3. Gives the reactions of sodium salts. See Chapter 18.

214

Tests for Purity
1. Acidity or alkalinity
2. Clarity and colour of solution
3. Chloride
4. Fluorosilicate
5. Sulphate
6. Loss on drying

Standard : It contains not less than 98.5 per cent and not more than 100.5 per cent of NaF, calculated with reference to the dried substance.

Assay : It is assayed by a non-aqueous titration. The sample is dissolved in acetic anhydride and glacial acetic acid by heating and cooled. It is titrated with 0.1M perchloric acid using crystal violet solution as indicator. End point is the appearance of a green colour. A blank titration (without the substance) is also done.

Storage : Store in well-closed containers, preferably in pyrex glass bottles. Aqueous solution should always be stored in pyrex glass bottles only. It should not be stored for more than six months.

Medicinal Use : *Preventive for dental caries and tooth decay.* It is considered to bond with tooth enamel and toughen it.

II. DENTIFRICES

Dentifrices are tooth powders and tooth pastes used to clean the accessible portions of teeth with or without a tooth brush. The following are the usual ingredients of a tooth powder:-

a) Abrasive
b) Surfactant
c) Flavour (s)
d) Sweetening agent

The abrasive dislodges the dental plaques and helps to remove them. It should be mildly abrasive for this purpose and not too abrasive as to cause erosion of the dental enamel. Precipitated calcium carbonate is the usual abrasive used, sometimes supplemented by the inclusion of dicalcium phosphate and other substances. A surfactant such as hard soap or sodium lauryl sulphate is included for cleaning the teeth. Flavours such as peppermint oil, cinnamon oil, clove oil, methyl salicylate etc.

are also inculded in small amounts so that the required mild flavour is imparted to the tooth powder without at the same time causing any irritation. Soluble saccharin is the usual sweetening agent. Sometimes the tooth powder may be coloured by adding a dye such as amaranth.

2. CALCIUM CARBONATE, $CaCO_3$

See Chapter 9.

3. DIBASIC CALCIUM PHOSPHATE, $CaHPO_4$ or $CaHPO_4.2H_2O$

Dibasic calcium phosphate or dicalcium phosphate is the anhydrous substance $(CaHPO_4)$ or a crystaline salt containing two molecules of water of hydration $(CaHPO_4.2H_2O)$.

Preparation : It is prepared by the interaction of secondary sodium phosphate (disodium hydrogen phosphate) and calcium chloride in a neutral solution.

$$Na_2HPO_4 + CaCl_2 = CaHPO_4\downarrow + 2NaCl$$

Properties : It is a white powder which is odourless and tasteless. It is stable in air. It is practically insoluble in water and alcohol but soluble in dilute hydrochloric acid and dilute nitric acid.

It dissolves in aqueous phosphoric acid and the solution on evaporation deposits crystals of calcium dihydrogen phosphate,

$$CaHPO_4 + H_3PO_4 = Ca(H_2PO_4)_2$$

Monocalcium phosphate is soluble in water and in this respect it differs from both dicalcium and tricalcium phosphates. It is official in I.P.

Official Tests for Identity

1. A solution in warm, dilute hydrochloric acid gives the reactions of calcium (see Chapter 18).

2. A solution in warm, dilute nitric acid gives the reactions of phosphates (see Chapter 18).

Tests for Purity

1. Acid -insoluble substances
2. Barium

216

3. Carbonate
4. Iron
5. Chloride
6. Sulphate
7. Arsenic
8. Heavy metals
9. Nitrate
10. Reducing substances
11. Proteinous impurities
12. Monocalcium and tricalcium phosphates

Carbonate is detected by adding to an aqueous solution of hydrochloric acid. No effervescence is produced.

Barium is limited by adding dilute sulphuric acid to an aqueous solution of the sample. The solution should not be more opalescent than a standard treated similarly.

Reducing substances are limited by acidifying with dilute sulphuric acid and adding 0.005M potassium permanganate. The pink colour of the solution should not be discharged. It is compared with a standard of calcium carbonate similarly treated.

Nitrate is detected by adding to an aqueous solution nitrogen-free sulphuric acid and indigo carmine solution and heating to boiling. The blue colour should not disappear.

Proteinous impurities are detected by heating the sample in a dry test tube. There should be no change in colour and no unpleasant odour is emitted due to the decomposition of proteinous impurities.

Monocalcium and tricalcium phosphates are limited by dissolving the sample in hydrochloric acid and titrating with 1 M sodium hydroxide solution using methyl orange as indicator.

Standard : Dibasic calcium phosphate contains not less than 30.9 per cent and not more than 31.7 per cent of Ca, calculated with reference to the ignited substance.

Assay : This is a complexometric assay. The sample is dissolved in water and hydrochloric acid and a known excess of 0.1M disodium edetate is added and diluted with water. It is neutralised with strong ammonia solution, ammonia buffer pH 10 and mordant black II mixture are added and the excess of disodium edetate is titrated with 0.1 M zinc sulphate.

The dibasic calcium phosphate is first converted into calcium chloride by dissolving in hydrochloric acid and complexed with disodium edetate. It is neutralised with strong ammonia solution and the pH is raised to 10 by adding ammonia buffer pH 10. At this pH only calcium complexation takes place. Mordant black is the indicator.

Storage: Since it is stable in air, store in well-closed containers.

Medicinal and Pharmaceutical Uses: *Calcium supplement, Pharmaceutical aid (excipient).*

Dibasic calcium phosphate may be used to partially replace precipitated calcium carbonate in formulas for tooth powders and tooth pastes. It is also used to treat phosphorus deficiency states.

4. STRONTIUM CHLORIDE, $SrCl_2$, $6H_2O$

Preparation: Strontium chloride is prepared by reacting hydrochloric acid with strontium oxide, hydroxide or carbonate.

$$SrO + 2HCl \rightarrow SrCl_2 + H_2O$$
$$Sr(OH)_2 + 2HCl \rightarrow SrCl_2 + 2H_2O$$
$$SrCO_3 + 2HCl \rightarrow SrCl_2 + H_2O + CO_2\uparrow$$

The solution is then filtered, concentrated and allowed to crystallize.

Properties: It consists of colourless, odourless crystals or white granules. It effloresces in dry air and is readily soluble in water and alcohol.

Storage: Since it effloresces in dry air, store in well-closed containers.

Medicinal and Pharmaceutical Use: *Desensitizer.*

It is used to reduce sensitivity of teeth to heat and cold. When there is tooth ache or tooth decay, teeth are more sensitive to heat and cold. In this connection, strontium chloride acts like zinc chloride. It is possible that they may act like local anaesthetics to prevent the perception of heat and cold by the teeth.

5. ZINC CHLORIDE, $ZnCl_2$

See page 178 (Chapter 10)

CHAPTER 12
MEDICAL GASES

1.OXYGEN, O_2

Oxygen is essential to animal and human life. It constitutes about 21 percent of the atmosphere and 50 percent of the terrestrial matter. Plants take up carbon dioxide and liberate oxygen during photosynthesis.

Preparation : Oxygen is usually prepared by the fractional distillation of liquid air. It is also prepared by the electrolysis of water. Since water is a non-conductor of electricity, sodium hydroxide solution is used. Iron electrodes are used and the oxygen and hydrogen produced are collected separately.

Physical and Chemical Properties

Oxygen is a colourless, tasteless and odourless gas. It is slighty heavier than air. It can be liquefied at -118.8°C. It is sparingly soluble in water (1 in 32) but is freely soluble in alcohol (1 in 3.5). Oxygen stimulates a glowing splinter to burn brightly with a flame. Oxygen is one of the most active elements. At about 5000°C, the molecular form of oxygen (O_2) dissociates into the atomic form (O) completely. The atomic form of oxygen is much more active than the molecular form. It is also formed during oxidation reactions such as those involving acidified potassium permanganate. Oxygen combines with most metals directly. If a catalyst is present, the reaction is stimulated to a great extent.

$$S + O_2 \triangleq SO_2\uparrow$$
$$C + O_2 \triangleq CO_2\uparrow$$
$$4Fe + 3O_2 \triangleq 2Fe_2O_3$$
$$2Mg + O_2 \triangleq 2MgO$$

Magnesium ribbon burns in oxygen forming magnesium oxide. Oxidative changes are brought about by oxygen of the atomsphere in paints, oils and fats etc., This can be prevented by including antioxidants in the preparations. Oxygen is official in I.P.

219

Official Tests for Identity

1. Oxygen causes a glowing splinter to burn brightly.

2. Oxygen is absorbed when it is shaken with alkaline pyrogallol solution. The solution turns dark brown.

3. When oxygen is mixed with an equal volume of nitric oxide, red fumes are produced (distinction from nitrous oxide).

Tests for Purity

Oxygen has to comply with the following tests for purity :-

1. Acidity or alkalinity
2. Carbon monoxide
3. Carbon dioxide
4. Halogens
5. Oxidising substances.

For *acidity or alkalinity,* the gas is passed through carbon dioxide-free water containing a specified quantity of $0.01M$ hydrochloric acid (solution 1). Another solution containing double the quantity of $0.01M$ hydrochloric acid is also prepared (solution 3). Finally an equal volume of just carbon dioxide-free water only is also taken (solution 2). Methyl red indicator solution is added to all the containers. The intensity of the colour in solution 1 should be between the colours seen in solutions 2 and 3 thereby indicating that the sample of oxygen gas being tested does not contain excess acidity or alkalinity.

For *carbon monoxide,* see the test given under carbon dioxide. For *carbon dioxide,* see the test given under nitrous oxide.

For *oxidising substances,* the gas is passed through a freshly prepared solution of soluble starch and potassium iodide containing a little glacial acetic acid. The colour of the liquid is not changed. If oxidising substances are present, they will oxidize potassium iodide to iodine which will give a blue colour with starch.

For *halogens,* the gas is passed through a dilute solution of silver nitrate. No opalescence (due to the formation of silver halides) should be produced.

Standard : Oxygen contains not less than 99 percent v/v of O_2.

Assay : This assay is based on the fact that certain substances such as pyrogallol in alkaline solution absorb oxygen completely and the volume of other gases such as nitrogen, argon or hydrogen can be measured easily. A special gas pipette and a gas burette are prescribed in the I.P. (see Appendix 3.49) for this assay.

A certain volume of the gas is drawn into the gas burette and allowd to mix with the absorption liquid. The volume of the residual gas is measured.

Storage : Oxygen should be stored under compression in appropriate metal cylinders with prescribed safety regulations. Valves should not be lubricated with oil or grease. The shoulder of the metal cylinder should be painted white and the rest is painted black. The name of the gas or the symbol "O_2" should be on the label and also painted on the shoulder of the cylinder.

Medicinal and Pharmaceutical Uses

Medical Gas. Oxygen is essential for breathing. Whenever there is any respiratory difficulty, as in asthma or pneumonia, oxygen is administered. It is also used during surgery. It is administered along with helium or with carbon dioxide. Liquid oxygen is used for removing warts.

2. CARBON DIOXIDE, CO_2

Carbon dioxide is present in the atmosphere to the extent of about 0.03%. It is a product of combustion, respiration and fermentation reactions.

Preparation

1. It may be prepared by heating alkali carbonates and bicarbonates.

$$2NaHCO_3 = Na_2CO_3 + CO_2\uparrow + H_2O$$

2. It may also be prepared by the action of acids on carbonates or bicarbonates.

221

$$Na_2CO_3 + H_2SO_4 = Na_2SO_4 + CO_2\uparrow + H_2O$$

Carbon dioxide is also formed from the products of combustion of coke, from fermentation and during the manufacture of lime by burning limestone in lime kilns.

Physical and Chemical Properties

Carbon dioxide is a colourless and odourless gas. It is freely soluble in water (1 in 1) and the aqueous solution, known as aerated water (soda) has a faintly acid taste. It is about one and a half times heavier than air. It can be easily liquefied under a pressure of about 50 to 60 atmospheres and this liquid becomes solid at -57.7^0C. The so- called "dry ice" is solid carbon dioxide.

Carbon dioxide does not support combustion. A burning splinter is extinguished when it is introduced into a jar containing carbon dioxide. It dissolves in water to form carbonic acid which is, however, unstable.

$$CO_2 + H_2O \rightleftharpoons H_2CO_3$$

Carbonic acid, being a dibasic acid, forms both acid and normal salts.

$$NaOH + H_2CO_3 = NaHCO_3 + H_2O$$
$$NaHCO_3 + NaOH = Na_2CO_3 + H_2O$$

Carbonic acid reddens blue litmus. When carbon dioxide is passed into a solution of calcium hydroxide (lime water), the solution turns milky due to the formation of calcium carbonate. On passing more carbon dioxide, the liquid becomes clear due to the formation of calcium bicarbonate. If this solution is heated, carbon dioxide is liberated and the solution again turns milky due to the reprecipitation of calcium carbonate.

$$Ca(OH)_2 + CO_2 = CaCO_3\downarrow + H_2O$$
$$CaCO_3 + H_2O + CO_2 = Ca(HCO_3)_2$$
$$Ca(HCO_3)_2 = CaCO_3 + H_2O + CO_2\uparrow$$

222

When passed through reduced coke, carbon dioxide is reducd to carbon monoxide.

$$CO_2 + C = 2CO$$

It is official in B.P.

Official Tests for Identity

1. Carbon dioxide extinguishes a burning splinter.
2. When the gas is passed through a solution of barium hydroxide, a white precipitate (barium carbonate) is produced. It dissolves with effervescence on the additon of dilute acetic acid

Tests for Purity

The B.P. requires that carbon dioxide should comply with the following tests for purity:-

1. Acidity
2. Phosphoric hydrides, hydrogen sulphide and organic reducing substances.
3. Carbon monoxide

Acidity is tested by passing the gas through carbon dixide-free water containing a little methyl orange indicator and 1% w/v of hydrogen peroxide. Then the dissolved carbon dioxide (which itself acts as acid) is flushed out by passing nitrogen for a long time. The colour of the solution is now compared with the colour obtained with another sample of carbon dioxide-free water mixed with 1% hydrogen peroxide and methyl orange indicator in the same way and to which a specified quantity of 0.01 M hydrochloric acid has been added.

Phosphoric hydrides, hydrogen sulphide and organic reducing substances are tested by passing the gas through ammoniacal silver nitrate solution. The solution is compared with the original reagent solution (ammoniacal silver nitrate solution) through which no gas has been passed. The test solution should not be darker than the reagent solution. If any dark colouration is seen, it may be due to silver phosphide, silver sulphide or metallic silver respectively.

Carbon monoxide in carbon dioxide is tested for by passing the carbon dioxide gas through first anhydrous silical gel impregnated with chromium (VI) oxide (which removes any ammonia and oily matter present in the sample), then through a concentrated solution of potassium hydroxide (which removes the carbon dioxide itself as potassium carbonate), and finally through phosphorous pentoxide dispersed on pumice (which removes higher oxides of nitrogen, halogens and moisture). The gas is then passed into a tube containing heated iodine pentoxide kept at 120°C which oxidizes carbon monoxide to carbon dioxide, itself getting reduced to iodine.

$$I_2O_5 + 5CO = I_2 + 5CO_2$$

The liberated iodine is absorbed in a solution of potassium iodide containing a little starch. It is titrated against 0.002 M (M/500) sodium thiosulphate solution. Since the iodine pentoxide is affected by other impurities also, they should be removed first. A blank titration, under the same conditions, after passing carbon dioxide–free air should be performed.

Standard : Carbon dioxide contains not less than 99 percent v/v of CO_2.

Assay : The B.P. prescribes a special gas burette for this assay (Appendix VIII J - p.A. 138). This burette is first flushed with the sample gas and finally filled with it. The absorption solution that is 40% w/v potassium hydroxide solution, is then sent into the burtte to absorb the carbon dioxide and the volume of the unabsorbed gas is measured.

Storage : Carbon dioxide should be kept liquefied under pressure in approved metal cylinders. The metal cylinder should be painted grey and carry a label stating 'carbon dioxide'. In addition, 'Carbon dioxide' or the symbol 'CO_2' should be stencilled in paint on the shoulder of the cylinder.

Medicinal and Pharmaceutical Uses

Medical Gas. Carbon dioxide (5%) is used along with oxygen to stimulate respiration when it is depressed in poisoning by carbon monoxide and by drugs such as morphine. It is used for manufacturing some chemicals such as sodium bicarbonate, sodium carbonate etc., Soda water (water containing carbon dioxide under pressure) acts as a carminative and promotes absorption in the stomach.

3. NITROUS OXIDE, N_2O

Preparation : Nitrous oxide is prepared by heating ammonium nitrate. Since ammonium nitrate may explode when strongly heated, a mixture of sodium nitrate and ammonium sulphate may be used.

$$NH_4NO_3 = N_2O\uparrow + 2H_2O$$

$$2NaNO_3 + (NH_4)_2SO_4 = 2N_2O\uparrow + 4H_2O + Na_2SO_4$$

The gas is collected over hot water. It may be purified by passing through ferrous sulphate solution (to remove higher oxides of nitrogen), caustic soda solution (to remove nitric acid) and concentrated sulphuric acid (to remove water vapour).

Physical and Chemical Properties

Nitrous oxide is a colourless, odourless and tasteless gas. It is about one and a half times heavier than air. It is soluble in water and freely soluble in alcohol. It is liquefied to a thin, mobile, colourless liquid which boils at -89.5^0C. The liquid freezes to a white solid at -102.4^0C. It produces exhilarating effects or 'hysterical laughter' when inhaled. Hence it is known as *'laughing gas'*. On heating it decomposes into nitrogen and oxygen.

$$2N_2O = 2N_2 + O_2$$

It does not support combustion. However since it is readily decomposed, the oxygen released from it supports the combustion of a burning splinter, burning phosphorous and burning sulphur.

$$C + 2N_2O = CO_2 + 2N_2$$

$$S + 2N_2O = SO_2 + 2N_2$$

Nitrous oxide is reduced to nitrogen when it is passed over hot copper.

$$Cu + N_2O = CuO + N_2$$

It is official in I.P.

Official Tests for Identity

1. A glowing wood splinter bursts into flame when introduced into the gas.
2. The gas is not absorbed by alkaline pyrogallol solution.

Tests for Purity

The following are the tests for purity prescribed in the I.P. for nitrous oxide :-

1. Acidity or alkalinity
2. Arsine and phosphine
3. Carbon dioxide
4. Carbon monoxide
5. Halogens and hydrogen sulphide
6. Nitric oxide and nitrogen dioxide
7. Oxidising substances
8. Water

Acidity or alkalinity is tested for in the same way as for oxygen. So see the test for purity in oxygen.

Arsine and phosphine are detected by passing the sample gas through a mercuric chloride paper attached to a glass tube as in the limit test for arsenic (see the Chapter on "Impurities and Limit Tests").

Carbon dioxide is tested by passing the gas through barium hydroxide solution. Any turbidity produced should not be more intense than that produced by adding the prescribed quantiy of sodium bicarbonate in carbon dioxide-free water to barium hydroxide solution.

See the test for purity for *carbon monoxide* in carbon dioxide. This is the same for nitrous oxide also.

Halogens and hydrogen sulphide are tested by passing the gas through a dilute solution of silver nitrate. Neither opalesence nor darkening is produced. If opalescence is produced, it is due to the presence of halides which produce the corresponding silver halides

226

Similarly darkening indicates hydrogen sulphide which forms the silver sulphide.

Nitric oxide and nitrogen dioxide are limited by a spectrophotometric test. First the higher oxides of nitrogen are oxidised to nitrous acid which is used to diazotise sulphanilic acid in acetic acid. Then it is coupled with N-1(1-naphthyl) ethylenediamine dihydrochloride in acetic acid. The colour obtained in the solution is compared with the colour obtained by adding a specified quantity of sodium nitrite to the reagent solution containing sulphanilic acid in glacial acetic acid mixed with N-(1-naphthyl) ethylenediamine dihydrochloride. Any red colour in the sample solution should not be more intense than that in the reference solution.

Oxidising substances are tested by passing the gas through potassium iodide solution containing a little starch. No (blue) colour is produced. Here oxidizing substances oxidise potassium iodide to iodine which gives the blue colour with starch.

Standard : Nitrous oxide contains not less than 95 percent v/v of N_2O in the gaseous phase.

Assay : In this assay also a special apparatus is used. The essence of this assay is that nitrous oxide is condensed by using liquid nitrogen and the non-condensible volume of the gas is measured.

Storage : Nitrous oxide is stored under compression in metal cyclinders of the type conforming to the appropriate safety regulations and at a temperature not exceeding 37⁰C. The cylinder is painted blue and carries a label with the name of the gas or N_2O which is also painted on the shoulder of the cylinder.

Medicinal and Pharmaceutical Uses

Medical Gas. General anaesthetic (inhalation) and analgesic.

It is a good inhalation anaesthetic which also acts as a good analgesic. It is used to carry out minor operations such as tooth ~~ctions and removal of boils and abscesses. It is also used for calming excited mental patients. It is used in a concentration of 60-80% along with oxygen in a concentration of 20-40%. Since it does not combine with haemoglobin, nitrous oxide is also used to measure the cerebral and coronary blood flow.

Nitrogen as such is not official either in the I.P. or the B.P. but it is widely used as an antioxidant and in the manufacture of many nitrogenous compounds.

4. NITROGEN, N_2

Nitrogen occurs in the atmosphere to the extent of 79 percent. It also occurs in large quantities as white salt petre ($NaNO_3$). Combined with hydrogen it occurs as ammonia and also in organic combination as proteins, aminoacids, alkaloids etc., in plant and animal tissues. It is also present as nitrates in the soil formed by the soil bacteria such as the nitrifying bacteria.

Preparation : Nitrogen may be obtained either by removing the oxygen from the atomspheric air or by decomposing compounds in which it may occur.

Oxygen may be removed from the atmospheric air by any one of the following methods:

(a) Burning phosphorus in air in a closed container.

(b) Passing air over red-hot copper filings.

(c) Passsing air through a solution of sodium hydrosulphite ($Na_2S_2O_4$) which will absorb oxygen.

(d) Shaking an alkaline solution of pyrogallol with air. Alkaline solution of pyrogallol absorbs oxygen.

Nitrogen may also be prepared by fractional distillation of liquid air.

Chemically nitrogen is also prepared by oxidation of ammonia with red hot copper oxide.

$$2NH_3 + 3CuO = N_2 + 3H_2O + 3Cu$$

Physical and Chemical Properties

Nitrogen is a colourless, odourless and tasteless gas. It is slightly lighter than air. It is only slightly soluble in water. It is not poisonous but

228

animals die in an atmosphere of nitrogen for lack of oxygen. It can be liquefied to a colourless liquid boiling at $-195.8^{0}C$. Nitrogen neither burns itself nor supports combustion.

Nitrogen is a very inert gas. It combines with other elements only with difficulty. With oxygen it combines only in the presence of lightning or when the mixture is passed through an electric arc.

$$N_2 + O_2 \rightleftharpoons 2NO$$

With hydrogen it combines under a pressure of 200-900 atmospheres and in the presence of a catalyst made of finely divided iron and molybdenum at $452^{0}C$.

$$N_2 + 3H_2 \rightleftharpoons 2NH_3$$

Even though nitrogen is non-combustible and is also not a supporter of combustion, burning magnesium or aluminium continues to burn in an atmosphere of nitrogen forming the corresponding nitride.

$$3Mg + N_2 = Mg_3N_2$$
$$\text{Magnesium nitride}$$

If the ash containing the nitride is moistened with water, the nitride is hydrolysed and the ammonia formed can be tested with red litmus.

$$Mg_3N_2 + 6H_2O = 3Mg(OH)_2 + 2NH_3\uparrow$$

Tests for Identity
1. Nitrogen is colourless, odourless and tasteless.
2. Nitrogen has no action on litmus and lime water.
3. The flame of a burning wood splinter when introduced into nitrogen is extinguished (put out).
4. Burning magnesium ribbon continues to burn in a jar of nitrogen.

Storage : Since nitrogen is a gas, it must be stored under pressure in a gas cyclinder tightly closed.

Medicinal and Pharmaceutical Uses : Its usual pharmaceutical use is to retard or prevent oxidation by providing an inert atmosphere in the containers containing certain medicaments such as ergometrine injection, some vitamin preparations and some fish liver oils. In these containers, the air is replaced by nitrogen.

It is also used for filling electric lamps. It is used in the manufacture of ammonia, nitric acid, calcium cyanamide and other nitrogen compounds. Liquid nitrogen is used to freeze water etc. Mercury thermometers used above 200^0C have nitrogen filled above the mercury column to decrease the evaporation of mercury and also to prevent its oxidation.

5. HELIUM, He

Helium is an inert gas present in the atmosphere to the extent of 0.000037% w/w. It is present in a concentration of 2% in the natural gas obtained from Canada and U.S.A. It is also present in ores of some radioactive elements such as uranium and thorium. Whatever may be the source, helium is always present in the free state.

Preparation : First a mixture of noble or inert gases is isolated from air which should have been already freed from dust, carbon dioxide, water vapour etc.,

For this purpose dry air is passed over heated copper when oxygen in the air is removed as copper oxide. Next the air is passed over heated magnesium which removes nitrogen as magnesium nitride. These two procedures are repeated again and again till oxygen and nitrogen are completely removed and the residual air is only a mixture of noble gases.

These noble gases are separated by using coconut charcoal which adsorbs each gas at a different temperature. The mixture of noble gases is sent into a double-walled glass bulb containing coconut charcoal placed in a bath at 373K and allowed to remain in contact with the charcoal for about half an hour. At this temperature, argon, krypton and xenon are adsorbed whereas neon and helium are unadsorbed. However when this mixture of neon and helium is allowed to remain in contact with another sample of coconut charcoal at 93K, only neon is adsorbed and helium is left free.

Helium can also be obtained by fractionation of liquid air. Liquid helium boils at 4K. It can also be obtained from natural petroleum gas by liquefaction and rectification at low temperatures. Helium is also obtained by heating monazite (mineral of thorium found abundantly in Kerala and Kanyakumari district of Tamilnadu) to 1273K or by heating with dilute sulphuric acid or KHSO4 and passing the gas over potassium hydroxide solution to free it from carbon dioxide.

Properties: Helium is a colorless, odourless and tasteless gas. After hydrogen it is the lightest substance known. It has a solubility of 1 in 72 in water. It is monatomic and can be liquefied under pressure.It is adsorbed by coconut charcoal at a low temperature.

Liquid helium exhibits some unusual properties. If helium is cooled below 2.18K, a new form of He called HeII is obtained. It exhibits unusual properties and is called as *degenerate gas or superfluid.* It behaves like a solid but with the properties of a gas. Its viscosity is very low and it flows in thin films of a few hundred atoms thick without friction. Its thermal conductivity is very high. It is able to rise against gravity and flow over the top of the container in which it is kept.

Helium was last official in B.P.1958.

Tests for Purity
　　1. Acidity or alkalinity
　　2. Oxidising substances
　　3. Reducing substances
　　4. Carbanaceous compounds
　　5. Specific gravity

Acidity or alkalinity and oxidising substances comply with the tests given under nitrous oxide.

For testing for *reducing substances* the gas is passed through a dilute solution of potassium permanganate. The colour should not be completely discharged.

Carbanaceous compounds are tested by passing the gas over activated copper heated to 600°C and then through barium hydroxide solution. Any carbanaceous compound present is oxidized to carbon dioxide which produces turbidity in the barium hydroxide solution. The turbidity is matched against a standard.

Specific gravity is determined by weighing a sample of the gas in a glass bulb.

Standard: Helium contains not less than 98% v/v of He.

Assay: Since likely impurities in helium such as nitrogen can be adsorbed by coconut charcoal cooled by liquid oxygen, a sample of the gas is introduced into a glass bulb containing coconut charcoal cooled by liquid oxygen. The unabsorbed gas (helium) is pumped out and measured.

Storage: Helium is kept at a pressure of 132 atmospheres i.e., at 2000 lbs per sq.inch in a metallic cylinder capable of withstanding pressure in a cool,dry place, The body and valve end of the gas cylinder should be painted brown. Cylinders containing oxygen and helium mixtures should have the body painted black and the valve end painted white and brown.

Medicinal and Other Uses

Medical Gas. A mixture of helium (79%) and oxygen (21%) is administered in cases of respiratory distress like asthma because helium offers less resistance than nitrogen.

Because of its lightness and non-inflammability, helium is used for inflating tyres of aeroplanes and for filling balloons.

CHAPTER 13
MAJOR INTRA AND EXTRA-CELLULAR ELECTROLYTES

Water forms the major part of the human body mass. Thus while the male contains about 60 per cent of water, the female contains about 51 per cent. This water is divided in the body into two major compartments-the extracelluar fluid (ECF) and the intracellular fluid (ICF). The ECF is further subdivided into intravascular fluid (plasma) which is present inside the blood vessels and the extravascular fluid outside the blood vessels which comprises of interstitial fluid, lymph etc. Intracellular fluid is the fluid present within the cells. Almost all cell membranes are freely permeable to water, that is they allow the passage of water freely.

ELECTROLYTE BALANCE

The plasma (that is, the blood) is in equilibrium with the extra cellular fluid outside the blood vessels known as the interstitial fluid. The, endothelium (membrane) of the blood vessels acts as a semipermeable membrane and allows the passage of water and most of the solutes in the blood.

Electrolytes are inorganic salts present in solution as charged ions that is, cations (positively charged) and anions (negatively charged). They are present in blood and maintain the osmotic pressure of the blood. Because of this osmotic pressure there is no passage of water across the cell membrane. Therefore it is essential that the osmotic pressure be maintained at a particular level so that blood may flow within the blood vessels without being attracted via the cell membrane into the interstitial fluid (extravascular fluid).

Actually the cell membrane separates two fluids (blood and interstitial fluid) of different composition but which have equal osmotic pressure. The plasma contains a large quantity of sodium ions and a

233

small quantity each of potassium, calcium and magnesium ions. The anions present include a good amount of chloride and bicarbonate and a small quantity of phosphate, organic anions and some amount of proteins. The table given below gives the actual quantity of the ions present in plasma in mEq/litre.

Electrolytes Present in Plasma

Cations (mEq/l)		Anions (mEq/l)	
Sodium	135-145	Chloride	98-106
Potassium	3.5-5	Bicarbonate	24-28
Calcium	4.5-5.3	Phosphate	2-5
Magnesium	1.5-2.0	Organic anions	3-6
		Proteins	15-20

Even though the cations and anions present in plasma help to maintain its osmotic pressure, their contribution in this regard is rather insignificant. The concentration of proteins in plasma is about 6 to 7 g in 100 ml and being unionised large molecules, the proteins help to maintain sufficient oncotic pressure, that is, osmotic pressure contributed by large molecules such as the colloids like proteins.

The volume of the extracellular fluid (ECF) including blood, its electrolyte concentration and its osmotic pressure are maintained within narrow limits. If this balance is disturbed in any way due to vomiting, diarrhoea or haemorrhage or any other condition leading to the accumulation or depletion of any or some of the ions, this should be rectified by administering the solution suitable for meeting the situation as given below:

1. Volume depletion (loss of sodium and water)

Here there is loss of fluid leading to dehydration. This may be caused by vomiting, diarrhoea or haemorrhage. This can be treated by using sodium chloride injection (0.9%) or balanced isotonic electrolyte solutions to restore the extracellular fluid volume.

2. Hypernatremia (loss of water in excess of sodium)

This may result from reduced intake of water or unusual water loss. Since water has been lost, there is an increase of osmotic pressure in both ECF and ICF. The best way of treat this condition is to give 5% dextrose injection to replace the water lost.

3. Hyponatremia (loss of sodium in excess of water)

This may result from conditions such as adrenocortical insufficiency, excessive sweating etc. This can be treated by giving sodium chloride injection (0.9%).

4. Oedema (Volume excess)

This is due to accumulation of excess of fluid in the interstitial space with salt retention. This is seen in patients with congestive heart failure, kidney disease etc. Diuretics are used to treat this condition.

From the above discussion, it should be clear that electrolyte balance of the extracellular fluid may be disturbed at times due to various reasons and it can be restored by administering the solutions of suitable electrolytes. The most important of these electrolytes are so--dium chloride, potassium chloride and their preparations.

1. SODIUM CHLORIDE, NaCl

Preparation

(a) From Sea Water: Sea water contains about 3 per cent of sodium chloride in addition to other substances. At high tide the sea water is allowed to flow into the shallow ponds where the less soluble material and suspended matters precipitate out. It then goes to the crystallizing pond. There it is evaporated so that the crystallized salt separates out. In the next pans, the more soluble salts such as magnesium sulphate, potassium iodide etc. are removed. The calcium and magnesium salts are removed by treating the brine with either soda ash (commercial anhydrous sodium carbonate) and lime or soda ash and caustic soda (sodium hydroxide) and allowing the precipitate to settle. The purified brine is concentrated and evaporated in triple effect evaporators.

(b) **From Underground Rock-salt Deposits:** Holes are drilled into the rock-salt beds and water is sent to run down the holes into the salt bed. The salt solution, now known as brine, is pumped to the surface and evaporated in triple effect evaporators. This is purified by a special lime soda process (refer above under method (a) and very pure sodium chloride is obtained.

(c) The purest form of salt (analytical grade) is now obtained by passing hydrogen chloride gas into a saturated solution of the salt. Very pure sodium chloride precipitates out. The crystals are centrifuged and dried.

Hydrogen chloride dissolves in water to form hydrochloric acid in which sodium chloride is only slightly soluble. The principle of solubility product also comes into play.

Physical Properties

Sodium chloride occurs in the form of colourless, transparent cubes or as a white, crystalline powder. It is odourless and has a saline taste. It is slightly hygroscopic possibly due to the presence of small amounts of magnesium or calcium chloride. It is freely soluble in water (1 in 2.8) and slightly soluble in alcohol.

Chemical Properties

1. Sodium chloride gives a curdy white precipitate of silver chloride with solution of silver nitrate:

   $$NaCl + AgNO_3 \longrightarrow AgCl\downarrow + NaNO_3$$

   The precipitate which is affected by light (i.e., photosensitive) is soluble in dilute ammonia and insoluble in nitric acid.

2. It reacts with sulphuric acid or phosphoric acid to give hydrochloric acid.

   $$2NaCl + H_2SO_4 \longrightarrow 2HCl + Na_2SO_4$$

236

3. Sodium chloride is rather easily oxidized to liberate free chlorine. For eg. heating with manganese dioxide and concentrated sulphuric acid produces chlorine.

$$2NaCl + MnO_2 + 2H_2SO_4 \longrightarrow MnSO_4 + Na_2SO_4 + 2H_2O + Cl_2$$

Electrolytic oxidation of sodium chloride (solution of sodium chloride) is useful in the production of sodium hydroxide and chlorine. It is official in I.P.

Official Tests for Identity

Give the reactions characteristic of sodium and of chlorides (see Chapter 18).

Tests for Purity

1. Acidity or alkalinity.
2. Arsenic
3. Iron
4. Heavy metals
5. Calcium and magnesium
6. Barium
7. Ferrocyanide
The above impurities might have been derived from the crude salt which is purified to give the official substance.
8. Loss on drying.
9. Iodide. Present in salt obtained from sea water.
10. Bromide.

Calcium and magnesium are determined by a complexometric titration with EDTA using eriochrome black T as indicator.

Bromide is limited by adding to an aqueous solution of the sample phenol red and chloramine solutions followed by sodium thiosulphate solution. Any violet colour produced should not be more intense than that of a solution of standard potassium bromide solution similarly treated.

237

Iodide is limited by adding to an aqueous solution starch solution, dilute sulphuric acid and sodium nitrite solution. No blue colour is produced. If iodide is present, it is oxidised by nitrous acid to iodine which will give blue colour with starch.

Ferrocyanide is tested by adding to an aqueous solution ferric ammonium sulphate in sulphuric acid and ferrous sulphate solution. Nc blue colour (due to Prussian blue) is produced within ten minutes.

Standard: Contains between 99.5 and 100.5 per cent of NaCl calculated with reference to the dried substance.

Assay: An accurately weighted quantity is dissolved in water and a known excess of 0.1M silver nitrate solution, dilute nitric acid and dibutyl phthalate are added. It is titrated with 0.1M ammonium thiocynate solution using ferric ammonium sulphate as indicator.

This is a modified Volhard's method. Sodium chloride is precipitated as silver chloride by the addition silver nitrate. Dibutylphthalate is added to coat the silver chloride so that it will not interfere with the titration of the excess of silver nitrate with 0.1M ammonium thiocyanate, since silver chloride reacts slowly with ammonium thiocyanate.

Previously (in I.P. 66) sodium chloride was assayed by direct titration in neutral solution with 0.1N silver nitrate using potassium chromate as indicator. The same cannot be used now since silvei chromate formed at the end point is soluble in acid.

$$AgNO_3 + NaCl = AgCl \downarrow + NaNO_3$$
$$AgNO_3 + NH_4SCN = AgSCN + NH_4NO_3$$

Storage: Since it may be slightly hygroscopic due to the presence of small amounts of calcium or magnesium chloride, store in tightly closed containers.

Medicinal Uses: *Electrolyte Replenisher.* Sodium chloride exerts the effect of both the chloride ion and the sodium ion. Deficiency of sodium chloride leads to "salt hunger".

It is used as a *fluid and electrolyte replenisher* in the form of various solutions such as Sodium Chloride Injection (Normal Saline), Compound Sodium Chloride Injection, Sodium Chloride Hypertonic Injection, Compound Sodium Chloride Solution and Sodiium Chloride and Dextrose Injection.

2. OFFICIAL PREPARATIONS OF SODIUM CHLORIDE

The following preparations of sodium chloride are official in the I.P. and are used to restore fluid and electrolyte balance in the body.

(a) Sodium Chloride Injection, I.P. *(Normal Saline)*

This is a sterile, isotonic solution of sodium chloride in water for injection. It contains 0.9%w/v of sodium chloride (150 millimoles each of sodium and chloride ions).

Storage: The injection should be stored in single dose containers made of glass or plastic. On keeping, small solid particles may separate in a glass container. Such an injection having such visible glass particles should not be used. A caution to this effect should be given on the label.

Medicinal Use: *Fluid and electrolyte replenisher and isotonic vehicle.*

(b) Sodium Chloride Hypertonic Injection, I.P. *(Hypertonic Saline)*

This is a sterile, hypertonic solution of sodium chloride in water for injection. It contains 1.60%w/v of sodium chloride or 270 millimoles each of sodium and chloride ions per litre.

Storage: The injection should be stored in single dose containers made of glass or plastic. On keeping small solid particles may separate in a glass container. Such an injection having such visible glass particles should not be used. A caution to this effect should be given on the label.

Medicinal Use: *Fluid and electrolyte replenisher.* Since this is a hypertonic injection, it should be given intravenously very slowly. It is administered when there is a severe electrolyte imbalance. Hypertonic saline is also used as a *sclerosing agent* for varicose veins.

(c) Compound Sodium Chloride Injection, I.P. (Ringer's Injection)

This contains 0.86% w/v of sodium chloride, 0.03% w/v of potassium chloride and 0.033% w/v of calcium chloride in water for injection, that is, it contains 147.5 mEq. (millequivalents) of sodium, 4 mEq of potassium, 4.5 mEq of calcium and 156 mEq of chloride ions per litre.

Storage: The injection should be stored in single-dose containers made of glass or plastic. When it is kept in glass containers, small solid particles may separate out. A solution containing such glass particles should not be used. A caution to this effect should be given on the label.

Medicinal Use: *Fluid and electrolyte replenisher.*

(d) Compound Sodium Chloride Solution, I.P. (Ringer's Solution)

This solution is a sterile solution of sodium chloride, potassium chloride and calcium chloride in purified water. It contains these salts in the same proportions as in the Compound Sodium Chloride Injection, I.P.

Storage: It should be stored in tightly-closed containers.

Medicinal Use: *Irrigation solution for external use.*

(e) Sodium Chloride and Dextrose Injection, I.P.

This is a sterile solution of sodium chloride and dextrose in water for injection. It may contain any strength of sodium chloride from 0.11% to 0.45% w/v and correspondingly from 5% to 2.5% w/v of dextrose so that the solution will be isotonic. About seven different solutions containing the quantities of sodium chloride and dextrose as given in the I.P. can be made subject to the condition that all the solutions should be isotonic.

Storage: The injection should be stored in single-dose containers in a cool place. Small solid particles may separate on keeping and such an injection should not be used. A caution to this effect should be given on the label.

Medicinal Use: *Fluid nutrient and electrolyte replenisher.* If the patient is also weak and his nutritional status is to be toned up, this injection containing dextrose in addition to sodium chloride may be administered.

Potassium

Potassium is the major intracellular cation. It is also present in plasma in a concentration of 3.4 to 5.6 mEq/l. Potassium is necessary for muscle contraction, enzyme action, nerve conduction and cell membrane function. It is also necessary for the proper functioning of the heart. Treatment with diuretics is the most common cause of hypokalaemia or depletion of potassium in the body. It is treated by giving potassium chloride which should be administered cautiously. Compound Sodium Chloride Injection, I.P. is used when other ions such as sodium and chloride are also to be supplemented.

Calcium

Calcium is present mostly in the ECF and its concentration in ECF is maintained within narrow limits by three factors:-
a) Release from or deposition on the bone
b) Tubular reabsorption in the kidney
c) Absorption from the intestine
In the plasma calcium is present mostly in the ionic state and also present bound to plasma proteins and also as the calcium salts of organic acids. Of these the ionic calcium is the most active and its absorption from the gut is regulated by the secretion of the parathyroid hormone and calcitonin. About 10 mg per cent of calcium is present in the human plasma.

However the content of intracellular calcium is comparatively very low, only 0.5 to 4 mcg per 100 ml. It is necessary for the proper

241

functioning of the metabolic processes in the cells and also necessary for the contraction of the muscles and for the proper secretion in the endocrine glands. Calcium is also essential for the formation of bones and teeth and for the coagulation of blood.

The usual causes of hypocalcaemia (low level of calcium in the ECF) may be due to vitamin D deficiency, hypoparathyroidism or chronic renal failure.

Phosphorus

Phosphorus occurs abundantly in cereals, pulses, fish, meat, milk and nuts. It is present in the body mostly in bones and to a small extent as inorganic ATP. Red blood cells contain more phosphorus than plasma. In the plasma it is present as inorganic phosphates, as esters of phosphoric acid and as phospholipids. It is necessary in all chemical reactions where phosphorylation, that is combination with phosphoric acid, takes place. It is also present in bone along with calcium as calcium phosphate. It is part of the structure of nucleus and cytoplasm in cells. Phosphates are involved in the regulation of the pH of the ECF. Energy is stored in the body in the form of phosphate bonds. ,

Magnesium

Magnesium is mostly present in bones, a small quantity (about 1%) in the ECF and the rest in the mitochondria of cells. In the plasma, the concentration of magnesium is between 1.5 and 2.5 mEq and about one third of this is bound to plasma proteins.

Magnesium is important for many enzyme actions and for coenzymes. Its effects are in many ways similar to that of calcium. Parenteral fluids containing magnesium as chloride or sulphate may be administered to treat chronic alcoholism.

3. POTASSIUM CHLORIDE, KCl

Preparation : (1) It is prepared from *carnallite* ($MgCl_2.KCl.6H_2O$). Along with carnallite, sodium chloride and magnesium sulphate also occur. So a process of fractional crystallisation is carried out and after removing the insoluble impurities, potassium chloride is crystallized out.

(2) Potassium chloride can also be prepared by adding potassium carbonate to hydrochloric acid and evaporating to crystallization.

$$K_2CO_3 + 2HCl = 2KCl + CO_2\uparrow + H_2O$$

Physical and Chemical Properties

Potassium chloride occurs as colourless, elongated, prismatic or cubical crystals or as a white, granular powder. It is odourless and has a saline taste. It is stable in air. It decrepitates on heating and sublimes when heated to the red hot condition. It is freely soluble in water and practically insoulble in alcohol and ether. An aqueous solution·of potassium chloride is neutral to litmus.

It has the same chemical properties as that of sodium chloride. It is official in I.P.

Official Tests for Identity

An aqueous solution gives the reactions of potassium and of chlorides. See Chapter 18.

Tests for Purity

1. Acidity or alkalinity.
2. Clarity and colour of solution
3. Bromides
4. Heavy metals
5. Arsenic
6. Barium
7. Iron
8. Sulphate
9. Loss on drying
10. Iodides
11. Calcium and magnesium

Bromides and Iodides: The tests are the same as for bromides and iodides in sodium chloride. Refer tests for purity for sodium chloride.

Calcium and magnesium are tested by adding dilute ammonia and sodium phosphate solutions. The solution should remain clear. If these impurities are present, opalescence due to calcium phosphate and magnesium ammonium phosphate will develop.

Standard: It contains not less than 99 per cent and not more than 100.5 per cent of KCl, calculated with reference to the dried substance.

Assay: By Mohr's method. An accurately weighed quantity is dissolved in water and titrated with 0.1M silver nitrate, using potassium chromate solution as indicator. Appearance of a pale red colour is the end point.

$$KCl + AgNO_3 = KNO_3 + AgCl\downarrow$$

Storage: Store in well-closed containers.

Medicinal Use: *Electrolyte replenisher.*

It is used along with sodium chloride and calcium chloride in Compound Sodium Chloride Injection, I.P. (Ringer's Injection) and Compound Sodium Chloride Solution, I.P. (Ringer's Solution) for restoring electrolyte balance. However potassium chloride solution irritates the gastric mucosa and may cause ulceration. So it must be well diluted before oral administration. It is also used as a diuretic and to treat hypopotassaemia (depletion of potassium in the body).

4. OFFICIAL PREPARATIONS OF POTASSIUM CHLORIDE

The following are the official preparations of potassium chloride

1. Compound Sodium Chloride Injection, I.P.
2. Compound Sodium Chloride Solution, I.P.

Refer under Sodium Chloride.

5. CALCIUM CHLORIDE, $CaCl_2.2H_2O$

Preparation : The hexahydrate is prepared first by adding a slight excess of pure calcium carbonate to hot, diluted hydrochloric acid and filtering after the effervescence ceases. The mixture is evaporated to a syrup and allowed to crystallize at a temperature below 10°C. The crystals are separated by suction and put into stoppered bottles. When this hexahydrate is heated to 200°C, it forms the dihydrate.

$$CaCO_3 + 2HCl + 6H_2O \longrightarrow CaCl_2.6H_2O + CO_2\uparrow + H_2O$$

Physical and Chemical Properties: Calcium chloride occurs as a white, crystalline powder or as hard fragments or granules. It is odourless and has a sharp, bitter, saline taste. It is deliquescent, that is, it absorbs moisture from the air rapidly and dissolves in the water forming a solution. It is freely soluble in cold water and very soluble in boiling water.

Calcium chloride normally forms several hydrates such as the monohydrate ($CaCl_2.H_2O$), the dihydrate ($CaCl_2.2H_2O$), the tetra hydrate ($CaCl_2.4H_2O$), and the hexahydrate ($CaCl_2.6H_2O$). All the hydrates lose water when heated and form a porous mass with variable water content. This porous mass, commonly but erroneously known as fused calcium chloride, is used for drying gases and liquids. Since it forms crystalline compounds with alcohols and ammonia gas, it is unsuitable to serve as drying agent for them. It is official in I.P.

Official Tests for Identity: An aqueous solution of the substance gives the reactions of calcium and of chlorides (refer Chapter 18).

Tests for Purity

1. Clarity and colour of solution
2. Acidity or alkalinity
3. Arsenic
4. Heavy metals
5. Aluminium and phosphate
6. Magnesium and alkali salts
7. Iron
8. Barium
9. Sulphate

Clarity and colour of solution has been prescribed to eliminate the possibility of the presence of any unreacted calcium carbonate from the method of preparation. A 10% w/v solution of the sample in water should be clear and colourless.

Aluminium and phosphate can be detected by adding to a solution of the sample dilute hydrochloric acid and phenolphthalein indicator and adding ammonia-ammonium chloride solution to neutralization and then in excess. The liquid is heated to boiling. No turbidity or precipitate is produced. Any aluminium present will be precipitated as aluminium hydroxide along with the phosphate.

Magnesium and alkali salts are tested by the same method which is used for calcium carbonate. See calcium carbonate.

Standard: Calcium chloride contains between 97 and 103 per cent of $CaCl_2.2H_2O$.

Assay: An accurately weighed quantity is dissolved in water and the solution is titrated with 0.05 M EDTA and adding just before the end point is reached sodium hydroxide solution and calcon mixture used as the indicator. The end point is marked by a change of colour from pink to full blue. This is a complexometric assay.

Storage: Since it is very deliquescent absorbing moisture from the atmosphere and dissolves in the water absorbed forming a solution, store in tightly closed containers.

Medicinal Use: *Calcium replenisher.* It is used in combinatiion with sodium chloride and potassium chloride in Compound Sodium Chloride Injection I.P. (Ringer's Injection) and Compound Sodium Chloride Solution, I.P. (Ringer's Solution).

6. CALCIUM GLUCONATE,
$[HOCH_2(CHOH)_4COO]_2Ca.H_2O$

Preparation: Calcium gluconate may be prepared by the oxidation of glucose to gluconic acid in the presence of calcium carbonate. The oxidation may be carried out either by bromine or by electrolytic oxidation with sodium bromide. An alternative method will be to prepare the gluconic acid first and then react it with calcium carbonate in boiling condition.

$$2HOCH_2-(CHOH)_4-COOH + CaCO_3 =$$
Gluconic acid

$$[HOCH_2-(CHOH)_4-COO]_2 Ca + CO_2\uparrow + H_2O$$
Calcium gluconate

Physical and Chemical Properties: Calcium gluconate occurs as a white, crystalline or granular powder. It is tasteless and odourless. It is stable in air. It loses its water of crystallization with decomposition above 100°C. It is soluble in cold water, freely soluble in boiling water and insoluble in ethyl alcohol, chloroform and solvent ether.

Calcium gluconate is decomposed by mineral acids to form gluconic acid which on dehydration forms the D-gluconolactone.

$$[HOCH_2 — (CHOH)_4 COO]_2 Ca + 2HCl$$

Cal. gluconate

$$\downarrow$$

$$HOCH_2(CHOH)_4COOH + CaCl_2$$

Gluconic acid

$$\downarrow -H_2O$$

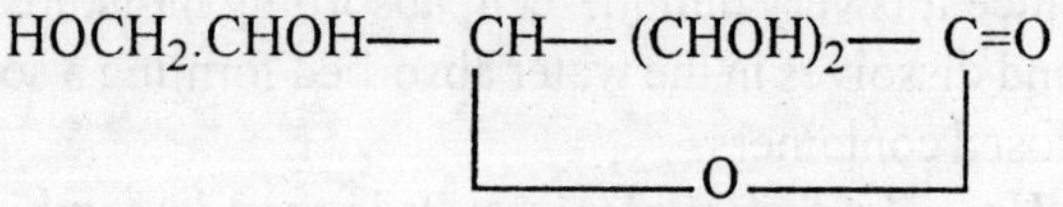

$$HOCH_2.CHOH— \underset{\underset{O}{\rule{6cm}{0.4pt}}}{CH— (CHOH)_2— C=O}$$

D - Gluconolactone

Calcium gluconate is official in I.P.

Official Tests for Identity

1. Gives the reactions characteristic of calcium (see Chapter 18).

2. To a solution of the substance in water, ferric chloride solution is added. A yellow colour is produced.

3. Complies with a thin layer chromatographic (TLC) identification test.

Tests for Purity

1. Clarity and colour of solution
2. Acidity or alkalinity
3. Arsenic
4. Heavy metals
5. Chloride
6. Sulphate
7. Sucrose and reducing sugars

Sucrose and reducing sugars such as dextrose may be present since gluconic acid is made by fermentation of sugar solutions. In this test any sucrose present is inverted by boiling a solution of the sample with dilute hydrochloric acid and adding potassium cupritartrate solution and boiling. No red precipitate is produced.

Standard: Contains not less than 98.5 per cent and not more than the equivalent of 102 per cent of $C_{12}H_{22}O_{14}Ca, H_2O$ (calcium gluconate).

Assay: This is complexometric assay. An accurately weighed quantity is dissolved in warm water and a definite quantity of 0.05 M magnesium sulphate solution and strong ammonia solution are added. The mixture is titrated with M/20 disodium ethylenediaminetetraacetate (EDTA or disodium salt of ethylenediaminetetraacetic acid or sodium edetate) using mordant black mixture as indicator. A blank titration taking only the definite quantity of 0.05M magnesium sulphate solution is done and this blank titre value is subtracted from the titre value earlier obtained for the assay.

Strong ammonia solution is added to raise and maintain the pH at 10, because at this pH only complexation takes place. Magnesium is added to give the indicator action, since the indicator does not give the wine red colour with calcium but only with magnesium. First calcium is complexed by EDTA and finally magnesium. The end point is the appearance of blue colour. The complexation of calcium by EDTA is given below :

Calcium - EDTA Complex

Storage : Store in well-closed container.

Medicinal and Pharmaceutical Use : *Electrolyte replenisher.* Calcium gluconate is administered in the form of tablets or injection in case of calcium deficiency.

7. CALCIUM LACTATE, $[CH_3.CH(OH)COO]_2 Ca, xH_2O]$

Preparation

1. Calcium lactate is prepared by adding a slight excess of calcium carbonate to hot, dilute lactic acid and boiling the mixture for at least half an hour. The boiling converts the anhydrides of lactic acid, that is lactide and lactyl-lactic acid, into lactic acid which, along with the free lactic acid, reacts with the calcium carbonate to form calcium lactate.

$$CaCO_3 + 2CH_3. CHOH. COOH = [CH_3. CH(OH). COO]_2 Ca + CO_2\uparrow + H_2O$$

The hot liquid is filtered and the filtrate is evaporated till crystallization takes place.

2. Calcium lactate may also be prepared by fermentation of a monosaccharide in milk with lactic acid bacilli and allowing the lactic acid formed to react with the added chalk (prepared calcium carbonate). Putrid (decomposing) cheese is the source for lactic acid bacilli. The mixture is allowed to ferment for two weeks at 30°C and the calcium lactate obtained is purified by recrystallization.

$$C_6H_{12}O_6 = 2CH_3CH(OH)COOH$$

Monosaccharide   Lactic acid

$$2CH_3CH(OH)COOH + CaCO_3 = [CH_3CH(OH)COO]_2 Ca + CO_2\uparrow + H_2O$$

Physical and Chemical Properties : Calcium lactate occurs as a nearly odourless white powder or as white granules without taste. It is somewhat efflorescent. When heated at about 120°C, it loses its water molecules and becomes anhydrous. It is soluble in cold water and readily soluble in hot water.

As far as chemical properties are concerned, it answers all the reactions of calcium and lactate. It is official in I.P.

Official Tests for Identity

1. An aqueous solution gives the reactions of calcium and of lactates. See Chapter 18.

2. An aqueous solution is acidified with sulphuric acid and warmed with potassium permanganate. It develops the odour of acetaldehyde. Sulphuric acid hydrolyses the calcium lactate to lactic acid which is oxidised to acetaldehyde by the potassium permanganate. The permanganate oxidation leads to fission of the molecule with consequent formation of acetaldehyde and carbon dioxide.

$$CH_3CH(OH)COOH \overset{O}{=} CH_3CHO + CO_2 + H_2O$$

Tests for Purity

1. Acidity or alkalinity
2. Arsenic
3. Iron
4. Heavy metals
5. Chloride
6. Sulphate
7. Reducing sugars
8. Loss on drying

Reducing sugars are limited by adding Fehling's solution (potassium cupri-tartrate solution) to an aqueous solution of the sample and boiling. Not more than a slight brick-red precipitate is produced. This means that a small amount of reducing sugars is permitted to be present. It can be seen that under method (2) of preparation, only a monosaccharide is converted by fermentation into lactic acid. Therefore a higher limit for reducing sugars is prescribed.

Standard: Contains between 98 per cent and 101 per cent of $C_6H_{10}CaO_6$, calculated with reference to the anhydrous substance.

Assay: Same as for calcium gluconate.

Storage: Since it is slightly efflorescent, store in tightly-closed containers.

Medicinal use: *Calcium replenisher.* It is given in the form of tablets.

8. DIBASIC CALCIUM PHOSPHATE

See Chapter 11.

9. TRIBASIC CALCIUM PHOSPHATE, $Ca_3(PO_4)_2$

Preparation: Tribasic calcium phosphate is prepared by the reaction between calcium chloride and secondary sodium phosphate in the presence of ammonia.

$$3CaCl_2 + 2Na_2HPO_4 + 2NH_4OH = Ca_3(PO_4)_2 + 4NaCl + 2NH_4Cl + 2H_2O$$

| Secondary sodium phosphate | Tribasic calcium phosphate | $2H_2O$ |

The white precipitate is washed with water until free from chloride and dried at 100°C.

Physical and Chemical Properties : Tribasic calcium phosphate consists of a variable mixture of normal, basic and acid calcium phosphates. It contains calcium equivalent to not less than 90 percent of $Ca_3(PO_4)_2$ (tribasic calcium phosphate), calculated with reference to the ignited substance.

It is a bulky, white amorphous or microcrystalline powder, it is odourless and insoluble in water and alcohol. It readily dissilves in dilute nitric acid and in dilute hydrochloric acid. It dissolves in solutions of salts and also in a solution of carbon dioxide. Alkalis precipitate it from an acid solution. Since it is almost completely insoluble in water, it undergoes few chemical reactions. However it acts as an antacid through an interesting mechanism. It ionizes slighty in contact with water even though it is insoluble in water. The phosphate ion, being a strong base, combines with hydrogen ions (from the hydrochloric acid secreted

in the stomach. It also combines with water to release OH⁻ions which
also neutralise the acid.

$$Ca_3(PO_4)_2 \rightleftarrows 3Ca^{2+} + 2PO_4^{3-}$$
$$PO_4^{3-} + HCl \rightleftarrows HPO_4^{3-} + Cl^-$$
$$PO_4^{3-} + HOH \rightleftarrows HPO4^{3-} + OH^-$$

Tribasic calcium Phosphate is official in I.P.

Official Tests for Identity: Gives the reactions charcteristic of
calcium and of phosphates (see Chapter 18).

Tests for Purity
1. Acid-insoluble substances
2. Water-solube substances
3. Carbonate
4. Chloride
5. Sulphate
6. Arsenic
7. Heavy metals
8. Iron
9. Proteinous impurities - see dibasic calcium phosphate
10. Water
11. Loss on ignition

Standard: Contains not less than 90% of calcium phosphates, calcu-
lated as $Ca_3(PO_4)_2$.
Assay: Same as for dibasic calcium phosphate.
Storage: Store in a well-closed container.
Medicinal and Pharmaceutical Uses: *Electrolyte replenisher and phar-
maceutical aid (excipient).* Sometimes it is used as a gastric antacid.

ACID - BASE BALANCE

The pH of the arterial blood is maintained at 7.4 and the pH of the
venous blood and interstitial fluid at 7.35. If the pH falls below 7.0

or rises above 7.8, the person concerned will die. Generally if the pH of the ECF goes below 7.4 the condition is known as acidosis and if it goes above 7.4 it is known as alkalosis. The acid base balance is a dynamic equilibrium and it is maintained by three factors:

1. Action of chemical buffers present in the blood such as carbonic acid and sodium bicarbonate.

2. Respiration which constantly removes carbon dioxide from the body.

3. Excretion through kidney of acid as well as base.

The following are the electrolytes used for maintaining the physiological acid-base balance:-

1. SODIUM ACETATE, $CH_3COONa, 3H_2O$

Preparation: Sodium acetate is prepared by neutralising acetic acid with either sodium bicarbonate or sodium carbonate. The solution is filtered and evaporated to crystallisation.

$$CH_3COOH + NaHCO_3 \longrightarrow CH_3COONa + H_2O + CO_2\uparrow$$

$$2CH_3COOH + Na_2CO_3 \longrightarrow 2CH_3COONa + H_2O + CO_2\uparrow$$

$$CH_3COOH + NaOH = CH_3COONa + H_2O$$

Physical and Chemical Properties

Sodium acetate occurs either as colourless crystals or as a white, granular powder. It is either odourless or has a slight acetous odour. It has a slightly saline and bitter taste. It is very soluble in water. When exposed to warm, dry air, it effloresces. Along with acetic acid, it acts as a buffer. When sodium acetate is heated, it dissolves in its own water of crystallization. On further heating the water is removed and it becomes solid. By careful heating to prevent charring it is melted and poured into a clean surface. The product now obtained is known as 'fused sodium acetate' which is used for some acetylation reactions.

When a mineral acid is added to sodium acetate, acetic acid is formed and the smell of vinegar is noticed.

$$CH_3COONa + HCl = CH_3COOH + NaCl$$

$$2CH_3COONa + H_2SO_4 = 2CH_3COOH + Na_2SO_4$$

Sodium acetate warmed with sulphuric acid and ethyl alcohol, gives ethyl acetate which has a fruity odour.

$$CH_3COOH + C_2H_5OH \xrightarrow{H_2SO_4} CH_3COOC_2H_5 + H_2O$$

When sodium acetate is ignited, it is converted into sodium carbonate.

$$2CH_3COONa, 3H_2O + 4O_2 \triangleq Na_2CO_3 + 6H_2O + 3CO_2\uparrow$$

It gives a deep red colour with neutral ferric chloride. Ferric acetate is formed.

$$FeCl_3 + 3CH_3COONa \rightleftharpoons (CH_3COO)_3Fe + 3NaCl$$

It is official in I.P.

Official Tests for Identity: Sodium acetate gives the reactions of sodium and of acetates (see Chapter 18).

Non-official Tests for Identity

1. Heat the substance in a test tube. It becomes liquid and then becomes solid. Finally it fuses at a high temperature. It emits non-inflammable vapours and leaves a residue of sodium carbonate. The residue answers the tests for sodium (see Chapter 18) and gives effervescence with acids.

2. When the solution of the substance is added to Ferric Chloride, T.S., a deep red colour is produced.

Tests for Purity

1. Clarity and colour of solution
2. pH
3. Arsenic
4. Calcium and magnesium
5. Heavy metals
6. Iron

7. Chloride
8. Sulphate
9. Reducing substances
10. Loss on drying

pH of a 5% aqueous solution should be between 7.5 and 9. *Calcium and magnesium* are limited by a complexometric titration. *Reducing substances* are limited by dissolving the substance in boiling water, acidifying with dilute sulphuric acid, adding 0.01 N potassium permanganate and boiling gently for five minutes. The pink colour is not entirely discharged. Potassium permanganate oxidises any reducing substances present, itself getting reduced to a colourless substance. *Loss on drying* is determined by drying the substance at 130°C. It should be between 39 and 40 per cent.

Standard: Sodium Acetate contains between 99 and 101 per cent of $C_2H_3NaO_2$ calculated with reference to the dried substance.

Assay: The assay is by a non-aqueous titration method. An accurately weighed quantity is dissolved in glacial acetic acid and acetic anhydride is added. Then after the addition of a further quantity of glacial acetic acid, it is titrated with 0.1N perchloric acid using 1-naptholbenzein solution as indicator. A blank titration also is done.

Storage: Since it effloresces in dry, warm air, store in tightly closed containers.

Medicinal Use: *Pharmaceutical aid (for peritoneal dialysis fluids).* It is also used as a *diuretic, urinary alkalizer and systemic antacid or alkalizer.* It acts as a systemic alkalizer because it is oxidised in the body to sodium bicarbonate.

$$CH_3COONa + 4(O) = NaHCO_3 + CO_2 + H_2O$$

2. POTASSIUM ACETATE, CH_3COOK

Preparation: Potassium acetate is prepared by neutralizing acetic acid with either potassium bicarbonate or potassium carbonate until effervescence ceases. The solution is evaporated to dryness and fused. While the mass is still warm, it is reduced to powder and bottled.

$$CH_3COOH + KHCO_3 \longrightarrow CH_3COOK + H_2O + CO_2\uparrow$$

Physical and Chemical Properties: Potassium acetate occurs either as colourless crystals or as a white, crystalline powder. It is odourless. However it may have a slight acetous odour especially when it is damp. It is deliquescent which means that it absorbs moisture very rapidly when it is exposed to air and also dissolves in the water absorbed to form a solution. It is very soluble in water.

Like sodium acetate, potassium acetate also, on strong ignition, evolves volatile, non-inflammable vapours and leaves a residue of potassium carbonate.

$$2CH_3COOK + 4O_2 \triangleq K_2CO_3 + 3H_2O + 3CO_2$$

The residue is alkaline to litmus and answers tests for potassium. It also gives effervescence with acids. It is official in B.P.

Official Tests for Identity : Potasssium acetate gives the reactions characteristic of potassium, and of acetates (see Chapter 18).

Tests for Purity
1. Alkalinity
2. Aluminium and calcium
3. Arsenic
4. Heavy metals
5. Sodium
6. Chloride
7. Sulphate
8. Loss on drying

Aluminium and calcium are limited by adding to an aqueous solution of the substance dilute ammonia and ammonium oxalate solutions. No preceipitate or turbidity is produced (due to the corresponding oxalates).

Since it is a deliquescent substance, *loss on drying* is prescribed. It should lose not more than 5% of its weight when dried to constant weight at 105°C.

Standard : Potassium acetate should contain between 99 and 101 per cent of $C_2H_3O_2K$, calculated with reference to the dried substance.

Assay : Potassium acetate is carbonised by heating and the resultant potassium carbonate (see Properties) is neutralised with excess of 0.5 N sulphuric acid and the excess of acid is backtitrated with 0.5 N sodium hydroxide using methyl orange as indicator.

Storage : Since it is very deliquescent, store in tightly closed containers.

Medicinal Uses: Like sodium acetate it is also converted into bicarbonate in the body. So it acts as a *diuretic and urinary alkalizer.* It is also used in solutions for haemodialysis and peritoneal dialysis.

3. SODIUM BICARBONATE, NaHCO$_3$

Refer Chapter 9.

SODIUM BICARBONATE INJECTION

This is official as Sodium Bicarbonate Intravenous Infusion in B.P. It is a sterile solution of sodium bicarbonate in water for injection. Intravenous infusions containing 1.26,1.4,2.74,4.2,5.0 and 8.4% w/v of sodium bicarbonate are available. A preparation containing 1.4% w/v of sodium bicarbonate contains 167 millimoles each of sodium and bicarbonate ions. It is sterilised by heating in an autoclave. Containers containing visible particles should not be used.

Medicinal Use : *Systemic alkalizer.* The injection is administered intravenously to raise the pH of the blood in acidosis due to diabetes mellitus and certain other diseases.

4. POTASSIUM BICARBONATE, KHCO$_3$

Preparation : Potassium bicarbonate is prepared in the same way as sodium bicarbonate. Potassium carbonate is dissolved in water and carbon dioxide is passed through it. Potassium bicarbonate is precipitated and it is washed and dried.

$$K_2CO_3 + CO_2 + H_2O = 2KHCO_3$$

Physical Properties : Potassium bicarbonate occurs in colourless, transparent, monoclinic prisms or as a white, granular powder. It is odourless and has a feebly alkaline, saline taste.

Chemical Properties : All the chemical properties given under sodium bicarbonate are applicable to potassium bicarbonate also. It was last official in I.P. 66.

Official Tests for Identity : Gives the reactions characteric of potassium and of bicarbonates. See Chapter 18.

Tests for Purity
  1. Reaction
  2. Normal carbonate
  3. Aluminium, calcium and insoluble matter
  4. Iron
  5. Heavy metals
  6. Sodium
  7. Arsenic
  8. Chloride
  9. Sulphate

As far as *reaction* is concerned, pH of a 1% solution should not be greater than 8.6. This test is given to exclude the presence of the normal carbonate. Only a 2% limit is allowed.

The limit of *normal carbonate* is further confirmed by adding to a solution of the substance a specific volume of 0.1N hydrochlorie acid and phenolphthalein solution. If normal carbonate is present beyond the limit prescribed, it will neutralise the added acid and also give a red colour with phenolphthalein immediately. No red colour should appear immediately.

For *aluminium, calcium and insoluble matter,* dilute ammonia solution is added to an aqueous solution of the substance, filtered and washed. The insoluble residue, if any, is ignited to constant weight and weighed. The corresponding hydroxides of aluminium and calcium may be precipitated if these metals are present.

Standard : Potassium Bicarbonate contains not less than 99 percent of $KHCO_3$.

Assay : An accurately weighed quantity is dissolved in water and titrated against 0.5N sulphuric acid, using methyl orange as indicator.

$$2KHCO_3 + H_2SO_4 = K_2SO_4 + 2CO_2 + 2H_2O$$

Storage : Store in a well closed container

Medicinal Use : *Electrolyte replenisher and antacid.*

5. SODIUM CITRATE, $Na_3C_6H_5O_7.2H_2O$

Preparation : Sodium citrate us prepared by reacting a solution of citric acid with either sodium carbonate or sodium bicarbonate. The effervescence is allowed to subside and the solution is evaporated to crystallization.

$$3NaHCO_3 + H_3C_6H_5O_7. H_2O = Na_3C_6H_5O_7.2H_2O$$
$$\text{Citric acid} \qquad \text{Sod. citrate} \qquad + 2H_2O + 3CO_2\uparrow$$

Physical and Chemical Properties

Sodium citrate consists of white, granular crystals or occurs as a white, crystalline powder. It is odourless and has a cool, saline taste. It is slighty deliquescent in moist air but effloresces slowly in dry air. It is freely soluble in cold water and very soluble in boiling water. It is slightly alkaline in aqueous solution.

When heated, it starts to lose water at about 100^0C and becomes anhydrous at about 150^0C. On strong heating, it carbonizes evolving non - inflammable gases with a pungent, acid odour and leaving a residue of sodium carbonate.

$$2Na_3C_6H_5O_7. 2H_2O + 9O_2 \triangleq 3Na_2CO_3 + 5H_2O + 9CO_2\uparrow$$

Sodium citrate is the salt of a strong base with a weak acid, that is citric acid which is a tricarboxylic hydroxy acid.

$$
\begin{array}{l}
CH_2COOH \\
| \\
C(OH)COOH \\
| \\
CH_2COOH
\end{array}
+ 3NaOH ==
\begin{array}{l}
CH_2COONa \\
| \\
C(OH)COONa. 2H_2O + H_2O \\
| \\
CH_2COONa
\end{array}
$$

or $Na_3C_6H_5O_7$ $2H_2O$
Sodium citrate

259

Because of the presence of the alcoholic hydroxyl group, sodium citrate possesses the property of sequestration or complexation. When added to blood, it sequesters the blood calcium as an undissociated organic complex and thus the coagulation of blood is prevented. Sodium citrate is official in I.P.

Official Tests for Identity : A solution in carbon dioxide - free water gives the reactions characteristic of sodium salts and of citrates (see Chapter 18).

Tests for Purity

1. Acidity or alkalinity.
2. Arsenic.
3. Heavy metals.
4. Chloride.
5. Sulphate.
6. Tartrate.
7. Oxalate.
8. Readily carbonisable substances.
9. Water.
10. Clarity and colour of solution.

Acidity or alkalinity is determined by titrating against either 0.05 M sulphuric acid or 0.1M sodium hydroxide, using thymol blue as indicator. The end point is more easily obtained with thymol blue than with phenolphthalein.

Readily carbonizable substances are detected by heating the substance with concentrated sulphuric acid in a water bath. Sodium citrate does not darken under these conditions but readily carbonisable substances will do. A standard is used for comparison.

Standard: Sodium citrate contains between 99 and 101 per cent of $Na_3C_6H_5O_7$, $2H_2O$ calculated with reference to the anhydrous substance.

Assay: It is assayed by a non-aqueous titration method in which it is dissolved in glacial acetic acid by warming and titrated with 0.1N perchloric acid after cooling. The end point is determined potentiometrically.

Storage: Since it deliquesces in moist air and effloresces in dry air, it must be kept in a tightly closed or airtight container.

Medicinal and Pharmaceutical Uses: *Systemic alkalizer and diuretic.* Sodium citrate is oxidized in the body to sodium bicarbonate. It is also used as an *anticoagulant.*

6. POTASSIUM CITRATE, $K_3C_6H_5O_7.H_2O$

See Chapter 9.

SODIUM LACTATE

Sodium lactate is a colourless thick liquid without odour. It is soluble in water. Usually it is available as a 70 to 80 per cent solution in water. It has the following structure:

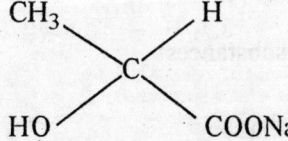

Since the central carbon is asymmetric, two stereoisomeric forms of D-lactate and L-Lactate are available. The racemic mixture (combination of both D- and L-forms) is present in the injection. The L-Lactate is converted in the body to sodium bicarbonate and so acts as a systemic alkalizer. In the I.P. racemic sodium lactate is made in the preparation of injection by reacting lactic acid with sodium hydroxide.

7. SODIUM LACTATE INJECTION

Preparation: This is an one-sixth molar solution which is approximately isotonic with blood serum. It is prepared by reacting sodium hydroxide and lactic acid and heating in an autocalave at 115°C to 116°C for one hour. By heating at a very high temperature it is possible to ensure that the lactic anhydride is fully hydrolysed to lactic acid which then reacts with sodium hydroxide along with the already present free lactic acid.

Then the pH is adjusted to a value of 5 to 7 with phenol red solution and the solution is made up to volume. It is filtered and immediately sterilised by heating in an autoclave.

Sodium Lactate Injection is a clear, colourless solution and it is official in I.P.

Official Tests for Identity

1. When the injection is warmed with potassium permanganate, it gives off acetaldehyde which can be recognised by its characteristic odour.

2. The injection is evaporated to dryness. The residue gives the reactions of sodium (refer Chapter 18).

Standard: Sodium Lactate Injection contains about 1.85 per cent w/v of $C_3H_5NaO_3$ (sodium lactate). (The injection is one-sixth molar and contains approximately 167 millimoles each of sodium and lactate).

Storage: Should be stored only in single-dose container of glass or plastic. On keeping, there may be separation of small particles in glass containers. So a caution should be given on the label that the injection should not be used if it contains visible particles.

Medicinal Use: *Fluid and electrolyte replenisher.* It is easily oxidised to sodium bicarbonate and so acts as a *systemic alkalizer.* Its advantages over sodium bicarbonate are that it can be readily sterilised and also that it does not produce systemic alkalosis like sodium bicarbonate.

8. AMMONIUM CHLORIDE , NH₄Cl

Refer Chapter 9.

AMMONIUM CHLORIDE INJECTION

Ammonium chloride injection is not official now. However it can be used as a *systemic acidifier* by injecting a 2% solution along with glucose. It acts by reducing the alkali reserve in the body and so is useful in reducing metabolic alkalosis. If it is given in large doses, it makes the urine acidic and acts as a diuretic also.

COMBINATIONS OF ORAL ELECTROLYTE POWDERS AND SOLUTIONS

In cholera there is a massive diarrohea with watery stools and also vomiting resulting in a marked depletion of sodium, potassium and bicarbonate leading to metabolic acidosis. Hence it is necessary to make good the water loss (dehydration) and electrolyte loss and correct the acidosis in addition to treatment with antibiotics etc. Even in cases of severe diarrohea (other than cholera), it may become necessary to correct the dehydration and electrolyte depletion. Normally this condition is treated with isotonic saline and isotonic sodium bicarbonate solution given intravenously.

Now it has been established that where facilities for intravenous therapy are not available, an oral glucose-electrolyte solution may be given and serves equally well. Addition of glucose to the electrolyte solution enhances the sodium and water absorption by the small intestine. This Oral Rehydration Therapy (O.R.T.) has several advantages:-

1. This oral treatment is very cheap, much cheaper than the intravenous solution.
2. No expertise is needed to give this by mouth. It can be given by anybody.
3. It is not necessary that the solution should be sterile.
4. Vomiting is easily corrected by the therapy itself.
5. Patients strong enough to drink take this easily.

The W.H.O. has recommended the following formula for oral rehydration therapy (O.R.T.):-

Sodium chloride	3.5 g
Potassium chloride	1.5 g
Sodium bicarbonate	2.5 g
Glucose (Anhydrous Dextrose, I.P.)	20.0 g
Boiled water, to make	100.0 ml

This contains sodium 90 mEq/l, potassium 20 mEq/l, chloride 80 mEq/l and bicarbonate 30 mEq/l. The constituents are mixed and supplied in sealed packets in the form of a ready-to-dissolve powder.

This formula may be slighty varied by including sodium citrate in place of sodium bicarbonate.

Sodium chloride	3.5 g
Potassium chloride	1.5 g
Sodium citrate	2.9 g
Dexrose (anhydrous)	20.0 g

The powder may be dissolved in boiled water and made upto one litre which is equivalent to 5 tumblerfulls (200 ml each). It contains the same proportions of electrolytes as in the previous formula except that this powder contains 9.9 mEq/l of citrate in place of the bicarbonate.

DOSAGE : Depending upon age and severity of dehydration.

Infants and Children : 1-2 litres (5-10 glasses) over a period of 24 hours.

Adults : 2-4 litres(10-20 glasses) over a period of 24 hours.

Sucrose may be used in place of glucose (dextrose) with equally good results. Starch or rice powder may also be used. We may recall here that our people have been using rice conjee as diet for patients suffering from diarrhoea.

In the light of the above a recently recommended method is to dissolve one pinch of salt and two teaspoons of sugar in a tumbler full of water and give it to the patient making the O.R.T., even simpler.

CHAPTER 14
ESSENTIAL AND TRACE IONS

Essential and trace ions include sodium, potassium, calcium, magnesium, phosphorus, chlorine, sulphur, iron, copper, manganese, chromium, zinc, molybdenum, cobalt, selenium, iodine and fluorine. Of these the first six, viz, sodium, potassium, calcium, magnesium, phosphorus, chlorine and sulphur are present in the body in relatively large amounts. The other minerals which are known as *trace elements or trace ions* occur in the body in relatively smaller quantities and are necessary for various biochemical functions in the body. These include iron, copper, manganese, zinc, chromium, molybdenum, cobalt, selenium, iodine and fluorine. This chapter deals with the trace elements, their functions and some of their important compounds and preparations.

IRON

Dietary sources of iron are cereals such as ragi and jowar, lentils and grams, soya beans, greens and green leafy vegetables, meat and liver, eggs, chocolate, pulses, wheat, oat meal etc., Daily dietary requirements are 10 mg for adult men, 15 mg for women and 5-10 mg for children.

Iron absorption mainly takes place in the small intestine, that is in the duodenum and the proximal jejunum. In the food stuffs, iron is usually in the ferric state but is reduced to ferrous state in the stomach. In the ferrous form iron is readily absorbed by diffusion across the mucosal barrier into the blood directly. This ferrous iron is reoxidized to ferric ions by a blue-copper *glycoprotein called ceruloplasmin or serum ferrioxidase. Fe^{3+} ions then bind to a protein apotransferrin to form transferrin which is carried to storage sites.*

If there is excess of iron, it is oxidized back to the ferric state in the mucosal cell. Now it is insoluble and combines with a protein known as *apoferritin* to form a complex called *ferritin* which is the storage form of iron. A mucosal barrier is established when apoferritin is saturated with iron. This is also called as the *ferritin curtain.* When this takes place, no more iron will be absorbed from the gut. Ferritin releases ferric iron into the blood and the iron is now bound to a protein and is known as transferrin and is stored in the liver, spleen and bone marrow. Diets rich in milk, antacids and tetracyclines interfere with the absorption of iron, that is, reduce its absorption.

Physiological Role

Iron is responsible for the transport, storage and utilization of oxygen in the body. Metalloporphyrins are complex compounds in which a metal ion is at the centre of a ring of four nitrogen atoms which are part of the pyrrole rings constituting a porphyrin group. The central metal ion in haemoglobin is iron.

Haemoglobin is actually a conjugated protein carrying four prosthetic groups. It contains four atoms of iron and has a molecular weight of about 67,000. In haemoglobin the iron is in the ferrous state. The ferrous ion can form co-ordinate linkages with ligands like O_2, CO, CN etc. The Fe^{2+} ion contains four unpaired electrons and it is able to take up four molecules of oxygen as given below :-

$$Hb + O_2 \rightleftharpoons HbO_2$$

$$HbO_2 + O_2 \rightleftharpoons Hb(O_2)_2$$

$$Hb(O_2)_2 + O_2 \rightleftharpoons Hb(O_2)_3$$

$$Hb(O_2)_3 + O_2 \rightleftharpoons Hb(O_2)_4$$

Thus haemoglobin can function as an efficient carrier of oxygen from the lungs to various parts of the body. However carbon monoxide (CO) and cyanide (CN^-) also can combine with haemoglobin. Since they are stronger field ligands than oxygen, they form complexes which are more stable than the complex formed by oxygen. So this explains how they are able to act as poisons.

Other haemoproteins which are able to act as enzymes participate in electron transport and tissue oxidation. The iron atoms in their prosthetic groups change from Fe^{3+} to Fe^{2+} and vice versa while transferring electron from an electron-donor to an electron-acceptor. Examples are *peroxidases, cytochromes, catalases* etc.,

There are also NHI (non-heme iron) proteins like ferritin which store iron in their prosthetic groups and also transferrin which is the carrier of Fe^{3+} ions in the blood.

Many iron-sulphur proteins act as NHI enzymes in which the iron and sulphur atoms participate in electron transfers during mitochondrial oxidations and hydroxylations of steroids and xenobiotics (foreign molecules). Examples are *thioredoxin of ribonucleotide reductase system and ferredoxin of renal mitochondrial cytochrome P_{450} hydroxylase system.*

Microsomal haemoproteins like cytochrome P_{450} monooxygenase are useful in detoxicating many xenobiotics like drugs (ex : warfarin), polycyclic aromatic hydrocarbons present in tobacco smoke and carcinogenic chemicals. They hydroxylate the xenobiotics by using the heme-iron as an electron-carrier.

COPPER

Dietary sources of copper are nuts, roots and tubers, greens and green leafy vegetables, lentils and legumes and liver. Daily dietary requirements are 1 mg for adults and 0.5 mg for children.

Copper is absorbed from food from the stomach and duodenum by being bound to small proteins like *metallothioneines* present in cells of the intestinal mucosa. This copper is taken by serum albumin from intestine to liver. This is the *direct-reacting copper*, since it can react with diethyldithiocarbamate directly and give a coloured complex. Some of the copper in the liver is combined with α-globulins. This is the *indirect-reacting copper* because it can react with diethyldithiocarbamate and give the coloured complex only after the copper is released from the protein by treatment with hydrochloric acid. The copper in the body is mainly present as *ceruloplasmin* which is a globulin which is a

267

blue copper-glycoprotein. This contains 6 copper atoms in each molecule, both as Cu^{2+} and Cu^+ ions. Other proteins which contain copper are *hepatocuprein* and *erythrocuprein*.

Physiological Role

a) **Role in iron utilization** : It has been found that simultaneous administration of iron and copper in anaemia helps to raise the haemoglobin concentration and reticulocyte count more quickly than when iron is administered alone. This is because of the fact that indirect-reacting copper such as the protein ceruloplasmin functions as *serum ferrioxidase* and helps to oxidize Fe^{2+} ions into Fe^{3+} ions which are transported to the bone marrow as transferrin for heme synthesis. In this case the Cu^{2+} ions in ceruloplasmin act as electron-acceptors to oxidize Fe^{2+} ions to Fe^{3+} ions.

b) **Destroying free radicals** : Just like tocopherols (vit.E) and carotenes, a copper-containing enzyme *cytoplasmic superoxide dismutase* present in liver, leucocytes, erythrocytes etc. combines with free radicals and converts them into oxygen and hydrogen peroxide.

c) **Role in oxidoreductase reactions** : Many copper-containing enzymes such as *oxidoreductases* and *dismutases* participate in redox reactions by accepting or donating electrons. For example *dopamine β-hydroxylase* is useful in catecholamine synthesis.

ZINC

Dietary sources of zinc are green, leafy vegetables, nuts, beans, unmilled cereals, roots and tubers, legumes, gingelly seeds, mustard seeds etc. Daily dietary requirements are 12-15 mg for adults and 4-10 mg for children.

Physiological Role

a) **Insulin storage and secretion** : In the β-cells of the pancreas, insulin is stored in the secretory vesicles combined with two Zn^{2+} ions which are linked to the thiol or imidazole sidechains of the aminoacids of insulin. Insulin is released into the blood as and when necessary from this combination and the circulating insulin does not have any

Zn^{2+} ions combined with it.

However some insulin preparations containing zinc are clinically used. These are insulin zinc suspensions and protamine zinc insulin. Insulin zinc suspensions are zinc compounds of insulin without a protein like protamine. Protamine zinc insulin is a complex of insulin with a suitable protamine and zinc.

b) **Removal of free radicals :** As mentioned under copper, the enzyme *cytoplasmic superoxide dismutase* is a copper–zinc protein present in liver, erythrocytes, leucocytes and neurons which combines with free radicals and converts them into innocuous compounds like oxygen and hydrogen peroxide.

c) **Zinc enzymes :** Zinc ions are constituents of many enzymes like *alcohol dehydrogenase, carbonic anhydrase, cytoplasmic superoxide dismutase, retinal reductase etc.,*

d) **Gustatory sensation :** Gustatory sensation refers to the taste sensation. Since a zinc-protein known as *gusten* is found to be involved in gustatory sensation, the acuity of the taste sensation comes down if there is zinc deficiency.

Zinc is stored in the liver, skin, muscles and bones after absorption from duodenum. The zinc stored in the liver is found to be combined with small proteins called metallothioneines.

CHROMIUM

Dietary sources of chromium are oil seeds like gingelly, cereals, nuts, mangos, meat, yeast, poppy seeds etc., Daily dietary requirement is of the order of 65-70 mcg.

Physiological Role : Chromium promotes glucose transport into the cells. Since it is a component of a glucose tolerance factor which promotes the binding of insulin to the cell membranes, the glucose transport into the cell is increased.

MANGANESE

Dietary sources of manganese are only from plants such as nuts, roots and tubers and green leafy vegetables. Daily dietary requirment is about 5 mg.

Manganese is stored in the liver combined with a protein, a β-globulin known as *transmanganin* in which form it is circulating in the blood also.

Physiological Role

a) **Component of enzymes:** Manganese is either a component or cofactor of many enzymes. Some of these are *cholinesterase, acetyl-CoA carboxylase, mitochondrial superoxide dismutase, glucose-6-phosphate dehydrogenase* etc.,

b) **Removal of free radicals :** Mn^{2+} ions like copper and zinc ions convert free radicals into H_2O_2 as components of mitochondrial superoxide dismutase.

c) **Carbohydrate metabolism :** Three enzymes of the oxidative phase of pentose metabolism and other enzymes like *isocitrate dehydrogenase, pyruvate carboxylase* are essential for carbohydrate metabolism. All these enzymes have Mn^{2+} as a cofactor.

d) **Role in the synthesis of extracellular matrices of connective tissues, tendons and bones :**

Mn^{2+} plays a role in the synthesis of mucopolysaccharide and proteoglycan being a part of the enzyme, *glycosyl transferase* which are essential for the formation of extracellular matrices of connective tissues, tendons and bones.

MOLYBDENUM

Dietary sources of molybdenum are only plant sources like oil seeds (gingelly and mustard), nuts and green leafy vegetables. Daily dietary requirements are 0.1-0.5 mg for adults and 0.02-0.25 mg for children.

Physiological Role

Molybdenum ions, MO^{6+}, are cofactors in some enzymes like *oxidoreductases* which take part in electron transfers. The enzyme *xanthine oxidase* catalyzes oxidation of xanthine and hypoxanthine to uric acid. *Sulphite oxidase* oxidizes inorganic sulphites to sulphates and *aldehyde dehydrogenase* catalyzes oxidation of aldehyde to alcohol.

SELENIUM

Dietary sources of selenium are milk, meat and plant sources. Daily requirements are 50-75 mg for adults and 20-30 mcg for children.

Physiological Role

a) Synergistic antioxidant action with tocopherols : Selenium and tocopherols promote each other's antioxidant action. Selenium also promotes tocopherol absorption. In turn tocopherols also protect the selenium present in the membrane selenoproteins from the actions of free redicals.

b) Anticancer effects : Selenium seems to have some anticancer effects as it destroys carcinogenic free radicals.

c) Protection against heavy metals : Selenium combines with heavy metals like cadmium and protects the body against the toxic effects of the heavy metals.

d) Role in T_3formation : Triodothyronine (T_3) is formed in the body by the partial deiodination of thyroxine (T_4). $T_4 5' - monodeiodinase$, an enzyme which is a selenoprotein, catalyzes this reaction.

SULPHUR

Daily dietary requirement of sulphur need not be stated since many proteins contain sulphur in their molecules. So adequate protein intake supplies the required sulphur to the body. Sulphur is present in the body in the form of inorganic sulphates and organic sulphur in the form of neutral sulphur and ethereal sulphates. There are many sulphur containing amnioacids such as cysteine, cystine and methionine, free as well as part of proteins. Sulphur occurs in many compounds such as vitamins like biotin and thiamine, mucopolysaccharides and coenzyme A and high energy sulphur compounds such as S-adenosylmethionine. The two chains A and B containing 21 and 30 aminoacids respectively of insulin are joined at two places through two disulphide bridges.

Physiological Role

a) **Stabilization of structure of proteins :** Disulphide bonds such as those mentioned in the case of insulin stabilize three dimensional structures of proteins. Two cysteine residuces join to form a cystine residue stabilizing the structures of secondary, tertiary and quarternary structures of many proteins.

b) **Sulphur-containg enzymes :** These enzymes also known as sulphydryl or thiol enzymes owe their activity to the active −SH group which participates directly in the binding to and subsequent action on the substrate. Examples are *cytosolic glucose 6-phosphate dehydrogenase and microsomal HMG-CoA reductase.*

c) **Role in methylations :** A high-energy sulphur compound like S-adenosylmethionine acts as a donor of methyl groups. The sulphur in the side chain of this compound contains a "labile" methyl group and transfers the methyl group more freely than any other compound. Even though there are many transmethylations facilitated by S-adenosylmethionine, two deserve particular mention, viz, the methylation of noradrenaline to adrenaline and nicotinamide to N-methylnicotinamide.

d) **Thioesterification :** Fatty acids are metabolised by conversion into their thioesters by −SH groups of enzymes like coenzyme A.

e) **Tissue redox reactions :** Iron-sulphur proteins and compounds like glutathione take part in tissue oxido − reductions involving electron transfers such as mitochondrial aerobic oxidations and detoxications of xenobiotics. The −SH functions as the donor of electrons.

f) **Detoxications of xenobiotics :** Xenobiotics are molecules foreign to the body such as drugs, insecticides, food adulterants, carcinogens etc. They are detoxified in different ways depending on their structure such as methylation, sulfation, conjugation, hydroxylation etc. Sulphur containing compounds are very useful for this purpose. For example phenols are sulfated. Quinoline is methylated. Drugs like isoniazid are acetylated. Carcinogenic hydrocarbons are conjugated. Policyclic aromatic hydrocarbons are hydroxylated.

IODINE

About 100 mcg of iodine is required daily for the normal synthesis of thyroid hormones. Sufficient supply of iodine is available from vegetables and animal muscle meat. Marine fish is a good source of iodine. Iodate-enriched bread and iodized table salt are also good sources now. Daily requirements are 100-140 mcg for adults and 60-100 mg for children.

Physiological Role

About 5-8 mcg of iodine is bound to plasma proteins and about 0.3 mcg present as inorganic iodide in the blood. However the thyroid gland contains about 12 mg of iodine, almost the whole of it bound to a protein known as thyroglobulin. The thyroid gland actively collects iodine from the blood through an iodide pump. It secretes two iodine containing hormones, *levothyroxine and liothyronine*.

Iodine deficiency goitre and hypothyroidism are the results of iodine deficiency. In addition to dietary iodine deficiency, two other factors may contribute to the deficiency. Ingestion of thiocyanate containing vegetables and vegetable products such as cabbage and mustard oil which inhibit the iodide intake and ingestion of foods containing thiocarbamide such as turnip and mustard seeds which inhibit the iodination of tyrosine present in thyroglobulin are these factors.

Hypothyroidism is marked by the lowering of the basal metabolic rate and congenital deficiency leads to cretinism in which growth is stunted and mental development is retarded. Excess secretion of the hormone produces thyrotoxicosis or hyperthyroidism marked by increase in basal metabolic rate, cardiac acceleration, restlessness and anxiety.

Hypothyroidism is treated by administration of dried thyroid gland and thyroid hormones whereas hyperthyroidism is treated by synthetic antithyroids.

The chemistry of some of the clinically used compounds of iron, zinc and iodine is detailed below :-

1.FERROUS FUMARATE, $\left[\begin{array}{c} HC-COO^- \\ {}^-OOCCH \end{array}\right] Fe^{2+}$ or $C_4H_2FeO_4$

Preparation : Ferrous fumarate is prepared by treating ferrous sulphate with sodium fumarate.

$$\underset{\text{Sodium fumarate}}{\begin{array}{c} HC.COONa \\ NaOOCCH \end{array}} + FeSO_4 = \underset{\text{Ferrous fumarate}}{\left[\begin{array}{c} HC-COO^- \\ {}^-OOCCH \end{array}\right] Fe^{2+}} + Na_2SO_4$$

Physical and Chemical Properties

Ferrous fumarate is a reddish-orange to reddish–brown fine powder. It may contains soft lumps which produce a yellow streak when crushed. It has a slight odour and a slightly astringent taste. It is slightly soluble in water.

It answers the tests for ferrous iron and for fumarate ion. It is assayed by titration with ceric ammonium sulphate using ferroin sulphate solution as indicator. Here the ferrous fumarate is oxidised.

It is official in I.P.

Official Tests for Identity

1. A small quantity of the sample is heated with diluted hydro chloric acid on a water bath for fifteen minutes, cooled and

274

filtered. The filtrate gives the reactions of ferrous salts (see Chapter 18).

2. The precipitate obtained in (1) above is washed with diluted hydrochloric acid and dried. It is suspended in sodium carbonate solution and potassium permanganate solution is added drop by drop. The permanganate is decolourised and a brownish solution is obtained.

3. A small quantity of the sample is mixed with resorcinol, a few drops of concentrated sulphuric acid are added and gently heatd. A deep red semisolid mass is obtained. It is added to a large volume of water. An orange-yellow solution without any fluorescence is obtained.

Tests for Purity

1. Arsenic
2. Heavy metals
3. Sulphate
4. Ferric iron
5. Loss on drying

Ferric iron is limited by allowing it to oxidize potassium iodide to iodine in acid medium. The iodine liberated is estimated by titrating with 0.1 M sodium thiosulphate.

Standard : Ferrous fumarate contains not less than 93 per cent and not more than 101 per cent of $C_4H_2FeO_4$ calculated with reference to the dried substance.

Assay : An accurately weighed quantity is dissolved in dilute sulphuric acid with the aid of gentle heat and titrated with 0.1N ceric ammonium nitrate, using ferroin sulphate as indicator. This is a redox titration and ferrous fumarate is oxidised to the ferric state by the ceric ammonium nitrate.

$$C_4H_2FeO_4 + H_2SO_4 = FeSO_4 + C_4H_4O_4$$

Ferrous fumarate   Fumaric acid

275

$$2Ce(NO_3)_4 + 2FeSO_4 + H_2SO_4 = Fe_2(SO_4)_3 + Ce_2(NO_3)_6$$

Ceric nitrate   Cerous nitrate

$$+ 2HNO_3$$

Storage : Store in a well-closed container.

Medicinal Use : *Haematinic.* It is useful in the prevention and treatement of iron-deficiency anaemias.

2. FERROUS GLUCONATE,

$[CH_2OH(CHOH)_4COO]_2$ Fe. $2H_2O$

Preparation : Glucose is oxidised by bacterial fermentation to gluconic acid. The gluconic acid so obtained is treated with ferrous carbonate to give ferrous gluconate. It is crystallized with 2 molecules of water of hydration and dried.

$$C_6H_{12}O_6 \xrightarrow{(O)} HC_6H_{11}O_7$$

Glucose   Gluconic acid

$$2HC_6H_{11}O_7 + FeCO_3 + H_2O = Fe(C_6H_{11}O_7)_2.2H_2O + CO_2\uparrow$$

Gluconic   Ferrous   Ferrous gluconate

acid   carbonate

Physical and Chemical Properties

Ferrous gluconate occurs as yellowish-grey or pale greenish yellow fine powder or granules. It has a slight odour like that of burnt sugar. It is fairly soluble in cold water and more soluble in warm water.

An aqueous solution is acid in reaction and it answers the reactions of ferrous salts and of the gluconate ion. It is assayed by titration with ceric ammonium sulphate solution like ferrous fumarate.

It is official in I.P.

Official Tests for Identity

1. A solution of the sample in water gives the reactions of ferrous salts (see Chapter 18).

2. To a small quantity of the sample are added water, glacial

276

acetic acid and freshly distilled phenylhydrazine. The mixture is heated on a water bath for thirty minutes. It is cooled and the inner surface of the test tube is scratched with a glass-rod until crystals of gluconic acid phenylhydrazide begin to form. After setting aside for ten minutes it is filtered. The precipitate is dissolved in hot water, mixed with a small amount of decolourising charcoal and filtered into a test tube. The filtrate is cooled and the inner surface of the test tube is scratched. White crystals of pure gluconic acid phenylhydrazide are obtained. They melt at about 202°C with decomposition.

Tests for Purity

1. Clarity of solution
2. pH
3. Arsenic
4. Barium
5. Ferric iron
6. Heavy metals
7. Chloride
8. Sulphate
9. Oxalic acid
10. Reducing sugars
11. Loss on drying

Ferric iron is limited in the same way as in the case of ferrous fumarate. *Oxalic acid* is limited by extraction with solvent ether from an acid solution of the substance and evaporation to dryness. To the residue are added acetic acid and calcium chloride solution. No turbidity is produced. If calcium is present it will be precipitated as white calcium oxalate forming the turbidity.

Reducing sugars may be present since ferrous gluconate is prepared from glucose. They are limited by their reaction with Fehling's solution after the removal of ferrous gluconate as ferrous sulphide by passing hydrogen sulphide. No red precipitate is formed within one minute.

277

Standard : Ferrous gluconate contains not less than 95 per cent and not more than 102 per cent $C_{12}H_{22}FeO_{14}$ calculated with reference to the dried substance.

Assay : It is assayed in the same way as ferrous fumarate by titration with 0.1M ceric ammonium nitrate. However the pretreatment of the sample involves the dissolving of the sample in dilute sulphuric acid and treating with sodium bicarbonate to produce carbon dioxide so that all the iron in the sample will be in the ferrous form without being oxidised to the ferric state. Ferroin sulphate is used as the indicator and the end point is marked by the disppearance of the red colour. See assay of ferrous fumarate for equations.

Storage : Since it is affected by light, store in well-closed light resistant containers.

Medicinal Uses : *Haematinic.* It is useful in the prevention and treatment of iron-deficiency anemias.

3. FERROUS SULPHATE, $FeSO_4,7H_2O$

Preparation : It is prepared by dissolving a slight excess of iron in dilute sulphuric acid and concentrating to get green crystals of ferrous sulphate.

$$Fe + H_2SO_4 = FeSO_4 + H_2\uparrow$$

On the manufacturing scale scrap iron is used.

Physical and Chemical Properties : This is crystalline ferrous sulphate containing seven molecules of water of hydration. It occurs in the form of transparent, green crystals or as a pale bluish-green, crystalline powder. It is odourless and has a metallic, astringent taste. It effloresces in dry air. When exposed to moist air, it is slowly oxidised and is coated with a brown basic ferric sulphate. When this takes place, the sample should not be used. It is soluble in water and practically insoluble in alcohol. Ferrous sulphate combines with alkali sulphates to form double salts. Ferrous ammonium sulphate. $FeSO_4(NH_4)_2SO_4.6H_2O$ is one such. It is used in analytical chemistry

Ferrous sulphate is oxidised by acidified potassium permanganate to ferric sulphate. This was used as the assay method for estimating ferrous sulphate. Ferrous sulphate is official in I.P.

Official Tests for Identity : Gives the reactions characteristic of ferrous salts and sulphates (refer Chapter 18).

Tests for Purity
1. pH : A.5% aqueous solution should have a pH between 3 and 4.
2. Arsenic
3. Copper, zinc and lead
4. Manganese
5. Clarity of solution
6. Chloride

Copper, zinc and lead are tested by preparing a special solution of the substance. *Copper* is tested by forming a coloured complex with sodium diethylidithiocarbamate in the presence of citric acid and ammonia and extracting the complex with carbon tetrachloride. The colour of the resulting solution is not greater than that of a standard dilute copper sulphate solution similarly treated. *Zinc* is extracted with dithizone, the zinc dithizonate is decomposed with hydrochloric acid and the liberated zinc is treated with potassium ferrocyanide solution to produce a turbidity (zinc ferrocyanide). The turbidity should not be greater than a turbidity produced with standard dilute zinc sulphate solution similarly treated. *Lead* is precipitated as lead sulphide with sodium sulphide in the presence of ammonia and potassium cyanide which keeps the other heavy metals complexed. The colour produced is compared with that produced in a standard lead solution similarly treated.

Manganese is tested by getting it oxidised to potassium permanganate by sodium periodate and comparing the colour with the colour of a standard solution of potassium permanganate similarly treated.

Standard : Contains not less than 98 percent and not more than the equivalent of 105 percent of $FeSO_4$. $7H_2O$.

1.Assay (I.P.'96): It is assayed by the same method used for ferrous gluconate. See ferrous gluconate.

2. Assay (I.P. '66): An accurately weighed quantity is dissolved in dilute sulphuric acid and titrated against 0.1N potassium permanganate. In this way ferrous sulphate is oxidised by the nascent oxygen from the acidified potassium permanganate to ferric sulphate. Potassium permanganate acts as its own indicator. Appearance of pale pink colour is the end point.

$$2KMnO_4 + 3H_2SO_4 = K_2SO_4 + 2MnSO_4 + 3H_2O + 5(O)$$

$$2FeSO_4 + H_2SO_4 + O = Fe_2(SO_4)_3 + H_2O$$

Ferrous   Ferric
sulphate   sulphate

$$\text{(or) } 10FeSO_4 + 2KMnO_4 + 8H_2SO_4 = 5Fe_2(SO_4)_3 + 2MnSO_4 \\ + K_2SO_4 + H_2O$$

Storage : Since it effloresces in dry air and is oxidised in moist air, store in tightly closed containers.

Medicinal Use : *Haematinic.* This is the most popular of the ferrous salts and also the cheapest.

4. DRIED FERROUS SULPHATE

This is a greyish white to buff-coloured powder with a metallic astringent taste. It dissolves slowly but completely in water. Otherwise it resembles ferrous sulphate.

Preparation : It is prepared by drying the crystalline salt in an oven at 40°C till it is loses the correct amount of water. It is mixture of hydrates and corresponds to the formula $FeSO_4 . 2H_2O$. It must be immediately put into a bottle and tightly stoppered.

Official Tests for Identity : Same as for Ferrrous Sulphate.

Tests for Purity : Same as for Ferrous Sulphate.

Assay : Same as for Ferrous Sulphate.

Standard: Contains not less than 86 percent and not more than 90 percent of $FeSO_4$.

Storage : Store in a tightly closed container.

Medicinal Use : *Haematinic, pharmaceutical aid.*

5. IRON AND AMMONIUM CITRATE (FERRIC AMMONIUM CITRATE)

Preparation: This can be considered in stages as given below:

1. Preparation of Ferric Hydroxide: Ferric hydroxide is prepared by the interaction between a ferric salt solution and an alkali such as ammonia, sodium hydroxide or sodium carbonate. The ferric salt solution should be added to the alkali with stirring and not vice versa. Ferric hydroxide is precipitated and it is collected by filtration and washed.

$$Fe_2(SO_4)_3 + 6NaOH = 2Fe(OH)_3 + 3Na_2SO_4$$
Ferric sulphate   Ferric hydroxide

2. Preparation of Ferric Citrate : Citric acid is added to the wet precipitate (which is not dried) to dissolve nearly the whole of the precipitate.

$$Fe(OH)_3 + H_3C_6H_5O_7 = FeC_6H_5O_7 + 3H_2O$$
Citric acid   Ferric citrate

3. Preparation of Ferric Ammonium Citrate

(a) Formation of Ferric Ammonium Citrate : A slight excess of ammonia is added and any undissolved ferric hydroxide is removed by filtration.

(b) Concentration : The filtrate is clear and reddish brown in colour. It is evaporated to a syrup, adding ammonia from time to time so that an excess of ammonia is maintained throughout the evaporation process.

(c) Scaling : Finally the syrup is painted on glass plates and dried below 40°C. Then it is scrapped off as scales (reddish brown). Green scales are obtained if excess of citric acid is used.

Physical and Chemical Properties : Iron and Ammoniam Citrate is a complex ammonium ferric citrate. It occurs as thin, transparent, dark-red scales or granules or as a brownish red granular powder. It is odourless and has an astringent taste. It deliquesces in air and is affected by light. It is very soluble in water and almost insoluble in alcohol. An aqueous solution does not give the normal reactions for iron. Only after acidification with hydrochloric acid, it gives the reactions for iron.

There is a view that ferric ammonium citrate is a solid sol of a basic colloidal complex, $FeC_6H_5O_7 \cdot 2Fe(OH)_3$ dispersed in ammonium citrate. It is assayed by treating with acidified potassium iodide. The acid releases the ferric iron in the ferric ammonium citrate and the ferric iron then oxidizes the potassium iodide to iodine which is estimated by titration against standard sodium thiosulphate solution.

$$2FeCl_3 + 2KI = I_2 + 2FeCl_2 + 2KCl$$

$$I_2 + 2Na_2S_2O_3 = 2NaI + Na_2S_4O_6$$

Ferric ammonium citrate is official in I.P.

Official Tests for Identity

1. Ignite gently and dissolve the residue in hydrochloric acid. The solution gives the reactions characteristic of ferric salts (see Chapter 18).

2. Warm with solution of sodium hydroxide. Ammonia is evolved and the solution gives the reactions characteristic of citrates (refer Chapter 18).

Tests for Purity
  1. Arsenic
  2. Lead
  3. Zinc
  4. Chloride
  5. Free ferric compounds
  6. Sulphate

Free ferric compounds are limited by adding to an aqueous

solution of the substance potassium ferrocyanide solution. No blue colour or precipitate is formed. If free ferric ions are present, they will react with potassium ferrocyanide to give a blue precipitate which is Prussian blue (Lassaigne's test for nitrogen is based on this). If, however, hydrochloric acid is added along with potassium ferrocyanide solution, a blue precipitate is got. This is because the acid decomposes the ferric ammonium citrate releasing ferric ions.

Standard : It contains not less 20.5 percent and not more than 22.5 percent of Fe.

Assay : An accurately weighed quantity is dissolved in water, acidified with sulphuric acid and warmed till the dark brown colour becomes yellow. The solution is cooled and one or two drops of 0.02M potassium permanganate solution are added so as to get a pink colour persisting for five seconds. Then hydrochloric acid and potassium iodide are added and the liberated iodine is titrated with 0.1M sodium thiosulphate using starch solution as indicator.

Ferric ammonium citrate is decomposed with sulphuric acid to give ferric ions. Any ferrous iron present is oxidised to the ferric state by adding drop by drop 0.02M potassium permanganate solution till the pink colour persists for just 5 seconds. It is enough if the colour persists only for a few seconds since decolourization of the permanganate after this period is due to the oxidation of the citric acid. The ferric iron then oxidizes potassium iodide in the presence of excess of hydrochloric acid to liberate iodine which is titrated with 0.1M sodium thiosulphate. See Physical and Chemical Properties for the equations.

Storage : Since it deliquesces in moist air and is also affected by light, store in tighty closed, light-resistant containers.

Medicinal Use : *Haematinic.* Because of its high solubility in water, it can be used in the form of syrups, elixirs etc.,

6. ZINC CHLORIDE

See Chapter 10.

7. POTASSIUM IODIDE

See Chapter 16.

8. STRONG IODINE SOLUTION

See Chapter 10.

9. IRON DEXTRAN INJECTION

Iron Dextran Injection is a sterile colloidal solution of a complex of ferric hydroxide with dextran of average molecular weight between 5000 and 7500.

Dextran is a common name applied to a group of bacterial polysaccharides prepared by growing a special strain of the organism *Leuconostoc mesenteroides* in a medium rich in sucrose. Dextran is a polysaccharide like starch and glycogen. However while the amylose part in starch is composed of unbranched chains of α-1:4 glucosidic linkages and glycogen also is made up mostly of α-1:4 glucosidic linkages, dextran contains both α-1:4 and α-1:6 glucosidic linkages with the latter preponderating. There may also be branchings which may be due to some α-1:3 and other types of linkages.

Dextrans contain molecules of widely varying size and varying molecular weights. Crude dextran has a molecular weight between 40 and 60 million and it must be hydrolysed by acid to give degraded dextrans. Clinical dextran is used as a plasma substitute. Dextran 40 injection contains dextrans of weight average molecular weight of about 40,000 whereas dextran 110 injection contains weight average molecular weight of about 1,10,000. These are close to the molecular weights of plasma proteins and so clinical dextran solutions have a colloidal osmotic pressure same as that of human plasma. Dextran has some advantages over plasma in that it can be stored without refrigeration for a long period, it can be sterilized and its use will not be the cause for transmitting viral hepatitis and jaundice which may happen sometimes in plasma transfusions.

As already stated, iron dextran injection is a sterile colloidal solution of a complex of ferric hydroxide with dextran of average molecular weight between 5000 and 7500. So it is obvious that in this case the dextran component is there not for use as a plasma substitute but only as a carrier for ferric iron in unionisable organic combination.Its use here is only as a *haematinic*. The molecular weight of the dextran is also low and not within the clinical range required for a plasma substitute.

Iron dextran injection is a dark brown solution. Even though the I.P. does not give any indication as to the concentration of iron that should be present, it is usually available as 5 ml ampoules containing 50 mg of elemental iron per ml.

Tests for Identity

1. To a diluted solution of the injection, 5M ammonia is added. No precipitate is produced. Since the iron is in organic combination and so is unionisable, no precipitate of ferric hydroxide is produced on the addition of ammonia.

2. A diluted solution of the injection is treated with a small quantity of hydrochloric acid, boiled for just 30 seconds and strong ammonia and hydrogen sulphide solution are added. Under these conditions iron is released from organic combination and is precipitated as ferric sulphide which is filtered.

   The filtrate is boiled with potassium cupri-tartrate solution after elimination of excess hydrogen sulphide by boiling. The solution should remain greenish and no precipitate should be produced. This proves that the earlier treatment with hydrochloric acid released only the iron and has not hydrolysed the dextrans to dextrose. So there is no reaction with potassium cupri-tartrate solution (Fehling's solution).Another portion of the filtrate is boiled with hydrochloric acid. Then it is treated with sodium hydroxide solution and potassium cupri-tartrate solution and boiled. A reddish precipitate is produced. Now the dextrans have been hydrolysed by the acid and the resulting dextrose gives the reaction with the Fehling's solution.

3. A diluted solution of the injection is boiled with concentrated hydrochloric acid for 5 minutes. The solution is cooled and an excess of strong ammonia solution is added and filtered. The precipitated ferric hydroxide is dissolved in dilute hydrochloric acid and diluted. The resulting solution answers the following test :- To this solution are added dilute hydrochloric acid and ammonium thiocyanate solution. It becomes blood-red in colour. Divide into two portions. Extract one with solvent ether. The ether layer becomes pink. To the other mercuric chloride solution is added. The colour disappears. This reaction is answered only by ferric salts and not by ferrous salts.

Tests for Purity
1. Arsenic
2. Heavy metals
3. Chloride
4. pH
5. Copper
6. Zinc
7. Iron absorption
8. Abnormal toxicity
9. Bacterial endotoxins
10. Other requirements

The procedures for performing the tests 1 to 2 are given in Chapter 21. The I.P. may also be referred to for pretreatment and other details. Mostly the pretreatment prescribes the procedure to be followed for oxidising and destroying the organic matter before proceeding with the limit tests.

Chloride : This is not the usual limit test for chlorides. Here the injection is mixed with nitric acid and titrated with 0.1M silver nitrate. The end-point is found out potentiometrically. The volume of 0.1M

286

silver nitrate required should be within the prescribed range given in the I.P. A very much higher limit for chloride is prescribed probably because there is a possibility of some hydrochloric acid, which might have been used for degrading the crude dextrans soon after fermentation to the required clinical range, still remaining in the final product.

Copper : In this limit test organic matter is destroyed by heating with concentrated nitric and sulphuric acids. The residue is digested with hydrochloric acid, made alkaline with ammonia and treated with sodium diethyldithiocarbamate. Any colour produced is compared with the colour produced in a standard, that is copper standard solution (10 ppm Cu) similarly treated. If the colour produced in the test is more, it fails the test. If it is less, it passes the test.

Zinc : In this test, a portion of the acid solution prepared for the copper test is mixed with sodium hydroxide solution and filtered. Zinc is present in the filtrate as sodium zincate $Zn(ONa)_2$. It is treated with potassium ferrocyanide solution. If zinc is present, a white opalesecnce may be produced which should be not more than that produced in a specific volume of zinc standard solution (25 ppm Zn) similary treated.

Iron absorption : This is a combined biological and chemical test to find out whether sufficient iron absorption takes place *in vivo* from the site of injection over a period of 7 days.

In the biological test, two rabbits are injected with the preparation in the leg muscle. After 7 days the rabbits are killed and the leg muscle dissected and examined. The muscle should be only lightly stained and no heavy black deposit of unabsorbed iron compounds is observed.

In the chemical test, the leg muscle pieces are extracted with sodium hydroxide solution and organic matter destroyed by heating with concentrated sulphuric acid and fuming nitric acid. The mixture is treated with ammonium citrate solution, ammonium thioglycollate solution and dilute ammonia solution. The absorbance of the resulting coloured solution is measured at 530 nm in a spectrophotometer. A reference standard curve is also prepared by taking different quantities of ferric ammonium sulphate solution containing 0.01% Fe and treating them

287

with the same reagents. The absorbance of the test is referred to this curve to find out the amount of Fe present in the leg. A blank is also done on the legs not injected with the iron preparation. Not more than 20% of injected iron should be present in the leg.

Abnormal toxicity and Bacterial endotoxins : These are biological and microbiological tests and should be done in the concerned laboratories.

Other requirements : The preparation should comply with the requirements of tests given under injectable preparations such as the test for pyrogens, test for sterility etc.,

Standard : Iron Dextran injection contains between 4.75 and 5.25 percent w/v of iron, Fe, and between 17 and 23% w/v of dextrans.

Assay : The assay is divided into two parts, one for ferric iron and the other for dextrans.

For iron : The injection mixed with sulphuric acid is passed through a column containing activated zinc amalgam and fitted with a sintered glass disc and washed with very dilute sulphuric acid. The combined eluates now contain ferrous iron formed by the reduction of the ferric iron by the zinc amalgam and the acid. The combined eluates are now titrated with 0.1M ceric ammonium sulphate solution using ferroin solution as indicator.

For dextrans : A diluted solution of the injection is mixed at 0^0C with anthrone in sulphuric acid and heated on a water bath for 5 minutes. It is cooled and its absorbance is measured at 625 nm. A green colour is formed.

A blank is prepared using water and its absorbance is measured. The corrected absorbance is referred to a calibration curve prepared by treating suitable amounts of dextrose in the same manner. Each g of dextrose is equivalent to 0.94 g of dextrans. Using the weight per ml of the injection, the percentage w/v of dextrans may be calculated.

CHAPTER 15
INORGANIC
PHARMACEUTICAL AIDS

Pharmaceutical aids or necessities are those substances which are used in the formulation and manufacture of various pharmaceutical preparations. They possess little pharmacological or therapeutic value of their own. They may be classified into (1) solvents and vehicles (2) diluents (3) suspending agents (4) emulsifying agents (5) clarifying and distributive agents (6) lubricants (7) soothing and protective agents (8) antioxidants (9) preservatives and (10) aids in the preparation of other substances.

1. Solvents and Vehicles: Solvents and vehicles give form and appearance to the preparation, for example, (a) Purified Water – used in the preparation of many pharmaceutical preparations such as solutions, mixtures, emulsions etc., (b) Water for Injection - used in the preparation of injections.

2. Diluents: These are substances used for diluting the potent active ingredient so that it can be administered in a convenient unit dosage form such as powders, tablets and capsules. Examples of inorganic substances used for this purpose are light kaolin, calcium phosphate etc. The diluents should be chemically inert and should not have any pharmacological action of their own.

3. Suspending agents: These compounds increase the viscosity of the vehicle, thereby enabling the insoluble, indiffusible powders to be suspended. Bentonite is an example. Three percent of bentonite is used in Calamine Lotion to suspend calamine and zinc oxide. Silica thickens water, benzene and turpentine.

4. Emulsifying agents: Emusifying agents or emulgents are substances which promote emulsions between oils and oily substances and water. The emulsions can be either oil in water or water in oil. Many medicinal substances and cosmetics are examples. Many of the emulgents possess high HLB value and can also act as wetting agents, solubilising agents etc. Sodium lauryl sulphate is a classic example.

5. Clarifying and Distributive Agents: Aromatic waters are prepared by dissolving a volatile oil in alcohol and adding the solution to a large volume of water. Since the oils have very low solubility in water, the liquid becomes turbid due to the presence of undissolved volatile oil. Addition of talc helps in the absorption of undissolved oil and a clear liquid is obtained on filtration eg. gripe waters. They usually contain a volatile oil such as dill oil.

6. Lubricants: A lubricant must be added to the granules before they are compressed into tablets. This is done so that the granules may flow freely into the die. The lubricant also improves the appearance of the tablet by giving it a shine. Examples of lubricants are talc, magnesium stearate etc.

7. Soothing and Protective Agents: Some substances are included in the formulation of dusting powders because they are able to give a soothing and protective effect to the skin. Talc, zinc oxide and zinc stearate are examples.

8. Antioxidants: Antioxidants are usually powerful reducing agents. They preserve the active ingredient of a preparation by combining with the oxygen or the oxidising agent themselves. Sodium metabisulphite is a classic example. It is included in the preparation of Adrenaline Tartrate Injection, I.P. 85 where it preserves the adrenaline from being oxidised and converted into an oxidation product. For the same reason it is an ingredient in Apomorphine Injection.

9. Preservatives: These substances preserve the active ingredient from microbial attack and consequent spoilage of the preparation. They are usually bacteriostatic and fungistatic. Sodium benzoate is used for this purpose in a concentration not exceeding 0.5 per cent. Examples of preparations where sodium benzoate is used as the preservative are Aluminium Hydroxide Gel, I.P., Milk of Magnesia, I.P. and many syrups.

10. Aids in the Preparation of Other Substances or Preparations: The following are a few examples of substances which are used in the preparation of other substances or preparations. Here the pharmaceutical aid is used for adjusting the pH to a definite value or for precipitating impurities or for keeping the active ingredient in the same reduced condition.

See the next page

Pharmaceutical aids	Used in the preparation
1. Ammonia Solution Strong	Strong Ammonium Acetate Solution
2. Borax	Vanishing creams.
3. Hypophosphorus acid	Syrup of ferrous iodide.
4. Lead monoxide	Extraction of caffeine from tea.

1. SODIUM BISULPHITE, $NaHSO_3$

Preparation: Sodium bisulphite is prepared by passing sulphur dioxide into a solution of sodium carbonate till the solution is saturated with sulphur dioxide. First the sulphur dioxide dissolves in water to form sulphurous acid which reacts with sodium carbonate to give sodium bisulphite.

$$SO_2 + H_2O \longrightarrow H_2SO_3$$
$$Na_2CO_3 + 2H_2SO_3 \longrightarrow 2NaHSO_3 + H_2O + CO_2\uparrow$$

Sodium bisulphite may be crystallized from the solution directly. Alternatively it may be precipitated as a white powder by the addition of alcohol.

Physical and Chemical Properties

Sodium bisulphite is a white powder or it may occur as white crystals. It has the odour of sulphur dioxide. It is soluble in water.

It reacts with acids to yield sulphurous acid.

$$NaHSO_3 + HCl \longrightarrow NaCl + H_2SO_3$$

It is a powerful reducing agent and reduces in acid solution iodine, permanganate, dichromate, halogens, hydrogen peroxide, ferric salts etc. itself getting oxidised to sodium bisulphate. The reaction with iodine is given below.

$$NaHSO_3 + I_2 + H_2O \longrightarrow NaHSO_4 + 2HI$$

291

Actually this is the assay method for sodium bisulphite.

Sodium bisulphite is sufficiently acidic to produce effervescence with sodium carbonate. Sodium sulphite is formed.

$$2NaHSO_3 + Na_2CO_3 \longrightarrow 2Na_2SO_3 + H_2O + CO_2\uparrow$$

Sodium bisulphite forms addition compounds with organic compounds containing carbonyl groups such as aldehydes and ketones.

$$\diagdown C=O \; + NaHSO_3 \longrightarrow \diagup\diagdown C \diagup^{OH}_{SO_3Na}$$

The organic compound is now converted into a water-soluble, stable, form which can be dissolved in water and injected. Sodium bisulphite is not an official compound.

Tests for Identity

1. Sodium bisulphite solution in water gives the reactions of sodium (see Chapter 18).

2. A solution of sodium bisulphite treated with hydrochloric acid turns a filter paper moistened with mercurous nitrate solution black.

   Sodium bisulphite liberates sulphur dioxide on treatment with hydrochloric acid and the sulphur dioxide reduces mercurous nitrate to mercury.

Storage : Sodium bisulphite is somewhat unstable in air releasing sulphur dioxide. So it should be stored in a tightly closed container.

Medicinal and Pharmaceutical Uses: Formerly sodium bisulphite was used as an *antioxidant preservative* in a concentration of 0.1-0.2% in certain injections such as adrenaline injection and phenylephrine injection. Now sodium metabisulphite has replaced sodium bisulphite in these preparations. As already stated sodium bisulphite is used to convert certain ketonic compounds into soluble sodium bisulphite compounds.

2. SODIUM METABISULPHITE, $Na_2S_2O_5.H_2O$

Preparation: Sodium metabisulphite is produced by passing sulphur dioxide into a hot concentrated sodium hydroxide solution and saturating it. Sodium bisulphite which is first formed is converted into sodium metabisulphite.

$$NaOH + SO_2 = NaHSO_3$$
$$2NaHSO_3 = Na_2S_2O_5 + H_2O$$

Physical and Chemical Properties

Sodium metabisulphite occurs as colourless prismatic crystals or as a white powder which may become yellowish on keeping. It has a sulphurous odour and an acid and saline taste. It contains one molecule of water of hydration. It slowly gets oxidised to sulphate on exposure to air. It is acid in reaction and is a powerful reducing agent. It is freely soluble in water.

On heating it decomposes into sodium sulphite and sulphur dioxide and for this reason may be considered as sodium sulphite with excess of sulphur dioxide to explain its reducing action.

$$Na_2S_2O_5 = Na_2SO_3 + SO_2\uparrow$$

It reduces iodine, permanganate, dichromate, ferric salts etc. Its reaction with iodine is used as the assay method.

$$2I_2 + Na_2S_2O_5 + H_2O = 4HI + 2NaHSO_4$$

It is official in I.P.

Official Tests for Identity

1. Yields the reactions characteristic of sodium salts. See Chapter 18.
2. A solution of the sample decolourises iodinated potassium iodide and the resulting solution gives the reactions of sulphates. See Chapter 18.

Tests for Purity

1. Acidity
2. Arsenic

293

3. Heavy metals
4. Iron
5. Thiosulphate

Iron in this substance is not limited by the usual thioglycollic acid limit test. Iron present is oxidised to the ferric state by bromine solution and treated with ammonium thiocyanate solution. Any red colour produced should not be darker than that produced with a definite quantity of standard solution of iron similarly treated.

Thiosulphate is limited by adding hydrochloric acid to the substance and boiling. Any turbidity produced should not be greater than that produced in a definite volume of 0.1N sodium thiosulphate similarly treated. When acid is added to thiosulphate, it decomposes to deposit sulphur.

$$Na_2S_2O_3 + 2HCl = 2NaCl + SO_2\uparrow + S\downarrow + H_2O$$

Sodium metabisulphite also is decomposed but in the following manner:-

$$Na_2S_2O_5 + 2HCl = 2NaCl + 2SO_2\uparrow + H_2O$$

Standard: Contains not less than 95% of $Na_2S_2O_5$.

Assay: An accurately weighed quantity is dissolved in known excess of 0.1M iodine, hydrochloric acid is added and the excess of 0.1M iodine is titrated with 0.1M sodium thiosulphate using starch solution as indicator towards the end of the titration.

$$2I_2 + Na_2S_2O_5 + 3H_2O = 4HI + 2NaHSO_4$$

Storage: Sodium metabisulphite should be kept in a tightly closed light resistant container in a dry place. On exposure to air and moisture it is slowly oxidised to sulphate with disintegration of crystals.

Medicinal and Pharmaceutical Uses

Antioxidant Preservative. It is used to stabilise injections of adrenaline tartrate and morphine and also adrenaline solution. It is also used in the preparation of photographic developers and as an antichlor after bleaching paper or cloth with chlorine.

3. SULPHUR DIOXIDE, SO_2

Preparation

1. Sulphur dioxide is produced when sulphur is burnt in air or oxygen.

$$S + O_2 \xrightarrow{\Delta} SO_2\uparrow$$

A small quantity of sulphur trioxide also is produced.

2. Sulphur dioxide is also produced by roasting metallic sulphides in air.

$$4FeS_2 + 11O_2 \xrightarrow{\Delta} 2Fe_2O_3 + 8SO_2\uparrow$$
$$Cu_2S + 2O_2 \xrightarrow{\Delta} 2CuO + SO_2\uparrow$$

3. It is also produced by reducing sulphuric acid with carbon or sulphur or copper.

$$2H_2SO_4 + Cu \longrightarrow SO_2\uparrow + CuSO_4 + 2H_2O.$$

Physical and Chemical Properties

Sulphur dioxide is a colourless gas with a pungent and irritating odour. It is non-inflammable and is soluble in water. Its aqueous solution is acid to litmus since sulphurous acid is formed. It is stable even at high temperatures.

However under the influence of a catalyst, it combines with oxygen to form sulphur trioxide.

$$SO_2 + O \longrightarrow SO_3$$

In direct sunlight as well as in the presence of a catalyst like camphor, sulphur dioxide forms addition compounds. It also forms a hydrate with 7 molecules of water ($SO_2.7H_2O$). The hydrate is obtained by cooling a saturated aqueous solution of sulphur dioxide.

It is a good reducing agnet. It reduces iodine and chlorine. It reduces potassium iodate to iodine and also discharges the colour of potassium permanganate solution.

$$I_2 + 2H_2O + SO_2 \longrightarrow H_2SO_4 + 2HI$$

$$SO_2 + Cl_2 \longrightarrow SO_2Cl_2$$
Sulphuryl chloride

$$2KIO_3 + 4H_2O + 5SO_2 \longrightarrow 2KHSO_4 + I_2 + 3H_2SO_4$$
$$2KMnO_4 + 2H_2O + 5SO_2 \longrightarrow K_2SO_4 + 2MnSO_4 + 2H_2SO_4$$

Tests for Identity

1. Sulphur dioxide has a characteristic, acrid odour.

2. Filter paper moistened with potassium iodate and starch solutions and dried and exposed to sulphur dioxide develops a blue colour. On continuous exposure, the blue colour disappears.

    This is due to the fact that potassium iodate is reduced to iodine by sulphur dioxide and the iodine gives the blue colour with starch. However on further exposure, the sulphur dioxide reduces iodine to hydrogen iodide (HI) and the blue colour disappears.

3. When moistened mercuric nitrate paper is brought into contact with sulphur dioxide, it turns black due to the reduction of mercuric nitrate to mercury.

Storage: Since sulphur dioxide is a powerful reducing agent, it reacts with oxygen of the atmosphere. Further it is also a gas. So it should be stored in a tightly closed container, preferably a cylinder.

Medicinal and Pharmaceutical Uses: Formerly sulphur dioxide was used as an *antioxidant preservative* because of its reducing action in certain easily oxidisable preparations. However it finds extensive use in bleaching wood pulp and straw. It is also used for fumigating rooms and in the manufacture of sugar and sulphuric acid. ·

(4) BENTONITE, Al_2O_3, $6SiO_2$, xH_2O

Properties: Bentonite is a native colloidal, hydrated aluminium silicate. It is a very fine, odourless, pale buff or cream-coloured powder. It should be free from gritty particles.

296

It is odourless and has a slightly earthy taste. It is insoluble in water but swells into a homogeneous mass. It is also insoluble in organic solvents but does not swell in them.

Chemically it is supposed to be Al_2O_3. $6SiO_2$, xH_2O but there are variations.

When water is added to bentonite, each particle is surrounded by a layer or shell of water. This produces a particle several times larger than the original particle. Swelling of mass results and bentonite can absorb up to 5 times its weight of water and its bulk may increase by twelve to fifteen times. Therefore it is used mainly as a suspending agent. Bentonite suspensions are thixotropic which means they are liquid when agitated or disturbed but solid when at rest. Bentonite is incompatible with acid solutions and also with polyvalent cations.

It is official in I.P.

Official Test for Identity

The sample is fused with anhydrous sodium carbonate, the residue dissolved in water and filtered. To the filtrate hydrochloric acid is added. A gelatinous precipitate is produced.

The residue is dissolved in dilute hydrochloric acid. The solution gives the reactions of aluminium salts. See Chapter 18.

Tests for Purity

1. pH
2. Heavy metals
3. Sedimentation volume
4. Swelling power
5. Coarse particles
6. Loss on drying

pH should be between 9 and 10.5 for a 2% w/v suspension in water. *Sedimentation volume* is found out by mixing the sample with light magnesium oxide and suspending in water. The suspension is placed in a 100 ml measuring cylinder. After 24 hours the volume of the clear supernatant liquid is not more than 2 ml. This means that this suspension is almost a permanent one and so is able to retain the original volume of 100 ml almost.

For finding out the *swelling power*, the sample is added in small quantities at intervals of 2 minutes to a solution of sodium lauryl sulphate in a 100 ml measuring cylinder. It is allowed to stand for 2 hours. The apparent volume of the sediment at the bottom of the cylinder should be not less than 24 ml. The presence of the wetting agent (sodium lauryl sulphate) promotes compatibility between the insoluble bentonite and water. *Loss on drying* should be not more than 15% for reasons stated under Heavy Kaolin.

Storage: Store in tightly-closed containers.

Medicinal and Pharmaceutical Uses: *Suspending Agent.* Bentonite is used to stabilize emulsion, as a detergent in cleaners, as a clarifying agent, as an adsorbent for colouring matter and as a suspending agent. Three per cent of bentonite is used as a suspending agent in Calamine Lotion. IP'66.

5. MAGNESIUM STEARATE.

Preparation : First sodium stearate is produced by adding a calculated quantity of stearic acid gradually to a hot solution of sodium hydroxide with constant stirring. The solution is cooled and the sodium stearate is converted to magnesium stearate by adding a solution of magnesium sulphate. The magnesium stearate which is now precipitated is collected, washed and dried.

$$C_{17}H_{35}COOH + NaOH = C_{17}H_{35}COONa + H_2O$$
$$\text{Stearic acid} \qquad\qquad\quad \text{Sodium stearate}$$
$$2C_{17}H_{35}COONa + MgSO_4 = (C_{17}H_{35}COO)_2Mg + Na_2SO_4$$
$$\text{Magnesium stearate}$$

Physical and Chemical Properties

Magnesium stearate is a very fine, white, light powder with a faint and characteristic odour. It is greasy to touch and is free from grittiness. It is insoluble in water and alcohol.

Actually magnesium stearate is not a single substance but is a mixture of magnesium salts. Stearic acid itself is prepared by the hydrolysis of fats and as such it is liable to contain not only stearic acid but also other fatty acids such as palmitic acid and oleic acid. So magnesium stearate contains also variable proportions of magnesium palmitate and magnesium oleate. It is decomposed by the addition of mineral acids to stearic acid, palmitic acid etc.

$$(C_{17}H_{35}COO)_2Mg + 2HCl = 2C_{17}H_{35}COOH + MgCl_2$$
$$\text{Stearic acid}$$

It is official in I.P.

Official Tests for Identity

The sample is mixed with ether, nitric acid and distilled water and heated under reflux until dissolution is complete. It is cooled and the aqueous layer is separated. The ether layer is washed with water and the water combined with the aqueous layer. The aqueous layer also is washed with ether. The ethereal layer is evaporated to dryness and the residue is dried at 105°C. The freezing point of the residue is not lower than 53°C. The aqueous layer gives reactions of magnesium salts. See Chapter 18.

In the above test, magnesium stearate is decomposed by nitric acid and the fatty acids (chiefly stearic acid) are extracted by ether. The fatty acids after removal from ether should melt at a temperature not lower than 53°C which means that it mostly consists of stearic acid only. The filtrate containing magnesium nitrate will answer tests for magnesium.

Tests for Purity

1. Acidity or alkalinity
2. Colour of solution
3. Clarity and colour of solution of the fatty acids
4. Acid value of the fatty acids
5. Free stearic acid
6. Zinc stearate
7. Heavy metals
8. Chloride
9. Sulphate
10. Loss on drying

Colour of solution is observed by taking the aqueous layer obtained under official Tests for Identity. It is not more intensely coloured than a reference solution given in an appendix.

Clarity and colour of solution of the fatty acids are observed by dissolving the residue obtained under the Identity Test in choroform. The solution should be clear and not more intensely coloured than a reference solution.

Acid value of the fatty acids is a determination of the fatty acids in the residue as per procedure given in the appendix and it should be between 195 and 210.

Free stearic acid is determined by dissolving the substance in choloroform, filtering and evaporating on a water bath. The residue is dissolved in neutralised ethanol (95%) and titrating with 0.1M sodium hydroxide using phenolphthalein as indicator. Free stearic acid is extracted by chloroform and estimated by titration with 0.1M sodium hydroxide.

Standard : Magnesium stearate contains not less than 3.8 percent and not more than 5 percent of Mg, calculated with reference to the dried substance.

Assay : This is by complexometry and is a back titration. The sample is dissolved in a mixture of butanol and ethanol. Ammonia, ammonia buffer pH 10, a measured volume of 0.1M disodium edetate and mordant black indicator are added, heated to 45 to 50°C and titrated with 0.1M zinc sulphate until the colour changes from blue to violet. A blank titration without the substance is also done.

Disodium edetate complexes the magnesium at pH 10 provided by the buffer and the excess of disodium edetate is found out by titration with 0.1M zinc sulphate. Since zinc sulphate will be excess at the end point, the indicator colour will change from blue to violet.

Storage: Store in well closed containers.

Pharmaceutical Use : *Pharmaceutical aid (lubricant).*

6. ZINC STEARATE
See page 172 (Chapter 10).

7. ALUMINIUM SULPHATE, $Al_2(SO_4)_3 \cdot xH_2O$
Aluminium sulphate contains a variable quantity of water of crystallization.

Preparation: (1) It is prepared by dissolving alumina or aluminium hydroxide in dilute sulphuric acid.

$$Al_2O_3 + 3H_2SO_4 \rightarrow Al_2(SO_4)_3 + 3H_2O$$

(2) On a large scale it is prepared by roasting kaolin or china clay and then dissolving in boiling sulphuric acid.

$$Al_2O_3.2SiO_2.2H_2O + 3H_2SO_4 \rightarrow Al_2(SO_4)_3 + 2SiO_2 + 5H_2O$$
$$\text{Kaolin}$$

The insoluble residue of sand is filtered and the solution is cooled so that crystals of aluminium sulphate separate out.

Properties: Aluminium sulphate occurs as colourless lustrous crystals or as a white, crystalline powder or mass. It is soluble in cold water, freely soluble in hot water and practically insoluble in ethanol(95%). As already stated, it contains a variable quantity of water of hydration.

Due to hydrolysis, its solution in water is acidic. It forms double salts known as alums with sulphates of alkali metals. On being heated, the water of crystallization is first lost and then it decomposes into alumina and sulphur trioxide.

$$Al_2(SO_4)_3.xH_2O \rightarrow Al_2(SO_4)_3 + 4H_2O$$
$$Al_2(SO_4)_3 \rightarrow Al_2O_3 + 3SO_3\uparrow$$

It is official in I.P.

Official Tests for Identity: A solution in water gives reaction 1 of aluminium salts and reactions of sulphates.

301

Tests for Purity

1. pH
2. Clarity and colour of solution
3. Alkaline and alkaline-earth metals
4. Ammonium salts
5. Arsenic
6. Heavy metals
7. Iron

pH of a 2% solution should be between 2.5 and 4. As already stated under properties this is the salt of a strong acid and a weak alkali. So in solution in water, it is hydrolysed and gives a distinctly acid reaction.

Alkaline and alkaline-earth metals, if present, are converted to their hydroxides by making them distinctly alkaline with ammonia using methyl red as indicator. Then it is filtered and the filtrate is evaporated to dryness and weighed.

Ammonium salts are detected by adding sodium hydroxide solution and heating on a water bath. There should be no odour of ammonia.

Standard : Aluminium sulphate contains between 51 and 59 percent of $Al_2(SO_4)_3$.

Assay : Same as for aluminium hydroxide gel. See Chapter 9.

Storage : Store in tightly closed containers

Pharmaceutical Use : *Pharmaceutical aid (mineral carrier for adsorbed vaccines, see alum).*

It is also used to purify water, as it has the capacity to coagulate colloidal solutions of various substances present in water. It is also used in tanning and as a mordant in dyeing and calico-printing.

8. SODIUM BENZOATE, C_6H_5COONa

Preparation: A solution of sodium carbonate is added to a hot concentrated solution of benzoic acid till the mixture is just alkaline to litmus.

$$2C_6H_5COOH + Na_2CO_3 = 2C_6H_5COONa + CO_2\uparrow + H_2O$$
Benzoic acid   Sodium benzoate

The solution is carefully evaporated and the residue granulated.

Physical and Chemical Properties: Sodium benzoate is a white, amorphous, granular or crystalline powder. It is odourless or has a faint odour of benzoin. It has an unpleasant, sweetish and saline taste.

When a fairly concentrated neutral solution of sodium benzoate is treated with dilute hydrochloric acid, a white precipitate of benzoic acid is produced.

$$C_6H_5COONa + HCl = C_6H_5COOH + NaCl$$
Benzoic acid

When heated alone, sodium benzoate chars. But when heated with powdered soda lime, it is decarboxylated and evolves vapours with an odour of benzene.

$$C_6H_5COONa + NaOH = C_6H_6 + Na_2CO_3$$
Benzene

When sodium benzoate is warmed with a mixture of alcohol and concentrated sulphuric acid, the characteristic odour of the ester ethyl benzoate is noticed.

$$2C_6H_5COONa + H_2SO_4 = 2C_6H_5COOH + Na_2SO_4$$

$$C_6H_5COOH + C_2H_5OH \overset{H_2SO_4}{=} C_6H_5COOC_2H_5 + H_2O$$
Ethyl benzoate

When treated with ferric chloride, sodium benzoate gives a buff coloured precipitate of ferric benzoate.

$$3C_6H_5COONa + FeCl_3 = (C_6H_5COO)_3Fe + 3NaCl$$
Ferric benzoate

Sodium benzoate is official in I.P.

303

Official Tests of Identity

1. A 10 percent w/v solution yields with test solution of ferric chloride a buff-coloured precipitate and with dilute hydrochloric acid, a white crystalline precipitate of benzoic acid.

2. Gives the reacitons characteristic of sodium and benzoates. See Chapter 18.

Tests for Purity

1. Acidity or alkalinity
2. Arsenic
3. Heavy metals.
4. Clarity and colour of solution
5. Loss on drying
6. *Chlorinated compounds* : This may be due to benzoic acid being manufactured from chlorinated derivatrives of toluene. It is done by dissolving the sample in sodium carbonate solution, evaporating to dryness and heating the residue below $400^{0}C$. till it is charred. The chlorine present is now converted to sodium chloride. It is extracted with water and dilute nitric acid and filtered. The filtrate must comply with the limit test for chlorides.

Standard : Sodium Benzoate contains not less than 99 per cent of $C_7H_5O_2Na$ (C_6H_5COONa) calculated with reference to the substance dried at. $105^{0}C$.

Assay : The assay is by a non-aqueous titration. The sample is dissolved in glacial acetic acid and titrated with 0.1M perchloric acid using 1-naphtholbenzein solution as indicator.

Storage : Store in a well-closed container.

Medicinal Use : *Antifungal Preservative.* It is used as a preservative in syrups, fruit juices and various foods and food materials.

9. SODIUM CARBOXYMETHYLCELLULOSE

Preparation: The molecule of cellulose is composed of a large number of β-D-glucopyranose units joined together.

About 2000 to 3000 glucose units corresponding to a molecular weight of about 3,00,000-5,00,000 are supposed to have gone into the structure of cellulose. However this figure is highly variable.

Sodium carboxymethylcellulose is prepared by reacting cellulose with sodium hydroxide and chloroacetic acid. Some of the hydroxyl groups are replaced by $-OCH_2COONa$ groups. The exact number of $-OCH_2COONa$ groups entering the cellulose molecule is variable. So different grades of sodium carboxymethyl (OCH_2COONa) cellulose are available and when dissolved in water, the solutions have viscosities ranging from 5 to 4000 centipoises. I.P. describes sodium carboxymethylcellulose as the sodium salt of a partially substituted poly(carboxymethyl)ether of cellulose.

Properties: It is a white or almost white granular powder which is odourless and hygroscopic It is easily dispersed in water forming a colloidal solution. It is practically insoluble in ethanaol, acetone, ether and toluene. It is official in I.P.

Official Tests for Identity

1. It is dispersesd in carbon dioxide-free water at 40 to 50°C. A colloidal solution is formed (solution A). To a portion of this solution, copper sulphate solution is added. A blue cotton-like precipitate is produced.
2. Solution A is boiled for a few minutes. No precipitate is produced.
3. Solution A gives the reactions of sodium salts. See Chapter 18.

305

Tests for Purity

1. pH
2. Clarity and colour of solution
3. Apparent viscosity
4. Arsenic
5. Heavy metals
6. Chloride
7. Sulphated ash
8. Loss on drying

pH of solution A shall be between 6 and 8. *Clarity and colour of solution* are limited by matching solution A against a reference standard. These two tests are designed to prevent contamination of the substance.

Apparent viscosity is determined by dissolving the substance in water at 90°C, diluting and stirring till solution is complete. The viscosity of this solution is found out using a rotating viscometer. The viscosity should be between 75 and 140% of the value given on the label.

In the *arsenic* test, the organic matter in the sample is destroyed by heating with concentrated nitric acid and concentrated sulphuric acid and finally with perchloric acid. Then the limit test for arsenic is carried out.

Sulphated ash is an indicator of the presence of any extraneous inorganic impurities other than sodium. It should be between 20 and 33.3%

Since sodium carboxymethylcellulose is hygroscopic, some amount of water is always present. So *loss on drying* is done by drying the sample in an oven at 105°C. It should be below 10%.

Standard : It contains not less than 6.5 per cent and not more than 10.8 per cent of Na, calculated with reference to the dried substance.

Assay : An accurately weighed quantity of the substance is dispersed in anhydrous glacial acetic acid by heating on a water bath for two hours. Then it is titrated against 0.1M perchloric acid. The end point is determined potentiometrically. This is a non-aqueous titration.

Storage : Since it is hygroscopic, store it in a well closed or tightly closed container.

Medicinal and Pharmaceutical Uses

Pharmaceutical aid (suspending agent, thickening agent and tablet excipient). It is also used as a bulk laxative.

10. SODIUM FORMALDEHYDE SULPHOXYLATE, $HOCH_2SO_2Na. 2H_2O$

Preparation : This is obtained when sodium hydrosulphite $Na_2S_2O_4$, is treated with a solution of formaldehyde.

| Sodium hydrosulphite | Formal dehyde | Sodium formaldehyde sulphoxylate | Formaldehyde sodium bisulphite |

Properties : It consists of white crystals or hard white masses. It has a characteristic, garlic like odour. It is freely soluble in water and slightly soluble in organic solvents such as chloroform, ether and ethanol. It is an extremely powerful reducing agent. It is official in I.P. It may contain a suitable stabilising agent such as sodium carbonate.

Official Tests for Identity

1. To an aqueous solution ammoniacal silver nitrate solution is added. Metallic silver is produced by reduction either as a finely divided grey precipitate or as a bright metallic mirror on the inner surface of the test tube.

2. The substance is added to a solution of salicyclic acid in concentrated sulphuric acid. A permanent deep red colour is produced.

Tests for Purity

1. Clarity and colour of solution
2. Alkalinity
3. pH
4. Iron
5. Sulphide
6. Sodium sulphite
7. Loss on drying

pH should be between 9.5 and 10.5 determined in a 2% solution in carbondioxide-free water.

The limit test for *iron* in this case is done in a different way. Ammonium thiocyanate is used for the development of the red colour and this is done after destroying the organic matter in the sample by heating it at 600°C in a muffle furnace.

Sulphide and sodium sulphite are impurities which might have been derived from the method of manufacture. *Sulphide* is tested by moistening lead acetate paper in a solution of the sample. No discolouration (due to lead sulphide) is seen within five minutes.

Sodium sulphite is tested by taking the solution left after assay of the sample is completed and adding formaldehyde solution and titrating with 0.1M iodine using starch solution as indicator.The amount of sodium sulphite is calculated by using the formula given in the I.P.

Since sodium formaldehyde sulphoxylate contains two molecules of water of crystallization, *loss on drying* is calculated by drying the sample in an oven at 105°C for 3 hours. It should not exceed 27 percent.

Standard: It should contain an amount of CH_3NaO_3S equivalent to not less than 45 percent and not more than 55 percent of SO_2, calculated with reference to the dried substance.

Assay: An aqueous solution of the sample is titrated with 0.1M iodine using starch solution as the indicator towards the end of the titration. Iodine oxidises sodium formaldehyde sulphoxylate.

Storage : Since it is a powerful reducing agent, store in a tightly closed non-metallic container.

Pharmaceutical Use : *Pharmaceutical aid (antioxidant).*

11. SODIUM METHYLPARABEN

Preparation : Sodium methylparaben can be prepared from 4-hydroxybenzoic acid which is isomeric with salicylic acid which is 2-hydroxybenzoic acid. 4-hydroxybenzoic acid itself is prepared by heating potassium salicylate and acidifying with hydrochloric acid. Then the 4-hydroxybenzoic acid is esterified with methanol in the presence of sulphuric acid. The methylester (methylparaben) is dissolved in sodium hydroxide solution to give sodium methylparaben.

| Pot. salicylate | 4-Hydroxy benzoic acid | Methyl paraben | Sodium methyl paraben |

Properties : Sodium methylparaben is a white, crystalline powder. It is odourless or almost odourless and hygroscopic. It is freely soluble in water, sparingly soluble in ethanol(95%) and practically insoluble in fixed oils. It is official in I.P..

Official Tests for Identity

1. The sample is dissolved in water and the solution acidified with concentrated hydrochloric acid. The precipitated methylparaben is washed and dried. The infared absorption spectrum of this should be concordant with the spectrum obtained from methylparaben RS (Reference Standard).

2. The precipitate obtained in the previous test on ignition gives the reactions of sodium salts. See Chapter 18.

Tests for Purity

1. pH
2. Clarity of solution
3. Chloride
4. Sulphate
5. Water

pH : A 0.1% solution of the sample should have a pH of 9.5-10.5. Since it is a sodium salt, its pH is on the alkaline side at which pH also it is active.

Water : Since it is hygroscopic, a test for water content is necessary. It should be not more than 5%.

Standard : Sodium methylparaben contains between 99 and 102 per cent of $C_8H_7NaO_3$, calculated with reference to the anhydrous substance.

Assay : An accurately weighed quantity of the sample is boiled under reflux with sodium hydroxide. Parahydroxybenzoic acid is liberated. To this are added potassium bromate and potassium bromide solutions and concentrated hydrochloric acid. This solution is known as bromine solution, since bromine is released. In the presence of acid, potassium bromate forms bromic acid and potasssium bromide forms hydrobromic acid. These react together and liberate bromine.

$$HBrO_3 + 5HBr = 3H_2O + 3Br_2$$

The liberated bromine brominates the benezene nucles of 4-hydroxybenzoic acid and forms 2,4,6-tribromophenol. The carboxyl group is displaced.

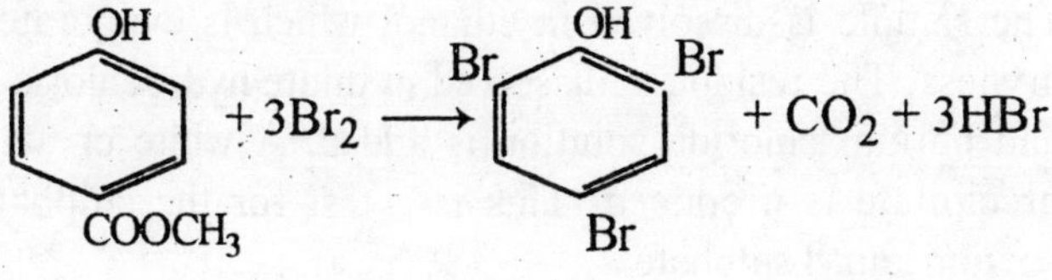

Then dilute potassium iodide solution is added. The excess of bromine liberates iodine from potassium iodide and it is titrated with 0.1M sodium thiosulphate. A blank titration is also done without the sample.

Pharmaceutical Use : *Pharmaceutical aid (antimicrobial preservative).* It is used as a preservative primarily to protect against yeast. Its effectiveness is more when it is used with propylparaben in the ratio 2:1.

12. SODIUM LAURYL SULPHATE ·

Preparation: Sodium lauryl sulphate is a mixture of sodium alkyl sulphates consisting mainly of sodium lauryl sulphate $[CH_3(CH_2)_{10}CH_2OSO_3Na]$. It is prepared by sulphating long-chain fatty alcohols such as commercial lauryl alcohol or dodecyl alcohol $(C_{12}H_{25}OH)$ and neutralizing with alkali to form the sodium salts. The alcohols are prepared by reduction of cocoanut oil by high pressure hydrogenation using the catalyst copper-chromium oxide.

Properties : Sodium lauryl sulphate occurs as white or light yellow crystals with a slight cocoanut-like fatty odour. It is freely soluble in water forming an opalescent solution and partly soluble in ethanol(95%) It is official in I.P.

Official Tests for Identity

1. Methylene blue solution and dilute sulphuric acid are added to an aqueous solution of the substance and dichloromethane is added and shaken. The dichloromethane layer is intensely blue.

2. The sample is dissolved in ethanol which is evaporated to dryness. The residue is dissolved in dilute hydrochloric acid and barium chloride solution is added. A white crystalline precipitate is produced. This is a test for the sulphate in sodium lauryl sulphate.

3. Gives reaction no.2 sodium salts. See Chapter 18.

Tests for Purity

1. Alkalinity
2. Non - esterified alcohols
3. Sodium Chloride and sodium sulphate

Alkalinity may arise from its method of manufacture. It is determined by titration of an aqueous solution with 0.1M hydrochloric acid using phenol red as indicator.

Non-esterified alcohols are the long chain fatty alcohols which escaped esterification during the preparation of sodium lauryl sulphate. The test is done by dissolving the sample in a mixture of alcohol (95%) and water and extracting repeatedly with n-pentane which is removed by evaporation on a water bath. The residue is dried at 105°C and weighed. Only up to 4% is allowed.

For *sodium chloride and sodium sulphate,* not more than a total of 8% is permitted. *Sodium chloride* is determined by dissolving in nitric acid and titrating with 0.1M silver nitrate using potassium chromate as indicator.

Sodium sulphate is determined by a titration. An aqueous solution is treated with a solution of dithizone in acetone. If the solution becomes red, nitric acid is added drop by drop till it becomes bluish green. Then dichloroacetic acid and acetone are added and titrated with 0.01M lead nitrate. End point is the appearance of a permanent orange-red colour.

Standard : Sodium lauryl sulphate contains not less than 85% of sodium alkyl sulphates, calculated as sodium lauryl sulphate.

Assay : To an aqueous solution of the sample are added chloroform, dilute sulphuric acid and dimethyl yellow-oracet blue B solution (indicator) and titrated with 0.004M benzethonium chloride solution until the chloroform layer acquires a permanent, clear green colour.

312

Pharmaceutical Uses: *Pharmaceutical aid - Anionic emulsifying agent.* It is a *surfactant* and is used for its foaming and cleansing activity in shampoos and dental preparations. It acts as an emulsifier and so is useful in preparing water-miscible ointment bases for cosmetic and pharmaceutical applications. Since it has a high HLB value, it is useful in various situations as a wetting agent, solubilising agent etc. also.

13. PURIFIED WATER, I.P.

Purified water is prepared from potable water either by distillation or by ion-exchange methods or by reverse osmosis or by any other suitable process. Ordinary potable water contains some amount of anions and cations whereas hard water contains a lot of magnesium and calcium salts. Purified water is prepared by using any one of the methods and should contain no anions and cations. Purified water only should be used for the manufacture of pharmaceutical formulations and hard water is totally unsuitable for this purpose.

Description: Purified water is a clear, colourless liquid. It is odourless and tasteless.

Tests for Purity

1. Acidity or alkalinity
2. Ammonium
3. Calcium and magnesium
4. Heavy metals
5. Chloride
6. Nitrate
7. Sulphate
8. Oxidisable substances
9. Residue on evaporation

Acidity or alkalinity is tested by adding to the water methyl red solution in a borosilicate glass flask. The resulting solution should not be red. To another borosilicate glass flask containing water, bromothymol blue solution is added. The resulting solution should not be blue. The limits of pH imposed by these tests on water are from pH 4.5 to 7. Borosilicate glass vessels should be used, as vessels made of ordinary glass may shed alkali and vitiate the test.

Some amount of ammonia is always present in the atmosphere and because of this purified water also may contain a small quantity of ammonia dissolved in it. Therefore a limit test for *ammonium* is prescribed. Nessler's Reagent or alkaline potassium mercuri-iodide solution is added to the sample and the colour obtained is compared with the colour obtained when the same reagent is added to a specified quantity of a solution of ammonium chloride.

Calcium and magnesium are limited by adding to the water sample ammonia buffer, mordant black II mixture and 0.01M disodium edetate. A pure blue colour is produced. If *both* calcium and magnesium are present in more quantity than what is allowed, a wine red colour is produced. This is a complexometric limit test.

Chloride is limited by adding to the water nitric acid and silver nitrate solution. The solution should be clear.

Nitrate is tested by adding to the water immersed in ice, potassium chloride solution, diphenylamine solution and sulphuric acid. It is heated on a water bath at 50°C and allowed to stand for 15 minutes. Any blue colour in the solution should not be more intense than a solution containing nitrate-free water and nitrate standard solution similarly treated.

Sulphate is limited by adding to the water dilute hydrochloric acid and barium chloride solution. The appearance of the solution should not change for at least one hour. If sulphate is present, an opalescence will develop.

Oxidizable substances are detected by adding acidified potassium permanganate solution and boiling. The solution should remain faintly pink. If oxidisable substances are present, the potassium permanganate is decolourised.

Residue on evaporation refers to limit for any non-volatile matter present in the sample of water. It is determined by evaporating the water on a water bath and drying to constant weight at 105°C. The residue should not be more than 0.001%.

Storage : Store purified water in well closed containers.

Pharmaceutical Use : It is mainly used as a *solvent*.

14. WATER FOR INJECTION

This water is meant for preparing injectable solutions and suspensions. It must be clearly understood that this is *distilled water free from pyrogens*. Water prepared by demineralisation through the use of ion-exchange materials is unsuitable for use as water for injection. Potable water is distilled in a neutral glass or metal still fitted with an efficient device for preventing the entrainment of droplets (such as an efficient baffle) to get water for injection. The baffle prevents the entrainment of droplets in the still and the distilled water obtained is pyrogen-free. However this is *not sterile*. It may be used for preparing aqueous injections which will be later sterilised in their final containers. Tests for purity are the same as for purified water but with the addition of one more test for pyrogens.

Water for Injection in Bulk has another test in addition, that is test for bacterial endotoxins.

15. STERILE WATER FOR INJECTION

Sterile water for injection is only water for injection, sterilized and suitably packed. It should not contain any antimicrobial or other substances. As for tests for purity, pH allowed is from 4.5 to 7.5. Higher limit of oxidizable substances and total solids (non-volatile matter) are permitted because of slight gains in these substances during sterilization. Sterile water for injection should also comply with tests for sterility and pyrogens. It is used as a solvent in the preparation of injections of medicaments (aqueous solutions and suspensions) by the method of aseptic processing.

16. ZINC CHLORIDE

See page 178 (Chapter 10).

CHAPTER 16
MISCELLANEOUS

I. SCLEROSING AGENTS

Sclerosing agents are some injections which are given to irritate and damage the wall of a vein resulting in its occlusion, ie., closing. This is done in the case of varicose veins. In these veins, the circulation is rather slow and the injection may remain undiluted for long. Hypertonic solutions of sodium morrhuate, quinine hydrochloride and ethanolamine oleate are used for this purpose. Hypertonic saline also may be used.

1. SODIUM CHLORIDE HYPERTONIC INJECTION, I.P. (HYPERTONIC SALINE)

See Chapter 13.

2. SODIUM TETRADECYL SULPHATE

Preparation : Sodium tertradecyl sulphate is prepared by sulphating tetradecyl alcohol ($C_{14}H_{29}OH$) and converting it into its sodium salt.

Properties : It is available only as a concentrate which is a clear, colourless aqueous gel. It is official in B.P.

Official Tests for Identity

1. It is identified by a gas chromatography test.
2. To an aqueous solution of the gel, are added methylene blue solution, dilute sulphuric acid and chloroform and shaken. The chloroform layer is intensely blue.
3. The substance is hydrolysed in hot ethanol solution with dilute hydrochloric acid and filtered. To the filtrate barium chloride solution is added. A white crystalline precipitate is produced.
4. Gives reaction no.2 of sodium salts. See Chapter 18.

317

Tests for Purity

1. Alkalinity
2. Non-esterified alcohols
3. Chloride
4. Sulphate
5. Sulphated ash

Non-esterified alcohols are those long chain fatty alcohols which are unsulphated and remain in the sample. An aqueous solution of the sample is extracted repeatedly with n-pentane. The extract is dried with anhydrous sodium sulphate, filtered and evaporated on a water bath. Finally the residue is dried at 105°C and weighed.

Standard : Sodium tetradecyl sulphate concentrate contains between 46 and 52% of sodium tetradecyl sulphate

Assay: An aqueous solution is treated with chloroform and dimidium bromide-sulphan blue mixed solution (indicator) and titrated against 0.004M benzethonium chloride solution until the pink colour of the chloroform layer is completely discharged and a greyish blue colour is produced. This is a non-aqueous titration.

Medicinal Use : *Sclerosing agent.*

II. EXPECTORANTS

Expectorants are drugs which enhance the secretion of the sputum by the air passages so that it is easier to remove the phlegm through coughing. They are used in cough mixtures for this purpose. They act either by increasing the bronchial secretion or by making it less viscous (mucolytic agents). Drugs such as ipecacuanha in small doses act as stimulant expectorants. They irritate the lining of the stomach which reflexly stimulates the production of sputum by the glands in the bronochial mucous membrane

Potassium iodide stimulates the gastric mucosa and reflexly increases the bronchial secretions. Ammonium chloride acts like potassium iodide but is less potent. Antimony potassium tartrate also is used as an expectorant.

1. AMMONIUM CHLORIDE
See page 124 (Chapter 9).

2. POTASSIUM IODIDE, KI

Preparation: Potassium iodide is prepared by adding a slight excess of iodine to a solution of potassium hydroxide to form a mixture of potassium iodide and potassium iodate. Potassium iodate is completely reduced to potassium iodide by heating with charcoal.

$$6KOH + 3I_2 = 5KI + KIO_3 + 3H_2O$$
$$KIO_3 + 3C = KI + 3CO$$

Physical and Chemical Properties: Potassium iodide occurs as large, transparent, colourless or white and somewhat opaque cubes or as a white, granular powder. It is odourless and has a saline and slightly bitter taste.It is stable in dry air. It is very soluble in water (1 in 0.7) and soluble in alcohol (1 in 23). Aqueous solutions of potassium iodide take up iodine, when the iodine is dissolved in them and form KI_3 which is in equilibrium with dissolved iodine.

$$KI_3 \rightleftarrows KI + I_2$$

Potassium iodide deliquesces slightly in moist air. It answers all the chemical reactions of the iodide ion (see Chapter 18).
It is official in I.P.

Official Tests for Identity: Gives the reactions characteristic of potassium and iodides (see Chapter 18).

Tests for Purity
1. Alkalinity
2. Arsenic
3. Heavy metals
4. Barium
5. Cyanide
6. Iodate
7. Loss on drying

8. Clarity and colour of solution
9. Iron
10. Thiosulphate

Alkalinity is expected from the method of preparation of the substance. It is determined by adding to an aqueous solution a definite volume of 0.01M sulphuric acid, using phenolphthalein as indicator. No colour is produced.

Barium is tested as usual by adding dilute sulphuric acid. No turbidity should develop.

Cyanide is tested by adding to an aqueous solution ferrous sulphate solution and sodium hydroxide solution and acidifying with hydrochloric acid. No blue colour (due to Prussian Blue) is produced.

Iodate is tested by adding dilute sulphuric acid and starch solution to an aqueous solution. No blue colour is produced. Iodate reacts with the potassium iodide to liberate iodine which will give the blue colour with starch.

Standard : Contains not less than 99.0 percent and not more than 100 percent of KI calculated with reference to the dried substance.

Assay : Same as for potassium iodide in Aqueous Iodine Solution. See Chapter 10.

Storage : Since it deliquesces slightly in moist air, store in a well closed container.

Medicinal and Pharmaceutical Uses

Expectorant and as a source of iodine. This is also an ingredient in many laboratory reagents such as Mayer's Reagent and Nessler's Reagent.

III. SEDATIVE

Hypnotics are drugs which produce sleep and so are used to treat cases of insomnia (sleeplessness). Sedatives are drugs which reduce excitment and produce sedation(calmness). The same drug may act as a hypnotic or sedative or both depending upon the dose. Hypnotics and sedatives depress the central nervous system for producing sleep and sedation.

POTASSIUM BROMIDE, KBr

Preparation : Bromine, in slight excess, is added to a concentrated solution of potassium hydroxide. Potasssium bromide and potassium bromate are formed. The solution is evaporated to dryness and the residue is heated with water, filtered and the filtrate evaporated to crystallisation.

$$6KOH + 3Br_2 = NaBrO_3 + 5NaBr + 3H_2O$$

$$NaBrO_3 + 3C = NaBr + 3CO$$

Physical and Chemical Properties

Potassium bromide occurs as colourless, translucent crystals or as white, cubical crystals or as a granular powder. It is odourless with a slightly bitter, sharp, saline taste. It is stable in air. It is freely soluble in water and slightly soluble in a alcohol. It crackles (or decrepitates) when heated and fuses at about 73^{0}C without decomposing. Aqueous solution of potassium bromide is neutral or weakly alkaline to litmus. It is not deliquescent like sodium bromide. It reacts with metals such as bismuth, antimony, lead, silver, mercurous mercury and cuprous copper to form the corresponding insoluble bromides. It is official in I P.

Official Tests for Identity : It gives the reactions of potassium and of bromides. See Chapter 18.

Tests for Purity

1. Acidity and alkalinity
2. Clarity and colour of solution
3. Bromates
4. Iodides
5. Heavy metals

6. Arsenic
7. Barium
8. Iron
9. Sulphate
10. Chlorides
11. Sodium
12. Calcium and magnesium
13. Loss on drying

The impurities of bromates, iodides and barium may result from the methods of manufacture.

Bromates are tested by adding dilute sulphuric acid and chloroform and shaking thoroughly. The chloroform layer should remain colourless. If bromates are present, they will react with the bromide in the presence of sulphuric acid and liberate bromine which will dissolve in the chloroform colouring it yellow or orange.

Iodides are tested by adding ferric chloride solution to an aqueous solution and heating on a water bath. It is cooled and shaken with chloroform. The chloroform layer should remain colourless. If iodides are present, they are oxidised to iodine which dissolves in the chloroform colouring it yellow or violet.

Barium is tested by adding to an aqueous solution of the substance dilute sulphuric acid. The solution should not develop any opalescence (due to barium sulphate).

Chlorides are tested by taking the solution available after completing the assay in which the potassium bromide is destroyed by oxidation with potassium permanganate (see assay below). The solution is treated with 0.1M silver nitrate and nitrobenzene and the excess of silver nitrate is titrated with standard 0.1M ammonium thiocyanate using ferric ammonium sulphate as indicator.

Calcium and magnesium are tested by adding to an aqueous solution of the substance dilute ammonia and sodium phosphate solution. The solution should remain clear. If calcium and magnesium are present, they will form insoluble calcium phosphate and magnesium ammonium phosphate respectively.

Sodium is tested by adding to an aqueous alcoholic solution potassium antimonate solution. No precipitate is formed within fifteen minutes. If sodium is present it will precipitate sodium pyroantimonate.

Standard : Potassium Bromide contains not less than 98% of KBr, calculated with reference to the dried substance.

Assay : An accurately weighed quantity is dissolved in water to form a dilute solution and heated to boiling after adding dilute sulphuric acid. While the solution is still boiling, it is titrated with 0.1N potassium permanganate added dropwise till the pink colour just persists.

Potassium permanganate oxidises potassium bromide to bromine.

$$2KMnO_4 + 10KBr + 8H_2SO_4 = 6K_2SO_4 + 2MnSO_4 + 5Br_2$$
$$+ 8H_2O$$

Storage : Store in well-closed containers.

Medicinal Use : *Sedative and anticonvulsant.*

IV. ANTIDOTES

1. SODIUM NITRITE, Na NO$_2$

Preparation : Sodium nitrite is usually obtained by reducing sodium nitrate.

1. By reducing sodium nitrate with carbon in the presence of lime which removes carbon dioxide as calcium carbonate.

    $$2NaNO_3 + C + Ca(OH)_2 \longrightarrow 2NaNO_2 + CaCO_3 + H_2O$$

2. By reducing sodium nitrate with lead at 450 to 500°C or better still with sulphur and sodium hydroxide.

    $$NaNO_3 + Pb \longrightarrow NaNO_2 + PbO$$
    $$3NaNO_3 + 2NaOH + S \longrightarrow 3NaNO_2 + Na_2SO_4 + H_2O.$$

Physical and Chemical Properties

Sodium nitrite occurs as colourless to slightly yellow crystals or as a slightly yellow, granular powder. It is odourless and has a mild saline taste. When exposed to the atmosphere, it deliquesces and is slightly oxidised to sodium nitrate. It is freely soluble in water and sparingly soluble in alcohol.

Aqueous solutions of sodium nitrite are alkaline because it is the salt of a weak acid (nitrous acid) and is appreciably hydrolysed in solution. Sodium nitrite is easily decomposed by acidification with dilute sulphuric acid to give nitric oxide (NO) which is readily oxidised by atmospheric oxygen to form nitrogen peroxide (NO_2).

$$2NaNO_2 + H_2SO_4 \rightarrow Na_2SO_4 + 2HNO_2$$
$$3HNO_2 \rightarrow H_2O + 2NO\uparrow + HNO_3$$
$$2NO + O_2 \rightarrow 2NO_2\uparrow$$

It behaves both as an oxidizing agent and as a reducing agent.

a. *As an oxidizing agent:* It oxidizes acidified potassium iodide to iodine and bleaches indigo.It oxidizes also stannous chloride to stannic chloride.

$$2HNO_2 + 2KI + H_2SO_4 \rightarrow I_2 + 2NO\uparrow + 2H_2O + K_2SO_4$$

b. *As a reducing agent :* It reduces acidified potassium permanganate and potassium dichromate solutions.

$$5NaNO_2 + 2KMnO_4 + 3H_2SO_4 \rightarrow 5NaNO_3 + K_2SO_4 + 2MnSO_4 + 3H_2O$$

In this reaction sodium nitrite is oxidised to sodium nitrate. This is the assay method for sodium nitrite. The known excess of potassium permanganate solution added is back titrated with decinormal oxalic acid solution.

It is official in I.P.1966.

Tests for Purity

1. A solution in water gives the reactions of sodium and of nitrites. See Chapter 18.

324

2. When sodium nitrite is treated with mineral acids or acetic acid, it gives brownish red fumes of nitrogen dioxide.

3. A solution of sodium nitrite in water, when added to potassium iodide containing a little starch solution gives a blue colour This is due to the oxidation of potassium iodide to iodine which gives the blue colour with starch.

Tests for Purity

1. Heavy metals
2. Chloride
3. Sulphate
4. Loss on drying
5. Reaction

Reaction: A solution in water is alkaline to litmus

Standard : Sodium nitrite contains not less than 97 percent of $NaNO_2$, calculated with reference to the substance dried over silica gel for four hours.

Assay : A solution of sodium nitrite is run into acidified 0.1N potassium permanganate. Always sodium nitrite solution must be run into potassium permanganate and not vice versa. This is because the nitrous acid formed decomposes quickly, losing oxides of nitrogen. The nitrous acid liberated is immediately oxidised before the above reaction can take place. For this the tip of the burette containing sodium nitrite solution should be immersed below the surface of the potassium permanganate solution.

$$NaNO_2 + H_2SO_4 = HNO_2 + NaHSO_4$$
$$HNO_2 + O = HNO_3$$

Excess of 0.1N oxalic acid is added, the mixture heated to 80°C and titrated with 0.1N potassium permanganate.

Storage : Since sodium nitrite is deliquescent and is slowly oxidised to sodium nitrate on exposure to atmosphere, it should be stored in tightly closed containers.

Medicinal and Pharmaceutical Uses

Antidote for Cyanide Poisoning. Sodium nitrite combines with haemoglobin of the blood to form methaemoglobin with which the cyanide forms cyanmethaemoglobin. In this form the cyanide is not toxic to the body. After the administration of nitrite, sodium thiosulphate is injected to convert the cyanide further to thiocyanate which is also not toxic.

Sodium nitrite is used as a vasodilator but rarely nowadays in view of its slow onset of action. It is also used in the manufacture of azo dyes and as a reagent in the laboratory.

2. SODIUM THIOSULPHATE, $Na_2S_2O_3.5H_2O$

Preparation : 1. One half of a concentrated solution of sodium carbonate is saturated with sulphur dioxide and the other half is added to it. Sodium sulphite is formed.

$$Na_2CO_3 + 2SO_2 + H_2O = 2NaHSO_3 + CO_2\uparrow$$

$$2NaHSO_3 + Na_2CO_3 = Na_2SO_3 + H_2O + CO_2\uparrow$$

Sodium thiosulphate solution is prepared by boiling sodium sulphite solution with flowers of sulphur and stirring till the alkaline reaction has disappeared.

$$Na_2SO_3 + S = Na_2S_2O_3$$

The excess of sulphur is filtered off and the filtrate evaporated to crystallization when crystals of sodium thiosulphate ($Na_2S_2O_3.5H_2O$) separate on slow cooling.

It can also be prepared by passing sulphur dioxide into sodium sulphide solution.

$$2Na_2S + 3SO_2 = 2Na_2S_2O_3 + S$$

Physical and Chemical Properties

Sodium thiosulphate occurs as large, colourless, monoclinic crystals or as a coarse, crystalline powder. It is odourless and has a saline taste. It is deliquescent in moist air and effloresces in dry air at temperatures above 33°C. It is very soluble in water and insoluble in alcohol. Aqueous neutral or alkaline solutions of the salt decompose on boiling because of reduction to sulphide and oxidation to sulphate.

At 56°C the salt melts in its water of hydration and at 100°C it becomes anhydrous. At 100°C decomposition of the salt begins and at 220°C it is completely converted into sulphur, sulphur dioxide, sodium sulphide and sodium sulphate.

$$4Na_2S_2O_3 \triangleq 3Na_2SO_4 + Na_2S_5$$
$$Na_2S_5 \triangleq Na_2S + 4S$$
$$Na_2S_5 + 4O_2 \triangleq Na_2S + 4SO_2\uparrow$$

Addition of a mineral acid such as hydrochloric acid to a solution of sodium thiosulphate produces thiosulphuric acid which immediately decomposes into sulphur, sulphur dioxide and water.

$$Na_2S_2O_3 + 2HCl = H_2S_2O_3 + 2NaCl$$
Thiosulphuric acid
$$H_2S_2O_3 = S\downarrow + SO_2 + H_2O$$

Silver nitrate gives with a very dilute solution of sodium thiosulphate a white precipitate which quickly changes colour to yellow, brown and finally black due to the formation of silver sulphide.

$$Na_2S_2O_3 + 2AgNO_3 = Ag_2S_2O_3\downarrow + 2NaNO_3$$
Silver thiosulphate
(white)

$$Ag_2S_2O_3 + H_2O = Ag_2S + H_2SO_4$$
Silver sulphide
(black)

Sodium thiosulphate is a good reducing agent and reduces halogens such as chlorine and iodine. It decolurises iodine solution and this is the method by which both iodine and sodium thiosulphate are assayed.

$$2Na_2S_2O_3 + I_2 = 2NaI + Na_2S_4O_6$$
Sodium tetrathionate

Upon the addition of a few drops of ferric chloride solution to a solution of sodium thiosulphate, a red colour appears and the colour disappears quickly. The red colour is due to the formation of ferric thiosulphate and the disappearance of the colour is due to the reduction of the ferric salt by the sodium thiosulphate.

A moderately concentrated solution of sodium thiosulphate gives a white precipitate of barium thiosulphate with barium chloride. No precipitate is obtained with calcium chloride since calcium thiosulphate is fairly soluble in water.

$$Na_2S_2O_3 + BaCl_2 = BaS_2O_3 + 2NaCl$$

It is official in I.P.

Official Tests for Identity

1. To an aqueous solution of the sample 0.1M silver nitrate is added. A white precipitate is produced and it becomes quickly yellowish and finally black.

2. To an aquous solution iodine is added. The colour is discharged.

3. To an aqueous solution hydrochloric acid is added. A gas is evolved and it turns starch-iodate paper blue. A precipitate of sulphur is also produced. Sulphur dioxide, which is produced, reduces iodate to iodine which gives the blue colour with starch.

4. An aqueous solution gives the reactions of sodium salts, see Chapter 18.

Non-official Test for Identity : Addition of Ferric Chloride T.S to an aqueous solution gives a dark red colour which quickly disappears.

Tests for Purity

1. pH
2. Arsenic
3. Heavy metals
4. Clarity and colour of solution
5. Chloride
6. Sulphate and sulphite
7. Sulphide.

In the case of *heavy metals*, the limit test is applied after pretreatment in the preparation of the solution of the substance.

Sulphate and sulphite (also *sulphide*) may arise from the method of manufacture. These are tested by oxidising the sodium thiosulphate with iodine solution and applying the limit test for sulphates. *Sulphide* is limited by adding to an aqueous solution a freshly prepared solution of sodium nitroprusside. The solution should not become violet.

Standard : Sodium thiosulphate contains not less than 99 per cent anad not more than 101 per cent of $Na_2S_2O_3 . 5H_2O$.

Assay : An accurately weighed quantity is dissolved in water and the solution is titrated with 0.05M iodine, using starch as indicator towards the end of the titration. Appearance of blue colour is the end point.

$$I_2 + Na_2S_2O_3 = Na_2S_4O_6 + 2NaI$$

Storage : Since it is deliquescent in moist air and efflorescent in dry air, it must be stored in tightly closed, air tight containers.

Medicinal and Pharmaceutical Uses

Antidote for Cyanide Poisoning. It is also used as an *antifungal* agent. Sometimes it is used as a cathartic. Due to its property of dissolving silver halides, it is used in photography for fixing under the name 'hypo'. During bleaching of textiles, it is used as an antichlor (that is , to remove excess of chlorine). It is also used in the extraction of gold and silver from their ores.

3. CHARCOAL

See Chapter 9.

V. RESPIRATORY STIMULANT

Reflex stimulation of the central nervous system is brought about by subjecting the patient to inhalation of substances like ammonium carbonate which gives off ammonia in conditions of syncope or fainting. In other words a person who has fainted is revived by keeping ammonium carbonate or any other volatile ammonium salt near his nose. These substances are also known as *smelling salts*.

AMMONIUM CARBONATE, $NH_4HCO_3.NH_4COONH_2$

Ammonium carbonate is also known as *ammonium sesquicarbonate and sal volatile*. It is a variable mixture of ammonium bicarbonate (NH_4HCO_3) and ammonium carbamate (NH_4COONH_2). It contains not less than 30 per cent of ammonia.

Preparation : Ammonium carbonate may be prepared by subliming a mixture of ammonium sulphate or ammonium chloride with chalk (calcium carbonate) in iron retorts and condensing the vapour in chambers lined with lead. The ammonia along with the ammonium carbonate is recovered by passing into sulphuric acid.

$$2(NH_4)_2SO_4 + 2CaCO_3 = NH_4HCO_3.NH_4COONH_2$$
$$+ NH_3 + H_2O + 2CaSO_4$$

Physical and Chemical Properties :

Ammonium carbonate consists of hard, translucent (semi-transparent), crystalline masses with a strong ammoniacal odour. It has a pungent and ammoniacal taste. It is soluble in water and partly soluble in alcohol. A residue of ammonium bicarbonate is found at the bottom of the alcoholic solution confirming the partial solubility. Aqueous solutions of the salt are alkaline.

When it is exposed to air, it partially dissociates and volatilises getting converted into porous opaque lumps or into a white powder. The residue is mainly ammonium bicarbonate. Ammonia and carbon dioxide are given off.

$$NH_4HCO_3. NH_4COONH_2 = 2NH_3\uparrow + CO_2\uparrow + NH_4HCO_3$$

The same result is produced by dissolving it in hot water.

When it is treated with dilute ammonia, it is readily converted to the normal carbonate $(NH_4)_2CO_3$.

$$NH_4HCO_3. NH_4COONH_2 + NH_4OH = 2(NH_4)_2CO_3$$

It is decomposed by the addition of any mineral acid. The acid may be added to the dry salt or to a solution of the salt in water.

$$NH_4HCO_3. NH_4COONH_2 + 3HCl = 3NH_4Cl + H_2O + 2CO_2\uparrow$$

Ammonium carbonate is not official in B.P. or I.P.

Tests for Identity

1. When a little of the salt is heated, it is volatilised and no charring takes place. When tested with moist litmus paper, the vapour is strongly alkaline.

2. When a dilute mineral acid is added to an aqueous solution of the salt, effervescence is produced.

Storage : Since it is very volatile, store in a tightly closed container.

Medicinal Uses : *Respiratory Stimulant.* As already stated, it is used for the revival of the fainted patients by reflex stimulation of their central nervous system by inhalation. It is also used as an expectorant and antacid.

CHAPTER 17
PREPARATION AND USES OF SOME INORGANIC REAGENTS IN ORGANIC SYNTHESIS

1. N-BROMOSUCCINIMIDE

Preparation: Succinimide can be prepared by heating either succinamic acid or succinamide.

Succinamic acid   Succinimide   Succinamide

Imides such as succinimide are tautomeric and form lactam and lactim which are similar to the keto and enol forms of β-Ketonic esters such as the acetoacetic ester. They are able to form these lactam and lactim because they possess the imido group $-CO-NH-CO-$.

Lactam   Lactim

The hydrogen atom in the lactim is labile and is weakly acidic. So the imides dissolve in alkali hydroxide solutions and form the corresponding metallic derivatives.

N-bromosuccinimide is formed when succinimide is allowed to react with bromine and sodium hydroxide at 0°C.

N - bromosuccinimide

Uses: N-bromosuccinimide is used for brominating olefinic compounds in the allyl position.

$$— CH_2— \ CH=CH— \ \longrightarrow —CHBr —CH = CH—$$

2. LITHIUM ALUMINIUM HYDRIDE

Preparation: Lithium aluminium hydride is prepared by treating an ethereal solution of lithium hydride with anhydrous aluminium chloride.

$$4 \ LiH + AlCl_3 = LiAlH_4 + 3 \ LiCl$$
$$\text{Lithium}$$
$$\text{aluminium}$$
$$\text{hydride}$$

Lithium hydride itself is obtained by heating lithium in a current of hydrogen strongly.

$$2 \ Li + H_2 = 2LiH$$

Uses: The reagent is used in ethereal solution. The following reductions are promoted by lithium aluminium hydride:-

$$R-CHO \ \longrightarrow \ R-CH_2OH$$
$$R_2CO \ \longrightarrow \ R_2CHOH$$
$$R-COOH \ \longrightarrow \ R-CH_2OH$$
$$R-Cl \ \longrightarrow \ R-H$$
$$R-COCl \ \longrightarrow \ R-CH_2OH$$
$$RCOOR \ \longrightarrow \ R-CH_2OH$$
$$R_2N-NO \ \longrightarrow \ R_2N-NH_2$$

It does not usually hydrogenate double bonds. A few examples are given below:-

1. It will reduce a triple bond to a double bond when the triple bond is adjacent to a propargylic hydroxyl group.

$$—C(OH)—C \equiv C— \ \xrightarrow{LiAlH_4} \ —C(OH)—CH \equiv CH—$$

2. In the synthesis of vitamin A, retinoic acid is reduced to vitamin A by lithium aluminium hydride.

$$CH=CH-\underset{\underset{CH_3}{|}}{C}=CH-CH=CH-\underset{\underset{CH_3}{|}}{C}=CH-COOH$$

Vit A_1, acid (Retinoic acid)

$\downarrow$ LiAlH$_4$

$$CH=CH-\underset{\underset{CH_3}{|}}{C}=CH-CH=CH-\underset{\underset{CH_3}{|}}{C}=CH-CH_2OH$$

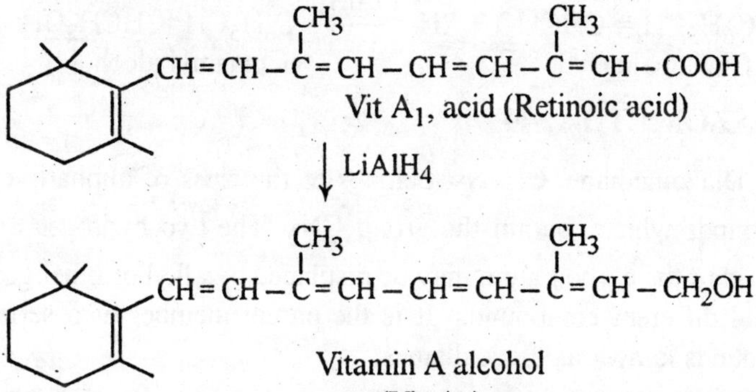

Vitamin A alcohol
(Vit A_1)

3. In the synthesis of vitamin D_3 or ergocalciferol starting from cholesterol, LiAlH$_4$ is used in the second stage for reducing the ketone at the 7th position into a secondary alcoholic group.

4. Oestrone may be reduced to oestradiol by catalytic hydrogenation or by aluminium isopropoxide or by LiAlH$_4$.

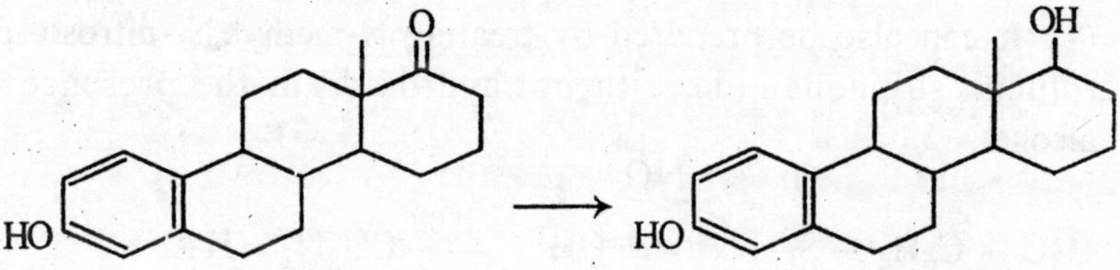

Oestrone   Oestradiol

5. The 11-keto group in cortisone can be readily reduced to the hydroxyl group by lithium aluminium hydride to form hydrocortisone.

6. Amino acids may be reduced to the amino alcohols directly by LiAlH$_4$.

7. In the determination of the structure of proteins, reduction of proteins with LiAlH$_4$ converts the free terminal carboxyl group to a primary alcoholic group. Hydrolysis produces an aminoalcohol which can be identified.

334

8. LiAlH$_4$ reduces cinnamaldehyde to cinnamyl alcohol. It reduces the —CHO group but does not reduce the ethylenic double bond.

$$C_6H_5CH = CHCHO + 2H \xrightarrow{\text{LiAlH}_4} C_6H_5CH=CHCH_2OH$$

Cinnamaldehyde   Cinnamyl alcohol

3. DIAZOMETHANE

Diazomethane, CH_2N_2, belongs to the class of aliphatic diazo compounds which contain the group $\text{C}N_2$. The two hydrogen atoms attached to the carbon atom may be displaced by alkyl or other groups to yield different compounds. It is the parent member of a series of compounds known as diazoalkanes.

Preparation: (1) It is prepared by the action of a base on N—nitroso—N—methylamide.

$$R—\overset{\overset{\textstyle O}{\|}}{C}—N\overset{NO}{\underset{CH_3}{<}} + OH^- \xrightarrow{\text{Ether}} R—\overset{\overset{\textstyle O}{\|}}{C}—O^- + CH_2N_2 + H_2O$$

N—Nitroso—N—methylamide   Diazomethane

(2) It can also be prepared by treating N-methyl N—nitroso—p—toluene sulphonamide with pot.hydroxide in the presence of alcohol.

$$H_3C — C_6H_4 — \overset{\overset{\textstyle O}{\|}}{\underset{\underset{\textstyle O}{\|}}{S}} — N\overset{NO}{\underset{CH_3}{<}} + OH^- \xrightarrow[\text{Ether}]{C_2H_5OH} CH_2N_2 + H_2O +$$

N—methyl—N—nitroso—p—toluene sulphonamide $H_3C—C_6H_4—\overset{\overset{\textstyle O}{\|}}{\underset{\underset{\textstyle O}{\|}}{S}}—O^-$

Uses: Diazomethane is a deep yellow gas which is very toxic. When pure, it is highly explosive. It is used in synthesis in ether solution.

(1) Methylation Reactions with Several Compounds

Diazomethane reacts with alcohols, phenols, amines and carboxylic acids in the presence of ether to introduce the methyl group in place of the hydrogen atom in the these compounds.

$$R\text{-}OH + CH_2N_2 \xrightarrow[BF_3]{Ether} R\text{-}OCH_3 + N_2$$
$$\text{Methyl ether}$$

$$C_6H_5OH + CH_2N_2 \xrightarrow{Ether} C_6H_5OCH_3 + N_2$$
$$\text{Anisole}$$

$$R-NH_2 + CH_2N_2 \xrightarrow[BF_3]{Ether} RNH\text{-}CH_3$$
$$\text{Methylamine}$$

$$R-COOH + CH_2N_2 \xrightarrow{Ether} R-COOCH_3 + N_2$$
$$\text{Methyl ester}$$

(2) It reacts with aldehydes to form the corresponding methyl ketone.

$$R\text{-}\overset{\overset{O}{\|}}{C}\text{-}H + CH_2N_2 \xrightarrow{Ether} R\text{-}\overset{\overset{O}{\|}}{C}\text{-}CH_3 + N_2$$
$$\text{Methyl ketone}$$

It reacts with ketones to insert the $-CH_2-$ group.

$$R\text{-}\overset{\overset{O}{\|}}{C}\text{-}R' + CH_2N_2 \xrightarrow{Ether} R\text{-}\overset{\overset{O}{\|}}{C}\text{-}CH_2\text{-}R' + N_2$$
$$\text{Higher ketone}$$

(3) Diazomethane also reacts with alkenes and alkynes.

$$CH_3CH=CHCH_3 + CH_2N_2 \xrightarrow[light]{UV} CH_3\text{-}CH\overset{\overset{H_2}{C}}{\text{---}}CH\text{-}CH_3 + N_2$$
$$\text{2-Butene} \qquad\qquad \text{1,2-Dimethylcyclopropane}$$

(4) It reacts with acid halides to give carboxylic acids with one more carbon atom.

$$R\text{-}\overset{\overset{O}{\|}}{C}\text{-}Cl + CH_2N_2 \rightarrow R\text{-}\overset{\overset{O}{\|}}{C}\text{-}CHN_2 + HCl$$
$$\text{Acid chloride} \qquad\qquad \text{Diazoketone}$$

$$R\text{-}\overset{\overset{O}{\|}}{C}\text{-}CHN_2 + H_2O \xrightarrow{Ag_2O} R\text{-}CH_2\text{-}\overset{\overset{O}{\|}}{C}\text{-}OH + N_2$$
$$\text{Carboxylic acid}$$

(5) It also reacts with alkanes to give the higher homologue.

$$CH_3CH_2CH_3 + CH_2N_2 \xrightarrow{hv} CH_3CH_2CH_2CH_3 + CH_3\overset{\overset{\displaystyle CH_3}{|}}{C}HCH_3$$

Propane   n-Butane   Isobutane

4. PERIODIC ACID

Periodic acid, also known as para-periodic acid, has the formula $HIO_4.2H_2O$ or H_5IO_6. It loses, on dehydration, water of crystallization to form dimeso-periodic acid, $H_4I_2O_9$ and metaperiodic acid, HIO_4. Finally it loses oxygen to form iodic acid, HIO_3.

Preparation: Para-periodic acid is prepared by suspending iodine in perchloric acid and heating.

$$2HClO_4 + I_2 + 4H_2O = 2H_5IO_6 + Cl_2$$

Perchloric acid   Para-periodic acid

Uses

It is a more powerful oxidizing agent than iodic acid and is used in organic chemistry for this purpose.

1. Determination of the Size of Ring in Sugars

Periodic acid is able to rupture 1:2-glycols.

$$R-CHOH-CHOH-R' \xrightarrow{HIO} R-CHO + R'-CHO$$

A free sugar is broken down completely.

$$CH_2OH-CHOH-CHOH-CHOH-CHO \xrightarrow{4HIO_4} H-CHO + 4H-COOH$$

                                         Formaldehyde   Formic acid

By finding out the periodic acid used and also the amount of formaldehyde and formic acid formed, the no.of free adjacent hydroxyl groups in a sugar can be found out.

2. Confirmation of the Structure of Sucrose

Sucrose is α-D-glucopyranosyl-β-D-fructofuranoside. The α-D-glucopyranose unit and the β-D-fructopyranose unit are joined by oxygen through the **carbonyl-carbon** atoms of both. Sucrose has no reducing property like **dextrose because** of this.

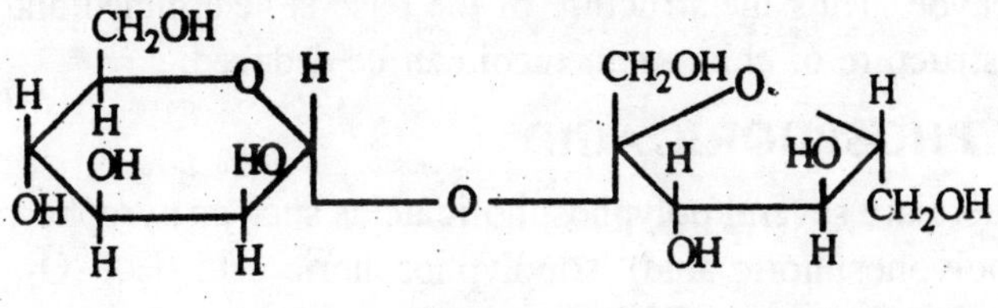

Sucrose

Oxidation of sucrose with periodic acid confirms this structure.

3. Determination of the Molecular weight of Cellulose :

Since cellulose is insoluble, its molecular weight cannot be determined by the usual methods like elevation of boiling point and depression of freezing point. For this purpose many end-group determination methods are used. One such is based on the periodate oxidation of cellulose. The terminal reducing unit of cellulose gives rise to two molecules of formic acid and one molecule of formaldehyde. The other reducing unit gives one molecule of formic acid. So totally three molecules of formic acid and one of formaldehyde are produced. Estimation of formic acid produced gives a chain length of approximately 1000 **glucose units.**

4. Determination of the Structure of Chloramphenicol :

Chloramphemicol has the following structure:

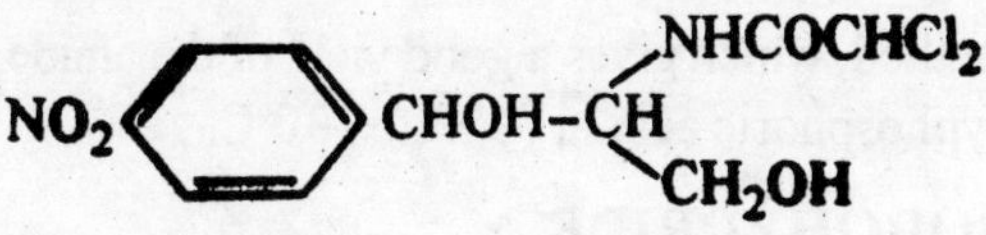

It is **hydrolysed to its** base given below:-

338

When this base is treated with periodic acid, two molecules of the base form one molecule each of ammonia, formaldehyde and p-nitrobenzaldehyde. Thus the structure of the base is determined and from that the structure of chloramphenicol can be deduced.

5. POLYPHOSPHORIC ACID

There are several polyphosphoric acids such as pyrophosphoric acid (dipolyphosphoric acid), tripolyphosphoric acid ($H_5P_3O_{10}$) and tetrapolyphosphoric acid ($H_6P_4O_{13}$).

Preparation: Pyrophosphoric acid is prepared by heating orthophosphoric acid to about 530K.

$$2H_3PO_4 = H_4P_2O_7 + H_2O$$

Uses: Aryl ketones react with hydroxylamine to form the corresponding ketoximes.

$$\underset{\text{Aryl ketone}}{\overset{Ar}{\underset{Ar}{>}}C=O} + \underset{\text{Hydroxylamine}}{H_2NOH} \longrightarrow \underset{\text{Aryl ketoxime}}{\overset{Ar}{\underset{Ar}{>}}C=NOH}$$

These ketoximes undergo rearrangement in the presence of dilute acids or PCl_5 to give N-substituted amides. This is called as *Beckmann Rearrangement.*

$$\overset{Ar}{\underset{Ar}{>}}C=NOH \xrightarrow{PCl_5} Ar-CO-NH-Ar$$
$$\text{N-Substituted amide}$$

An alternative method, which gives a good yield of the amide, is to heat the oxime in polyphosphoric acid at 95°C to 130°C.

6. SODIUM BOROHYDRIDE

Preparation: It is prepared by heating a mixture of NaH and $(CH_3)_3$ BO_3 at 225-275°C in the right proportions.

$$4NaH + B(OCH_3)_3 = NaBH_4 + 3NaOCH_3$$
$$\text{Sod. borohydride } \quad \text{Sod. metnoxide}$$

339

The borohydride is extracted with liquid ammonia in which the bye product sodium methoxide is insoluble.

Uses: Sodium borohydride is a good reducing agent. It differs from lithium aluminium hydride in many respects and acts more selectively. For example aldehydes and ketones are reduced to alcohols but ester, nitro, cyano and amido groups are not reduced. Some examples are given below:-

1. Determination of the Structure of Polysaccharides:

For determining the structure of any polysaccharide, it has to be degraded. The first step in this process is oxidation of the polysaccharide with periodic acid. The aldehyde groups produced by this oxidation may be reduced to primary alcohols by sodium borohydride.

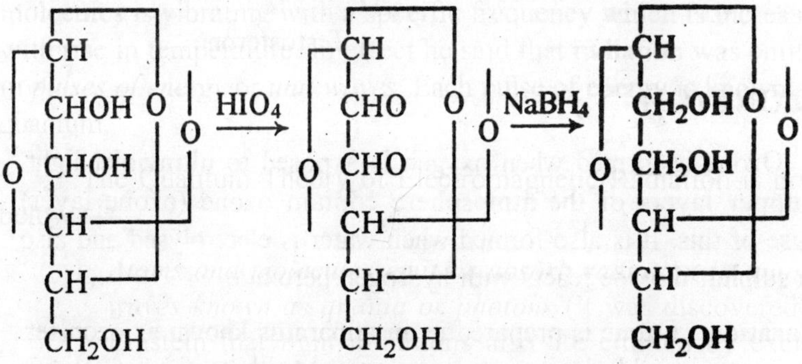

$$
\begin{array}{ccc}
\text{CH} & & \text{CH} & & \text{CH}\\
\text{CHOH} & \xrightarrow{\text{HIO}_4} & \text{CHO} & \xrightarrow{\text{NaBH}_4} & \text{CH}_2\text{OH}\\
\text{CHOH} & & \text{CHO} & & \text{CH}_2\text{OH}\\
\text{CH} & & \text{CH} & & \text{CH}\\
\text{CH} & & \text{CH} & & \text{CH}\\
\text{CH}_2\text{OH} & & \text{CH}_2\text{OH} & & \text{CH}_2\text{OH}
\end{array}
$$

Then it is hydrolysed with acid, methylated and so on.

2. Determination of the Structure of Cellulose.

In one method for the determination of the structure of cellulose, it is reduced by sodium borohydride which reduces the terminal reducing unit. It is followed by periodate oxidation.

3. Conformational Analysis of Steroids.

In the conformational analysis of steroids catalytic hydrogenation in neutral medium produces equatorial alcohol if the ketone is unhindered. Sodium borohydride also gives the same result.

4. Synthesis of Testosterone from Dehydroepiandrosterone.

In this synthesis, dehydroepiandrosterone is first oxidised to androsten - 4 - ene - 3:17 dione. The latter is reduced to testosterone by sodium borohydride.

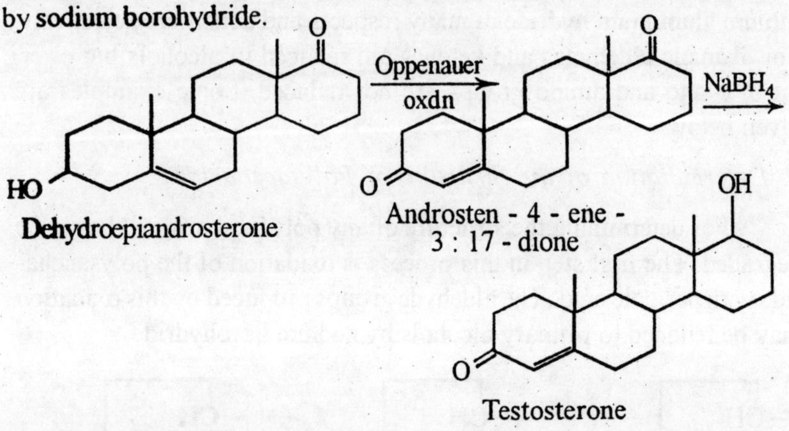

Dehydroepiandrosterone

Androsten - 4 - ene -
3 : 17 - dione

Testosterone

7. OZONE (O_3)

Ozone is formed when oxygen is exposed to ultraviolet light. The upper layers of the atmosphere contain ozone (ozone layer) because of this. It is also formed when water is electrolysed and also when sulphur dioxide reacts with hydrogen peroxide.

Preparation : Ozone is prepared in an apparatus known as ozoniser. In the ozoniser cold, dry oxygen is subjected to the action of electric discharges. Two types of ozonisers, viz, Siemen's ozoniser and Brodie's ozoniser are used. In the electrolytic method, acidified water is subjected to electrolysis with a high current density using a platinum anode and a gas which contains upto 95 percent ozone (the rest being oxygen) is collected at the anode.

Uses

1. Oxidation with Ozone

Ozone adds across double bonds to form an *ozonide*, when it is passed through an alkene in an inert solvent.

$$\underset{\text{Ethylene}}{\overset{\displaystyle CH_2}{\underset{\displaystyle CH_2}{\|}}} + O_3 \rightarrow \underset{\text{Ethylene ozonide}}{\overset{\displaystyle CH_2 —O—CH_2}{\underset{\displaystyle O————O}{\big|\qquad\big|}}}$$

On warming with zinc and water, ozonides break at the double bond and form aldehydes, ketones or both.

$$\overset{\displaystyle CH_2—O—CH_2}{\underset{\displaystyle O————O}{\big|\qquad\big|}} \xrightarrow[+H_2O]{Zn} CH_2{=}O + O{=}CH_2$$
$$\text{Formaldehyde (2 molecules)}$$

$$\underset{\text{2-Methyl-2-butene}}{(CH_3)_2C = CH\text{-}CH_3} \xrightarrow[Zn+H_2O]{O_3} \underset{\text{Acetone}}{(CH_3)_2C{=}O} + \underset{\text{Acetaldehyde}}{O = CH\text{-}CH_3}$$

This method of preparing the ozonide and decomposing to get carbonyl compounds is known as *ozonolysis*.

2. In a similar manner alkynes undergo ozonolysis. They first react with ozone to give ozonides which are decomposed with water to give diketones. The latter are also oxidised to carboxylic acids by the hydrogen peroxide produced during the reaction.

$$\underset{\text{Alkyne}}{R{-}C \equiv C{-}R'} + O_3 \rightarrow R{-}\overset{\displaystyle \frown}{\underset{\displaystyle O—O}{C—C}}{-}R' \xrightarrow{H_2O}$$
$$\text{Ozonide}$$

$$R{-}\overset{\|}{\underset{O}{C}}{-}\overset{\|}{\underset{O}{C}}{-}R' \xrightarrow{H_2O_2} \underset{\text{Carboxylic acids}}{R{-}COOH + HOOC{-}R'}$$

8. THIONYL CHLORIDE

This is the acid chloride of sulphurous acid, $SO(OH)_2$ or H_2SO_3.

Preparation

(1) It is produced by the action of sulphur trioxide on sulphur monochloride.

$$SO_3 + S_2Cl_2 = SOCl_2 + SO_2 + S$$
$$\text{Thionyl chloride}$$

(2) It may also be prepared by reacting phosphorus pentachloride with sulphur dioxide.

$$SO_2 + PCl_5 = SOCl_2 + POCl_3$$

Uses : Thionyl chloride is used for replacing the hydroxyl group in organic compounds by chlorine.

For example alcohols react with thionylchloride in the presence of pyridine to form alkyl chlorides. The hydrogen chloride formed as a bye product is absorbed by pyridine.

$$R-OH + SOCl_2 \xrightarrow{\text{Pyridine}} R-Cl + SO_2 + HCl$$

9. ALUMINIUM ISOPROPOXIDE

Aluminium isopropoxide has the formula $[(CH_3)_2CHO)_3]Al$. It is also called as Meerwein-Ponndorf-Verly reagent.

Preparation: It is prepared by the action of aluminium amalgam or aluminium shavings on isopropanol.

$$(CH_3)_2 CHOH \xrightarrow{Al/Hg} [(CH_3)_2CHO]_3Al$$

Uses: Aluminium isopropoxide is a good reducing agent.

(1) Reduction of both aldehydes and ketones to alcohols may be done by means of the Meerwein–Ponndorf–Verley reduction. The carbonyl compound is heated with aluminium isopropoxide in isopropanol. The isopropoxide is oxidized to acetone which is removed from the equilibrium mixture by slow distillation.

$$R_2CO + [(CH_3)_2CHO]_3Al \rightleftharpoons (R_2CHO)_3Al + CH_3COCH_3 \xrightarrow[H_2SO_4]{Dil}$$
$$R_2CHOH$$
$$\text{Alcohol}$$

This reducing agent is specific for the carbonyl group and so may be used for reducing aldehydes and ketones containing a reducible group such as a nitro group or double bond.

(2) It reduces cinnamaldehyde to give cinnamyl alcohol. In this reaction it reduces the –CHO group only but does not reduce the ethylenic double bond.

$$C_6H_5CH = CHCHO + 2H \xrightarrow{\ [(CH_3)_2\ CHO]_3Al\ } C_6H_5CH = CHCH_2OH$$
Cinnamaldehyde   Cinnamyl alcohol

(3) In the synthesis of the antibiotic chloramphenicol from p-nitroacetophenone ($O_2NC_6H_4COCH_3$), the keto group is reduced to a secondary alcohol by the use of aluminium isopropoxide.

10. ALUMINIUM TERTIARY BUTOXIDE

Aluminium t-butoxide has the formula $[(CH_3)_3CO]_3$ Al.

Preparation: It is prepared by the action of aluminium amalgam or aluminium shavings on tertiary butyl alcohol.

$$(CH_3)_3\ COH \xrightarrow{\ Al/Hg\ } [(CH_3)_3CO]_3Al$$
Tertiary butyl alcohol

Uses: *(1) Oppenauer Oxidation*

In this process, ketones can be obtained from secondary alcohols when the secondary alcohols are refluxed with excess of acetone in the presence of aluminium tertiary butoxide as catalyst.

This method is very useful for oxidizing unsaturated secondary alcohols since double bonds are not affected.

344

2. Oppenauer oxidation involving aluminium tertiary butoxide in acetone is very much used in steroid chemistry for synthesis as well as for structural elucidation.

For example in the synthesis of testosterone from cholesterol, the penultimate step involving the oxidation of the secondary alcohol at the third position to a ketone and the shifting of the double bond from the 5,6-position to the 4,5-position is carried out using Oppenauer oxidation only.

Testosterone

Oppenauer oxidation is also used in the conversion of pregnenolone to progesterone (last step in the synthesis of progesterone) from stigmasterol, cholesterol and diosgenin. It is also the penultimate step in the synthesis of certain other steroids such as deoxycorticosterone from pregnenolone and used for the same purpose.

11. SODAMIDE

Preparation: Sodamide is prepared by passing a current of dry ammonia gas over sodium metal kept in an iron tube at $600 - 675$ K.

$$2Na + 2NH_3 \longrightarrow 2NaNH_2 + H_2$$
$$\text{Sodamide}$$

Uses

1. Acetylene may be prepared by the action of ethanolic KOH on ethylene dibromide.

$$BrCH_2CH_2Br + KOH \xrightarrow{C_2H_5OH} CH_2=CHBr + KBr + H_2O$$

$$CH_2 = CHBr + KOH \xrightarrow{C_2H_5OH} CH \equiv CH + KBr + H_2O$$

Instead of ethanolic KOH, sodamide can be used. Bye-products are less and the yield is also better.

$$-CHBr\,CHBr- + 2NaNH_2 \longrightarrow -C \equiv C- + 2NaBr + 2NH_3$$

2. Sodio derivatives are obtained when ketones are treated with sodamide in ether solution.

$$CH_3COCH_3 + NaNH_2 \longrightarrow \left[CH_3\overset{O^-}{\underset{|}{C}} = CH_2 \right] Na^+ + NH_3$$

3. Sodamide in liquid ammonia solution reacts with carboxylic acid esters containing α-hydrogen atoms to form the acid amide and a condensation product involving two molecules of the ester. For example ethyl acetate gives acetamide and acetoacetic ester.

$$CH_3COOC_2H_5 + NaNH_2 \longrightarrow CH_3CONH_2 + C_2H_5ONa$$
$$\text{Acetamide}$$

$$CH_3COOC_2H_5 + NaNH_2 \longrightarrow NH_3 + [CH_2COOC_2H_5]^- Na^+$$
$$\xrightarrow{CH_3COOC_2H_5} CH_3COCH_2COOC_2H_5 + C_2H_5OH$$
$$\text{Acetoacetic ester}$$

4. Alkyl cyanides with α-hydrogen atoms can be condensed with esters in the presence of sodamide if the reaction takes place in ether solution.

$$CH_3CN + NaNH_2 \xrightarrow{CH_3CH_2COOC_2H_5} CH_3CH_2COCH_2CN + C_2H_5OH$$

5. Sodamide is also used in the synthesis of indigotin.

12. SODIUM AZIDE

Preparation: Sodium azide can be prepared by heating a solution of sodium nitrate in liquid ammonia along with sodamide to about 365K.

$$NaNO_3 + 3NaNH_2 \longrightarrow NaN_3 + 3NaOH + NH_3$$

Sodamide   Sodium azide

Uses

The Curtius rearrangement involves the following steps :-

ester $\longrightarrow$ hydrazide $\longrightarrow$ azide $\longrightarrow$ urethan $\longrightarrow$ NH$_2$

So in this series of reactions, a carboxylic ester is finally converted into an amino group. For example the synthesis of an a-aminoacid can be carried out as below :-

$$\text{R.CH}\genfrac{}{}{0pt}{}{\text{COOK}}{\text{COOC}_2\text{H}_5} \xrightarrow{N_2H_4} \text{R.CH}\genfrac{}{}{0pt}{}{\text{COOK}}{\text{CONHNH}_2} \xrightarrow{HNO_2} \text{R.CH}\genfrac{}{}{0pt}{}{\text{COOH}}{\text{CON}_3} \xrightarrow{C_2H_5OH}$$

                           Acid azide

$$\text{R.CH}\genfrac{}{}{0pt}{}{\text{COOH}}{\text{NHCOOC}_2\text{H}_5} \xrightarrow{HCl} \text{R.CH (NH}_2\text{) COOH}$$

                α–Aminoacid

It is possible to prepare glycine, alanine, phenylalanine and valine by this method.

However by treating an acid chloride with sodium azide, we can prepare the acid azide used in the Curtius rearrangement and the reaction proceeds as below :-

$$\text{R.CH}\genfrac{}{}{0pt}{}{\text{COOK}}{\text{COCl}} + NaN_3 \longrightarrow \text{R.CH}\genfrac{}{}{0pt}{}{\text{COOK}}{\text{CON}_3} \xrightarrow{C_2H_5OH}$$

                        Acid azide

$$\text{R.CH}\genfrac{}{}{0pt}{}{\text{COOK}}{\text{NH.COOC}_2\text{H}_5} \xrightarrow{HCl} \text{R.CH (NH}_2\text{) COOH}$$

                α–Aminoacid

CHAPTER 18

OFFICIAL IDENTIFICATION TESTS FOR ANIONS AND CATIONS

Identification tests are given in the I.P. 1996 for identifying the cations and anions of the inorganic substances included in the I.P. in monographs. Even though it is stated that these tests are not necessarily sufficient to establish absolute proof of identity, yet we can be reasonably sure that the substance being tested is nothing but the substance claimed on the label, if it answers these tests for identification. When there is a doubt, these tests are highly useful for establishing identity. The tests for all the anions and cations given in the I.P. are included here to give a comprehensive idea to the student. Even though a number of tests are given, the I.P. usually requires in the monograph of the drug, the performance of one or two tests only for each radical. However one is not precluded from doing the other tests also to establish identity if he so chooses.

IDENTIFICATION TESTS FOR ANIONS

ACETATES

1. The sample is heated with an equal quantity of oxalic acid. Acetic acid with its characteistic odour is liberated.

2. The sample is heated with a little concentrated sulphuric acid and ethyl alcohol. The ester ethyl acetate, which can be recognised by its odour, is evolved.

3. To an aqueous solution of the sample are added successively lanthanum nitrate solution, decinormal iodine and dilute ammonia solution. The mixture is heated carefully to boiling. After a few minutes either a blue precipitate is formed or a dark blue colour develops.

BENZOATES

1. To a neutral, aqueous solution of the sample is added a little Ferric Chloride T.S. A dull yellow precipitate, which is soluble in solvent ether, is formed.

348

2. A little of the sample is moistened with a little concentrated sulphuric acid in a test tube. When the bottom of the tube is gently warmed, no charring takes place. A white sublimate is deposited on the inner walls of the tube.

3. An aqueous solution of the sample is treated with a little concentrated hydrochloric acid. A precipitate is obtained. It is crystallised from water and dried under reduced pressure. It melts at about 122°C.

BICARBONATES AND CARBONATES

1. Solutions of bicarbonates, on boiling liberate carbon dioxide whcih turns lime water milky. Carbonates do not give this reaction.

2. Solutions of bicarbonates give no precipitate with magnesium sulphate solutions but on boiling a white precipitate is produced. Solutions of carbonates give with magnesium suphate solution a white precipitate at room temperature. The white precipitate is magnesium carbonate.

   In the test for bicarbonates, the soluble magnesium bicarbonate first formed decomposes on boiling to magnesium carbonate.

3. Aqueous solutions of carbonates and bicarbonates liberate carbon dioxide on being heated gently with dilute acetic acid. The gas is passed through barium hydroxide solution. A white precipitate of barium carbonate is formed. It dissolves on adding an excess of dilute hydrochloric acid.

BROMIDES

1. An aqueous solution of the sample is treated with a little dilute nitric acid and a little silver nitrate solution. A curdy, pale yellow precipitate is formed. It is slightly soluble in dilute ammonia.

2. An aqueous solution of the sample is treated with chlorine solution. Bromine is evolved. The bromine solution is divided into two parts. To one part add 2 or 3 drops of chloroform. A reddish solution is formed in the chloroform

layer. To the other part phenol solution is added. A white precipitate (of tribromophenol) is formed.

CARBONATES: Refer under Bicarbonates.

CHLORIDES

1. Solutions of chlorides give with dilute nitric acid and silver nitrate solution a curdy, white precipitate of silver chloride. It is soluble in dilute ammonia solution but insoluble in dilute nitric acid.

2. A little of the sample in a test tube is mixed with a little potassium dichromate and a little concentrated sulphuric acid. A filter paper moistened with a dilute solution of diphenylcarbazide solution is placed over the opening of the test tube. The paper turns violet-red.

CITRATES

1. Neutral solutions of citrates, boiled with an excess of calcium chloride solution, give a white granular precipitate of calcium citrate. It is soluble in acetic acid.

2. An aqueous solution of the sample is mixed with acidified potassium permanganate solution and warmed till the colour of the permanganate is discharged. It is mixed with a little sodium nitroprusside solution in 2N sulphuric acid and sulphamic acid. It is made alkaline by adding strong ammonia solution drop by drop till the sulphamic acid is completely dissolved. Further addition of ammonia solution gives a violet colour changing to violet-blue.

IODIDES

1. Solutions of iodides give with dilute nitric acid and silver nitrate solution a curdy, yellow precipitate of silver iodide which is insoluble in dilute ammonia and in dilute nitric acid.

2. Iodides, when heated with sulphuric acid and potassium dichromate, produce violet coloured iodine. When a few ml of chloroform are added and shaken and allowed to settle, the choroform layer is coloured violet or violet-red.

350

3. Solutions of iodides give with mercuric chloride solution a dark red precipitate (mercuric iodide). This is very soluble when excess of potassium iodide is added (potassium mercuri iodide is formed).

LACTATES

To an aqueous solution of the substance bromine water and dilute sulphuric acid are added and heated on a water bath till the colour is discharged. To this mixture ammonium sulphate and a solution of sodium nitroprusside in 1M sulphuric acid are added. Finally without mixing, strong ammonia solution is added and allowed to stand for thirty minutes. A dark green ring appears at the place (interface) where the two liquids meet.

NITRATES

1. To an aqueous solution of the substance mixed with a little concentrated sulphuric acid is added ferrous sulphate solution through the sides of the test tube. A brown colour is formed at the interface of the two liquids.

2. A small quantity of the substance is added to a mixture of nitrobenzene and concentrated sulphuric acid. It is allowed to stand for five minutes and cooled in ice water while water and sodium hydroxide solution are added slowly with stirring. Then acetone is added, shaken and allowed to stand. The upper layer shows an intense violet colour.

NITRITES (I.P.'66)

1. Nitrites give off red fumes when heated with diluted sulphuric acid (nitrogen dioxide is liberated).

2. When dilute sulphuric acid, potassium iodide solution and starch solution are added to a solution of a nitrite, a blue colour is produced (potassium iodide is oxidised by the nitrous acid to iodine which gives the blue colour with starch).

3. A deep brown colour is produced when ferrous sulphate solution is added to a nitrite solution.

4. Solutions of nitrites, when treated with urea and dilute sulphuric acid, give off carbon dioxide which turns lime water milky.

351

PHOSPHATES

Solutions of orthophosphates give the following reactions :-

1. Solution of an orthophosphate at pH 7 gives a light yellow precipitate with silver nitrate solution. THe precipitate is readily soluble in dilute ammonia solution and dilute nitric acid. The yellow colour is not changed by boiling.

2. Solution of an orthophosphate when mixed with ammonia and magnesium sulphate solution, gives a white crystalline precipitate (magnesium ammonium phosphate).

3. Solution of an onthophosphate gives with dilute nitric acid and molybdate solution on warming a canary yellow precipitate (ammonium phosphomolybdate is produced).

SALICYLATES

1. To a neutral solution of the substance Ferric Chloride T.S. is added. A violet colour is produced. The colour remains even after the addition of dilute acetic acid.

2. Concentrated hydrochloric acid is added to an aqueous solution of the substance. Salicylic acid is precipitated. It is recrystallised from hot water and dried in vaccum. It melts at about 159°C.

3. Bromine solution is added to a solution of the substance. A cream-coloured precipitate(of tribromosalicylic acid) is formed,

SILICATES

The substance is mixed with sodium fluoride and concentrated sulphuric acid in a platinum or lead crucible using a copper wire. The crucible is covered with a thin, transparent plastic disc. A drop of water is suspeneded on the underside of the plastic disc and the crucible is warmed gently. After sometime a white ring is formed around the water drop.

Sodium fluoride and sulphuric acid react to form hydrofluoric acid (HF) which converts the silicate into gaseous silicon tetrafluoride (SiF_4). This gas dissolves in the water drop and is hydrolysed into gelatinous silicic acid and fluosilicic acid. These acids form the white ring around the drop of water.

SULPHATES

1. Solutions of sulphates give with barium chloride solutions a white precipitate (barium sulphate) which is insoluble in hydrochloric acid.

2. Solutions of sulphates give with solution of lead acetate a white precipitate (lead sulphate). It is soluble in ammonium acetate solution and also in sodium hydroxide solution.

3. To a suspension of barium sulphate in test (1) is added iodine solution. The suspension remains yellow but is decolourised by adding stannous chloride solution drop by drop. The mixture is boiled. No coloured precipitate is formed.

TARTRATES

1. Tartrates, when heated with concentrated sulphuric acid, char rapidly evolving carbon dioxide and carbon monoxide. The latter burns with a blue flame when ignited.

2. When a drop of ferrous sulphate solution is added to a solution of a tartrate acidified with acetic acid followed by a few drops of hydrogen peroxide, a transient yellow colour is produced. When sodium hydroxide solution is added drop by drop, a purple violet colour is produced.

3. Solutions of tartrates, mixed with potassium bromide solution and resorcinol solution and sulphuric acid, give an intense blue colour on warming cautiously. When the cooled solution is continuously poured into water, a red colour is obtained.

THIOSULPHATES

1. To an aqueous solution of the substance concentrsted hydrochloric acid is added. A white precipitate which soon turns yellow (sulphur) is produced. Sulphur dioxide which can be recognised by its odour is evolved.

353

2. Ferric chloride T.S. is added to a solution of the substance. A dark violet colour is produced and it quickly disappears.

3. Iodine solutions are decolourised by the addition of thiosulphate solutions. The decolourised solutions do not give the reactions of sulphates.

4. Bromine solution is decolourised by thiosulphate solution. The decolourised solution gives the reactions of sulphates.

IDENTIFICATION TESTS FOR CATIONS

ALUMINIUM

1. To an aqueous solution of the substance, dilute hydrochloric acid and thioacetamide reagent are added. There is no precipitate. Dilute sodium hydroxide solution is added drop by drop. A gelatinous white precipitate is formed. More dilute sodium hydroxide solution is added. The precipitate is redissolved. Ammonium chloride solution is now added. The gelatinous white precipitate reappears.

2. A small quantity of ammonium acetate solution and a small quantity of mordant blue-3 solution are added to a solution of the substance. An intense purple colour is produced.

3. Dilute ammonia is added to an aqueous solution of the substance until a faint precipitate is produced. Then quinalizarin in sodium hydroxide solution is added. The mixture is heated to boiling, cooled and acidified with excess of acetic acid. A reddish-violet colour is produced.

AMMONIUM

1. When ammonium salts are heated with sodium hydroxide solution, ammonia is produced. Ammonia can be easily recognised by its strong, pungent and characteristic odour. It truns moist red litmus paper blue.

2. To the solution of the ammonium salt light magnesium oxide is added. Ammonia is evolved and it is passed through a dilute solution of (0.1M) hydrochloric acid containing

methyl red till the colour of the solution becomes yellow. A freshly prepared sodium cobaltinitrite solution is added to this. A yellow precipitate (of ammonium sodium cobaltinitrite) is formed.

ANTIMONY

The substance is dissolved in a solution of sodium potassium tartrate with gentle heating and cooled. Sodium sulphide solution is added drop by drop to this solution. A reddish-orange precipitate is produced and it dissolves on the addition of sodium hydroxide solution.

ARSENIC

An aqueous solution of the substance is heated on a water bath with an equal volume of hypophosphorus reagent. A brown precipitate is formed.

BARIUM

1. In the flame test, barium salts burn in a non luminous flame with a yellowish-green colour. It appears blue when viewed through a green glass.

2. The substance is dissolved in dilute hydrochloric acid and dilute sulphuric acid is added. A white precipitate (of barium sulphate) is formed. It is insoluble in nitric acid.

BISMUTH

1. Dilute hydrochloric acid is added to the substance and it is boiled and cooled. It is diluted with water. A white or slightly yellow precipitate (of bismuth oxychloride) is formed. Sodium sulphide solution is added to this. The colour of the precipitate turns brown (due to the formation of bismuth sulphide).

2. Dilute nitric acid is added to an aqueous solution of the substance, heated to boiling and cooled. When thiourea solution is added to this, an orange-yellow colour or an orange precipitate is produced. Sodium fluoride solution is now added. The solution is not decolourised within thirty minutes.

CALCIUM

1. Solutions of calcium salts in acetic acid give no precipitate when potassium ferrocyanide solution is added. However, on adding ammonium chloride, a white, crystalline precipitate is formed.

2. Solutions of calcium salts give, with ammonium oxalate solution, a white precipitate (of calcium oxalate) which is soluble in hydrochloric acid but sparingly soluble in acetic acid.

3. Calcium salts, dissolved in hydrochloric acid and neutralised with sodium hydroxide, give with ammonium carbonate solution a white precipitate (of calcium carbonate) which, after boiling and cooling is insoluble in ammonium chloride solution.

COPPER

Official Tests (I.P.'66)

1. Solutions of copper salts give a brownish-black precipitate with hydrogen sulphide (a precipitate of cupric sulphide is formed). This precipitate is insoluble in dilute hydrochloric acid and also in sodium hydroxide solution. It is also almost insoluble in ammonium sulphide solution but it is decomposed and dissolved by boiling nitric acid.

2. Solutions of copper salts give with sodium hydroxide solution a light blue precipitate. This precipitate becomes brownish-black on boiling (blue cupric hydroxide first formed is converted finally to brownish-black cupric oxide).

3. Solutions of copper salts give with potassium iodide solution a brownish precipitate or a brown aqueous liquid which gives a deep blue colour with starch solution.

4. Strong solutions of copper salts give with ammonium thiocyanate solution a black precipitate. This black precipitate becomes white on the addition of sulphurous acid (the

black cupric thiocyanate first formed is reduced to white cuprous thiocyanate).

5. Solutions of copper salts give with dilute ammonia solution a greenish-blue precipitate. This readily dissolves in excess of ammonia solution forming a deep blue solution (cupric hydroxide formed dissolves in excess of ammonia to form blue cuprammonium complex).

6. Solutions of cupric salts give with potassium ferrocyanide solution a reddish-brown precipitate or, in very dilute solution, a reddish-brown colour (copper ferrocyanide is formed).

IRON

I. FERRIC SALTS

1. To an aqueous solution of a ferric salt is added potassium ferrocyanide solution. An intense blue precipitate is produced. It is insoluble in dilute hydrochloric acid.

2. To an aqueous solution of a ferric salt, add dilute hydrochloric acid and ammonium thiocyanate solution. It becomes blood-red (ferric thiocyanate) in colour. Divide into two portions. Extract one with solvent ether. The ether layer is pink. To the other add mercuric chloride solution. The colour disappears.

3. Solution of a ferric salt, strongly acidified with acetic acid gives with a 0.2 per cent solution of 7-iodo-8-hydroxyquinoline-5-sulphonic acid a stable green colour.

II. FERROUS SALTS

1. To an aqueous solution of a ferrous salt, dilute sulphuric acid and solution of 1, 10-phenonthroline are added. An intense red colour is produced. It is discharged when ceric ammomnium sulphate solution is added.

2. Solution of a ferrous salt gives with potassium ferricyanide solution a dark blue precipitate. It is insoluble in dilute hydrochloric acid. But it is decomposed by sodium hydroxide solution.

3. Solution of a ferrous salt gives with potassium ferrocyanide solution a white precipitate. This rapidly turns blue and is insoluble in dilute hydrochloric acid.

LEAD

1. Solution of a lead salt in acetic acid gives with potassium chromate solution a yellow precipitate of lead chromate. It is insoluble in sodium hydroxide solution.

2. Solution of a lead salt in acetic acid diluted with water, gives with potassium iodide solutions a yellow precipitate. It is heated to boiling and allowed to cool. The precipitate is reformed in yellow, glistening plates (golden spangles of lead iodide).

MAGNESIUM

1. An aqueous solution of the substance gives a white precipitate (magnesium hydroxide) on adding ammonia. When ammonium chloride is added, it dissolves. When disodium hydrogen phosphate solution is added, a white crystalline precipitate (magnesium ammonium phosphate) is formed.

2. Titan yellow solution and sodium hydroxide solution are added to an aqueous solution of the substance. A bright red turbidity appears. It is gradually changed to a bright red precipitate.

MERCURY

1. A well-scraped copper foil is immersed in a solution of the substance. A dark grey stain coats the copper foil. On rubbing it becomes shiny. (deposit of mercury). The dried copper foil is heated in a test tube. The spot of stain disappears.

2. Potassium iodide solution is added to a solution of the substance. A red precipitate (mercuric iodide) is produced and it is soluble when excess of potassium iodide is added (potassium mercuri iodide is formed - *mercuric compound)*. Instead of the red precipitate a yellow precipitate may also be produced. It becomes green on standing (*mercurous compound)*

3. Dilute sodium hydroxide solution is added to the solution of the substance. A dense, yellow precipitate (of yellow mercuric oxide) is produced (mercuric compound).

4. Dilute hydrochloric acid is added to a solution of the substance. A white precipitate (mercurous chloride) is a produced. On adding dilute ammonia, it becomes immediately black (a mixture of mercurous oxide and mercury is produced).

POTASSIUM

1. Solution of a potassium salt mixed with dilute acetic acid and a freshly prepared solution of sodium cobaltinitrite gives a yellow or orange-yellow precipitate immediately (a double salt of potassium sodium cobaltinitrite is formed).

2. No precipitate is formed when solution of a potassium salt is heated with sodium carbonate solution. Sodium sulphide solution is added. Still no precipitate is formed. It is cooled in ice, tartaric acid solution is added and allowed to stand. A white crystalline precipitate is formed.

3. A small quantity of the substance is ignited and dissolved in water. To this platinic chloride solution and a little dilute hydrochloric acid are added. A yellow crystalline precipitate (of potassium chloroplatinate) is formed. When it is ignited, it leaves a residue of potassium chloride and platinum.

SILVER

Dilute hydrochloric acid is added to a solution of a silver salt. A curdy white precipitate (of silver chloride) is formed. It is soluble in dilute ammonia. Potassium iodide solution is added. A yellow precipitate (of silver iodide) is formed. It is soluble in nitric acid.

SODIUM

1. An aqueous solution of the substance is mixed with potassium carbonate solution and heated to boiling. No precipitate is formed. Freshly prepared potassium antimonate

solution is now added and heated to boiling. It is allowed to cool in ice water and the inside of the test tube is rubbed with a glass rod. A dense, white precipitate is formed. It is disodium pyroantimonate, nearly insoluble in water, which is formed in a neutral or slightly alkaline solution.

2. The solution of the substance is acidified with dilute acetic acid and a large excess of magnesium uranylacetate solution is added. A yellow, crystalline precipitate (which is a triple acetate) is formed.

ZINC

1. An aqueous solution of a zinc salt is mixed with sodium hydroxide solution. A white precipitate (of zinc hydroxide) is formed. More sodium hydroxide solution is added. The precipitate dissolves (this is due to the formation of sodium zincate). Ammonium chloride solution is now added. The solution remains clear. Sodium sulphide solution is added. A floculent, white precipitate is formed. This is due to the fact that ammonium sulphide (formed from ammonium chloride and sodium sulphide) precipitates white zinc sulphide from neutral, alkaline or faintly acid solution of a zinc salt.

2. Solutions of zinc salts, acidified with dilute sulphuric acid and mixed with one drop of very dilute copper sulphate solution and a small quantity of ammonium mercuri-thiocyanate solution, give a violet precipitate.

3. Solutions of zinc salts give with potassium ferrocyanide solution a white precipitate of zinc ferrocyanide. It is insoluble in dilute hydrochloric acid.

Section B
PRACTICAL

CHAPTER 19
PREPARATION AND QUALITY CONTROL OF SOME INORGANIC PHARMACEUTICALS

1. ALUMINIUM HYDROXIDE GEL, I.P.

A. Preparation

Principle

To prepare the aluminium hydroxide gel, a hot solution of potash alum is added slowly to a hot solution of sodium carbonate and not vice versa. The precipitate of aluminium hydroxide is washed thoroughly in hot water till it is free from sulphate. The gel is then adjusted to required volume with distilled water.

$$3N\ a_2CO_3 + 2KAl(SO_4)_2 + 3H_2O = 3Na_2SO_4 + K_2SO_4$$
$$+ 2Al(OH)_3\downarrow + 3CO_2\uparrow$$

Procedure

1. *Dissolve about 9.5 g of sodium carbonate in about 100 ml of hot water in a 400 ml beaker.*

2. *Dissolve about 17 g of potash alum in 100 ml of hot water in a 250 ml beaker.*

3. *Add the alum solution to the sodium carbonate solution slowly with stirring and not vice versa.*

4. *Decant the supernatant liquid into the sink.*

5. *Add enough hot water to replace the water decanted. Stir well.*

6. *Decant the clear supernatant liquid and wash the precipitate with more hot water till the washed water does not answer tests for carbonate and sulphate (carbonate*

362

may be tested by adding dilute hydrochloric acid to the washed water. No effervesence should be produced. Sulphate may be tested by adding to the washed water dilute hydrochloric acid and barium chloride solution).

7. *Add enough water to produce the required volume of 100 ml.*

B. Quality Control

Tests for Identity

A solution of the preparation in dilute hydrochloric acid gives the reactions of aluminium. First take about 10 ml of the gel and add enough quantity of dilute hydrochloric acid to produce a clear solution.

1. *To about 2 ml of the solution, add thioacetamide reagent. There is no precipitate. Then add a dilute solution of sodium hydroxide. A gelatinous white precipitate is produced. Add more of the dilute sodium hydroxide solution. The precipitate is dissolved. Add ammonium chloride solution. The gelatinous white precipitate reappears.*

2. *To about 2 ml of the solution add ammonium acetate solution and mordant blue-3 solution. An intense purple colour is produced.*

3. *To about 2 ml of the solution, dilute ammonia is added till a faint precipitate is produced. Then add quinalizarin in sodium hydroxide solution. Heat the mixture to boiling, cool and acidify with excess of acetic acid. A reddish violet colour is produced.*

Tests for Purity

The following tests for purity should be done for aluminium hydroxide gel :-
1. Arsenic
2. Heavy metals
3. Chloride

4. Sulphate
5. pH
6. Neutralising capacity
7. Microbial limits

The procedure for performing the tests 1 to 4 are given in Chapter 21. The I.P. also may be consulted.

Test No. 5 (pH) may be done by using a properly calibrated pH meter or by using pH indicator papers. The pH should be between 5.5 and 8.

Test for Neutralising Capacity

Principle : Neutralising Capacity is determined by allowing the gel to remain in contact with 0.1M hydrochloric acid at 37^0C in a thermostatically controlled bath and measuring the pH at successive time intervals. Finally the concentration of the acid is increased further and the neutralizing capacity of the gel is found out by determining the remaining acid by titration with 0.1M sodium hydroxide after one hour.

Procedure

1. *Weigh accurately 5 g of the gel and add 100 ml of water. Mix and heat to 37^0C.*

2. *Add exactly 100 ml of 0.1M hydrochloric acid previously heated to 37^0C and stir continuously, maintaining the temperature at 37^0C.*

3. *Find the pH of the solution at 37^0C after 10 minutes. It should be not less than 1.8*

4. *Again find the pH of the solution after 15 minutes. It should be not less than 2.3.*

5. *Again find the pH of the solution after 20 minutes. It should be not less than 3.*

6. *In all the above three measurements the pH should not exceed 4.5.*

7. *Add 10 ml of 0.5 M hydrochloric acid previously heated to 37^0C.*

364

8. *Then titrate with 0.1M sodium hydroxide till a pH of 3.5 is obtained. Not more than 50 ml of 0.1M sodium hydroxide should be required to raise the pH to 3.5.*

This test has been designed to simulate conditions in the stomach. The test for *microbial* limits may be done in a microbiology laboratory.

II. ZINC OXIDE, I.P.

A. Preparation

Principle : Zinc carbonate is prepared first by reacting zinc sulphate with a boiling solution of sodium carbonate. The precipitated basic zinc carbonate, $2ZnCO_3.3Zn(OH)_2$, is collected, washed to remove sulphate, dried and finally gently ignited. It loses carbon dioxide and water, leaving zinc oxide as the residue.

$$2ZnCO_3.3Zn(OH)_2 = 5ZnO + 2CO_2\uparrow + 3H_2O.$$

However zinc oxide may also be prepared by reacting any soluble zinc salt with sodium bicarbonate. In this reaction, normal zinc carbonate is formed. It is ignited gently to give zinc oxide.

$$ZnSO_4.7H_2O + 2NaHCO_3 = ZnCO_3 + Na_2SO_4 + CO_2\uparrow + 8H_2O$$
$$ZnCO_3 \stackrel{\Delta}{=} ZnO + CO_2\uparrow$$

Preparation

1. *Dissolve 16 g of zinc sulphate in 50 ml of water in a 250 ml beaker.*
2. *Dissolve 16.8 g of sodium bicarbonate in another 50 ml of water in a 250 ml beaker.*
3. *Add the sodium bicarbonate solution to the zinc sulphate solution stirring well.*
4. *Filter the zinc carbonate formed.*
5. *Wash the precipitate with water till the filtrate does not answer test for sulphate (test with dilute hydrochloric acid and barium chloride solution).*

365

6. Collect the precipitate and dry it well.

7. Heat the precipitate gently at first and then strongly. Cool and weigh.

8. Continue the heating, cooling and weighing till a constant weight is obtained.

B. Quality Control

Tests for Identity

1. When strongly heated, zinc oxide gets a yellow colour which disappears on cooling.

2. Dissolve zinc oxide in dilute hydrochloric acid. The solution gives the following reactions of zinc :-

a. To 2 ml of the above solution, add sodium hydroxide solution. A white precipitate (of zinc hydroxide) is produced. Add more sodium hydroxide solution. The precipitate dissolves (this is due to the formation of sodium zincate). Add ammonium chloride solution. The solution remains clear. Add sodium sulphide solution. A flocculent white precipitate is formed. This is due to the fact that ammonium sulphide (formed from ammonium chloride and sodium sulphide) precipitates white zinc sulphide from neutral, alkaline or faintly acid solution of a zinc salt.

b. To 2 ml of the above solution, add dilute sulphuric acid, one drop of very dilute copper sulphate solution and one drop of ammonium mercurithiocyanate solution and mix well. A violet precipitate is formed.

c. To 2 ml of the above solution, add potassium ferrocyanide solution. A white precipitate of zinc ferrocyanide is formed. Add a little dilute hydrochloric acid. It is insoluble.

Tests for Purity

1. Alkalinity

2. Carbonates and substances insoluble in acids

3. Arsenic
.4. Iron
5. Lead
6. Loss on ignition

Common impurities such as arsenic and iron may be tested and limited by the limit tests detailed in Chapter 21.

Other Tests

1. Alkalinity

 (a) Weigh accurately 1 g of the prepared zinc oxide and add it to 10 ml of boiling water. Shake well.

 (b) Add 1 ml of phenolphthalein solution and filter.

 (c) See whether the filtrate is red. If it is red, then titrate with 0.1 M hydrochloric acid till it becomes colourless.

 (d) If the titre value is more than 3 ml, the sample fails the test. If it is less than 3 ml, then it passes the test and the alkalinity in the sample is within the limit prescribed.

2. Carbonates and substances insoluble in acids are limited by suspending the sample in water and adding dilute hydrochloric acid. No effervescence is seen. If effervescence is produced, it indicates the presence of carbonates and the substance fails the test.

 The solution should also be clear and colourless and not opalescent. Even if it is opalescent, it should not be more opalescent than *opalescence standard OS2* (details can be had by referring to p.A.78-Appendix 6.2 of I.P.).

 1. Weigh accurately 1 g of the sample and dissolve in 15 ml of 2M hydrochloric acid.

 2. No effervescence is produced in the solution.

 3. It should also be colourless. If it is opalescent, it should not be more opalescent than opalescence standard OS2.

 4. If effervescence is produced, the sample fails the test. This indicates the presence of carbonate (zinc carbonate not converted to oxide).

367

5. *If the solution is more opalescent than opalescence standard OS2, the sample fails the test. It indicates the presence of substances insoluble in acids.*

3. *Lead* is not limited by the usual dithizone test in I.P. It is tested by adding glacial acetic acid and potassium chromate solution. The solution should remain clear. If lead is present, a yellow colour (lead chromate) is produced.

Dissolve 2 g of the sample in a mixture of 20 ml of water and 5 ml of glacial acetic acid. Add 0.25 ml of potassium chromate solution. The solution should remain clear to pass the test. If the solution has a yellow colour, it fails the test.

4. *Loss on ignition : Weigh accurately 2 g of the substance, place it in a tared crucible and ignite at 500°C in a muffle furnace. After one hour, cool the crucible in a desiccator and weigh. Ignite again for 1 hour, cool and weigh again and again till a constant weight is obtained. Calculate the percentage loss in weight by using the formula given below :-*

$$\frac{(a-b) \times 100}{c}$$

Where a = weight of sample + crucible
b = weight of residue + crucible
c = weight of sample

The sample passes the test if the loss on ignition is not more than 1%. The sample fails the test if the loss on ignition is more than 1%.

III. BARIUM SULPHATE, I.P.

A. Preparation
Principle

It is prepared by treating a cold, dilute solution of any soluble barium salt such as barium chloride with dilute sulphuric acid

$$BaCl_2 + H_2SO_4 = BaSO_4\downarrow + 2HCl$$

The precipitate is filtered, washed with water till free from chloride and dried.

Preparation

1. Dissolve 42 g of barium chloride accurately weighed in 50 ml of distilled water.
2. Add to this 220 ml of dilute sulphuric acid and stir well.
3. Filter through a funnel fitted with a filter paper.
4. Wash the precipitate on the filter with distilled water repeatedly till the washed water does not answer test for chloride (test with dilute nitric acid and silver nitrate solution).
5. Dry the precipitate in an air oven at a temperature below 80°C. Cool and weigh the precipitate.

B. Quality Control

The following tests should be carried out on the sample prepared to find out its identity and purity:-

Tests for Identity

Boil 0.2 g of the sample with 5 ml of a 50%w/v solution of sodium carbonate for 5 minutes, add 10 ml of water and filter (the precipitate on the filter contains barium carbonate). Reserve the residue for test (2). Acidify the filtrate with dilute hydrochloric acid. The solution now gives the reactions of sulphates given below:-

(a) To 2 ml of the solution add barium chloride solution. A white precipitate of barium sulphate is formed.

(b) To 2 ml of the solution add lead acetate solution. A white precipitate of lead sulphate is formed. Divide into 2 parts. To one part add ammonium acetate solution. To the other part add sodium hydroxide solution. The precipitate dissolves in both the solutions.

(c) To the suspension of barium sulphate obtained in test (a) above add iodine solution. The suspension is now *yellow. Add stannous chloride solution. It is decolourised. Boil the mixture. No coloured precipitate is formed.*

2. *Wash the residue obtained in test no. (1) three times with successive small quantities of water. To the residue add 5 ml of dilute hydrochloric acid. Filter and to the filtrate add 0.3 ml of dilute sulphuric acid. A white precipitate is formed. Add to this dilute sodium hydroxide solution. It is insoluble.*

Sulphate component of the barium sulphate is tested by test (1) while the barium component is tested by test (2).

Test for Purity
1. Acidity or alkalinity
2. Arsenic
3. Heavy metals
4. Phosphate
5. Sulphide
6. Acid-soluble substances
7. Soluble barium salts
8. Bulkiness

The procedures for performing the arsenic and heavy metals limit tests are given in Chapter 21. The I.P. may be also be consulted for pretreatment and other details.

Acidity or alkalinity : Heat 5 g of the sample with 20 ml of carbon dioxide-free water for 5 minutes and filter. (Prepare carbon dioxide-free water by boiling distilled water and cooling the same, keeping the container closed). To 10 ml of the filtrate add 1 drop of bromothymol blue solution. If the solution has a yellow colour, titrate with 0.01M (M/100) sodium hydroxide solution till a light blue colour is formed. If the solution has a blue colour, titrate with 0.01M (M/100) hydrochloric acid till a yellow colour is formed. Not more than 0.5 ml of either 0.01M hydrochloric acid or 0.01M sodium hydroxide should be required for the sample to pass the test. If more than 0.5 ml of the acid or alkali is required, the sample fails the test.

Phosphate : Phosphate is limited by the usual ammonium molybdate test. A hot nitric acid extract of the substance is mixed with ammonium molybdate solution. No yellow precipitate is produced.

Boil 1 g of the sample with a mixture of 3 ml of concentrated nitric acid and 5 ml of water for 5 minutes. Add water to restore the original volume. Filter through filter paper previously washed with dilute nitric acid. Add to the warm filtrate an equal volume of ammonium molybdate solution.

The substance passes the test if no yellow precipitate is formed. The substance fails the test if a yellow precipitate is formed.

Sulphide : Sulphide is tested by boiling the substance with dilute hydrochloric acid. Lead acetate paper is exposed to the vapour coming out. The paper should not darken. Any sulphide present is converted into hydrogen sulphide which will darken the lead acetate paper by forming lead sulphide.

Boil 10 g of the sample with a mixture of 10 ml of dilute hydrochloric acid and 90 ml of water for 10 minutes. Expose a lead acetate paper to the vapour.

If the paper does not become dark, the sample passes the test. If the paper becomes dark, the sample fails the test.

Acid - soluble substances : Cool the mixture obtained in the test for sulphide. Add water to restore the orginal volume. Filter through a filter paper previously washed with a mixture of 10 ml of dilute hydrochloric acid and 90 ml of water. Evaporate 50 ml of the filtrate to dryness on a water bath and add 2 drops of concentrated hydrochloric acid and 10 ml of hot water. Filter again through acid-washed paper. Wash the filter paper with 10 ml of hot water. Evaporate the combined filtrate and washings. Dry the residue at 105°C. Cool and weigh. Calculate the percentage w/w of the residue using the formula given below :-

$$\% \ of \ acid\text{-}soluble \ substances = \frac{a \times 100}{10}$$

where a is the weight of the residue.

371

If it is less than 0.3%, the substance passes the test. If it is more than 0.3%, the substance fails the test.

Soluble barium salts : These are tested by digesting the residue obtained in the test for acid-soluble substances with water and filtering through a filter paper moistened with dilute hydrochloric acid. Dilute sulphuric acid is added to the filtrate and set aside for 30 minutes. No turbidity should be produced (due to barium sulphate obtained from any barium salts).

Digest the residue obtained in the test for acid-soluble substances with 10 ml of water.

Filter through a filter paper previously washed with a mixture of 10 ml of dilute hydrochloric acid and 90 ml of water.

To the clear filtrate add 0.5 ml of dilute sulphuric acid and set aside for 30 minutes.

If no turbidity is produced in 30 minutes, the sample passes the test. If any turbidity is produced within 30 minutes, the sample fails the test.

Bulkiness: The test for bulkiness is done by suspending the substance in water in a 50 ml graduated cylinder and shaking for 5 minutes. If it is allowed to stand for 15 minutes, it should not settle below the 15 ml mark indicating that the sample has sufficient bulkiness.

Place 5 g of the sample accurately weighed in a 50 ml graduated cylinder (measuring cylinder).

Add water to 50 ml.

Shake the mixture for 5 minutes and allow to stand for 15 minutes.

If the substance does not settle below the 15 ml mark at the end of 15 minutes, it passes the test.

If the substance settles below the 15 ml mark after 15 minutes, it fails the test.

IV. CALCIUM CARBONATE, I.P.

A. Preparation

Principle

It is prepared by mixing boiling solutions of calcium chloride and sodium carbonate.

$$CaCl_2 + Na_2CO_3 = CaCO_3\downarrow + 2NaCl$$

The precipitated calcium carbonate is filtered, washed free from chloride and dried.

Preparation

1. Dissolve about 22 g of anhydrous calcium chloride in boiling water.

2. Dissolve about 17 g of anhydrous sodium carbonate in boiling water.

3. Add the sodium carbonate solution to the calcium chloride solution and mix well.

4. Cool and filter on a calico filter.

5. Wash the precipitate on the filter with distilled water till the filtrate is free from chloride.

6. Dry the precipitate at 105°C in an air oven.

B. Quality Control

Tests for Identity

Pretreatment : Dissolve 5 g of the sample in 80 ml of 2M acetic acid. Wait till the effervescence stops. Boil the solution for 2 minutes, cool, dilute to 100 ml with 2M acetic acid and filter, if necessary, through a tared sintered glass filter. Keep any residue on the filter for the test for substances insoluble in acetic acid.

The filtrate gives the following reactions of calcium:-

1. To 5 ml of the solution add 1ml of glacial acetic acid and 0.5ml of potassium ferrocyanide solution. The solution remains clear. Add about 50 mg of ammonium chloride. A white, crystalline precipitate is formed.

2. *To 5 ml of the solution add 0.2 ml of a 2% w/v solution of ammonium oxalate. A white precipitate is obtained. Divide it into two parts. To one part add dilute acetic acid. It is only sparingly soluble in acetic acid. Add conc. hydrochloric acid to the other part. It is completely soluble and a clear solution is obtained.*

3. *Test for Carbonate : Suspend 0.1 g of the substance in 2 ml of water. Add 2 ml of 2M acetic acid and close the tube immediately with a glass tube bent at two right- angles. Heat gently and collect the gas in 5 ml of 0.1M barium hydroxide in another test tube. A white precipitate is formed. Add to this excess of dilute hydrochloric acid. The precipitate dissolves and a clear solution is obtained.*

Tests for Purity

1. Arsenic
2. Heavy metals
3. Chloride
4. Sulphate
5. Iron
6. Substances insoluble in acetic acid
7. Magnesium and alkali metals
8. Barium
9. Loss on drying

The procedures for performing the tests 1 to 5 are given in Chapter 21. The I.P. may also be consulted for pretreatment and other details.

Substances insoluble in acetic acid : These are determined by allowing the sample to react with acetic acid till effervescence ceases. Then the solution is boiled, cooled, diluted and filtered through a sintered glass filter. The residue is washed repeatedly with hot water, dried and weighed.

The residue should be already available in a tared sintered glass filter (see Pretreatment under Tests for Identity). If there is any residue, wash it with 5 ml of hot water four times. Dry it at 100°C in an air oven for 1 hour. Find the weight of the residue. It should not be more than 10 mg or 0.2% to pass the test.

If it is more than 10 mg, the sample fails the test.

Magnesium and alkali metals: In this test, the calcium carbonate in the sample is removed as calcium oxalate by dissolving in dilute hydrochloric acid, adding dilute ammonia and acetic acid, heating the solution and adding ammonium oxalate solution. The precipitated calcium oxalate is filtered off. The filtrate contains the oxalates of magnesium and alkali metals. Dilute sulphuric acid is added to the filtrate converting magnesium and alkali metals, if any, to their sulphates. It is evaporated to dryness and weighed.

Dissolve 1 g of the sample in 10 ml of dilute hydrochloric acid. Neutralise this solution by adding dilute ammonia solution. Heat the solution to boiling and add 50 ml of hot ammonium oxalate solution. Cool, dilute to 100 ml with water and filter. To 50 ml of the filtrate add 1.5 ml of dilute sulphuric acid. Evaporate to dryness on a water bath. Heat the residue to redness. Allow to cool and weigh.

The weight of the residue should be not more than 10 mg for the sample to pass the test.

The sample does not pass the test if the weight of the residue is more than 10 mg.

Barium : Barium is detected by dissolving the sample in dilute acetic acid and adding calcium sulphate solution. If barium is present, it will be precipitated as barium sulphate.

Dissolve 0.6 g of the sample in 10 ml of 2M acetic acid by boiling. Cool and add 10 ml of calcium sulphate solution.

The sample passes the test if the solution remains clear for not less than 15 minutes.

The sample fails the test if the solution becomes turbid or opalescent within 15 minutes.

Loss on ignition: Weigh 1g of the sample in a tared crucible and dry the same in an oven at 200°C. Weigh after cooling and calculate the percentage loss in weight.

The sample passes the test if the loss on drying is not more than 2%.

The sample fails the test if the loss on drying is more than 2%.

V. POTASSIUM CITRATE, I.P.

A. Preparation

Principle

Potassium citrate is prepared by neutralizing a solution of citric acid with either potassium carbonate or potassium bicarbonate. The effervescence is allowed to subside and the solution is evaporated to crystallization.

$$3KHCO_3 + H_3C_6H_5O_7.H_2O = K_3C_6H_5O_7.H_2O + 3CO_2\uparrow + 3H_2O$$

Preparation

1. *Weigh about 21 g of citric acid and dissolve in 100 ml of water.*

2. *Weigh about 30 g of potassium bicarbonate and slowly add to the citric acid solution little by little stirring well.*

3. *Stir well and allow the effervescence to subside.*

4. *Test the solution with phenolphthalein indicator solution and adjust the pH to be between 8.3 and 10 (pH range of phenolphthalein indicator) by adding either citric acid or potassium bicarbonate to the solution.*

5. *Evaporate the solution and allow the potassium citrate to crystallize. Do not overheat lest the potassium citrate is charred.*

B. Verifying the Quality of the Product

Tests for Identity

Prepare a 10% w/v (10 g in 100ml) solution of the sample in carbon dioxide-free water prepared from distilled water. Let us call it solution A. It gives the reactions of potassium salts and also the reactions of citrates.

Reactions of Potassium Salts

1. To 1ml of solution A add 1ml of dilute acetic acid and 1ml of a freshly prepared 10% w/v solution of sodium cobaltnitrite. A yellow or orange-yellow precipitate is produced immediately (a double salt of potassium sodium cobaltnitrite is formed).

2. Heat 2 ml of solution A with 1ml of sodium carbonate solution. No precipitate is formed. Add a drop of sodium sulphide solution. Still no precipitate is formed. Cool in ice, add 2 ml of a 15% solution of tartaric acid and allow to stand. A white, crystalline precipitate is formed.

3. Ignite (heat strongly) a few mg of the sample. Cool and dissolve in the minimum quantity of water. To this solution add 1ml of platinic chloride solution and 1ml of concentrated hydrochloric acid. A yellow, crystalline precipitate (potassium chloroplatinate) is produced. Collect this precipitate, dry and ignite. A residue of potassium chloride and platinum is left.

Tests for Purity

1. Arsenic
2. Heavy metals
3. Chloride
4. Sulphate
5. Acidity or alkalinity
6. Sodium
7. Oxalate

8. Readily carbonisable substances
9. Water
10. Clarity and colour of solution

The procedures for performing the tests 1 to 4 are given in Chapter 21. The I.P. may also be referred to for pretreatment and other details.

Acidity or alkalinity : To 10 ml of solution A add 0.1 ml of dilute phenolphthalein solution. Titrate with 0.1M hydrochloric acid or 0.1M sodium hydroxide.

If not more than 0.2 ml of either 0.1M hydrochloric acid or 0.1M sodium hydroxide solution is required to change the colour of the solution, the sample passes the test.

If more than 0.2 ml is required, the sample fails the test.

Refer under **preparation** in which the pH of potassium citrate is adjusted to be between 8.3 and 10 by using phenolphthalein indicator solution.

Clarity and Colour of solution: Examine solution A. If it is clear and colourless, the sample passes the test. Otherwise it fails.

Sodium is determined by a method using atomic absorption spectrophotometry.

Oxalate

1. *Dissolve 0.4 g of the sample, accurately weighed, in 4 ml of water.*

2. *Add 3 ml of concentrated hydrochloric acid and 1g of granulated zinc and heat on a water bath for 1 minute.*

3. *Allow to stand for 2 minutes and decant into 0.25 ml of a 1% solution of phenylhydrazine hydrochloride.*

4. *Heat to boiling, cool rapidly and add an equal volume of concentrated hydrochloric acid and 0.25 ml of potassium ferricyanide solution.*

5. *Shake and allow to stand for 30 minutes.*

6. *Observe whether any pink colour is produced.*

7. Compare the pink colour with the pink colour in another solution obtained by treating 4 ml of a 0.005% solution of oxalic acid in the same manner and at the same time (repeat steps 2 to 6).

8. If the pink colour is not more intense than the pink colour obtained in the control, the sample passes the test. If the pink colour is more intense than the pink colour obtained in the control, the sample does not pass the test.

Readily carbonisable substances: This test is done by adding to the sample concentrated sulphuric acid and heating on a water bath at 90°C for one hour. The colour of the solution is compared with a standard coloured solution coloured by using ferric chloride, copper sulphate and cobalt chloride solutions and dilute hydrochloric acid. If readily carbonisable substances are present, they will be charred and carbonised by the sulphuric acid.

1. Weigh 0.2 g of the sample accurately.

2. Add to this 10 ml of concentrated sulphuric acid and heat on a water bath at 90°C for 60 minutes.

3. Cool rapidly.

4. Compare the colour obtained with the colour in the reference solution YS2 or GYS2 given in Appendix 6.2 (the procedure for preparing these standards are given on pages A-78 and A-79 of I.P.). The colours of the standards YS2 and GYS2 are yellow and greenish yellow respectively.

Water : Since potassium citrate is hygroscopic, a liberal limit for water is prescribed in the I.P.

Water content is determined by using aquametry (Karl Fischer Titration Method). For details see Appendix 3.24 of the I.P., pages A-48 and A-49.

Water content should be between 4 and 7%.

VI. BORIC ACID, I.P.

A. Preparation
Principle

Boric acid is prepared by decomposing borax with a mineral acid like sulphuric acid. The boric acid is allowed to crystallize after filtration, washed free from soluble sulphate and dried.

$$Na_2B_4O_7 + H_2SO_4 + 5H_2O = Na_2SO_4 + 4H_3BO_3$$

Preparation

1. Dissolve 20 g of borax in 100 ml of water. Heat, if necessary, to dissolve.

2. Add to this solution about 10 ml of conc.sulphuric acid slowly and with constant stirring.

3. Cool and filter. Wash the precipitate on the filter with water till the filtrate is free from sulphate.

4. Dry the precipitate between folds of filter paper.

B. Quality Control
Tests for Identity

1. Take 5 ml of methanol and add a few drops of concentrated sulphuric acid. Dissolve 0.1g of the sample in this by gently warming. Ignite the solution. A flame with a green border burns at the top of the tube (this is due to the formation of methyl borate).

2. Dissolve 3 g of the sample in 90 ml of boiling distilled water. The solution is faintly acid.

Tests for Purity

1. Arsenic
2. Sulphate
3. Heavy metals
4. Clarity and colour of solution
5. Solubility in ethanol

6. pH
7. Loss on drying

The procedures for performing the tests 1 to 3 are given in Chapter 21. The I.P. may also be referred to for any pretreatment and other details.

Clarity and colour of solution and *solubility in ethanol* are tested by dissolving the sample in boiling water and boiling ethanol (95%) respectively. The solutions should be clear and colourless (clarity and colour of solution) or at the most slightly opalescent when compared with a standard (solubility in ethanol). These are tests to exclude metallic borates and insoluble impurities generally.

Clarity and colour of solution: Weigh 3.5 g of the sample and dissolve it in boiling water (100 ml). The solution should be clear and colourless as per Appendix 6.1 of the I.P. In the I.P., it is mentioned that a liquid is considered clear if its clarity is the same as that of water or of the solvent being used for preparing the solution or if its opalescence is not more than that of opalescence standard OS1.

Solubility in Ethanol : Weigh 1g of the sample and dissolve it in 10 ml of boiling ethanol (95%). The solution is not more opalescent than opalescence standard OS2 (see I.P.)

pH : The solution prepared in identification test no. 2 should have a pH between 3.8 and 4.8. Use a pH meter or pH indicator papers for determining the pH.

Loss on Drying: Since boric acid does not contain any water of crystalization nor is hygroscopic or deliquescent, a very low limit of 0.5% is fixed for this test.

Weigh 1g of the sample and dry it in a tared weighing bottle in a desiccator containing silica gel for 5 hours. See Appendix 8.6 of the I.P. Calculate the percentage of weight loss. If the loss is less than 0.5%, the sample passes this test. If it is more than 0.5%, it fails the test.

VII. MAGNESIUM SULPHATE, I.P.

A. Preparation

Principle

Magnesium sulphate is prepared by dissolving either magnesium oxide or magnesium carbonate in dilute sulphuric acid and evaporating the solution when the heptahydrate ($MgSO_4.7H_2O$) crystallizes out as efflorescent needle-like crystals or rhombic prisms. The anhydrous salt is obtained by heating the hydrate at about 200°C.

$$MgO + H_2SO_4 = MgSO_4 + H_2O$$
$$MgCO_3 + H_2SO_4 = MgSO_4 + CO_2 + H_2O$$

Preparation

1. *Weigh 8 g of magnesium oxide.*
2. *Separately add 20 ml of concentrated sulphuric acid to about 100 ml of water.*
3. *Add the magnesium oxide gradually and with stirring to the diluted acid.*
4. *Evaporate the solution, concentrate it to about one-fourth of its volume and cool.*
5. *Filter the magnesium sulphate precipitated out and dry between folds of filter paper.*

B. Quality Control

Tests for Identity

Gives reactions of magnesium and of sulphates.

Reactions of Magnesium

Dissolve about 15 mg of the sample in 2 ml of water. Add 1 ml of dilute ammonia solution. A white precipitate is formed (magnesium hydroxide). Add 1 ml of 2M ammonium chloride solution. The precipitate is dissolved. Add 1ml of 0.25M disodium hydrogen phosphate solution. A white, crystalline precipitate (magnesium ammonium phosphate) is formed.

Reactions of Sulphates

1. *Dissolve about 50 mg of the substance in 5 ml of water. Add 1ml of dilute hydrochloric acid and 1ml of barium chloride solution. A white precipitate (barium sulphate) is formed.*

2. *Add 0.1 ml of iodine solution to the suspension obtained at the end of the above test. The suspension becomes yellow (distinction from sulphides and dithionites). Add, drop by drop, stannous chloride solution. It loses its colour (distinction from iodates). Boil the mixture. No coloured precipitate is formed (distinction from selenates and tungstates).*

3. *Dissolve about 50 mg of the substance in 5 ml of water. Add 2 ml of lead acetate solution. A white precipitate (lead sulphate) is formed. Divide it into two parts. To one part add ammonium acetate solution. To the other part add sodium hydroxide solution. In both the cases the precipitate is dissolved.*

Tests for Purity

1. Arsenic
2. Iron
3. Heavy metals
4. Chloride
5. Clarity and colour of solution
6. Acidity or alkalinity
7. Loss on drying

The procedures for performing tests 1 to 4 are given in Chapter 21. The I.P. may also be referred to for any pretreatment and other details.

Acidity or Alkalinity: Weigh 5 g of the sample and dissolve in sufficient carbon dioxide-free water to produce 50 ml (solution A). To 10 ml of solution A add 0.05 ml of phenol red solution. Titrate with either 0.01M (M/100) hydrochloric acid or 0.01M sodium hydroxide. Not more than 0.2 ml of any one of them should be required to change the colour from yellow to red or from red to yellow. The pH of the solution should be between 6.8 and 8.4 to comply with this test. If only 0.2 ml or less is required of either of the two solutions to change colour, the sample passes the test. If more than 0.2 ml is required to change the colour, the substance fails the test.

Loss on Drying : The substance is dried to constant weight initially at 110°C to 120°C and then at 400°C. It loses about 48 to 52 per cent of its weight. All the water molecules ($7H_2O$) are lost.

Weigh accurately about 0.5 g of the sample in a tared crucible and dry in an oven at 110° to 120°C for 1 hour and then at 400°C to constant weight. Calculate the percentage loss in weight.

If the loss on drying is between 48 and 52%, the substance passes the test. If the loss is below or above these limits, the substance fails the test.

VIII. FERROUS SULPHATE, I.P.

A. Preparation

Principle

Ferrous sulphate is prepared by dissolving a slight excess of iron in dilute sulphuric acid and concentrating to get green crystals.

$$Fe + H_2SO_4 = FeSO_4 + H_2\uparrow$$

Preparation

1. *Add about 20 ml of concentrated sulphuric acid to about 100 ml of water. Cool.*

2. *Add about 12 g of iron filings to the acid solution with stirring.*

3. *Concentrate to about one fourth the volume and cool.*

4. *Filter and dry the crystals between folds of filter paper. Keep in a container tightly closed.*

B. Quality Control

Tests for Identity

Gives reaction A of ferrous salts and also the reactions of sulphates.

Reaction A of Ferrous Salts

Dissolve about 10 mg of the substance in 2 ml of water. Add 2 ml of dilute sulphuric acid and 1ml of a 0.1% solution of 1, 10-phenanthroline. An intense red colour is produced. Add a slight excess of 0.1M ceric ammonium sulphate. The red colour is discharged.

Reactions of Sulphates

Do the tests given under Magnesium Sulphate in this Chapter.

Tests for Purity

1. Arsenic
2. Chloride
3. pH
4. Clarity of solution
5. Copper
6. Lead
7. Zinc
8. Manganese

The procedures for performing the tests 1 to 2 are given in Chapter 21. The I.P. may also be referred to for any pretreatment and other details.

pH : pH should be between 3 and 4. Since ferrous sulphate is the salt of a strong acid and a weak base, it tends to be slightly acidic in solution.

Weigh 5 g of the sample and dissolve in 100 ml of distilled water. Find the pH of the solution using a pH meter or indicator papers.

385

If the pH is between 3 and 4, the sample passes the test. Otherwise it fails.

Clarity of Solution : If some of the ferrous sulphate is oxidised to the ferric sulphate, the clarity of the solution will be affected.

Weigh 2.5 g accurately and dissolve in carbon dioxide-free water. Add 0.5 ml of 1M sulphuric acid and dilute to 50 ml with water (solution A).

The substance passes the test if the solution is not more opalescent than opalescence standard OS2. See Appendix 6.1 of the I.P. See also under Boric Acid in this Chapter.

Copper : Copper is tested by forming a coloured complex with sodium diethyldithiocarbamate in the presence of citric acid and ammonia and extracting the complex with carbon tetrachloride. The colour of the resulting solution is not greater than that of a dilute copper sulphate solution similarly treated.

Pretreatment: Weigh 8 g of the sample accurately and dissolve it in 40 ml of concentrated hydrochloric acid. Add 10 ml of concentrated nitric acid and 15 ml of water. Transfer to a separating funnel and shake with four quantities (each 30 ml) of ether and discard (reject) the ether extracts. Heat the acid solution on a water bath to remove the dissolved ether. Cool and add sufficient water to produce 100 ml (solution B).

To 10 ml of solution B, add 1g of citric acid. Make alkaline with dilute ammonia solution. Add 25 ml of water and 5 ml of sodium diethyldithiocarbamate solution. Extract succesively with 5, 3 and 2 ml quantities of carbon tetrachloride. Mix the carbon tetrachloride extracts and add sufficient carbon tetrachloride to produce 100 ml.

Prepare another solution by treating 4 ml of copper standard solution (10 ppm Cu) and 7.5 ml of water in the same manner (50 ppm.)

Copper standard solution (10 ppm Cu) is prepared by diluting 1 volume of a 0.393% solution of cupric sulphate to 100 volumes with water.

If the test solution is not more intensely coloured than the standard solution, the sample passes the test.

If the test solution is more intensely coloured than the standard solution, the sample fails the test.

Zinc : Zinc is extracted with dithizone, the zinc dithizonate is decomposed with hydrochloric acid and the liberated zinc is treated with potassium ferrocyanide solution to produce a turbidity (zinc ferrocyanide). The turbidity should not be greater than a turbidity produced with standard dilute zinc sulphate solution similarly treated.

To 2.5 ml of solution B (see under Copper-pretreatment) add 1g of citric acid and 1g of recorcinol. Neutralise the solution with dilute ammonia solution using thymol blue solution as indicator. Shake for 1 minute with two quantities, each of 20 ml, of dithizone solution. To the combined extracts add 10 ml of 0.1M hydrochloric acid and shake for 1 minute. Separate the acid layer, add 3 ml of 1M hydrochloric acid and 20 ml of ammonium chloride solution. Adjust the volume to 50 ml with water. Add 1 ml of potassium ferrocyanide solution and allow to stand for 15 minutes.

Prepare a standard turbidity by taking 10 ml of zinc standard solution (10 ppm zinc) and mixing with 4 ml of 1M hydrochloric acid, 20 ml of ammonium chloride solution and water. Add to this mixture 1 ml of potassium ferrocyanide solution and sufficient water to produce 50 ml (500 ppm).

Any turbidity produced in the test should not be greater than that produced in the standard to pass the test.

If the turbidity produced in the test is greater than that in the standard, the substance fails the test.

Note: Zinc standard solution (10 ppm zinc) is prepared by diluting 1 volume of zinc standard solution (100 ppm Zn) to 10 volumes with water.

Zinc standard solution (100 ppm) is prepared by dissolving 0.440 g of zinc sulphate (accurately weighed) in water containing 1 ml of 5M acetic acid and adding sufficient water to produce 100 ml.

Lead: Lead is precipitated as lead sulphide with sodium sulphide in the presence of ammonia and potassium cyanide which keeps the other heavy metals complexed. The colour produced is compared with that produced in a standard lead solution similarly treated.

Make 25 ml of solution B (see under Copper-pretreatment) alkaline with dilute ammonia solution. Add 1 ml of potassium cyanide solution and sufficient water to produce 50 ml. Add 0.1 ml of sodium sulphide solution. Stir well.

Prepare a standard solution by mixing 10 ml of concentrated hydrochloric acid, 0.5 ml of concentrated nitric acid, 5 ml of lead standard solution (20 ppm Pb) and 0.1 ml of sodium sulphide solution. Add sufficient water to produce 50 ml (50 ppm).

Note : *Lead Standard solution (20 ppm Pb)* is prepared by diluting 1 volume of lead standard solution (100 ppm Pb) to 5 volumes with water.

Lead standard solution (100 ppm Pb) is prepared by diluting 1 volume of lead standard solution (0.1% Pb) to 10 volumes with water.

Lead standard solution (0.1% Pb) is prepared by dissolving 0.400 g of lead nitrate (accurately weighed) in water containing 2 ml of concentrated nitric acid and adding sufficient water to produce 250 ml.

If the turbidity produced in the test is not more intensely coloured than that in the standard, the substance passes the test.

If the turbidity produced in the test is more intensely coloured than that in the standard, the substance fails the test.

Manganese: Manganese is tested by getting it oxidised to potassium permanganate by sodium periodate and comparing the colour with the colour of a standard solution of potassium permanganate similarly treated.

Weigh accurately 1g of the sample and dissolve it in 40 ml of water. Add 10 ml of concentrated nitric acid and boil until red fumes are evolved. Add 0.5 g of ammonium persulphate and boil for 10 minutes. Discharge any pink colour by the dropwise addition of a 5% w/v solution of sodium sulphide and boil until the odour of sulphur dioxide, if any, is eliminated. Add 10 ml of water, 5 ml of phosphoric acid and 0.5g of sodium periodate. Boil for one minute and allow to cool.

Prepare a standard solution by taking 1 ml of 0.02M potassium permanganate and subject it to the same procedure outlined in the preceding para as in the case of the sample. Compare the colour in the test with that in the standard (0.1%)

If the test solution is not more intensely coloured than the standard solution, the substance passes the test.

If the test solution is more intensely coloured than the standard solution, the substance fails the test.

Note : *0.02 M potassium permanganate* may be prepared as below:-

Dissolve 3.2 g of potassium permanganate in 1000 ml of water. Heat on a water bath for 1 hour. Allow to stand for 2 days and filter through glass wool. The solution may be standardised as given below:-

Pipette out 25 ml of the solution into a glass-stoppered flask, add 2 g of potassium iodide and 10 ml of 1M sulphuric acid. Titrate the liberated iodine with standard 0.1M sodium thiosulphate using 3 ml of starch solution as indicator added towards the end of the titration. Do a blank titration (that is, without the potassium permanganate) and make any correction in the titre value, if necessary. Calculate the actual strength of the 0.02M potassium permanganate.

CHAPTER 20
TESTS FOR PURITY

1. SWELLING POWER IN BENTONITE

Principle : When water is added to bentonite, each particle is surrounded by a layer or shell of water. This produces a particle several times larger than the original particle. Swelling of mass results. Bentonite can absorb upto 5 times its weight of water and its bulk may increase by twelve to fifteen times. Bentonite is insoluble in water but swells into a homogeneous mass.

To find out the swelling power, the sample is added in small quantities at intervals of 2 minutes to a solution of sodium lauryl sulphate in a 100 ml measuring cylinder. It is allowed to stand for 2 hours. The apparent volume of the sediment should be not less than 24 ml. The presence of the wetting agent (sodium lauryl sulphate) promotes compatibility between the insoluble bentonite and water.

Procedure

1. *Dissolve 1g of sodium lauryl sulphate in 100 ml of water and transfer to a 100 ml graduated or measuring cylinder having a diameter of 3 cm.*

2. *Weigh accurately 2 g of the sample of bentonite and add it in small quantities every 2 minutes to the above solution. Allow each portion to settle.*

3. *Set aside for 2 hours.*

4. *Find out the apparent volume of the sediment at the bottom of the cylinder.*

Observation : The observation is *one* of the two given below:-

1. The apparent volume of the sediment is 24 ml or more.

or

2. The apparent volume of the sediment is less than 24ml.

Report : 1. The report may be *one* of the two given below:-

    1. The sample passes the test.

    2. The sample does not pass the test.

2. ACID NEUTRALIZING CAPACITY OF ALUMINIUM HYDROXIDE GEL

Principle : Aluminium hydroxide reacts with hydrochloric acid to form aluminium chloride.

$$Al(OH)_3 + 2HCl = AlCl_3 + 3H_2O$$

This means that aluminium hydroxide can act as a good antacid and will be able to neutralise the acid in the stomach.

Neutralizing capacity is determined by allowing the gel to remain in contact with 0.1M hydrochloric acid at 37°C in a thermostatically controlled bath and measuring the pH at successive time intervals. Finally the concentration of acid is increased further and the neutralizing capacity of the gel is found out by determining the remaining acid by titration with 0.1M sodium hydroxide after one hour.

Procedure

1. *Take 100ml of water in a 250 ml beaker and add 5 g of the sample to it.*

2. *Place the beaker in a thermostatic water bath and adjust to get 37°C in the suspension in the beaker.*

3. *Add 100 ml of 0.1M hydrochloric acid, previously heated to 37°C.*

4. *Stir continuously maintaining the temperature at 37°C.*

5. *Measure the pH of the solution at 37°C with the help of a pH meter after 10, 15 and 20 minutes and record the same. The pH should not be more than 1.8 after 10 minutes, 2.3 after 15 minutes and 3 after 20 minutes. The pH at any time should not be more than 4.5.*

6. *Add 10 ml of 0.5M hydrochloric acid, previously heated to 37°C.*

7. *Stir continuously for one hour maintaining the temperature at 37°C.*

8. *Titrate with 0.1M sodium hydroxide. This is a potentiometric titration. So titrate till a pH of 3.5 is attained.*

Observation : *One* of the two given below may be observed:-

1. Not more than 50 ml of 0.1M sodium hydroxide is required for the titration.

or

2. More than 50 ml of 0.1M sodium hydroxide is required for the titration.

Report : Based on the above observation, *one* of the two reports may be submitted.

1. The sample passes the test.

or

2. The sample does not pass the test.

Note: *1. Aluminium hydroxide gel (5 g) should be accurately weighed.*

2. *The temperature of the contents in the beaker should be maintained at 37°C throughtout the experiment.*

3. *The volumetric solutions used, viz. 0.1M and 0.5M hydrochloric acid and 0.1M sodium hydroxide should be exactly of the same strength. If not, solution of a higher strength may be prepared, assayed and diluted to the required strength.*

3. AMMONIUM SALTS IN POTASH ALUM

Alum of the pharmacopoeia is potash alum which is a double salt of aluminium sulphate and potassium sulphate with 12 molecules of water of hydration. Alum can also be prepared by using ammonium sulphate in the place of potassium sulphate. So a test for ammonium salts is prescribed.

Procedure

Test	Standard
1. Weigh accurately 1g of the sample (potash alum) and dissolve in 1000 ml of ammonia-free water in a beaker.	Pipette out 1ml of dilute solution of ammonium chloride (Nessler's).
2. Pipette out 10 ml of the solution into a Nessler cylinder and add 40 ml of ammonia-free water.	Add 50 ml of ammonia-free water.
3. Add 2 ml of alkaline potassium mercuri-iodide solution.	Add 2 ml of alkaline potassium mercuri-iodide solution.
4. Stir well with a glass rod.	Stir well with a glass rod.

Observation

Any *one* of the two may be observed:-

1. The colour produced in the test is not deeper than the colour produced in the standard.

2. The colour produced in the test is deeper than the colour produced in the standard.

Report: According to the observation recorded above, any *one* of the following may be given as report:-

1. The sample passes the test.

or

2. The sample does not pass the test.

Note: The following solutions will have to be prepared for this test:-

1. Solution of Ammonium Chloride (Nessler's)

Dissolve 3.15 g of ammonium chloride (accurately weighed) in sufficient quantity of ammonia-free water to produce 1000 ml. The solution may be prepared in a 1000 ml volumetric flask.

2. Dilute Solution of Ammonium Chloride (Nessler's)

Pipette out 10 ml of the above solution into a 1000 ml volumetric flask. Add sufficient quantity of ammonia-free water to produce 1000 ml, stopper and mix well.

4. ADSORPTION POWER IN HEAVY KAOLIN

Principle : Adsorption power in heavy kaolin is found out by shaking the sample powder with a solution of methylene blue and allowing to settle. It is centrifuged and the supernatant liquid is diluted with water to a definite volume. The solution should not be more intensely coloured than a standard solution of methylene blue prepared for the purpose. If the adsorption power of the sample is good, most of the dye would have been adsorbed by it and the colour of the solution will be less intense than that of the standard solution.

Test	Standard
1. Pipette out 10 ml of a 0.37% w/v solution of methylene blue into a groundglass-stoppered test tube.	*1. Take 0.003% w/v solution of methylene blue in a 100 ml volumetric flask.*
2. Add 1g of the sample and shake for 2 minutes. Allow to settle.	*2. Adjust to the mark. Stopper and mix.*
3. Centrifuge and pipette out 1ml of the supernatant liquid into a 100 ml volumetric flask.	
4. Dilute with water to 100 ml. Stopper and mix.	
5. Compare the colour with the colour of the standard.	

Observation : *One* of the two given below may be observed.

1. The colour of the solution in the test is *not* more intense than the colour of the solution in the standard.

2. The colour of the solution in the test is more intense than the colour of the solution in the standard.

Report: Based on the above observation, *one* of the two given below may be submitted as report:-

1. The sample passes the test.

or

2. The sample does not pass the test.

Note: The following solutions should be prepared for this test:-

1. 0.37% w/v solution of methylene blue

Weigh accurately 370 mg of methylene blue and dissolve in enough quantity of water in a 100 ml volumetric flask. Dilute to the mark, stopper and mix.

2. 0.003% w/v solution of methlyene blue

Weigh accurately 30 mg of methylene blue and dissolve in enough quantity of water in a 100 ml volumetric flask. Dilute to the mark, stopper and mix.

Pipette out 10 ml of this solution into a 100 ml volumetric flask and dilute to the mark. Stopper and mix. This is 0.003% w/v solution of methylene blue.

5. PRESENCE OF IODATE IN POTASSIUM IODIDE

Principle : Iodate in potassium iodide is tested by adding dilute sulphuric acid and starch solution to an aqueous solution of the sample. No blue colour should be produced. Iodate, if present, reacts with potassium iodide in the presence of acid and liberates iodine which will give the blue colour with starch.

$$2KI + H_2SO_4 = 2HI + K_2SO_4$$
$$2KIO_3 + H_2SO_4 = 2HIO_3 + K_2SO_4$$

$$5HI + HIO_3 = 3I_2 + 3H_2O$$

Procedure

1. Weigh 0.5 g of the sample accurately and dissolve in 10 ml of carbon dioxide-free water in a boiling tube. (Carbon dioxide-free water is prepared by boiling distilled or purified water and cooling. The container should be kept closed while cooling).

2. Add 0.15 ml of dilute sulphuric acid from a 1ml graduated pipette and one drop of iodide-free starch solution. (For preparing iodide-free starch solution, triturate in a glass mortar 1g of soluble starch with 5 ml of distilled or purified water and add, stirring continuouly, to 100 ml of boiling water. Prepare immediately before use.)

Observation : *One* of the two given below may be observed.
   1. No blue colour is produced within 2 minutes.
                          or
   2. Blue colour is produced within two minutes.

Report: Based on the above observation, *one* of the following may be reported.
   1. The sample passes the test.
                          or
   2. The sample does not pass the test.

6. FERRIC IRON IN FERROUS GLUCONATE

Principle : Ferric iron in ferrous gluconate is limited by allowing it to oxidize potassium iodide in the presence of acid to iodine. The iodine liberated is estimated by titrating with 0.1M sodium thiosulphate.

$$2FeCl_3 + 2KI = I_2 + 2FeCl_2 + 2KCl$$

$$I_2 + 2Na_2S_2O_3 = Na_2S_4O_6 + 2NaI$$

1% of ferric iron is permitted to be present.

Procedure

1. *Take 100 ml of freshly boiled and cooled water in a glass-stoppered conical flask and add 10 ml of concentrated hydrochloric acid.*

2. *Weigh accurately 5 g of the sample and add to the contents in the flask.*

3. *Add 3 g of potassium iodide, shake well and allow to stand in the dark for 5 minutes.*

4. *Titrate the liberated iodine with 0.1M sodium thiosulphate using starch solution as the indicator.*

Calculation : Calculate the amount of ferric iron present as impurity using the following equation. Each ml of 0.1M sodium thiosulphate is equivalent to 0.005585g of ferric iron:-

$$\frac{T \times N \times 0.005585 \times 100}{5}$$

where T = Titre Value

N = Normality of 0.1M sodium thiosulphate.

Report: See whether the amount of ferric iron is within the permitted 1% or more and submit your report:-

1. The amount of ferric iron is below 1%. So the sample passes the test.

   or

2. The amount of ferric iron is more than 1%. So the sample fails the test.

7. REDUCING SUGARS IN FERROUS GLUCONATE

Principle : Reducing sugars may be present since ferrous gluconate is prepared from glucose. They are limited by their reaction with Fehling's solution after the removed of ferrous gluconate as ferrous sulphide by passing hydrogen sulphide. No red precipitate is formed within one minute.

Procedure

1. *Dissolve 0.5 g of the sample, accurately weighed, in 10 ml of distilled or purified water and make alkaline with dilute ammonia solution (use red litmus paper).*

2. *Pass hydrogen sulphide into the solution and allow to stand for 30 minutes.*

3. *Filter and wash the precipitate with 5 ml of water and again with another 5 ml of water.*

4. *Combine the filtrate and washings and acidify with dilute hydrochloric acid (use blue litmus paper). Add 2 ml of dilute hydorchloric acid extra.*

5. *Boil the solution till the vapours coming out of the tube do not darken lead acetate paper (this is to drive out the dissolved hydrogen sulphide. If it is present, it will give a dark brown colour with lead acetate paper).*

6. *Boil further to concentrate the solution to about 10 ml.*

7. *Cool and add 10 ml of sodium carbonate solution.*

8. *Set aside for 5 minutes, filter and dilute the filtrate to 100 ml in a volumetric flask. Mix well.*

9. *To 5 ml of the filtrate (pipetted out), add 2 ml of potassium cupri-tartrate solution (Fehlings's solution) and boil for 1 minute.*

Observation : Write *one* of the observations given below:-

1. No red precipitate is produced.

or

2. A red precipitate is produced.

Report: In accordance with the observation obtained, submit the corresponding report:-

1. The sample passes the test.

or

2. The sample does not pass the test.

CHAPTER 21
LIMIT TESTS

Limit tests are quantitative or semi–quantitative tests which are designed to detect and control small quantities of impurities which are likely to be present in the substance.

These tests require a standard containing a definite amount of impurity to be set up at the same time and under the same conditions of the test experiment. In this way, it is possible to compare the amount of the impurity in the substance with a standard of known concentration and find out whether the impurity is within or excess of the limit prescribed.

For this purpose these tests make use of simple comparisons of opalescence, turbidity or colour with standards as prescribed in the pharmacopoeias. By taking different quantities of the test substance it is possible to vary the limits of the impurities permitted for each substance. No numerical values are given for the permitted limits because other impurities also may interfere with the tests. Variations in time and method of performing the tests also influence the tests.

Limit Test for Chlorides (I.P. 1996)

Aim: To perform the limit test for chlorides on the given sample labelled as Dextrose I.P. and report on its standard.

Principle: The limit test for chlorides is based on the well-known reaction between silver nitrate and soluble chlorides forming a precipitate of silver chloride which is insoluble in dilute nitric acid. The opalescence produced depends upon the amount of chlorides present in the sample. It is compared with the opalescence produced in a standard solution containing the prescribed quantity of chloride similarly treated. If the opalescence in the sample is less than that in the standard, it passes the test and is declared as standard. If it is more, it fails the test and is declared as substandard. The test is done in Nessler cylinders.

399

$$Cl^- + AgNO_3 = AgCl \downarrow + NO_3^-$$

Procedure : Take two 50 ml Nessler cylinders. Label one as "Test" and the other as 'Standard'.

Test	Standard
1. Dissolve the specified quantity of the substance or take the specified volume of the solution as directed in the text in the Nessler cylinder. (10 ml of a 20% w/v solution for dextrose).	Pipette out 10 ml of Chloride Standard Solution (25 ppm Cl) into the Nessler cylinder. Add 5 ml of water.
2. Add 10 ml of dilute nitric acid.	Add 10 ml of dilute nitric acid
3. Dilute to 50 ml with water.	Dilute to 50 ml with water.
4. Add 1 ml of 0.1M silver nitrate solution.	Add 1 ml of 0.1M silver nitrate solution.
5. Stir immediately with a glass rod and allow to stand for five minutes protected from light (keep in a dark place).	Stir immediately with a glass rod and allow to stand for 5 minutes protected from light (keep in a dark place).

Observation: Observe whether the test has a greater opalescence than the standard or lesser opalescence than the standard. Write *one* of the following:

1. When viewed transversely against a black background the opalescence produced in the test is *not more intense* than the standard opalescence:

or

2. When viewed transversely against a black background the opalescence produced in the test is *more intense* than the standard opalescence.

   Report: Write *either* one of the following according to the observation that you got:

400

1. The sample (of dextrose) *passes* the test. As far as this limit test is concerned, it is *standard*.

or

2. The sample (of dextrose) *does not pass* the test. It is *substandard*.

Note: *Chloride standard solution (25 ppm Cl)* is prepared by diluting exactly 5 volumes of a 0.0824% w/v solution of sodium chloride to 100 volumes with distilled water and mixing well.

List of Some Substances for which Limit Test for Chlorides is Prescribed in I.P. 1996

1. Calcium carbonate
2. Calcium gluconate
3. Calcium lactate
4. Dextrose
5. Heavy magnesium carbonate
6. Light magnesium carbonate
7. Magnesium hydroxide
8. Heavy magnesium oxide
9. Light magnesium oxide
10. Magnesium sulphate
11. Potassium citrate
12. Sodium acetate
13. Sodium dihydrogen phosphate dihydrate
14. Sodium bicarbonate
15. Sodium citrate
16. Sodium phosphate
17. Sodium salicylate
18. Sodium thiosulphate
19. Zinc sulphate

Limit Test for Sulphates (I.P.1996)

Aim: To perform the limit test for sulphates on the given sample labelled as Sodium Bicarbonate, I.P. and report on its standard.

Principle: The limit test for sulphates is based on the reaction between barium chloride and soluble sulphates in the presence of dilute hydrochloric acid or dilute acetic acid. The opalescence produced in the test is compared with the opalescence produced in a standard containing a known quantity of sulphate and similarly treated. Barium sulphate reagent which contains barium chloride, sulphate-free alcohol and a small quantity of potasium sulphate is used as the reagent and is made *in situ*. The i̇ lusion of the small quantity of potassium sulphate in the reagent increases the sensitivity of the test. Alcohol prevents supersaturation and a more uniform opalescence develops. The test substance passes the test if the opalescence produced in it is not more intense than the opalescence produced in the standard. If the opalescence in the test is greater in intensity, it fails the test.

$$SO_4^{2-} + BaCl_2 = BaSO_4\downarrow + 2Cl^-$$

Procedure: Take two 50 ml Nessler cylinders. Label one as 'Test' and the other as 'Standard.'

Test	Standard
1. Pipette into the Nessler cylinder 1.5 ml of Ethanolic Sulphate Standard Solution (10 ppm SO_4).	Pipette into the Nessler cylinder 1.5 ml of Ethanolic Sulphate Standard Solution (10 ppm SO_4).
2. Add 1 ml of 25% w/v solution of barium chloride. Mix well and allow to stand for one minute.	Add 1 ml of 25% w/v solution of barium chloride. Mix well and allow to stand for one minute.
3. Pipette into this solution 15 ml of the solution of the substance prepared as directed in the monograph. (For sodium bicarbonate, 1 g is dissolved in 10 ml of distilled water, neutralised with hydrochloric acid and diluted to 15 ml).	Pipette into this solution 15 ml of Sulphate Standard Solution (10 ppm SO_4).
4. Add sufficient distilled water to produce 50 ml	Add sufficient distilled water to produce 50 ml.

5. Stir immediately with a glass rod and allow to stand for five minutes	Stir immediately with a glass rod and allow to stand for five minutes.

Observation: Observe whether the opalescence produced in the test is more intense than the opalescence produced in the standard and write *either one* of the following :-

1. When viewed transversely against a black back-ground, the opalescence produced in the test is *not more intense* than the opalescence in the standard.

or

2. When viewed transversely against a black back-ground, the opalescence produced in the test is *more intense* than the opalescence in the standard.

Report: Report *one* of the following according to the observation of (1) or (2) :-

1. The sample passes the test. It is *standard* as far as this test is concerned.

or

2. The sample does not pass the test. It is *substandard*.

Note: *Ethanolic Sulphate Standard solution (10 ppm SO_4)* is prepared by diluting 1 volume of 0.181% w/v solution of potassium sulphate in ethanol (30%) to 100 volumes with ethanol (30%). *Sulphate Standard Solution (10 ppm SO_4)* is prepared by diluting 1 volume of 0.181% w/v solution of potassium sulphate in distilled water to 100 volumes with distilled water.

List of Some Substances for which Limit Test for Sulphates is Prescribed in I.P. 1996

1. Calcium carbonate
2. Calcium gluconate
3. Anhydrous citric acid
4. Dextrose
5. Heavy magnesium carbonate
6. Light magnesium carbonate
7. Heavy magnesium oxide
8. Light magnesium oxide
9. Potassium chloride

10.Potassium citrate
11.Potassium iodide
12.Potassium permanganate
13.Sodium acetate
14.Sodium acid phosphate
15.Sodium bicarbonate
16.Sodium citrate
17.Sodium phosphate
18.Sodium salicylate
19.Sodium thiosulphate

Limit Test for Iron (I.P.1996)

Aim: To perform the limit test for iron on the given sample labelled as Sodium Chloride, I.P. and report on its standard.

Principle: The test depends on the reaction between ferrous iron and thioglycollic acid in the presence of ammonia when a pale pink to deep reddish colour is produced. Ferric iron is reduced to ferrous iron by the thioglycollic acid and the compound produced is ferrous thioglycollate. Citric acid forms a soluble complex with iron and prevents its precipitation by ammonia as ferrous hydroxide. Ferrous thioglycollate is colourless in neutral or acid solutions. The colour develops only in the presence of alkali. It is stable in the presence of air but fades when exposed to air due to oxidation to the ferric compound. Therefore the colours should be compared immediately after the time allowed for full development of colour is over. The following reactions take place:-

$$2Fe^{3+} + 2CH_2SHCOOH = 2Fe^{2+} + \begin{array}{c} SCH_2COOH \\ | \\ SCH_2COOH \end{array} +2H^+$$

Ferric iron Thioglycollic acid · · · Ferrous iron

$$2Fe^{2+} + 2CH_2SHCOOH = \begin{array}{c} CH_2SH \\ | \\ CO.O \end{array} \begin{array}{c} O.CO \\ Fe \\ HS \end{array} CH_2 + 2H^+$$

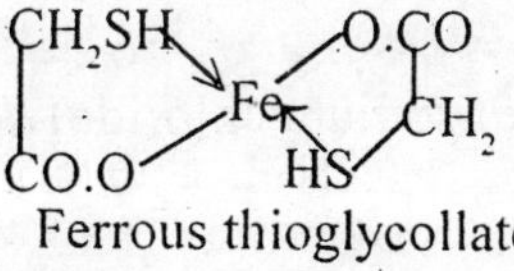

Ferrous thioglycollate

404

Procedure: Take two 50 ml Nessler cylinders. Label one as Test and the other as 'Standard'.

Test	Standard
1. Dissolve the specified quantity of the substance (2 g of sodium chloride) in 20 ml of water prescribed in the monograph in a Nessler cylinder.	Dilute 2 ml of Standard Iron Solution (20 ppm Fe) with 20 ml of water in a Nessler cylinder.
2. Add 2 ml of a 20% w/v solution of iron - free citric acid and 0.1 ml of thioglycollic acid and mix.	Add 2 ml of a 20% w/v solution of iron-free citric acid and 0.1 ml of thioglycollic acid and mix.
3. Make alkaline with iron-free ammonia solution	Make alkaline with iron-free ammonia solution
4. Dilute to 50 ml with water.	Dilute to 50 ml with water.
5. Allow to stand for five minutes.	Allow to stand for five minutes.

Observation: Observe whether the colour produced in the test is not more intense than the standard colour and write *either one* of the following:-

1. The colour produced in the test is *not more intense* than the standard colour.

or

2. The colour produced in the test is *more intense* than the standard colour.

Report: Write *either one* of the following according as you have the observation of (1) or (2).

1. The sample (of sodium chloride) *passes* the test. So it is *standard* for this test.

or

2. The sample (of sodium chloride) *does not pass* the test. So it is *substandard*.

Note: *Iron Standard Solution (20 ppm Fe)* is prepared by diluting 1 volume of 0.1726% w/v solution of ferric ammonium sulphate in 0.05 M sulphuric acid to 10 volumes with water. This contains iron in the ferric state.

List of Some Substances for which Limit Test for Iron is Prescribed in I.P.1996

1. Calcium carbonate
2. Calcium chloride
3. Calcium lactate
4. Dibasic calcium phosphate
5. Tribasic calcium phosphate
6. Glycerin
7. Heavy magnesium carbonate
8. Light magnesium carbonate
9. Heavy magnesium oxide
10. Light magnesium oxide
11. Magnesium sulphate
12. Phosphoric acid
13. Potassium chloride
14. Sodium acetate
15. Sodium bicarbonate
16. Sodium chloride
17. Zinc oxide
18. Zinc sulphate

Limit Test for Heavy Metals (I.P. 1996)

This limit test is for detecting and limiting the impurity of heavy metals likely to be present in many drugs. The heavy metals are precipitated as their sulphides by the addition of either hydrogen sulphide or sodium sulphide solution under specified conditions. A dark brown to light brown colour is produced depending upon the amount of heavy metals present. This is compared with the colour produced in a standard prepared by taking a specified quantity of standard lead solution and similarly treating it. The test solution and the standard solution are prepared in 50 ml Nessler cylinders and are diluted to the mark. Since many heavy metals are likely to be present, lead is chosen as the standard to represent all the heavy metals.

The precipitation is carried out at a pH of 3 to 4 by adjustment with dilute acetic acid for substances which are precipitated as their sulphides in moderately acid conditions (Method A). Organic compounds like benzocaine should be treated specially with mineral acids and ignited to destroy organic matter. The residue is extracted with hot water and adjusted to a pH of 3 to 4 as in Method A and the limit test is done on this solution containing the extracted heavy metals as in Method A (Method B). When no clear solution can be obtained with the test substance (eg: acetazolamide) by dissolving in acid as under Method A or Method B, the substance may be dissolved in sodium hydroxide solution for obtaining a clear solution. Using this solution the limit test is done under alkaline conditions. Almost all the heavy metals are precipitated under these conditions as their sulphides (Method C). Where there is the likelihood of other impurities present in the substance interfering in the usual sulphide test, the heavy metals are allowed to react with thioacetamide at a pH of 3.5 producing a brown colour (Method D).

Aim: To perform the limit test for heavy metals on the given sample labelled as Boric Acid, I.P.and report on its standard.

Principle: This limit test is for detecting and limiting the impurity of heavy metals. The heavy metals are precipitated as their sulphides by the addition of hydrogen sulphide or sodium sulphide solution. The sample is dissolved in acid or alkali for making a solution. If acid is used, the pH is adjusted to a value of 3 to 4 by adding either dilute acetic acid or dilute ammonia solution. The test is done in two 50 ml Nessler cylinders. The test solution is prepared in one cylinder and a standard solution is prepared in the other cylinder taking the prescribed volume of standard lead solution. The reagent solution is then added to both and they are diluted to the mark and mixed. After standing for five minutes, they are compared.

Method A

Procedure: Take two 50 ml Nessler cylinders. Label one as 'Test Solution' and the other as 'Standard Solution'

407

Test Solution	Standard Solution
1. Place 25 ml of the solution prepared for the test as directed in the individual monograph (for boric acid, dissolve 1g of the sample in 2 ml of dilute acetic acid and add enough distilled water to make up to 25 ml) in the Nessler cylinder.	Pipette out 2 ml of Standard Lead Solution (20 ppm Pb) into the Nessler cylinder and dilute with distilled water to 25 ml.
2. Adjust with either dilute acetic acid Sp or dilute ammonia solution Sp to a pH between 3 and 4.	Adjust with either dilute acetic acid Sp or dilute ammonia solution Sp to a pH between 3 and 4.
3. Dilute with water to about 35 ml and mix.	Dilute with water to about 35 ml and mix.
4. Add 10 ml of freshly prepared hydrogen sulphide solution and mix.	Add 10 ml of freshly prepared hydrogen sulphide solution and mix.
5. Dilute with water to 50 ml and allow to stand for five minutes.	Dilute with water to 50 ml and allow to stand for five minutes.

Observation: Observe whether the test solution has a darker colour than that of the standard and write one of the following :-

1. When viewed downwards over a white surface, the colour produced in the test solution is *not more intense* than that produced in the standard solution

or

2. When viewed downwards over a white surface, the colour produced in the test solution is *more intense* than that produced in the standard solution

Report: Write *one* of the following reports according to the observation made :-

1. The sample *passes* the limit test. So it is *standard* for this test

or

2. The sample *does not pass* the limit test. So it is *substandard*.

Note : The Lead Standard Solutions required for these tests (Methods A to D) are prepared as below :-

1. *Lead Standard Solution (20 ppm Pb)* is prepared by diluting 1 volume of Lead Standard Solution (100 ppm Pb) to 5 volumes with water. Lead Standard Solution (100 ppm Pb) itself is prepared by diluting 1 volume of Lead Standard Solution (0.1% Pb) to 10 volumes with water. Lead Standard Solution (0.1% Pb) is prepared by dissolving 0.400 g of lead nitrate in water containing 2 ml of concentrated nitric acid and adding sufficient water to produce 250 ml.

2. *Lead Standard Solution (1 ppm Pb) and Lead Standard Solution (2 ppm Pb)* are prepared by diluting 1 volume of Lead Standard Solution (10 ppm Pb) to 10 volumes and 5 volumes respectively with water. Lead Standard Solution (10 ppm Pb) is prepared by diluting 1 volume of Lead Standard Solution (100 ppm Pb) to 10 volumes with water.

List of Some Substances for which Limit Test for Heavy Metals is Prescribed in I.P. 1996.

Method A

Aluminium hydroxide gel
Dried aluminium hydroxide gel
Aluminium sulphate
Aminophylline
Ammonium chloride
Analgin
Ascorbic acid
Barium sulphate
Boric acid
Calcium carbonate
Calcium chloride
Calcium gluconate
Calcium lactate
Calcium levulinate
Dibasic calcilum phosphate

Tribasic calcium phosphate
Citric acid monohydrate
Anhydrous citric acid
Dextrose
Glycerin
Lactose
Magnesium chloride
Magnesium sulphate
Phosphoric acid
Potassium chloride
Potassium citrate
Potassium iodide
Sodium benzoate
Sodium bicarbonate
Sodium chloride
Sodium hydroxide
Sodium phosphate

Method B

Benzocaine
Cellulose acetate phthalate
Frusemide
Isoniazid
Saccharin
Sodium aminosalicylate
Sodium ascorbate

Method C

Acetazolamide
Disulfiram
Paracetamol
Prophythiouracil
Quinalbarbitone sodium

Method D

Allopurinol
Bentonite
Heavy kaolin
Light kaolin

Lactic acid
Heavy magnesium carbonate
Light magnesium carbonate
Magnesium hydroxide
Magnesium hydroxide oral suspension
Magnesium stearate
Magnesium trisilicate
Propylene glycol
Pyridoxine hydrochloride
Riboflavine sodium phosphate
Saccharin sodium
Salicylic acid
Colloidal silicon dioxide
Sodium acetate
Sodium carboxymethylcellulose
Sodium dihydrogenphosphate dihydrate
Titanium dioxide
Purified water

Limit Test for Arsenic (I.P.1996)

Aim: To perform the limit test for arsenic on the given sample labelled as Dextrose, I.P. and report on its standard.

Principle: The test substance is dissolved in hydrochloric acid or an aqueous solution or extract is acidified. Some substances have to be specially treated for making a solution suitable for the test. The arsenic present in the sample is converted to either arsenious acid or arsenic acid depending on its valency state. Then it is further treated with a reducing agent such as stannous chloride. Arsenic acid is reduced to arsenious acid. In the I.P., stannated hydrochloric acid (stannous chloride mixed with hydrochloric acid) is added to the substance.

$$H_3AsO_4 = H_3AsO_3$$
Arsenic acid   Arsenious acid

Potassium iodide which is also added forms hydriodic acid which also reduces arsenic acid to arsenious acid.

411

The arsenious acid is further reduced to arsine by nascent hydrogen produced by the action of granulated zinc and hydrochloric acid.

$$H_3AsO_3 + 6H = AsH_3 \uparrow + 3H_2O$$
$$\text{Arsine}$$

When arsine comes into contact with dry paper saturated with mercuric chloride, it produces a yellow stain.

$$2AsH_3 + HgCl_2 = Hg \Big\langle \begin{array}{c} AsH_2 \\ \\ AsH_2 \end{array} + 2HCl$$

Yellow Or brown stain

The intensity of the stain is compared by daylight with a standard stain which is similarly and simultaneously prepared by taking a specified quantity of dilute arsenic solution in place of the test substance. If the test stain is less in intensity of colour than the standard stain, the sample passes the test.

All the reagents used excepting strong and dilute arsenic solutions should be arsenic-free and are designated as AsT. A standard prepared by taking 1 ml of dilute arsenic solution AsT and compared with the test stain produced by taking 10 g of the test substance indicates that the permitted limit of arsenic is 1 part per million.

Apparatus: The apparatus consists of a wide-mouthed glass bottle (about 100 ml capacity) or conical flask fitted with a rubber bung or ground glass stopper. A glass tube of specified dimensions is passed through the rubber bung. The internal diameter (5 mm) is important and should be uniform throughout. The tube is open at the upper end but tapers to a small diameter at the lower end. Near the lower end a small hole is present to allow condensed moisture to escape.

(See the figure on the next page).

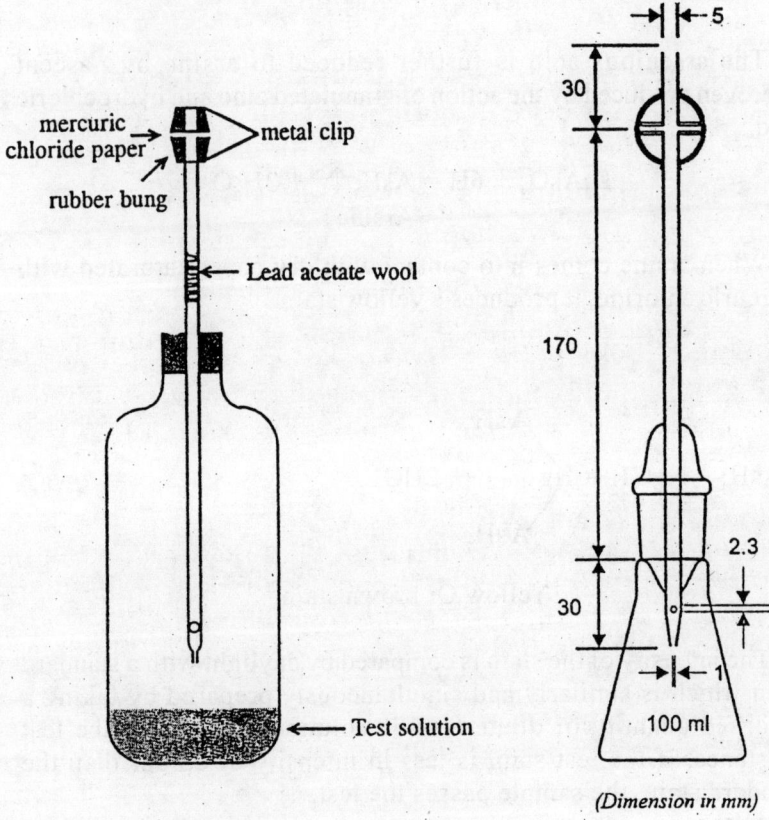

mercuric chloride paper →
metal clip

rubber bung

← Lead acetate wool

← Test solution

→| |←—5

30

170

30

2.3

→| |←—1

100 ml

(Dimension in mm)

Apparatus for Limit Test for Arsenic

The tube is packed lightly with cotton wool saturated with lead acetate solution and dried. This is to trap any hydrogen sulphide which may be produced during the reaction, if any sulphur impurity is present in the substance.

The mercuric chloride paper is fixed at the upper end of the tube between two rubber bungs by means of a spring clip. The two rubber bungs contain the tube in two parts and the mercuric chloride paper is correctly positioned between them.

Procedure: Take two 120 ml wide-mouthed bottles or conical flasks with the attachments and label one as 'Test' and the other as 'Standard.'

Test	Standard
1. Weigh accurately 10 g of the sample and dissolve in 50 ml of water. Transfer to the bottle or flask.	Take in the bottle or flask accurately 1 ml of Arsenic Standard Solution (10 ppm As). Add 50 ml of water.
2. Add 10 ml of stannated hydrochloric acid AsT.	Add 10 ml of stannated hydrochloric acid AsT.
3. Add 5 ml of 1M potassium iodide and 10 g of zinc AsT.	Add 5 ml of 1M potassium iodide and 10 g of zinc AsT.
4. Place the co;rk immediately over the bottle with the attachments and immerse the bottle in a water bath at a suitable temperature.	Place the cork with the attachments over the bottle and immerse the bottle in a water bath at a suitable temperature.
5. Allow the reaction to go on for forty minutes.	Allow the reaction to go on for forty minutes.

Obervation: Compare by daylight the depth of colour in the test stain with the standard stain. Report *either one* of the following:

1. The test stain is *more intense* than the standard stain.
or
2. The test stain is *not more intense* than the standard stain.

Report: Report *either one* of the following according to the observation:

1. The sample *does not pass* the test. It is *substandard*.
or
2. The sample *passes* the test. It is *standard* for this test.

Note: To prepare *Arsenic Standard Solution (10 ppm As)*, dissolve 0.330 g of arsenic trioxide in 5 ml of 2M sodium hydroxide and dilute to 250 ml with water. Dilute 1 volume of this solution to 100 volumes with water.

List of Some Substances for Which Limit Test for Arsenic is Prescribed in I.P.1996

1. Aluminium sulphate
2. Ammonium chloride
3. Barium sulphate
4. Calcium chloride
5. Calcium gluconate
6. Calcium levulinate
7. Citric acid monohydrate
8. Anhydrous citric acid
9. Dextrose
10. Hydrochloric acid
11. Heavy kaolin
12. Light kaolin
13. Lactic acid
14. Lactose
15. Magnesium chloride
16. Magnesium sulphate
17. Magnesium trisilicate
18. Potassium chloride
19. Potassium citrate
20. Potassium iodide
21. Sodium acetate
22. Sodium acid phosphate
23. Sodium chloride
24. Sodium citrate
25. Sodium phosphate
26. Sodium thiosulphate
27. Tartaric acid
28. Zinc sulphate

MODIFIED PROCEDURES FOR CERTAIN LIMIT TESTS

1. CHLORIDE AND SULPHATE IN POTASSIUM PERMANGANATE

Principle : If these limit tests are done in the usual way, it will be difficult to make any observation, since the sample itself (potassium permanganate) is highly coloured. So potassium permanganate is eliminated by reduction with alcohol. This can be called as *pretreatment.*

The sample is dissolved in water and heated on a water bath. Alcohol is added. It is filtered to remove the precipitated manganese dioxide. The filtrate is colourless and can be used for performing the limit tests for chloride and sulphate in the usual way.

$$2KMnO_4 + 3CH_3CH_2OH = 2KOH + 2MnO_2 + 3CH_3CHO + 2H_2O$$

Procedure

    a. Dissolve 1.5 g of the sample, accurately weighed, in 50 ml of distilled water.

    b. Heat on a water bath and add gradually 6 ml of ethanol 95%.

    c. Cool, dilute to 60 ml with distilled water and filter. The filtrate (solution A) is colourless.

For Limit Test for Chlorides : Take 40 ml of solution A and do the limit test for chlorides.

For Limit Test for Sulphates : Take 10 ml of solution A and do the limit test for sulphates.

2. CHLORIDE AND SULPHATE IN SODIUM BICARBONATE

Principle : Here the *pretreatment* consists of neutralising the sodium bicarbonate with an appropriate mineral acid and using the neutralised solution for the particular limit test. In the case of limit test for chlorides, the sample is dissolved in distilled water and neutralised with nitric acid.

$$NaHCO_3 + HNO_3 = NaNO_3 + CO_2\uparrow + H_2O$$

In the case of limit test for sulphates, the sample is suspended in distilled water and neutralised with hydrochloric acid.

$$NaHCO_3 + HCl = NaCl + CO_2\uparrow + H_2O$$

In both cases, the solutions should be stirred well and the effervescence should be allowed to subside.

Procedure

For Limit Test for Chlorides

    a. *Weigh accurately 1.25 g of the sample and dissolve it in 15 ml of distilled water.*

    b. *Add 2 ml of concentrated nitric acid.*

    c. *Apply the limit test for chlorides to this solution.*

For Limit Test for Sulphates

    a. *Weigh accurately 1g of the sample and suspend it in 10 ml of distilled water.*

    b. *Neutralise with concentrated hydrochloric acid adding it gradually till the effervescence ceases.*

    c. *Dilute to 15 ml with distilled water.*

    d. *Do the limit test for sulphates with this solution.*

3 . LIMIT TEST FOR CHLORINATED COMPOUNDS IN SODIUM BENZOATE

Principle : Chlorinated compounds as impurity may be due to benzoic acid being manufactured from chlorinated derivatives of toluene. It is done by dissolving the sample in sodium carbonate solution, evaporating to dryness and heating the residue at a temperature below 400°C till it is charred. The organic matter has been destroyed and the chlorine present is converted to sodium chloride. It is extracted with

417

water and dilute nitric acid and filtered. The filtrate must comply with the limit test for chlorides.

Procedure

a. Dissolve 0.33 g of the sample, accuratr'y weighed, in 5 ml of 0.5M sodium carbonate.

b. Evaporate to dryness and heat the residue till it is completely charred, keeping the temperature below 400°C.

c. Extract the residue with a mixture of 10 ml of distilled water and 12 ml of dilute nitric acid. Filter.

d. The filtrate complies with the limit test for chlorides (do the limit test).

4. CHLORIDE AND SULPHATE IN SODIUM SALICYLATE

Principle : For doing these two limit tests, a solution of sodium salicylate in carbon dioxide-free water (solution A) should be prepared. For chloride limit test, nitric acid is added which decomposes the sodium salicylate and releases salicylic acid which is filtered. The limit test for chlorides is then applied to the filtrate.

Procedure

Pretreatment : Weigh 10 g of the sample accurately and dissolve it in enough quantity of carbon dioxide-free water and making up to 100 ml with more carbon dioxide-free water (carbon dioxide-free water may be prepared by boiling distilled water and cooling it, keeping the container closed.)

For Limit test for Chloride :

a. Take 25 ml of solution A and add 15 ml of distilled water

b. Add 10 ml of 2M nitric acid and filter.

c. Do the limit test for chlorides on the filtrate.

For Limit test for Sulphates :

a. Take 2.5 ml of solution A and add 125 ml of distilled water.

b. Do the limit test for sulphates.

CHAPTER 22

SYSTEMATIC QUALITATIVE ANALYSIS OF INORGANIC SALTS

If any inorganic salt, whose identity is not known, is given, the student should be in a position to do some tests and find out what inorganic salt it is. For this purpose a regular systematic procedure incorporating all the tests including confirmatory tests should be used for identifying the various acidic and basic radicals. It must be clearly understood that in the case of a single salt as soon as the basic tests for an acid radical are answered, further tests for confirming its identity should be done. This means that the student should not waste his time doing other tests for other acidic radicals which are going to be negative any way. The same goes for basic radicals also. Suppose a second group metal is found to be present as indicated by group analysis, then the metals in the second group only should be tested. If any one metal in the group answers the tests positively, further tests, if any, should be confined to establishing and confirming the presence of this metal only.

However in the case of mixtures of inorganic salts such as a four radical mixture (which obviously consists of two acid radicals and two basic radicals), tests should be done further as given in the systematic procedure till the second acidic radical and the second basic radical are identified after finding out the first acidic and the first basic radicals. Then confirmatory and special tests for these two acidic and two basic radicals only may be done.

The systematic procedure given in the following pages consists of two parts. The first part deals with the tests for acidic radicals mainly and the second part deals with the tests for basic radicals.

SYSTEMATIC QUALITATIVE ANALYSIS

EXPERIMENT	OBSERVATION	INFERENCE
1. Colour and appearance a) Colour	a) Yellow colour	May be a chromate.
	b) Blue colour	May be a copper salt.
	c) Green colour	May be a copper. chromium or nickel salt.
	d) Flesh colour or pale pink colour	May be a manganese salt.
	e) Pink colour	May be a cobalt salt.
	f) Pale green colour	May be a ferrous salt.
	g) Brown colour	May be a ferric salt.
	h) White or colourless	Absence of all the above salts.
2. Action of Heat Take a pinch of the substance in a test tube and heat strongly in a Bunsen flame	**A gas is evolved** a) **Colourless gas.** Pass this gas into lime water by connecting a L-tube. Lime water turns milky.	May be a carbonate or an oxalate.
	b) **Reddish brown gas.** Turns starch-iodide paper blue.	May be a nitrate
	c) **Colourless, pungent gas.** Turns red litmus paper blue and also gives white fumes when a glass rod dipped in concentrated	May be an ammonium salt.

EXPERIMENT	OBSERVATION	INFERENCE
	hydrochloric acid is exposed to it.	
	d) **Colourless gas** which burns with a blue flame	May be an oxalate.
	e) **Colourless gas** with an irritating odour which gives white fumes when a glass rod dipped in ammonia is exposed to it.	May be a chloride.
	f) **Greenish yellow gas.** Turns starch-potassium iodide paper blue when it is exposed to it.	May be a chloride.
	g) **Reddish brown gas.** Turns fluorescein paper red.	May be a bromide.
	h) **Reddish brown gas.** Does not turn fluorescein paper red but turns ferrous sulphate paper brown .	May be a nitrate.
	i) **Colourless gas.** Turns acidified potassium dichromate paper green.	May be a sulphide or sulphite or thiosulphate.
	Charring takes place ie, the salt on heating becomes completely black.	May be a tartrate.

EXPERIMENT	OBSERVATION	INFERENCE
	A sublimate is seen on the cooler upper parts of the test tube.	
	a) The sublimate is white.	May be an ammonium, arsenic, antimony or mercury salt.
	b) The sublimate is yellow.	May be a thiosulphate.
	A colour change is seen.	
	a) White to yellow	May be a lead salt.
	b) Yellow when hot and white when it is cooled.	May be a zinc salt.
	c) Changes to black.	May be a copper or cobalt or nickel salt.
	d) Brown when hot and yellow when cold.	May be a bismuth salt.
	e) Turns brown.	May be a cadmium salt.
3.Solubility Test To a pinch of salt in a test tube is added excess of distilled water and shaken well. It is allowed to settle.	Soluble in water. No deposit is seen.	May be a sodium, potassium or ammonium salt. May be a chloride, sulphate or nitrate.
4. Flame Test A small quantity of the salt is made into a paste with a little concentrated hydro-chloric acid in a watch glass. A small quantity of this	a) Golden yellow colour.	May be a sodium salt.
	b) Brick red colour.	May be a calcium salt.
	c) Crimson red colour.	May be a strontium salt.

EXPERIMENT	OBSERVATION	INFERENCE
paste is introduced on a platinum loop (or at the end of a glass rod) into the nonluminous part of the flame of the Bunsen burner. The colour imparted to the flame is noted.	d) Lilac colour.	May be a potassium salt.
	e) Apple green colour.	May be a barium salt. May also be a borate.
	f) Green or bluish green colour.	May be a copper salt.
5. Charcoal Cavity Test.		
In the cavity of the charcoal block a little of the substance mixed with twice the amount of sodium carbonate is placed. It is heated by blowing a flame continuously through the Bunsen burner by a blow pipe. The salt mix is moistened with a drop of water before starting the heating.	a) A white powder only is left.	May be an aluminum or zinc salt.
	b) An incrustation is left. It is yellow when hot and white when cold.	May be a zinc salt.
	c) Brown incrustation only.	May be a cadmium salt.
	d) A brilliant, white metallic bead is left.	May be a silver salt.
	e) White brittle globules in white incrustation are seen.	May be an antimony salt.
	f) Grey metallic particles are left.	May be a nickel or cobalt or iron or manganese salt.
	g) Greyish-white globules are present in a yellow incrustation. The globules mark paper just like a black lead pencil. The incrustation is yellow when cold but orange-red when hot.	May be a lead salt.

423

EXPERIMENT	OBSERVATION	INFERENCE
	h) Pinkish-white globules with yellow incrustation are seen.	May be a bismuth salt.
	i) Red metallic scales are got.	May be a copper salt.
If only a white powder is got as in (a) above, moisten it with a drop of cobalt nitrate solution and heat.	a) Pink colour is got.	May be a magnesium salt.
	b) Green colour is got.	May be a zinc salt.
	c) Blue colour is got.	May be an aluminium salt. May also be a phosphate, arsenate or borate.
	d) No colour is got.	Not a zinc, aluminium or magnesium salt.
6. Action of Dilute Hydrochloric Acid.	a) Brisk effervescence is seen. A colourless gas comes out. When passed into lime water, it turns the lime water milky.	May be a carbonate.
	b) A colourless gas with a small of rotten eggs comes out. It turns lead acetate paper black and alkaline sodium nitroprusside paper blue.	May be a sulphide.

EXPERIMENT	OBSERVATION	INFERENCE
	c) A colourless gas with a pungent and irritating odour comes out. It turns acidified potassium dichromate paper green.	May be a sulphite.
	d) A colourless gas, the same as in (c) above, comes out. It turns acidified potassium dichromate paper green. The solution in the test tube becomes turbid due to the separation of sulphur. After sometime, there is a pale yellow deposit at the bottom.	May be a thiosulphate.
	e) A colourless gas comes out. It turns brown when it comes into contact with air.	May be a nitrite.
	f) No reaction.	Carbonate, sulphide, sulphite, thiosulphate and nitrite are absent.
7. **Action of Dilute Sulphuric Acid and Potassium Permanganate.**		

EXPERIMENT	OBSERVATION	INFERENCE
A small amount of the salt is added to potassium permanganate solution acidified with dilute sulphuric acid.	a) The pink colour is discharged (the colour disappears immediately).	May be a reducing agent like a ferrous or a stannous salt. May also be a sulphide, sulphite, thiosulphate or nitrite.
	b) The pink colour is discharged slowly.	May be an iodide, bromide or chloride.
	c) The pink colour is discharged only on heating.	May be an oxalate.
	d) Pink colour is not discharged even on heating.	Ferrous salt, stannous salt, sulphide, sulphite, thiosulphate, oxalate etc. absent.
8. Action of Concentrated Sulphuric Acid. A few drops of concentrated sulphuric acid are added to a little amount of the substance and heated.	a) Charring takes place. A black solution is left.	May be a tartrate.
	b) Two gases are evolved. One (CO) burns with a blue flame. The other (CO_2) turns lime water milky.	May be an oxalate.
	c) A colourless gas is evolved. It gives a white precipitate when a glass rod dipped in water is exposed to it. The inside of the test tube has an oily appearance.	May be a fluoride.

426

EXPERIMENT	OBSERVATION	INFERENCE
	d) A colourless gas is evolved. It forms white fumes in moist air and also with a glass rod dipped in ammonia.	May be a chloride.
	e) A reddish-brown gas is evolved. It turns fluorescein paper red.	May be a bromide.
	f) Violet vapours are evolved. They turn starch-iodide paper blue.	May be an iodide.
	g) A colourless gas which later turns reddish-brown is evolved. It turns ferrous sulphate paper brown but does not turn fluorescein paper red.	May be a nitrate.
	h) No characteristic reaction.	Absence of tartrates, oxalates etc.
9. Action with Concentrated Sulphuric Acid and Manganese Dioxide. A small quantity of the substance is mixed with a pinch of manganese dioxide. A few drops of concentrated	a) Greenish-yellow gas is evolved. It turns starch-potassium iodide paper blue.	May be a chloride.
	b) Reddish brown gas is evolved. It turns fluorescein paper red.	May be a bromide
	c) Violet vapours are evolved. They	May be an iodide.

EXPERIMENT	OBSERVATION	INFERENCE
sulphuric acid are added and heated.	turn starch paper blue.	
10. **Action with Concentrated Sulphuric Acid and Copper Turnings.**	a) Reddish-brown gas is evolved. It turns ferrous sulphate paper brown. It does not turn fluorescein paper red.	May be a nitrate.
	b) Reddish brown gas is evolved. It turns fluorescein paper red.	May be a bromide.
11. **Action of Sodium Hydroxide Solution.**		
A few drops of sodium hydroxide solution are added to a small quantity of the substance and heated.	A colour gas with a pungent, ammoniacal smell is evolved. It gives white fumes when a glass rod dipped in concentrated hydrochloric acid is exposed to it. It also turns red litmus blue.	May be an ammonium salt.
12. **Ammonium Molybdate Test.**		
A small quantity of the substance is dissolved in one ml of concentrated nitric acid and one ml of ammonium molybdate solution is added.	a) A canary yellow precipitate is formed in the cold on shaking or when slightly heated.	May be a phosphate.
	b) Yellow precipitate is obtained	May be an arsenite

EXPERIMENT	OBSERVATION	INFERENCE
	only on boiling the solution.	May be an arsenite.
	c) A yellow solution or yellow precipitate is obtained only on vigorous boiling.	May be an arsenate.
13. Action with Concentrated Sulphuric Acid and Ethyl Alcohol. A small quantity of the substance is heated with a few drop of concentrated sulphuric acid and one ml of ethyl alcohol. A burning splinter is brought to the mouth of the test tube.	A gas is evolved. It burns with a green-edged flame.	May be a borate.

14. SODIUM CARBONATE EXTRACT TEST

About 1 gram of the substance is mixed with about 3 grams of sodium carbonate in a beaker or China dish. 15 ml of distilled water are added. It is boiled for about 15 minutes and filtered. The filtrate is used for the following tests:—

A. Appearance of the Extract	It is yellow in colour.	May be a chromate.
B. A small volume of the extract is neutralised with dilute nitric acid. Silver nitrate solution is added.	a) A curdy white precipitate is got. It dissolves when dilute ammonia is added to it.	May be a chloride.
	b) A pale yellow precipitate is got. It is sparingly	May be a bromide.

429

EXPERIMENT	OBSERVATION	INFERENCE
	soluble in dilute ammonia.	
	c) A yellow precipitate is got. It is insoluble in dilute ammonia.	May be an iodide.
C. Barium Chloride Test A small volume of the extract is neutralised with dilute hydrochloric acid and barium chloride solution is added.	a) A white precipitate is got. It is insoluble when concentrated hydrochloric acid is added to it.	May be a sulphate.
	b) A white precipitate is got. It is soluble in concentrated hydrochloric acid.	May be a sulphite.
D. Calcium Chloride Test A small volume of the extract is neutralised with dilute acetic acid. One ml of calcium chloride solution is added.	A white precipitate is obtained.	May be an oxalate or a fluoride.
To the white precipitate formed is added dilute potassium permanganate solution	The pink colour of the permanganate is discharged.	May be an oxalate.
already acidified with dilute sulphuric acid and boiled.	Pink colour is not discharged.	May be a fluoride.

EXPERIMENT	OBSERVATION	INFERENCE
E. Brown Ring Test About one ml of the extract is neutralised with dilute sulphuric acid. It is boiled and cooled. Freshly prepared ferrous sulphate solution is added. Then concentrated sulphuric acid is added slowly through the sides of the test tube.	A brown ring is formed at the interface or junction of the two liquids.	May be a nitrate.
F. Silver Mirror Test About one ml of the extract is neutralised with dilute nitric acid, boiled and cooled. Ammonia is added followed by one ml of Tollen's reagent (ammoniacal silver nitrate) and the solution is heated in a water bath.	Silver mirror is formed on the inner sides of the test tube.	May be a tartrate.
G. Sulphide Test About one ml of the extract is neutralised with dilute hydrochloric acid, boiled and cooled. Then pass	a) Yellow precipitate is obtained immediately.	May be an arsenite.
	b) Yellow precipitate is got only after passing	May be an arsenate.

EXPERIMENT	OBSERVATION	INFERENCE
hydrogen sulphide gas through the solution.	the gas for a long time.	

Confirmatory Tests for Acid Radicals

Arsenate

1. Add to a dilute solution of the sample 1 ml of concentrated hydrochloric acid and 2 ml of a 20% w/v solution of potassium iodide. The solution turns reddish brown due to the liberation of iodine.

2. To a dilute solution of the sample add 1 ml of ammoniacal silver nitrate solution. A reddish-chocolate precipitate is produced.

3. To a dilute solution of the sample add 1 ml of solution of magnesium ammonio-sulphate (ammoniacal magnesium sulphate). A white, crystalline precipitate is produced.

Arsenite

1. Add to a dilute solution of the sample a pinch of sodium bicarbonate. Add 1 ml of solution of iodine. The colour of iodine is discharged.

2. To a dilute solution of the sample add 1 ml of ammoniacal silver nitrate solution. A yellow precipitate is produced.

Borate

Make a paste of a small quantity of the sample with concentrated sulphuric acid and ethyl alcohol and introduce a small quantity of it into the blue flame of the Bunsen burner. It burns with a green flame.

Bromide

Dissolve about 10 mg of the sample in 2 ml of water and add 1 ml of chlorine solution. Bromine is liberated. Divide the solution into two parts. To one part add two or three drops of chloroform. The chloroform layer is coloured reddish brown. To the other part add phenol solution. A white precipitate is produced.

Carbonate

1. Suspend 0.1 g of the substance in a test tube in 2 ml of water. Add 2 ml of 2N acetic acid. Close the tube immediately using a stopper fitted with a glass tube with L-shape. Heat gently and collect the gas in 5 ml of 0.1N barium hydroxide. A white precipitate is produced. Add a little dilute hydrochloric acid. The precipitate dissolves.

2. To a solution of the substance add 1 ml of magnesium sulphate solution. A white precipitate is produced.

3. To a solution of the substance add 1 ml of solution of mercuric chloride. A brownish-red precipitate is produced.

Chloride

Take 10 mg of the substance in a test tube and add 0.2 g of potassium dichrdomate and 1 ml of concentrated sulphuric acid. Place a filter-paper strip moistened with 0.1 ml of diphenylcarbazide solution over the mouth of the test tube. The paper turns violet red.

Chromate

1. To a pinch of the substance add 1 ml of dilute hydrochloric acid, 1 ml of hydrogen peroxide solution and 1 ml of amyl alcohol. A blue colour is produced.

2. To a small quantity of the substance add 1 ml of dilute hydrochloric acid and diphenylcarbazide solution in alcohol. A violet to red colour is produced.

Fluoride

Mix 0.1 g of the substance with 0.1 g of borax and enough concentrated sulphuric acid to form a paste. Introduce into the oxidizing part of the Bunsen flame. The Bunsen flame is coloured green.

Iodide

1. To 0.2 ml of a solution of the substance, add 0.5 ml of 2N sulphuric acid, 0.2 ml of potasium dichromate solution, 2 ml of water and 2 ml of chloroform. Shake for a few seconds and allow to stand. The chloroform layer is coloured violet or violet red.

433

2. To 1 ml of the solution of the substance add 0.5 ml of mercuric chloride solution. A dark red precipitate is formed. Add excess of potassium iodide solution. The precipitate dissolves forming a clear solution.

3. Add 1 ml of solution of the substance to 1 ml of potassium iodate solution and 1 ml of dilute acetic acid. Iodine is liberated. Divide into two parts. To one part add 1 ml of chloroform. The chloroform layer is coloured reddish-violet. To the other part add 0.5 ml of starch solution. Immediately a blue colour is produced.

5. Add 1 ml of chlorine water to 1 ml of solution of the substance. Iodine is liberated. Divide into two parts. To one part add 1 ml of chloroform. The chloroform layer is coloured reddish-violet To the other part add 0.5 ml of starch solution. A blue colour is produced.

Nitrate

1. To a solution of the substance add cautiously 1 ml of concentrated sulphuric acid and a crystal of brucine. A red colour is produced.

2. To a solution of the substance add 1 ml of solution of sodium hydroxide. Boil for one minute. Then add a pinch of zinc powder and 1 ml of solution of sodium hydroxide. Boil and test the gas evolved with red litmus paper. It turns blue. Expose a filter paper impregnated with mercurous nitrate solution. Darkening of the paper is seen.

3. To a mixture of 1 ml of nitrobenzene and 0.2 ml of concentrated sulphuric acid add a small quantity of the substance. Allow to stand for five minutes and cool in ice water while adding slowly with stirring 5 ml of water and then 5 ml of sodium hydroxide solution. Add 5 ml of acetone, shake and allow to stand. The upper layer shows an intense violet colour.

Nitrite

1. Add to a solution of the substance a few drops of dilute sulphuric acid and 1 ml of solution of potassium iodide and 0.5 ml of starch solution. A blue colour is produced.

434

2. Add 0.5 ml of solution of ferrous sulphate to 0.5 ml of a solution of the substance. A deep brown colour is produced.

3. Add 10 mg of urea and 0.5 ml of dilute sulphuric acid to 0.5 ml of a solution of the substance. Pass the gas evolved into lime water. Lime water turns milky.

4. Add 2 drops of 5% thiourea solution to 0.5 ml of a solution of the substance and warm. Add a drop of dilute hydrochloric acid and one drop of ferric chloride solution. A blood red colouration is produced.

Oxalate

1. Boil the substance with 1 ml of dilute sulphuric acid and a small quantity of manganese dioxide. There is brisk effervescence and carbon dioxide is produced. Pass the gas into lime water. Lime water turns milky.

2. To 1 ml of solution of the substance add barium chloride solution. A white precipitate is formed.

Phosphate

1. To 5 ml of a solution of the substance, add 5 ml of silver nitrate solution. A light yellow precipitate is produced. Divide into parts. To one part add dilute ammonia. The precipitate dissolves. To the other part add dilute nitric acid. The precipitate dissolves.

2. Mix 1 ml of a solution of the substance with 1 ml of ammoniacal magnesium sulphate solution. A white, crystalline precipitate is produced.

3. Mix 1 ml of a solution of the substance with 1 ml of barium chloride solution. A white precipitate is produced.

Sulphate

Dissolve about 50 mg of the substance in 5 ml of lead scetate solution. A white precipitate is formed. Divide the precipitate into two parts. To one part add ammonium acetate solution. The precipitate is soluble. To the other part add sodium hydroxide solution. The precipitate dissolves.

Sulphide

1. To a solution of the substance add 0.5 ml of a freshly prepared solution of sodium nitroprusside mixed with a little sodium hydroxide solution. A violet colour is produced.

2. To a solution of the substance add silver nitrate solution. A black precipitate is produced.

Sulphite

1. To a solution of the substance add iodine solution. The iodine solution is decolourised. The solution gives the reactions for sulphates.

2. To a solution of the substance add lead acetate solution. A white precipitate is produced. Add cold, dilute nitric acid. The precipitate dissolves. Boil the solution. A white precipitate is produced.

3. To a solution of the substance add bromine water and barium chloride solution. Bromine is decolourised and a white precipitate is produced. Add concentrated hydrochloric acid. The precipitate is insoluble.

Thiosulphate

1. Dissolve 0.1g of the substance in 5 ml of water and add 2 ml of ferric chloride test solution. A dark violet colour is produced. It quickly disappears.

2. To a solution of the substance add iodine solution. It is decolourised. The solution does not answer the reactions of sulphates.

3. To a solution of the substance add bromine water. It is decolourised. The solution answers the reactions of sulphates.

4. To a solution of the substance add lead acetate solution. A white precipitate soluble in excess of the reagent is produced. On boiling the suspension a black precipitate is produced.

5. To a solution of the substance add silver nitrate solution. A white precipitate is produced. It becomes black quickly.

Tartrate

1. Dissolve about 20 mg of the substance in 5 ml of water and add 0.1 ml of 1% solution of ferrous sulphate and 0.1 ml of hydrogen peroxide solution. A transient yellow colour is produced. Add dilute sodium hydroxide solution drop by drop. An intense blue colour is produced.

2. Heat 0.1 ml of a solution of the substance in a water bath for about ten minutes with 0.1 ml of potassium bromide solution, 0.1 ml of a solution of resorcinol and 3 ml of concentrated sulphuric acid. A dark blue colour is produced. Cool the solution and pour into water. A red colour is produced.

GROUP ANALYSIS OF COMMON CATIONS

For identifying the basic radicals of inorganic salts, the metallic radicals or cations are divided into six groups. This grouping is based on the solubilities of their salts. So the procedure here is to add a reagent to a solution of the salt and get a precipitate. If a precipitate is obtained in group I on adding the group reagent which is cold, dilute hydrochloric acid, it means that the inorganic salt being tested contains a cation falling within group I. There are three metals in this group. So one has to test further to find out which of these three metals is the actual basic radical forming part of the inorganic salt being tested.

However if no precipitate is got in group I, it indicates that the inorganic salt does not contain a cation of group I. Now we can test for group II by passing hydrogen sulphide into the solution of the salt got after testing for group I. If a precipitate is now obtained, it means that a cation of group II is present. We can proceed further by testing for all the cations listed in group II and identify the correct one. However if no precipitate is formed in group II, we will have to test for group III (with the reagent meant for group III) using the same solution obtained after testing for group II and so on. In the case of group VI, there is no group reagent but the cations can be tested individually by performing individual tests meant for each.

The following is a list of the groups, cations in the groups and group reagents :—

Group No	Cations in the Groups	Group Reagent(s) Used
I	Pb^{2+} Hg_2^{2+} and Ag^+	Cold, dilute hydrochloric acid.
IIA	Hg^{2+},Cu^{2+}, Pb^{2+}, Cd^{2+} and Bi^{3+}. Lead is not completely precipitated in group I, because the precipitate of lead chloride formed is partially soluble in cold water. So it is precipitated in group II as lead sulphide.	Cold, dilute hydrochloric acid and hydrogen sulphide.
IIB	Sb^{3+}, Sb^{5+}, As^{3+}, As^{5+}, Sn^{2+} and Sn^{4+}	
III	Al^{3+}, Fe^{3+} and Cr^{3+}	Ammonium chloride solution and dilute ammonia.
IV	Mn^{2+},Co^{2+},Zn^{2+} and Ni^{2+}	Ammonium chloride solution, dilute ammonia and hydrogen sulphide.
V	Ca^{2+}, Sr^{2+} and Ba^{2+}	Dilute ammonia and ammonium carbonate solution.
VI	Mg^{2+}, NH_4^+, Na^+ and K^+	Nil

Interference of Certain Anions in Systematic Cation Analysis

Certain anions, if present, interfere with the systematic analysis of cations by the above scheme. They don't allow the precipitation of the cations in their groups by complexing them or they may get precipitated themselves in some groups causing confusion These anions are known as "interfering anions" or as "eliminating radicals".

438

This complication is not present as long as the inorganic salt is in acid solution. This is because the salts of the 'interfering anions' are soluble in acids. So there will be no problem as far as the first and the second group testing is concerned since dilute hydrochloric acid is used as the group reagent or as one of the group reagents. However arsenite and arsenate may be precipitated in group II and give a false signal. Other interfering radicals may get precipitated in the III group and other succeeding groups.

So, after identifying the acid radicals, the interfering radicals should be eliminated by using special methods and the eliminated salt only should be used for the identification of the metallic radicals by means of systematic group analysis as outlined above. If this is not done, then the interfering acid radicals will get precipitated in the various groups and give false signals leading to the conclusion that some metallic radical is present simply because a precipitate (due to the interfering acid radical) is got in that particular group. So the above scheme for the systematic qualitative analysis of the cations can be used only after ensuring that no eliminating radical is present or if present, care has been taken to eliminate the same and use the 'eliminated' salt. The following is a list of the interfering anions':—

1. Arsenite
2. Arsenate
3. Borate
4. Chromate
5. Fluoride
6. Oxalate
7. Phosphate
8. Tartrate
9. Thiosulphate

Of these, anions of organic acids such as tartrates and to some extent oxalates and acetates prevent the precipitation of cations by 'sequestration'. Thus these cations are not precipitated in their usual groups. The detailed procedure for the elimination of these interfering anions is dealt with separately at the end of this chapter.

It is suggested that the group analysis may be done initially with 'known' salts to become familiar with the reactions and reaction products.

First a solution of the inorganic salt should be made. For this take the inorganic salt if it contains no eliminating radical or the eliminated salt (if it contains any interfering radical) and dissolve it in *any one* of the following solvents in which it is soluble :-

1. Cold water
2. Hot water
3. Cold, dilute hydr;ochloric acid
4. Hot, dilute hydrochloric acid
5. Cold, dilute nitric acid
6. Hot, dilute nitric acid
7. Concentrated hydrochloric acid
8. Concentrated nitric acid

After the solution is made, the group analysis for cations may be started by testing for Group I as given on page. 441.

Table 1

Analysis of Group I (Silver group)

To 2 ml of the solution, add 1 ml of cold, dilute hydrochloric acid. A precipitate is formed. Heat, then cool and filter. Wash the precipitate and add the washing to the filtrate kept separate.

RESIDUE	FILTRATE
Add 1 ml of water to the residue and boil. Filter rapidly. Separately take the residue and the filtrate for further testing. Residue contains mercurous chloride and silver chloride. Filtrate contains lead chloride.	*Keep this for the analysis of the II group.*

From the RESIDUE (mercurous chloride and silver chloride)

RESIDUE	FILTRATE
Shake with 3 to 4 ml of dilute ammonia and filter.	This contains dissolved lead chloride (soluble in hot water). *Cool the filtrate. Slowly the crystals of lead chloride separate out. Heat well till the crystals are redissolved. Add 2 to 3 drops of amm. acetate and one drop of pot. chromate solution. A yellow chromate solution. A yellow ppt.*

From the lead chloride filtrate

LEAD

Ammonium acetate is added to keep the lead in solution. It is finally precipitated as yellow lead chromate.

After shaking residue with dilute ammonia and filtering

RESIDUE	FILTRATE
Residue contains black metallic mercury. *Add to the residue 3 drops of Conc. HCl and one drop of Conc. HNO₃. To the clear filtrate, add 2 to 3 drops of stannous chloride solution. A white precipitate is formed. It slowly turns grey.*	Filtrate contains soluble silver-ammonia complex. *Warm and Add 2 to 3 drops of dilute nitric acid. A white precipitate is formed.*
MERCUROUS MERCURY	**SILVER**
The concentrated acids dissolve the black ppt. to give mercuric chloride which is reduced by the stannous chloride first to white mercurous chloride and then to grey metallic mercury.	Silver chloride is converted into a soluble complex by ammonia. The complex is decomposed when nitric acid is added and silver chloride is reformed as a white ppt.

Confirmatory Tests For Group I Metals

1. Lead

(a) To one drop of the test solution, add two drops of dilute sodium hydroxide solution, one drop of saturated bromine water and two drops of dilute ammonia. Then add two drops of benzidine (0.05% solution) in 10% acetic acid. A *blue* colour is produced.

(b) Add 1 ml of strong ammonia to one ml of the test solution. Then add one or two crystals of potassium cyanide and two drops of dithizone solution (5 mg of dithizone or diphenylthiocarbazone in 100 ml of chloroform). Immediately a rose-red colour is produced.

(c) Make a solution of the test substance (5 mg) in one ml of acetic acid. Dilute with water to 3 ml. Add one ml of potassium iodide solution (20%). Heat to boiling and allow to cool (the precipitate is reformed as yellow, glistening plates (golden spangles of lead iodide).

In the first reaction a complex with benzidine is produced. In the second reaction the lead-dithizone complex is formed. In the third reaction the lead iodide that is formed in the cold, dissolves in hot water and comes out as glistening plates on cooling.

2. Mercurous Mercury

(a) Add one drop of dilute hydrochloric acid to the test solution and then add one drop of a strong solution of sodium nitrite. A black colour is produced.

(b) Dissolve 10 mg of the salt in enough dilute nitric acid avoiding excess of acid. Immerse a bright copper foil in this solution. It gets coated with a deposit of mercury which on rubbing becomes bright.

3. Silver

(a) To one drop of the test solution add two drops of ammonium carbonate solution and one drop of 1% potassium chromate solution. A red ring of silver chromate is produced.

442

(b) To one drop of the test solution, add one drop of concentrated hydrochloric acid, two drops of 2% manganese sulphate solution. A black stain is produced. The black stain is due to the formation of manganese dioxide along with metallic silver.

(c) To one ml of test solution add one ml of dilute hydrochloric acid. A curdy white precipitate of silver chloride is formed. Add one ml of dilute ammonia. The precipitate dissolves. Add one ml of potassium iodide solution. A yellow precipitate of silver iodide is formed.

TABLE 2.1
Analysis of Group II

To the filtrate from group I, add one or two drops of hydrogen-peroxide solution. Dilute to about 3 to 4 ml. [Hydrogen peroxide oxidises Sn^{2+} (stannous) to Sn^{4+} (stannic)]. Neutralise with dilute ammonia using litmus paper and add one or two ml of dil. HCl. Heat and pass hydrogen sulphide till it is saturated with H_2S. Filter. Test the residue and filtrate separately as given below:—

RESIDUE	FILTRATE
Contains sulphides of both copper and tin sub- groups. *Boil with 1 to 2 ml of 2N NaOH. Filter. Wash the residue with water and add the washed water to the filtrate.* (The sulphides of tin sub-group metals such as arsenic, antimony etc. are soluble in alkali. Stannic sulphide is also soluble in alkali. So the residue contains only the sulphides of the copper sub-group metals, whereas the filtrate will contain the sulphides of tin sub-group metals.	*Reserve the filtrate for group III examination.*

RESIDUE	FILTRATE
This contains only the sulphides of copper sub-group metals. *Use Table 2.2 for identifying these metals.*	This contains only the sulphides of tin sub-group metals. *Neutralise the filtrate by using dil. HCl and litmus paper. Heat and filter. Reject the filtrate. Reserve the precipitate consisting of the sulphides of tin sub-group metals. Use Table 2.3 for further testing.* (On adding HCl, the sulphides of tin sub-group metals are reprecipitated).

443

Table 2.2.

Analysis of Group II-A (Copper Sub-Group)

Wash the residue obtained in Table 2.1 with water to remove the alkali. Reject the washed water. Add 2 ml of dilute nitric acid and boil. Add 2 drops of dilute sulphuric acid, mix and filter. (The sulphides of lead, copper and bismuth dissolve in hot, dilute nitric acid forming nitrates. The black mercuric sulphide is converted into a white precipitate which is a double complex of mercuric nitrate and mercuric sulphide. The white precipitate may also contain some lead sulphate which is formed by the oxidation of lead sulphide. So the white precipitate may contain mercuric mercury and some of the lead. The filtrate may contain the nitrates of lead, copper and bismuth formed from their sulphides).

RESIDUE	FILTRATE
(The residue contains HgS and $PbSO_4$). *Wash the residue with a little water. Filter and reject the filtrate. Add 5 drops of saturated ammonium acetate solution and boil. Filter.* (NH_4OAc is added to keep the lead in solution). *Test both the residue and the filtrate.*	(Contains the nitrates of copper, cadmium and bismuth). *Add ammonia to a slight excess. Boil and filter. Test both the residue and the filtrate.*

RESIDUE branch (left)

RESIDUE	FILTRATE
Add aqua regia (3 drops of Conc. HCl and one drop of Conc. HNO_3). Boil and dilute with one ml. of water. Add 2 drops of stannous chloride. A white or grey precipitate is obtained.	*Add one drop of dilute acetic acid and 2 drops of potassium chromate. A yellow ppt. is produced.*
MERCURIC MERCURY	**LEAD**
(The concentrated acids dissolve the mercuric sulphide to form mercuric chloride which is reduced by the stannous chloride first to white mercurous chloride and then to grey metallic mercury.	(Lead is precipitated as yellow lead chromate).

FILTRATE branch (right)

RESIDUE	FILTRATE	
Add dil. HCl till the residue is dissolved. Add 3 drops of sodium stannite solution. Black and also white precipitates are formed.	*Divide the filtrate into two parts. Test as below:*	
	I	**II**
	(If copper is present, the filtrate appears blue due to the formation of a blue cuprammonium complex). Add dilute acetic acid and potassium ferrocyanide solution. A reddish brown ppt. is formed.	*To the other part add potassium cyanide solution. Dilute with water and pass H_2S. A yellow precipitate is formed.*
BISMUTH	**COPPER**	**CADMIUM**
(From the bismuth salt, metallic bismuth (black) is formed by reduction. Some white bismuth hydroxide is also formed).	(The reddish-brown ppt. is copper ferrocyanide).	(Copper is kept complexed by KCN and cadmium is precipitated as cadmium sulphide.)

Confirmatory Tests For Group II A (Copper Sub-Group) Metals

1. Mercuric Mercury

(a) To one ml of the test solution add a crystal of ammonium thiocyanate and a crystal of cobalt acetate. A blue colour is produced.

(b) To one ml of the test solution add sodium hydroxide solution. A yellow precipitate (of yellow mercuric oxide) is formed.

(c) Make the test solution neutral by adding dilute ammonia and using litmus paper. To one ml of the neutral test solution add potassium iodide solution. A scarlet precipitate is produced. Add more of the potassium iodide solution. The precipitate dissolves and a clear solution is produced.

2. Lead

Do the confirmatory tests given for LEAD under group I.

3. Bismuth

(a) To the test solution add dilute hydrochloric acid, boil and cool. Dilute with water. A white or slightly yellow precipitate (of bismuth oxychloride) is formed. Add sodium sulphide solution. The precipitate becomes brown (due to the formation of bismuth sulphide).

(b) Add dilute nitric acid to the test solution and add one drop of 5% aqueous solution of thiourea. A yellow or orange yellow colour is produced.

4. Copper

(a) To the test solution add sodium hydroxide solution. A light blue precipitate is formed. Boil the precipitate. It becomes brownish-black (blue cupric hydroxide first formed is converted finally to brownish-black cupric oxide)

(b) To the test solution add dilute acetic acid and potassium iodide solution. A brownish precipitate or a brown colour is formed. One drop of this gives a blue colour with

445

starch solution (iodine is liberated in the first reaction and it gives the blue colour with starch)

(c)   To one drop of the test solution add one drop of ammonium mercurithiocyanate reagent. A violet precipitate is produced (ammonium mercurithiocyanate reagent can be made by dissolving 4.5 g of ammonium thiocyanate and 4 g of mercuric chloride in 50 ml of water). .

5. Cadmium

To one drop of the test solution acidified with acetic acid containing one drop of cadion 2B reagent (4-nitronaphthalene-diazoamino-azobenzene in ethanol and one drop of 2N KOH). A brigh pink spot is produced. It is encircled with blue colour.

Table 2.3
Analysis of Group II-B (Tin Sub-Group)

Heat the precipitate obtained by treating the filtrate as given in Table 2.1 with concentrated hydrochloric acid. Dilute with water and filter. Wash the residue with diluted hydrochloric acid and add the washed water to the filtrate. (Arsenic sulphide is insoluble in conc. HCl. So it forms the residue. The other two sulphides, that is tin sulphide and antimony sulphide dissolve in conc.HCl and are present in the filtrate).

RESIDUE	FILTRATE	
This contains only arsenic sulphide. *Add ammonium carbonate solution and stir until dissolved. Add dilute HCl. Yellow precipitate is produced.*	This contains stannic (tin) chloride and antimony trichloride. Divide into two portions.	
	(1)	**(2)**
	To the filtrate add a small quantity of iron filings or zinc dust. Warm till the metal is dissolved. Add mercuric chloride solution. A silky white or grey precipitate is produced.	To the filtrate add 1 g of solid oxalic acid. Boil and pass H_2S. An orange red precipitate is formed.
ARSENIC	**TIN**	**ANTIMONY**
Arsenic sulphide dissolves in ammonium carbonate solution but it is reprecipitated when dilute HCl is added	The iron or zinc metal reduces stannic chloride to stannous chloride which reduces mercuric chloride to either white or grey mercury.	Oxalic acid forms a stable complex with tin so that tin sulphide is not precipitated. Under these conditions only antimony sulphide is precipitated.

Confirmatory Tests for Group II-B (Tin Sub-Group) Metals

1. Arsenic

(a) To one portion of the residue obtained in Table 2.3 add conc. HNO_3 and boil. Add 3 to 4 drops of silver nitrate solution and then add dilute ammonia drop by drop. A reddish brown precipitate is formed (nitric acid oxidises the arsenous sulphide to arsenic acid which is converted to the reddish brown silver arsenate by the silver nitrate).

(b) To another portion of the residue add a small piece of zinc and dil.HCl. Place a piece of mercuric chloride paper over the mouth of the test tube. After some time the mercuric chloride paper has a yellow or brown stain (refer Limit Test for Arsenic).

(c) To another portion of the residue add strong ammonia, hydrogen peroxide solution and 10% $MgCl_2$ or $MgSO_4$ solution. Slowly evaporate and heat finally till no more fumes are evolved. Add to the residue one or two drops of stannous chloride solution. A brown or black precipitate or colour is produced.

2. Tin

To the test solution add concentrated HCl, ferric chloride solution, tartaric acid solution and an alcoholic solution of dimethylglyoxime. Add dilute ammonia. A red colour is produced.

Tartaric acid is added to complex iron and prevent its precipitation as ferric hydroxide.

3. Antimony

(a) To the test solution add a few drops of phosphomolybdic acid solution in water. After sometime a blue colour is produced.

(b) To the test solution add sodium potassium tartrate solution and sodium sulphate solution. A rdddish orange precipitate is produced. It dissolves when dilute sodium hydroxide solution is added to it.

(c) To the test solution add granulated zinc and dilute hydrochloric acid. Heat. Hold a cold porcelain tile against the gas coming out of the mouth of the test tube. It gets a dark, metallic deposit. It dissolves when a solution of chlorinated soda is added to it. The gas is stibine.

(d) To the test solution add dilute nitric acid and filter, if necessary. Add 5 per cent pyrogallol solution to the filtrate. A white, microcrystalline precipitate is produced.

(c) To the test solution add iron wire and boil. A thick, flaky, black precipitate of metallic antimony separates.

Table 3
Analysis of Group III (Iron Group)

Boil the filtrate from Table 2.1 to half its volume (Boiling is necessary to expel all the H.S. No H$_2$S should be present when ammonia is going to be added since group IV metals will be precipitated). Add Conc. HNO$_3$ and boil (Ferrous iron is oxidised to ferric iron by the nitric acid so that all the iron may be precipitated as ferric hydroxide only and not as ferrous hydroxide which is partially soluble in water. When testing for group IV is done, these ferrous ions will interfere). Add saturated solution of ammonium chloride and dilute ammonia with shaking. Filter. Test both the residue and the filtrate.

RESIDUE					FILTRATE
Suspend the precipitate in water. Add sodium peroxide and mix well. Boil for a few minutes and filter. Divide the residue into two parts and test as below. Divide the filtrate also into two parts and test as below:-					*Reserve the filtrate for testing for group IV.*
RESIDUE	**RESIDUE**	**FILTRATE**	**FILTRATE**		
The residue consists of reddish brown ferric hydroxide. Add dil. HCl and potassium ferrocyanide solution. A blue precipitate is formed.	The residue may contain some amount of MnO$_2$ also. Add to the residue a pinch of PbO$_2$ and Conc. HNO$_3$. Boil and dilute with water. Allow to settle. A pink colour is produced.	If the filtrate is yellow, it indicates chromium. To the filtrate add dil. acetic acid and lead acetate solution. A yellow precipitate is produced.	To the filtrate add dil. HCl till it is acidic and also ammonium chloride solution and ammonium hydroxide solution. A white gelatinous precipitate is produced.		
IRON	**MANGANESE**	**CHROMIUM**	**ALUMINIUM**		
[Fe(OH)$_3$ is dissolved by HCl and it combines with potassium ferrocyanide to give prussian blue. It is insoluble in dil. HCl].	(Actually manganese belongs to group IV and is partially precipitated here as MnO$_2$. It is finally oxidised to pink HMnO$_4$ (permanganic acid).	(Yellow lead chromate is produced).	(A gelatinous precipitate of aluminium hydroxide is produced).		

450

Confirmatory Tests For III Group (Iron Group) Metals

1. Iron

(a) To the residue add dil. HCl till it is dissolved. Then add ammonium thiocyanate solution. A blood red colour is produced. Divide into two portions. Extract one portion with solvent ether. The ether layer becomes pink. To the other add mercuric chloride solution. The colour disappears.

(b) Dissolve the residue in enough dil. HCl and add potassium ferricyanide solution. A reddish-brown colour is produced.

(c) Dissolve the residue in enough dil. HCl and strongly acidify with dilute acetic acid. Add a 0.2 per cent solution of 7-iodo-8- hydroxyquinoline-5-sulphonic acid. A stable green colour is produced.

(d) Dissolve the residue in enough dil. HCl and add ammonium nitrosophenylhydroxylamine solution. A reddish-brown precipitate is formed. Extract with solvent ether. The colour is transferred to the ether layer.

2. Manganese

See under group IV.

3. Chromium

(a) To the filtrate add dil. H_2SO_4, amyl alcohol and 6% hydrogen peroxide. Shake well. A blue colour is seen in the amyl alcohol layer. It is due to the formation of the peroxide CrO_5.

(b) To the test solution add a little dil. HCl and saturated solution of $K_2S_2O_8$ and silver nitrate solution. Allow to remain for about 3 minutes and add 1% solution of diphenylcarbazide in alcohol. A red or violet colour is produced.

4. Aluminium

(a) To the filtrate add dilute hydrochloric acid till it is acidic. Then add a solution of alizarin S 0.1% in water and either dilute ammonia or sodium hydroxide solution to slight excess. A red lake is produced.

The gelatinous $Al(OH)_3$ produced adsorbs the dye and forms a red lake.

(b) To the filtrate add dil. HCl and thioacetamide reagent. There is no precipitate. Add dilute sodium hydroxide solution drop by drop. A gelatinous white precipitate is formed. Add more dilute sodium hydroxide solution. The precipitate is dissolved. Add ammonium chloride solution. The gelatinous white precipitate reappears.

(c) To the filtrate add ammonium acetate solution and mordant blue-3 solution. An intense purple colour is produced.

Table 4
Analysis of Group IV (Zinc Group)

To the filtrate obtained in TABLE 3 add a little ammonium chloride solution and dilute ammonia and pass H_2S till the precipitation is completed. Heat for a few minutes and filter. Wash the residue with water and add the washed water to the filtrate. (Sulphides of zinc group metals, are precipitated and are present in the residue). Test the residue only.

RESIDUE	FILTRATE
Digest with very dilute hydrochloric acid (equal quantities of dil.HCl and water) and filter. (Cobalt sulphide and nickel sulphide are not soluble in very dilute HCl whereas zinc sulphide and manganese sulphide dissolve. So here the residue contains cobalt and nickel and the filtrate contains zinc and manganese). Test the residue further. Test also the filtrate.	Reserve this for analysis of groups V and VI.

RESIDUE side:

FILTRATE
(Contains Zn^{2+} and Mn^{2+}). Boil to expel H_2S. Add NaOH solution to excess and filter. (Zn^{2+} dissolves in NaOH solution forming sodium zincate and Mn^{2+} is precipitated as $Mn(OH)_2$ which has a pale brown colour). Test both the residue and the filtrate.

RESIDUE	FILTRATE
(Contains $Mn(OH)_2$). Add to the residue Conc.HNO_3 and lead dioxide. Boil. Dilute with water and allow to stand. A pink colour is produced.	(Contains Zn^{2+}). (1) Pass H_2S through the filtrate. White precipitate of zinc sulphide is produced. (2) To the filtrate add acetic acid and potassium ferrocyanide solution. White precipitate of zinc ferrocyanide is formed.
MANGANESE	**ZINC**
$Mn(OH)_2$ is oxidised to pink permanganic acid ($HMnO_4$). See also Table 3.	

Left RESIDUE analysis:

(Contains CoS and NiS). Add Conc.HCl and a crystal of $KClO_3$ (or one drop of Conc.HNO_3). Boil and evaporate to dryness. Dissolve in water and divide into two portions.(CoS and NiS are made soluble by oxidation with $KClO_3$ or Conc.HNO_3. The excess of oxidizing agent is destroyed by HCl and completely removed by evaporation).

COBALT	NICKEL
To one portion add ammonium thiocyanate and amyl alcohol and shake. The alcohol layer is coloured blue. (Vogel's reaction).	To the other portion add dimethylglyoxime reagent and dilute ammonia. A rose-red or scarlet precipitate is formed.
(Cobalt forms a deep blue complex soluble in amyl alcohol. Ni^{2+} does not interfere).	Ni^{2+} forms a complex with dimethylglyoxime in ammonia solution. Co^{2+} does not interfere.

453

Confirmatory Tests For Group IV (Zinc Group) Metals

1. Cobalt

(a) To the test solution add ammonium chloride, dilute ammonia and potassium ferricyanide solution. A reddish-brown precipitate is produced.

(b) To the test solution add NaOH solution. A blue colour rapidly changing to green is produced. Boil. The colour changes to pink.

(c) To the test solution add potasium chloride, potassium nitrite and acetic acid. A yellow precipitate (of potassium cobaltinitrite) is formed.

2. Nickel

(a) To the test solution add potassium ferrocyanide solution. A greenish-white precipitate (of nickel ferrocyanide) is produced.

(b) To the test solution add potassium ferricyanide solution. A greenish-yellow precipitate (of nickel ferricyanide) is produced.

(c) To the test solution add potassium cyanide solution. A yellowish-green precipitate (of nickel cyanide) is produced. It dissolves when excess of the reagent is added.

(d) To the solution add NaOH solution. A pale green precipitate [of nickel hydroxide, $Ni(OH)_2$] is produced. It is insoluble when excess of NaOH solution is added. Add dilute ammonia. The precipitate dissolves and a blue solution [containing the complex $Ni(NH_3)_6 (OH)_2$] is formed.

(e) To the test solution add sod.carbonate solution. A green precipitate (of basic nickelous carbonate) is formed. Add dilute ammonia. The precipitate dissolves and a blue solution is produced.

3. Manganese

(a) To the residue add a little dil. HCl to dissolve. Add sodium carbonate solution. A white precipitate is produced. It turns brown on exposure to air.

(b) To the residue add a little dil. HNO_3 and sodium bismuthate. Mix or stir well. A pink colour is produced. Here Mn^{2+} is oxidized to pink permanganic acid.

4. Zinc

(a) Pass H_2S through the test solution. A white precipitate of zinc sulphide is produced. Dissolve the precipitate in a few drops of Conc. HNO_3. Add one drop of cobalt nitrate solution. Soak a filter paper in it and dry. Burn the filter paper. The colour of the ash obtained is green.

(b) Add to the test solution sodium hydroxide solution. A white precipitate is formed. Add more NaOH solution. The precipitate dissolves. Add ammonium chloride solution. The solution remains clear. Add sodium sulphide solution. A flocculent, white precipitate is formed.

(c) To the test solution add dil. H_2SO_4 and one drop of very dilute copper sulphate solution and mercuric ammonium thiocyanate solution, A violet precipitate is formed.

Table 5
Analysis of Group V (Calcium Group)

To the filtrate obtained from group IV add dilute nitric acid and evaporate to dryness (This is to expel the H_2S and also to decompose and volatilise away the ammonium salts). Dissolve the residue in a little dil. HCl added to slight excess. Add dilute ammonia. (Ammonia is added to convert any bicarbonate present to carbonate). Add saturated ammonium carbonate solution filter. (The residue contains the carbonates of the V group metals). Test the residue as below:

RESIDUE	FILTRATE
(Contains the carbonates of Ba^{2+}, Sr^{2+} and Ca^{2+}). *Add enough acetic acid to dissolve. Add potassium chromate solution and filter.* (Only barium chromate is precipitated. Strontium and calcium chromates remain in solution). Divide the filtrate into two portions.	*Reserve this for examination of group VI.*

RESIDUE	FILTRATE
(The residue is pale yellow and it is barium chromate). *Add Conc. HCl to make a paste and introduce into the oxidizing part of the Bunsen flame. It burns with an apple green flame.*	(Contains Ca^{2+} and Sr^{2+}). *Add calcium sulphate solution. Boil and allow to stand.* A white precipitate is formed. (Calcium sulphate with a higher solubility in water precipitates strontium sulphate with a lower solubility).

RESIDUE	FILTRATE
	Add ammonium oxalate solution followed by dilute ammonia. A white precipitate is formed (Calcium oxalate is formed).

BARIUM	STRONTIUM	CALCIUM

Confirmatory Tests For V Group Metals

1. Barium

To the residue of barium chromate add dil. HCl to dissolve and add dilute sulphuric acid. A white precipitate is produced.

2. Strontium

Mix the white precipitate obtained above (for strontium) with a little Conc. HCl to make a paste and introduce a little of the paste through a platinum loop into the oxidizing portion of the Bunsen flame. A crimson red colour is imparted to the flame.

3. Calcium

Dissolve the precipitate (of calcium oxalate) obtained above in enough dilute HCl and add dilute sulphuric acid. A white precipitate (of calcium sulphate) is produced. The precipitation takes place only when a concentrated solution of calcium salt is used.

TABLE 6

Analysis Of Group VI (Magnesium Group) Metals

This group includes metals like magnesium, sodium and potassium and also the ammonium radical. As already stated, there is no common group reagent for this group as in the case of other groups. The three metals and the ammonium radical are identified and confirmed by doing individual reactions.

Evaporate to dryness the filtrate obtained in group V, add conc. HNO_3, evaporate again cautiously and ignite till no more fumes are evolved. (Any ammonium salt present is expelled as nitrous oxide by igniting with Conc.HNO_3). Extract the residue with water and divide into three portions for the testing of magnesium sodium and potassium.

(1)	(2)	(3)	(4)
To one portion add ammonium chloride solution, dilute ammonia and sodium acid phosphate solution. A white crystalline precipiate is formed.	To another portion add a concentrated solution of tartaric acid and alcohol. A white, crystalline precipitate is formed	To the third portion and zinc uranyl acetate, acetic acid and alcohol. A yellow, crystalline precipitate is formed.	To a pinch of the substance add sodium hydroxide solution and boil. A gas with a strong, pungent and characteristic odour is evolved. It turns moist red litmus paper blue.
MAGNESIUM	**POTASSIUM**	**SODIUM**	**AMMONIUM**
Magnesium ammonium phosphate is precipitated in the presence of NH_4Cl and NH_3. NH_4Cl is added to prevent the precipitation of $Mg(OH)_2$.	Potasium bitartrate which is insoluble in alcohol is precipitated.	Sodium zinc uranyl acetate is formed. It is sparingly soluble in alcohol.	Ammonia gas is evolved.

458

Confirmatory Tests For Group VI Metals

1. Magnesium

(a) To the test solution add dil. HCl. Mix well and add magneson reagent (one or two drops) and sodium hydroxide solution. A blue precipitate is formed.

Magneson is p-nitrobenzene-azo-resorcinol. It becomes blue in alkaline solution. The $Mg(OH)_2$ formed (on adding NaOH solution) adsorbs the dye.

(b) Repeat the above reaction with Titan yellow. A red lake is formed in a similar way.

(c) To the test solution add sodium hydroxide solution and diphenylcarbazide solution. A pink precipitate is produced.

2. Potassium

(a) To the test solution add silver nitrate solution and a small crystal of sodium cobaltinitrite. A yellow precipitate is produced.

The test substance should not contain any halide. If halide is present, silver nitrate should not be added. The yellow precipitate is still formed but rather slowly. The yellow precipitate is a double salt of potassium sodium cobaltinitrite.

(b) To the test solution add perchloric acid. A white, crystalline precipitate (of potassium perchlorate) is formed.

(c) To the test solution add dilute hydrochloric acid and chloroplatinic acid and alcohol. A yellow, crystalline precipitate of potassium chloroplatinate insoluble in 80% alcohol is produced.

(d) To the test solution add saturated solution of picric acid. Yellow, crystalline precipitate of potassium picrate is formed.

(e) To the neutral test solution add dipicrylamine solution and a drop of sodium hydroxide solution. An orange-red colour is produced.

459

(f) Mix a pinch of the substance with conc. HCl in a watch glass or china dish to make a paste. Introduce a small quantity on a platinum loop into the oxidizing part of the Bunsen flame and view through a blue glass.

A violet colour is seen to be imparted to the flame. Seeing through blue glass (cobalt glass) is necessary to eliminate the interference of the golden yellow colour imparted by any sodium salt present.

3. Sodium

(a) To the test solution add acetic acid, alcohol and magnesium uranyl acetate. A yellow, crystalline precipitate is formed.

(b) Repeat the above test with cobalt uranyl acetate. A yellow, crystalline precipitate is formed.

(c) To the test solution add a little alcohol and an alkaline solution of potassium antimonate. First a white, amorphous precipitate of sodium antimonate is formed. It rapidly becomes crystalline (forming disodium pyroantimonate). It is nearly insoluble in water and more insoluble in aqueous-alcoholic medium.

(d) In the flame test, sodium imparts a golden yellow colour to the flame.

4. Ammonium

A little of the substance is dissolved in water and filtered. To the filtrate add a few drops of Nessler's Reagent followed by a few drops of sodium hydroxide solution. A yellow to brown colour or precipitate is produced.

Elimination of Interfering Radicals

As already stated, it is necessary to eliminate interfering radicals (of which a list has already been given) and use the 'eliminated' salt for the systematic qualitative group analysis of cations. The following are the methods of elimination of the various interfering radicals:—

1. Oxalate and Tartrate

A small quantity of the salt is heated in a broken china dish at first gently and later strongly and ignited. The oxalate or tartrate is decomposed to the carbonate or oxide. The residue is extracted with hot, dilute hydrochloric acid and filtered.

If there is a residue on the filter, it is used for analysis of group I cations. The filtrate is used for analysis of basic radicals of other groups.

2. Thiosulphate

Thiosulphate can be easily decomposed by adding a mineral acid to a solution of the thiosulphate. Add concentrated hydrochloric acid to a solution of the substance and boil till no sulphur dioxide is evolved. Sulphur is precipitated. Filter while it is hot. The filtrate is used for group analysis. Reject the residue.

3. Fluoride, Chromate and Borate

Mix a little of the substance with conc. HCl and evaporate to dryness. Repeat this 4 or 5 times. Digest the residue with dilute HCl and filter, if necessary. If there is a residue, use it for analysis of group I metals. Use the filtrate for analysis of other groups.

The fluoride is decomposed to hydrofluoric acid which is volatilised off whereas the borate is converted to boric acid which is volatilised off in steam. The chromate is converted into chromium (III) chloride which is also volatilised off at $379.5°K$.

4. Arsenite

Arsenious sulphide is precipitated when hydrogen sulphide is passed through a solution containing any arsenite or arsenate. To eliminate arsenite, pass H_2S through the solution obtained after testing for group I. Filter the precipitate of arsenious sulphide and pass H_2S again through the filtrate till no more precipitate is formed.. The filtrate may be used for the testing for group III and subsequent groups.

5. Arsenate

Arsenate is eliminated in the same way as arsenite. To the filtrate obtained after testing for group I, add conc. HCl and a crystal of potassium iodide (which reduces arsenate to arsenite through the HI formed), boil and pass H_2S. The arsenite is precipitated as arsenious sulphide. Follow the same procedure as in the case of arsenite. The iodine liberated from potassium iodide should be volatilised off before passing H_2S.

6. Phosphate

Phosphates, if present, may be precipitated as the phosphates of III, IV, V and magnesium of the VI group when the test solution is made alkaline for analysis of group III. So upto the testing of groups I and II, there is no interference from phosphate. The interference starts only from group III. So phosphate present in an inorganic salt should be eliminated before the analysis of group III and subsequent groups. This can be done by precipitating and removing the phosphate as ferric phosphate or as bismuth phosphate or as zirconium phosphate.

(a) Removal of Phosphate as Ferric Phosphate

The filtrate got from group II contains a lot of hydrogen sulphide. This should be removed completely. *This can be done by boiling the filtrate well to expel* H_2S. *Add one or two drops of conc.HNO_3 and boil again. Take one drop of this solution and mix with one drop of potassium thiocyanate solution. If iron is present, a blood red colour is produced.* So now the inorganic salt may be examined further for iron.

If no iron is present (indicated by no blood-red colour being formed with potassium thiocyanate), *add solid ammonium chloride and dilute ammonia to the filtrate. Ammonia should be in slight excess. Neutralise the ammoniacal solution by adding dilute acetic acid and add a slight excess.* Thus an acetic acid-acetate buffer solution is produced. Under these conditions all III group metals are precipitated as their phosphates. *So if a precipitate is formed, regular group III analysis can be carried out.* However all the phosphate may not be fully precipitated.

If no precipitate is formed, add to the solution neutral ferric chloride solution drop by drop till the solution becomes deep reddish-brown in colour. Neutral ferric chloride solution may be ob-

462

tained by adding dilute ammonia to the ferric chloride solution till a very slight precipitate of [Fe(OH)₃] is formed. This may be filtered off and the filtrate may be used as the neutral ferric chloride solution. Alternatively the solution may be boiled to expel any excess ammonia present and used as the neutral ferric chloride solution.

Dilute with water and boil for ten minutes and filter. The residue may be examined for aluminium and chromium. The filtrate may be used for analysis of groups IV, V and VI. However the filtrate must be tested for the absence of phosphate (ammoniu molybdate test).

To the filtrate add dilute ammonia so that the excess of fer chloride may be precipitated as ferric hydroxide and removed filtration. The filtrate obtained here only must be used for t analysis of groups IV, V and VI.

(b) Removal of Phosphate as Bismuth Phosphate

Phosphate may also be eliminated by precipitating it as bi muth phosphate from a very dilute acid solution.

Evaporate the filtrate from group II nearly to dryness to ex pel the H₂S. Add a little dilute HNO₃ and evaporate nearly to dry ness again. Dilute with water and neutralise with dilute ammonic Add dilute HNO₃, boil gently and add a dilute solution of bismut. nitrate drop by drop till all the phosphate is precipitated as bismut phosphate. Digest to coagulate the precipitate and filter. The fil trate may be tested with a drop of bismuth nitrate solution for com pletion of precipitation. Reject the residue.

Bismuth phosphate is insoluble in dilute HNO₃ but is solubl in dilute HCl. So repeated boiling with dilute HNO₃ is done to re move any chloride present as volatile HCl.

Pass H₂S through the filtrate to remove bismuth as bismu sulphide. Filter and use the filtrate for the analysis of groups II IV, V and VI. Add to the filtrate ammonium chloride and dilute am monia solution.

(c) Removal of Phosphate as Zirconium Phosphate.

Proceed in the same way as in the case of (b) above, that is upto the stage of adding dilute HNO₃ and boiling to remove H₂S

463

and Cl⁻.Then add saturated ammonium chloride solution and either zirconium oxychloride or zirconium oxynitrate solution. Filter and test the filtrate (by adding one drop of zirconium oxychloride or zirconium oxynitrate solution) for complete precipitation of phosphate and complete the precipitation, if necessary. Filter. Repeat the process, if necessary. Use the filtrate for the analysis of Groups III, IV, V and VI. Add ammonium chloride and dilute ammonia in excess to the filtrate.

APPENDIX

Names, Symbols and Atomic Weights of Elements
$^{12}C = 12$

Element	Symbol	Atomic Weight	Element	Symbol	Atomic Weight
Aluminium	Al	26.98154	Manganese	Mn	54.9380
Antimony	Sb	121.75	Mercury	Hg	200.59
Arsenic	As	74.9216	Molybdenum	Mo	95.94
Barium	Ba	137.33	Nitrogen	N	14.0067
Bismuth	Bi	208.9804	Oxygen	O	15.9994
Boron	B	10.81	Palladium	Pd	106.4
Bromine	Br	79.904	Phosphorus	P	30.97376
Cadmium	Cd	112.41	Platinum	Pt	195.09
Calcium	Ca	40.08	Potassium	K	39.0983
Carbon	C	12.011	Ruthenium	Ru	101.07
Cerium	Ce	140.12	Selenium	Se	78.96
Chlorine	Cl	35.453	Silicon	Si	28.0855
Chromium	Cr	51.996	Silver	Ag	107.868
Cobalt	Co	58.9332	Sodium	Na	22.98977
Copper	Cu	63.546	Strontium	Sr	87.62
Fluorine	F	18.998403	Sulphur	S	32.06
Gold	Au	196.9665	Technetium	Tc	(97)
Helium	He	4.00260	Thallium	Tl	204.37
Hydrogen	H	1.0079	Tin	Sn	118.69
Iodine	I	126.9045	Titanium	Ti	47.90
Indium	In	114.82	Tungsten	W	183.85
Iron	Fe	55.847	Uranium	U	238.029
Lanthanum	La	138.9055	Vanadium	V	50.9414
Lead	Pb	207.2	Xenon	Xe	131.30
Lithium	Li	6.941	Zinc	Zn	65.38
Magnesium	Mg	24.305	Zirconium	Zr	91.22